THE BRITISH OMBUDSMAN

THE BRITISH OMBUDSMAN

FRANK STACEY

CLARENDON PRESS · OXFORD

1971

Oxford University Press, Ely House, London W.1

GLASGOW   NEW YORK   TORONTO   MELBOURNE   WELLINGTON
CAPE TOWN   SALISBURY   IBADAN   NAIROBI   DAR ES SALAAM   LUSAKA   ADDIS ABABA
BOMBAY   CALCUTTA   MADRAS   KARACHI   LAHORE   DACCA
KUALA LUMPUR   SINGAPORE   HONG KONG   TOKYO

PRINTED IN GREAT BRITAIN
BY WILLIAM CLOWES & SONS, LIMITED
LONDON, BECCLES AND COLCHESTER

PREFACE

In this book I have attempted to do three things: to describe and analyse the campaign which led up to the decision by the Wilson Government to set up a Parliamentary Commissioner; to study the drafting of the Parliamentary Commissioner Bill and its passage through both Houses of Parliament; and to evaluate the operation of the Parliamentary Commissioner in his first four years of office. It is then, in a sense, three books in one. It is a study of the policy-making process; it is a study, in depth, of the legislative process; and it is a study of a major reform in our system of government.

I have called the book *The British Ombudsman* although the Parliamentary Commissioner Act does not mention the word 'Ombudsman'. Indeed, some of the Ministers who introduced the Bill frowned upon any use of this word. But the Press always speak of the 'Ombudsman', and many members of the public would not recognize the title 'Parliamentary Commissioner for Administration'. He is, therefore, by usage, the 'British Ombudsman'.

I have benefited very much, in preparing Part One of the book, from interviews and discussion with Sir John Whyatt, Tom Sargant, Norman Marsh, Louis Blom-Cooper, Dr. Donald Johnson, Mrs. Lilian Hardern, George K. Young, Geoffrey Marshall, and Peter Shore. Professor F. H. Lawson helped me a great deal by correspondence.

On Parts Two and Three of the book, discussions with the Parliamentary Commissioner, Sir Edmund Compton, were particularly valuable. The following all gave me very helpful and stimulating interviews when they were Ministers in the Wilson Government: Lord Gardiner, Richard Crossman, Niall MacDermot, Fred Mulley, and Sir Eric Fletcher. Douglas Houghton, whom I interviewed when he was Chairman of the Parliamentary Labour Party, was most helpful and encouraging.

Many other Members of Parliament have given me freely of their time. I wish particularly to thank the following for the interviews and assistance they gave me: Alexander Lyon, Sir Hugh Munro-Lucas-Tooth, Sir John Foster, David Weitzman, Michael English, Paul Rose, Donald Anderson, Denis Coe, and William Wells.

I cannot mention by name all the Civil Servants who gave me interviews, but I would like to thank particularly Sir Philip Allen and Kenneth Couzens. My discussions with Kenneth Couzens were always most interesting and enjoyable, particularly when, as quite often happened, we were not in agreement.

For all those who helped me, I wish to make it clear that the responsibility for all statements of fact and opinion in the book is entirely my own.

University College of Swansea   FRANK STACEY
April 1971

CONTENTS

viii   *Contents*

LIST OF ABBREVIATIONS

Cmnd.   Command Paper.
H.C.Deb.   House of Commons Debates.
H.L.Deb.   House of Lords Debates.

Part One

THE BACKGROUND TO THE PARLIAMENTARY COMMISSIONER BILL

I

THE ORIGINS

IN July 1957 few people in Britain had heard of the Ombudsman. Sweden had acquired an Ombudsman in 1809, Finland in 1919, and Denmark in 1954. But in Britain, in the first half of 1957, it would have been difficult to find anyone who thought that this Scandinavian institution, with the strange-sounding title, had any relevance to the problem of safeguarding the rights of the citizen in his dealings with government departments.

This problem was, even so, very much in the public eye in July 1957. This was the month in which the Franks Report appeared. The Report of the Committee on Administrative Tribunals and Enquiries, to give it its full title, was a turning-point in more ways than one. Set up to consider the constitution and working of administrative tribunals and inquiries, it made a series of important recommendations most of which were implemented, either by the Tribunals and Inquiries Act of 1958 or by departmental circulars. It helped to produce a regularization of the vast congeries of administrative tribunals which had grown up in Britain as part of the development of the Welfare State. One of its chief recommendations was that there should be two standing Councils on Tribunals, one for England and Wales and one for Scotland. In fact, one Council on Tribunals was set up with a Scottish Committee. Since it was established the Council has carried out a continued supervision of the working of administrative tribunals and inquiries, and has advised upon the constitution of new tribunals and inquiries in the attempt to ensure that the principles laid down by the Franks Committee continue to be followed.

Yet the Franks Committee Report was partly a disappointment in that it made no proposals for new machinery for considering complaints against the administration where there is no statutory provision for a regular tribunal or inquiry. The Committee was not at fault in making no such recommendation. In fact it was precluded by its terms of reference from so doing.[1]

This was surprising to many since it was widely thought that the Franks Committee had been set up because of public disquiet over the Crichel Down Affair which had led to the resignation of the Minister of Agriculture, Sir Thomas Dugdale, in 1954. In fact, this affair, which concerned the refusal of the Ministry to return to its previous owner land that had been requisitioned before the Second World War, was a matter, in law, of the exercise of ministerial discretion, although, in fact, of the exercise of discretion by Civil Servants somewhat remote from the Minister's control.

The landowner, Lieutenant-Commander Marten, only secured redress after a long campaign by his local M.P. There was no administrative tribunal or inquiry to which he could have appealed and therefore, without any doubt, the Crichel Down type case was not a matter for the Franks Committee.

Many of those who gave evidence to the Franks Committee were nevertheless concerned with this type of case, but the Committee felt bound to reply that its terms of reference prevented it from making recommendations in this field. For example, Professor W. A. Robson gave evidence to the Committee advocating a general administrative appeal tribunal.[2] His suggestion was that this body should have jurisdiction not only to hear appeals from administrative tribunals but also appeals (to quote the Report) 'against harsh or unfair administrative decisions in that considerable field of

---

[1] The terms of reference of the Committee were:

'To consider and make recommendation on:

(a) the constitution and working of tribunals other than the ordinary courts, constituted under any Act of Parliament by a Minister of the Crown or for the purposes of a Minister's functions.

(b) the working of such administrative procedures as include the holding of an enquiry or hearing by or on behalf of a Minister on an appeal or as the result of objections or representations, and in particular the procedure for the compulsory purchase of land.'

[2] W. A. Robson was Professor of Public Administration at the London School of Economics from 1947 to 1962. He was a Lecturer there from 1926 to 1933 and Reader in Administrative Law from 1933 to 1946. In 1928 he published a pioneering study, *Justice and Administrative Law*. This work has been reissued in many subsequent editions and has played a major part in bringing about reform in the British administrative tribunal system. His many other works in the field of public administration include *The Government and Misgovernment of London* (1939), *Nationalised Industry and Public Ownership* (1960), and *Local Government in Crisis* (1966).

administration in which no special tribunal or enquiry procedure is provided'.[1]

The Committee's response to this proposal was to say in their Report: 'We have much sympathy with the desire to provide machinery for hearing appeals against administrative decisions generally. As we have already explained in Part I, however, our terms of reference do not cover all administrative decisions but only those reached after a special statutory procedure involving an enquiry or hearing.'[2] The Committee then went on to discuss his proposal in so far as it lay within their terms of reference, in that the general administrative appeal tribunal which he advocated would hear appeals from administrative tribunals and inquiries. They concluded that they did not favour this suggestion for two reasons. First, it would mean that appeals would lie 'from an expert tribunal to a comparatively inexpert body, and we see little advantage in this' and, second, because it would create two systems of law in this country: administrative law in which final determination would be made by the general administrative appeal tribunal, and ordinary law in which the High Court and the House of Lords were the final authority.[3]

Professor Robson's proposal for a general administrative appeal tribunal was clearly modelled on the machinery of the *Conseil d'État* in France. The role of the *Conseil d'État* was not overlooked by the Franks Committee. They heard evidence (on Day 27) from M. Letourneur, a member of the *Conseil d'État* and, on the same day, from Professor C. J. Hamson.[4]

Professor Hamson's study of the *Conseil d'État* in his book, *Executive Discretion and Judicial Control. An Aspect of the Conseil d'État*, published in 1954, had been influential in changing opinion among lawyers in Britain about administrative tribunals.[5] British lawyers had been nurtured on Dicey, who had declared in 1885 that bodies like the *Conseil d'État* and other continental systems of administrative law and administrative tribunals were inconsistent with English tradition and customs and that the idea of them was

[1] Cmnd. 218, Report of the Committee on Administrative Tribunals and Enquiries, p. 28 at para. 120.

[2] Cmnd. 218, p. 28 at para. 121.   [3] Cmnd. 218, pp. 28–9 at paras. 121–3.

[4] C. J. Hamson has been Professor of Comparative Law at Cambridge University since 1953.

[5] C. J. Hamson, *Executive Discretion and Judicial Control. An Aspect of the French Conseil d'État* (Stevens, 1954).

'utterly unknown to the law of England'.[1] Dicey had maintained that the *Conseil d'État*, as part of the executive branch, was bound to be less favourable to the rights of the citizen than were the British Common Law Courts. Hamson was able to show that this was not, in fact, the case and that, indeed, the *Conseil d'État*, as an adjudicating body within the executive and consisting in part of lawyers and in part of administrators, was able, often, to secure more effective redress for the citizen than is possible through the Common Law Courts in Britain.

Here, again, the Franks Report marked a turning-point. It marked a move away from Dicey in its recognition of the need for a system of administrative tribunals in Britain and for organizing this system on the basis of regular and coherent principles. On the other hand, the Report took what may be described as a 'residual Diceyan position' in its decision not to advocate a reform which would create two systems of law: one for the ordinary courts and one for the administrative courts.

A word may be appropriate here about the possibilities which existed for improving judicial control of administrative action. Opportunities for reform there were, and are, but it is not realistic to suppose that the courts alone could provide adequate redress of grievances for the citizen against government departments. For one thing, the courts are not equipped to review, or even properly ascertain, the facts in many kinds of case. For another, litigation is inevitably expensive. If the citizen's remedy lay only through the courts, this would be irksome even to the well-to-do claimant, and prohibitive to the person of small or moderate means, unless the system of legal aid were to be expanded far beyond its present limits. Even so, judicial process would be a heavy-handed, as well as expensive, method of investigation and redress.

The evidence submitted to the Franks Committee was appearing in print before the publication of the Franks Report. It was through reading this evidence that Professor F. H. Lawson decided to make what was to prove the seminal proposal for establishing an Ombudsman-type institution in Britain. Professor Lawson had been joint editor of the *Journal of Comparative Legislation*.[2] During this period

---

[1] A. V. Dicey, *Introduction to the Study of the Law of the Constitution*, 10th ed., p. 203.
[2] Professor F. H. Lawson was Professor of Comparative Law at Oxford University from 1948 to 1964. He was joint editor of the *Journal of Comparative Legislation and International Law* from 1948 to 1952 and of the *International and Comparative Law*

he became familiar with some of the work of Swedish lawyers on the functioning of the Swedish Ombudsman. He now decided that a form of Ombudsman might be the answer to the problem of how to provide redress against harsh behaviour by government officials.

He wrote a short article and sent it to *The Times*, in the form of a letter, advocating the appointment of an Inspector-General of Administration. This Officer would have the same tenure and relation to Parliament as the Comptroller and Auditor-General. He would investigate complaints of maladministration made by citizens against government departments, local authorities, administrative tribunals, and the ordinary courts (in so far as they exercise administrative functions). If he found a complaint to be justified, and he could not otherwise obtain satisfaction for the complainant, the Inspector-General would either take legal proceedings or report the matter to a committee of the House of Commons, similar to the Public Accounts Committee.

Professor Lawson acknowledged that his proposal was modelled on the practice in Sweden 'where two such officers have long been appointed by Parliament for civil and military affairs respectively, but I have introduced modifications to suit our conditions'.[1] He also commented that his proposal bore a fairly strong resemblance to the institution of the Prokuratura in the Soviet Union, 'the officers of which have many other tasks besides the prosecution of offenders'.[2]

The Times did not publish Professor Lawson's letter. The editor sent it back to him with a note saying that it was not topical. This curious notion of what was topical led, not for the first time, to *The Times* being scooped by the *Manchester Guardian*. Shortly after the publication of the Franks Report, the *Manchester Guardian* published, on 6 and 7 August, two articles by Professor David Mitrany.[3] The first of these articles was entitled 'Protecting the Citizen I—The Swedish System', and the second 'Protecting the

Quarterly from 1952 to 1955. Probably his best known work (written jointly with Sir D. L. Keir) was *Cases in Constitutional Law* (1st ed. 1928, 5th edn. 1967).

[1] See *Public Law*, Vol. II, p. 93.

[2] Ibid.

[3] David Mitrany was born in 1888 in Bucharest. He studied at the London School of Economics and from 1919 to 1922 was on the editorial staff of the *Manchester Guardian*. His subsequent academic career culminated in his appointment as Professor in the School of Economics and Politics at the Institute for Advanced Studies, Princeton. Many of his writings have been in the field of international politics. See for example: D. Mitrany, *A Working Peace System* (Chicago, Ill., Quadrangle Books, 1966).

Citizen II—A Warden of Rights'. The articles consisted almost entirely of description of the ways in which the Swedish *Justiteom-budsman* functions. Professor Mitrany made no clear proposal for a British version of the Ombudsman apart from a suggestion, at the end of his second article, that, in a country as large as Britain, it might be necessary to have more than one Ombudsman, their spheres being decided 'along the lines of administrative sectors. It might not be a bad beginning here to have such an omnipresent Commissioner of Justice for the nationalized services, and another for the social services.'

These articles were influential. Louis Blom-Cooper, for example, later to play an important part in spreading the Ombudsman idea, was one of those whose interest was first aroused by Mitrany's articles in the *Manchester Guardian*. Nevertheless, the direct line of influence comes from Professor Lawson's memorandum. This, as we have seen, had been returned to him by *The Times*. Professor Lawson then decided to send it to J. A. G. Griffith, editor of the journal *Public Law*.[1] Griffith published the memorandum as part of the editor's notes, although he, of course, acknowledged Professor Lawson's authorship. The text of the memorandum was the same as the text of the letter submitted to *The Times*.[2]

Public Law was, at that time, a new journal. It had been founded in 1956 by a group of lawyers interested in constitutional and administrative law. Its appearance, of itself, was an indication of the revolution in thinking among British lawyers and of the move away from strict Diceyan ideas. Its editor, J. A. G. Griffith, was part author, with H. Street, of *Principles of Administrative Law*, a textbook of administrative law in Britain which first appeared in 1952.[3] Street was a member of the editorial board of *Public Law*, which also included Professor Lawson himself, Professors C. J. Hamson, W. A. Robson, J. D. B. Mitchell, and E. C. S. Wade as well as Sir Ivor Jennings, who was at that time Master of Trinity Hall, Cambridge, and K. C. Wheare, Rector of Exeter College, Oxford, who had been a member of the Franks Committee.

[1] J. A. G. Griffith has been Professor of English Law at the London School of Economics since 1959. He has been editor of *Public Law* since its foundation in 1956.
[2] See *Public Law*, Vol. II (1957), pp. 92–5.
[3] J. A. G. Griffith and H. Street, *Principles of Administrative Law* (Pitman. 1st edn. 1952, 4th edn. 1967). Harry Street was Professor of Law at Nottingham University from 1952 to 1956, Professor of Public Law and Common Law at Manchester University from 1956 to 1960, and has been Professor of English Law there since 1960.

Some of the members of the editorial board of *Public Law*, notably Professors Lawson, Hamson, and Street, were also members of the Council of 'Justice', an organization which had been set up in 1957. Professor Lawson submitted his memorandum on the Inspector-General to the Executive Committee of 'Justice' at the end of 1957. The Executive Committee decided to appoint a subcommittee, chaired by Professor Lawson, to carry out research on his proposal. This subcommittee led directly to the creation of another committee of 'Justice' and to the Whyatt Report, which provided the model upon which the Parliamentary Commissioner Act of 1967 was to be based.

'Justice' was, therefore, the pressure group which played the crucial part in getting a Parliamentary Commissioner established in Britain. Its organization and role therefore deserve close scrutiny. But before turning to it, it is interesting to note how similar Professor Lawson's original proposal for an Inspector-General is to the office of Parliamentary Commissioner, as established by the 1967 Act, and in what ways it differs from it. The similarities are as follows. Professor Lawson proposed that the Inspector-General should be able to investigate complaints of maladministration. He should report to a committee of the House of Commons similar to the Public Accounts Committee and he would 'like the Comptroller and Auditor-General, almost inevitably be a higher civil servant nearing the end of his career' and as such 'he would, while preserving impartiality and independence, not only have experience of administration, but be able to speak to officials in departments as one of themselves.'[1] Finally, the Inspector-General would have access to all the relevant documents in official possession.

In all these respects the Parliamentary Commissioner for Administration, established in 1967, exactly fits in with Professor Lawson's 1957 proposals. In the following respects, however, the Parliamentary Commissioner's powers differ: first, he does not have power to institute judicial proceedings; second, he can only inquire into complaints against a stated list of, and not all, government departments; third, he cannot inquire into complaints against local authorities, administrative tribunals, or the courts. Finally, he cannot receive complaints direct from members of the public but only through M.P.s. Several of these limitations were in fact to be

---

[1] See *Public Law*, Vol. II, p. 94.

suggested by the Whyatt Report published by 'Justice' in 1962. It is to the part played by 'Justice' that we now turn.

'JUSTICE'

The organization known as 'Justice' had its formal foundation meeting in London on 4 June 1957. But, informally, it had been in being since December 1956. In that month lawyers of the three main political parties had, on the initiative of Peter Benenson, agreed to form an *ad hoc* alliance to try to secure fair trials for people accused of treason in Hungary and South Africa. They took 'Justice' as their title. The closing months of 1956 were a period of great intellectual and moral ferment in Britain. The Eden Government's ultimatum to Egypt at the end of October, followed by the Anglo-French military operation at Port Said, had shocked and dismayed a great many people in Britain, of all political parties. Hard upon the Suez Crisis, came the Soviet invasion of Hungary and brutal repression of the democratic rising there. At the same time came news of a trial which was to be held in South Africa in which a large number of the opponents of the Nationalist Government were accused of treason.

The events in Hungary and South Africa had created situations in which the lawyers, joining together in 'Justice', felt they had a duty to make use of their expertise. With the help of funds given by Christian Action, they sent out Gerald Gardiner to attend the preliminary hearing of the mass treason trial which opened in Johannesburg just before Christmas 1956. On his return to Britain, Gardiner reported to a meeting of 300 lawyers in a hall in the City of London.[1]

To Hungary 'Justice' sent Peter Benenson who, during a week's visit, was able to meet Hungarian judges and lawyers and attend part of one political trial. They also sent, in February 1957, representatives, including Sir Hartley Shawcross, Gerald Gardiner, John Foster M.P., and F. Elwyn Jones M.P., to a conference called by the International Commission of Jurists at the Hague to discuss the continuing legal repression in Hungary.

During all this activity, the members of the *ad hoc* 'Justice' committee became aware that their own objectives were very

---

[1] Gerald Austin Gardiner was made a life peer in 1963. He was called to the Bar in 1925. He was Chairman of the General Council of the Bar in 1958 and 1959. In the Wilson Government he was Lord Chancellor from 1964 to 1970.

similar to those of the International Commission of Jurists (as summarized at that time in the Commission's *Bulletin*) 'to seek to foster understanding of and respect for the Rule of Law'. The idea was therefore put forward that 'Justice' should become the British Section of the International Commission of Jurists.

This Commission is a non-governmental international organization which has consultative status with the United Nations, UNESCO, and the Council of Europe.[1] Its members are, in most cases, either former Supreme Court Judges or former Ministers of Justice. For example, Vivian Bose, one of its two Honorary Presidents in 1970, was a former Judge of the Supreme Court of India. Philippe Boulos was a former Minister of Justice of the Lebanon and Lord Shawcross was a former British Attorney-General. A minority of its members are practising judges: for example, in 1970, Terje Wold was Chief Justice of the Supreme Court of Norway.

The Secretary-General of the Commission, in 1970, was Sean MacBride who had at one time been Minister of Foreign Affairs of the Republic of Ireland. In January 1957, its Secretary-General was Norman Marsh.[2] He it was who on 16 January 1957 met representatives of the Inns of Court Conservative and Unionist Society, the Society of Labour Lawyers, and the Association of Liberal Lawyers. The three societies each agreed to nominate three of their members for inclusion in the council of a permanent organization which would be completed, after further consultation, by the Commission issuing invitations to a number of British solicitors and professors of law. Sir Hartley Shawcross, who was the British member of the Commission, was invited to become Chairman.[3]

---

[1] The office of the International Commission of Jurists is in Geneva.

[2] Norman Stayner Marsh was called to the Bar in 1937. From 1947 to 1960 he was a lecturer in law at Oxford University. He was Secretary-General of the International Commission of Jurists from 1956 to 1958 and Director of the British Institute of Comparative Law from 1960 to 1965. Since 1965 he has been a Law Commissioner. (For the Law Commission see below p. 322.)

[3] Hartley William Shawcross was made a Knight in 1945 and a life peer in 1959. He was called to the Bar in 1925 and from 1927 to 1934 was Senior Law Lecturer at Liverpool University. He practised as a barrister on the Northern Circuit and in 1939 became a Q.C. He was Labour M.P. for St. Helens from 1945 to 1958. In the Attlee Government, he held office first as Attorney General from 1945 to 1951. Early in this period, he became famous as the Chief Prosecutor for the U.K. at the International Tribunal at Nuremberg set up to try the Nazi leaders accused of war crimes. From April to October 1951 he was President of the Board of Trade. In the House of Lords he sits as a cross-bencher. He is a director of several large companies, including Shell, E.M.I., and Rank–Hovis–McDougall. He has continued to be Chairman of 'Justice' from its inception.

So, the Council of 'Justice' was completed and its constitution approved on 4 June 1957.[1] Tom Sargant, who had given voluntary help to the society in its early stages, was appointed part-time Secretary. The objects of 'Justice' as set out in the constitution are stated to be:

to uphold and strengthen the principles of the Rule of Law in the territories for which the British Parliament is directly or ultimately responsible; in particular to assist in the maintenance of the highest standards of the administration of justice and in the preservation of the fundamental liberties of the individual;

to assist the International Commission of Jurists as and when requested in giving help to people to whom the Rule of Law is denied and in giving advice and encouragement to those who are seeking to secure the fundamental liberties of the individual;

to keep under review all aspects of the Rule of Law and to publish such material as will be of assistance to lawyers in strengthening it.[2]

The annual reports of 'Justice' show how it has endeavoured to pursue these objectives, internationally, within the British Commonwealth, and in home affairs. In the early years it tended to give more time to international activities and to assisting people whose rights before the law were denied or threatened in such places as South Africa, Ghana, Northern Rhodesia, Nyasaland, and Nigeria.

As time has gone on, it has tended to concentrate more on home affairs. Thus, in the first Annual Report, which appeared in June 1958, approximately half a page of the report was given over to describing the activities of 'Justice' in the international field, approximately half a page to activities in the colonial territories, and half a page to home affairs. In the thirteenth Annual Report, which appeared in June 1970, two pages reported international activities, two pages reported activities in the Commonwealth, and twenty-three pages were concerned with activities in Britain.[3]

This change in the emphasis of the activities of 'Justice' must be accounted for partly by the declining area for which the United

---

[1] 'Justice', First Annual Report, June 1958, p. 1.

[2] Second Annual Report of 'Justice', June 1959, p. 1.

[3] In the case of each report, the space given to the domestic organization of 'Justice', membership, finance, etc., has been ignored.

Kingdom was responsible as a colonial power, partly by the interests of participating lawyers which would naturally be strongest in home affairs, and partly by the inevitable tendency for a group like 'Justice' to be brought into the Government's informal network of advisory agencies. Lord Shawcross commented in his Foreword to the Eleventh Annual Report that much of the time of 'Justice''s new standing committees had been spent in 'preparing answers to working papers and questionnaires put out by the Law Commission or by Departmental Committees'.[1] The following were the standing committees to which Lord Shawcross referred: a committee on Administrative Law, a committee on Evidence, on the Trial of Personal Injury Cases, on Crown Privilege, on Civil Justice, on the Right of Privacy, on Complaints against the Legal Profession, and on Criminal Justice.

The total membership of 'Justice' has always been small. In June 1958, the total membership was 375, made up of 10 members of the judiciary, 100 barristers, 183 solicitors, 33 university teachers of law, and 25 associate members (non-lawyers). The balance of membership was made up of 16 firms of solicitors and 8 associate corporate members (including four National Trade Unions).[2] In 1970 the total membership had grown to 1,655. Of these, 53 were members of the judicial branch (active or retired), 391 were barristers, 520 were solicitors, 153 were academic lawyers, 137 were law students or articled clerks, and 206 were associate members. In addition there were 80 individual members from overseas and 115 corporate members.[3]

While, then, the total membership remained small, two points should be made about it. First, the proportion of members of the legal profession who belong to 'Justice' is by no means insignificant. Second, its membership has always included some very high-powered people.

For example, in 1963, the Council of 'Justice' included two future Ministers in the Wilson Government: Gerald Gardiner, who was to be Lord Chancellor from October 1964 to 1970 (Chairman of the Executive Committee) and F. Elwyn Jones, who was to be Attorney General for the full lifetime of the Wilson Government (a joint Hon. Treasurer). It included two prominent Conservative M.P.s, both of

---

[1] 'Justice', 11th Annual Report, 1968, p. 2.
[2] See 'Justice', 1st Annual Report, 1958, p. 1.
[3] 'Justice', 13th Annual Report, 1970, p. 27.

whom were to be active in the standing committee on the Parliamentary Commissioner Bill in 1966: John Foster (Vice-Chairman of the Council) and William L. Roots (member of the Council). It also included two prominent Liberal M.P.s: Roderic Bowen (one of the joint Hon. Treasurers) and Emlyn Hooson (member of the Council).

The finances of 'Justice' have always been exiguous. The sources of finance are threefold: members' subscriptions, donations, and receipts from the Annual Ball which in 1970, as in previous years, was held at the Savoy Hotel.

The nerve-centre of 'Justice' is to be found in its small office in Crane Court, off Fleet Street, in the City of London. On the wall behind the table, where committees of 'Justice' confer, is a tiled mural specially designed and executed by Mrs. Charlotte Gerard. On the left of the mural is a dark, forbidding prison. In front of it a huge, driverless bulldozer, with gaping maw, pursues some naked men, women, and children who are running towards a standing, bearded figure helped by a kneeling angel. The prison and the bulldozer represent the unfeeling machinery of the modern state which (in the words of 'Justice''s own description of the mural) is 'threatening to crush and engulf the common man, who is fleeing for protection to a Mosaic figure upholding Justice and administering it with Mercy'.

If one is to classify 'Justice' as a pressure group one can say according to the author's own analysis that it is an 'ideas group'.[1] Or one can say with S. E. Finer that it is a 'cause group'.[2] But it is an ideas group of a very special kind. It is drawn predominantly from members of one occupational group—the lawyers in their four branches: judges, barristers, solicitors, and academics. It includes many members who have a very high expertise and prestige. It has been highly influential: not least in its campaign to get a form of Ombudsman established in Britain.

---

[1] See F. Stacey, *The Government of Modern Britain* (Clarendon Press, 1968), p. 320.
[2] See S. E. Finer, *Anonymous Empire. A Study of the Lobby in Great Britain* (2nd edn. Pall Mall, 1966), p. 3.

II

'JUSTICE' AND THE WHYATT REPORT

PROFESSOR Lawson sent his memorandum advocating an Inspector-General of Administration to Tom Sargant, the Secretary of 'Justice', late in 1957. The Council of 'Justice' considered the memorandum and decided to set up a subcommittee with Professor Lawson as Chairman to examine the proposal. Its terms of reference were to consider 'a proposal to institute a public office, similar to those established in Scandinavian countries, to which complaints against harsh and unjust acts of the administration can be made'.[1]

The subcommittee met once and decided that it was necessary to gather more information about the working of Ombudsmen in Scandinavia. Professor Lawson had an enthusiastic ally in Tom Sargant, who assisted the committee. Sargant, who is not a lawyer, but is a Justice of the Peace, had been a member of the Commonwealth Party during the war.[2] He had long been in favour of a 'Ministry of Stupidities', a special government department which would look into complaints of bureaucratic muddle and unfairness in the government machine. The idea of an Ombudsman therefore appealed to him strongly.

During the summer of 1958 details were collected for the subcommittee of the working of Ombudsmen in Sweden, Denmark, and Finland. The subcommittee also obtained a summarized translation of a report of a Norwegian inquiry into the advisability of setting up an Ombudsman in Norway.[3]

---

[1] 'Justice', First Annual Report, June 1958, p. 4.

[2] The Commonwealth Party came into existence during the latter years of the Second World War as a result of frustrations occasioned by the party truce under which the Labour Party did not fight Conservative-held seats at by-elections and vice versa. The Commonwealth Party was an idealistic left-wing party with a considerable middle-class following. After the war, many of its leading personalities, following the example of Sir Richard Acland, joined the Labour Party.

[3] 'Justice', Second Annual Report, June 1959, p. 3.

At the same time, in the summer of 1958, there appeared in the journal of the International Commission of Jurists an article by Professor S. Hurwitz, the Danish Ombudsman, on the work of his office. This article had been specially commissioned in 1957 by Norman Marsh, the Secretary-General of the Commission. Professor J. A. G. Griffith arranged for the same article to appear in the Autumn 1958 number of *Public Law*.[1]

The Council of 'Justice' then invited Professor Hurwitz to come to Britain to lecture on the work of his office. He came over in November 1958 and gave lectures at meetings arranged by 'Justice' in the City of London, in Oxford, Bristol, Nottingham, and Manchester.[2] The lectures attracted little publicity and to some of the organizers the outcome seemed disappointing. But interest in the Ombudsman was widening. For example, Louis Blom-Cooper, a member of 'Justice', had been trying to persuade the *Observer* to publish some articles on the Ombudsman in Scandinavia. The editor did not, at first, take to the idea, but when Hurwitz visited Britain, it did interest him and he then agreed to Blom-Cooper's suggestion.[3]

Blom-Cooper went to Scandinavia in the Spring of 1959. He visited Denmark, Sweden, and Norway. He interviewed the Ombudsmen in Denmark and Sweden and discussed proposals for an Ombudsman in Norway. On his return, he wrote two articles which the *Observer* published on 31 May and 7 June 1959. The articles set out in clear and persuasive form the background to the Ombudsman systems in Scandinavia, the success which Hurwitz had achieved as Danish Ombudsman since 1954, and the need for an Ombudsman in Britain.

These articles first got the idea of an Ombudsman off the ground in Britain. From then on, the word 'Ombudsman' came into general use as someone who could look into grievances in an impartial manner. Governments, and many politicians, in Britain were indeed slow to realize how well the essence of the idea had been grasped by the informed public here.

Meanwhile the subcommittee formed by 'Justice' to look into the Ombudsman proposal had temporarily suspended its activities.

[1] S. Hurwitz, 'The Danish Parliamentary Commissioner', *Public Law*, Autumn 1958, pp. 236–53.

[2] See 'Justice', Second Annual Report, June 1959, p. 3.

[3] Dr. Louis J. Blom-Cooper Q.C. is Joint Director of the Legal Research Unit at Bedford College, London University.

At a second meeting, in 1958, the subcommittee had decided that further research was needed into the feasibility of establishing an Ombudsman in Britain. A full-scale inquiry would be necessary and since 'Justice' did not have enough funds to launch one it would be necessary to secure the support of a charitable foundation for this purpose.

In June 1959, Lord Shawcross announced at the Annual General Meeting of 'Justice' that the Council was going to set on foot such an inquiry as soon as they had the necessary funds. But all through the summer and autumn of 1959 approaches to one foundation after another brought no response. Then aid came to the 'Justice' campaign in a quite unexpected way. A Conservative M.P., Dr. Donald Johnson, had put down a question to the Prime Minister asking him if he had given further consideration to a memorandum he had sent him suggesting the appointment of a Parliamentary Commissioner after the Scandinavian model.

The background to this question was very strange, but it has been fully described by Dr. Donald Johnson himself in two of his own books.[1] Dr. Johnson, besides being a medical man as well as a publisher and an M.P., had at one time owned the Marlborough Arms Hotel at Woodstock in Oxfordshire. In October 1950 he was, with his wife, taking over personal control of this hotel from his manager when he was, as he later decided, the victim of a doping plot. He implies in his book that the plot was connected with the activities of an international vice operator who, he later discovered, had frequently stayed at the hotel. As a result, Dr. Johnson concludes, of the clandestine administration of drugs in his and his wife's drinks, they both began to behave so peculiarly that he was certified as insane and taken to a mental hospital, while his wife was taken away to friends.

From then on, Dr. Johnson had a double grievance against 'the authorities': first that he had been taken to a mental hospital against his will and had some difficulty in securing his release, second that when he asked the Chief Constable of Oxfordshire to investigate the doping to which he had been subjected, the Chief Constable refused. When Dr. Johnson was elected Conservative M.P. for Carlisle at the General Election of 1955, he interested himself particularly in moves to reform the laws dealing with mental health,

[1] See particularly Donald McI. Johnson, *A Cassandra at Westminster* (Johnson, 1967) pp. 118–33.

and in the methods by which the citizen could secure more effective redress against officialdom.

In 1958 he read in a newspaper that Dr. Hurwitz was coming to Britain, at the invitation of 'Justice', to give a series of lectures. Dr. Johnson then got into touch with Tom Sargant, whom he already knew, and asked for further information. He then decided to go to Denmark where he saw Hurwitz who showed him how the office of Ombudsman operated. On his return to Britain, Dr. Johnson put down a question to the Prime Minister and also sent him a memorandum enlarging on the terms of the question.[1]

This was the memorandum to which he referred in the parliamentary question which was down to receive a written answer from the Prime Minister in November 1959. The Lord Chancellor's office was the government department which was given the task of producing an answer to Dr. Johnson's question. The officials in the Lord Chancellor's office, knowing, themselves, very little about the Ombudsman, decided to ring Tom Sargant in the 'Justice' office to see if he could help them. He told them something of what he knew and added that 'Justice' was about to carry out an inquiry into the feasibility of establishing an Ombudsman in Britain. He did not say that they had not yet secured the funds to make possible such an inquiry.

So it came about that the Lord Chancellor's office drafted the Prime Minister's written answer to Dr. Johnson's question in the following terms:

I have given further consideration to the memorandum submitted to me by my hon. Friend. There would be many constitutional and practical difficulties in the way of adopting the Scandinavian system in view of the very different constitutional and other circumstances of this country. I understand, however, that a group of lawyers is to undertake a serious and objective study of the matter, and I think it would be well to wait until the results of this study are known before coming to any final conclusion.[2]

This answer was an immense boon to 'Justice'. It gave their projected inquiry a quasi-official status. They could point out, when asking for funds, that the Prime Minister had said that his Govern-

---

[1] Dr. Donald Johnson was Conservative M.P. for Carlisle from 1955 to 1966. As a Liberal, he had unsuccessfully fought constituencies in four earlier elections. He was born in 1903 and was medical officer of the Cambridge University expedition to East Greenland in 1926 and of the Grenfell Mission in Labrador from 1937 to 1939.

[2] H.C. Deb. Vol. 612, Col. 68.

ment was waiting for the results of the 'Justice' inquiry. Working from this much more favourable position, 'Justice' was able, early in 1960, to secure the necessary funds through donations from Mr. and Mrs. Neville Blond and the Isaac Wolfson Foundation.[1]

The next task was to find someone suitably qualified to direct the inquiry. They were fortunate in securing the services of Sir John Whyatt who had just retired as Chief Justice of Singapore.[2] Sir John Whyatt had a very high status as a recently retired colonial judge, he had a knowledge of administration, and a strong attachment to the principle that justice should prevail over *raison d'État*.

Sir John Whyatt was assisted by an advisory committee. The original intention had been that Sir Hartley Shawcross would be Chairman of the Committee. In fact, he was not able to attend any meetings and Norman Marsh, who had originally been appointed Deputy Chairman, became Chairman. One of the other members had been nominated on Sir John's initiative. This was Sir Sydney Caine who was at that time Director of the London School of Economics.[3] He was a personal friend of Sir John's. The latter valued his experience of administration and was not disappointed in the contribution he made in the Advisory Committee. Dr. H. W. R. Wade made up the fourth full member of the Advisory Committee and supplied some of the academic expertise.[4]

There were, in addition, two distinguished people who were consulted during the research although they were not members of the Advisory Committee. These were Lord Devlin[5] and Sir Oliver Franks. Lord Devlin was an old friend of Sir John Whyatt's and

[1] 'Justice', Third Annual Report, June 1960, p. 5.

[2] Sir John Whyatt was born in 1905. He entered the Colonial Legal Service in 1937. From 1951 to 1955 he was Attorney General and Minister for Legal Affairs in Kenya. From 1955 to 1958 he was Chief Justice of Singapore. After completing his inquiry for 'Justice' he was made Judge of the Chief Court for the Persian Gulf where he served from 1961 to 1966. He was Director of Studies of the Overseas Government Legal Officers Course in London from 1966 to 1967.

[3] Sir Sydney Caine was Director of the London School of Economics from 1957 to 1967. He was Vice-Chancellor of the University of Malaya from 1952 to 1956 and previously had a distinguished career as a Civil Servant in the Colonial Office and the Treasury.

[4] H. W. R. Wade was a Lecturer in Law at Cambridge University from 1947 to 1961. In 1961 he was appointed Professor of English Law at Oxford. His publications include *Administrative Law* (Clarendon Press, 2nd edn., 1967) and *Towards Administrative Justice* (Ann Arbor, Michigan University, 1963).

[5] Lord Devlin was a Justice of the High Court, Queen's Bench Division, from 1948 to 1960. He was Lord Justice of Appeal from 1960 to 1961 and a Lord of Appeal in Ordinary from 1961 to 1964. In 1964 he was appointed Chairman of the Press Council.

had been at school with him. Sir John did not know Sir Oliver Franks well but greatly admired his abilities. He also provided an invaluable link with the Franks Report and was to contribute an influential foreword to the Whyatt Report.

Sir John Whyatt began his inquiry by making contact with the Permanent Secretaries of what he considered to be the key government departments which would be affected by the appointment of a Parliamentary Commissioner. These were the Ministries of Housing and Local Government, of Education, Health, and Agriculture, the Board of Trade, the Scottish Office, the Post Office, and the War Office. He did not approach the Foreign Office or the Colonial Office on the ground that these were departments which had little contact with the general public in the United Kingdom. He also excluded the Ministry of Pensions and National Insurance because it had a well-developed tribunal system.

The Treasury was also, obviously, a key department but here he had contact not with one of the Joint Permanent Secretaries but with the Treasury Solicitor, Sir Harold Kent, with whom he had useful talks. In the key departments which he had selected he saw, in most cases, the Permanent Secretary, but in some cases his deputy. The departments were all very helpful. Some Permanent Secretaries had prepared a memorandum discussing the implications for their department of the appointment of an Ombudsman. Of all the Permanent Secretaries, the most co-operative and interested was Dame Evelyn Sharp, Permanent Secretary of the Ministry of Housing and Local Government. Sir John also found the Permanent Secretary at the Scottish Office, and his colleagues, exceptionally helpful.

After seeing the Permanent Secretaries, Sir John prepared memoranda including recommendations for the Report. He then discussed these with the members of the Advisory Committee. The main proposals in the Report were decided by the Advisory Committee, although Sir John himself wrote the final text of the Report.

In addition to talking to top Civil Servants, Sir John also consulted members of the John Hilton Bureau at Cambridge. This organization had been set up during the Second World War and had long been financed by the *News of the World*. It existed to give advice to members of the public particularly in their dealings with central departments and local authorities. At the peak of its activities, the full-time staff of the Bureau included five solicitors, four barristers, three income tax specialists, and seven experts in national insurance questions, as well as some former officials of local authorities.

A group of organizations which he consulted was the Citizens' Advice Bureaux. He talked to officers of several Bureaux as well as to the Secretary of the Standing Conference of Citizens' Advice Bureaux in London. Sir John Whyatt also visited Denmark and Sweden to consult the Ombudsmen in those countries. He spent about two weeks in Denmark and paid a short visit to Sweden.

The main part of the work of the inquiry was undertaken by Sir John Whyatt himself assisted by his secretary Miss Corinne Lyman. The research assistants who helped him were employed on a part-time basis. Some, like Philip Allott, who was waiting to go into the Foreign Service, worked on specific aspects of the Report, others, like Roy Duffell, and Anders Hald, helped by translating Scandinavian documents.

Clearly, the inquiry was made on a meagre budget, but what was lacking in numbers of full-time staff was made up by the experience and ability of the Director, Sir John Whyatt, and of the members of his Advisory Committee. The Report issued was realistic yet bold in overall conception, although cautious in many of its detailed proposals.

THE WHYATT REPORT

The Report was a bold one in two principal ways. In the first place, it clearly asserted that it was carrying on where the Franks report left off. The Franks committee had been precluded by its terms of reference from considering complaints against the acts of administrators, where there was no statutory provision for an administrative tribunal or inquiry to consider the complaint. This was the gap to which the Whyatt Committee addressed themselves and Sir Oliver Franks, in his foreword, himself gave his blessing to their Report. Their proposals, he said, 'are skilfully elaborated in the Report and deserve the consideration of a wide circle of readers'.[1]

Second, the Report was a bold one in its advocacy of two major reforms to meet the situation left after Franks. It proposed a large extension of the system of administrative tribunals to consider complaints against the discretionary actions of administrators, and the establishment of the British equivalent to an Ombudsman to look

[1] Whyatt Committee, *The Citizen and the Administration : The Redress of Grievances*. A Report by 'Justice' (Stevens, 1961), p. xii.

into complaints of maladministration. The Report argued for these major reforms in a very cogent and lucid way. Indeed, Sir John Whyatt's Report may well be called 'one of the great non-state papers'.

The Report was cautious, however, in the following ways. First, it proposed that a Minister should be able to veto any proposed investigation by the Ombudsman, or Parliamentary Commissioner.[1] Second, it suggested that the Parliamentary Commissioner should normally only be allowed to examine the outward and inward correspondence, in a department, when investigating a case. He would only be allowed to see the internal minutes relating to a case, if he declared that he would be unable to carry out his duties efficiently without so doing. If the Minister did not then concede him this right, Parliament would have to be asked to require the disclosure of the internal minutes.[2]

These two proposals, if adopted in the subsequent legislation, would have gravely limited the effectiveness of the British Parliamentary Commissioner. Fortunately, the 1967 Act was more radical in its approach. The Act contains no provision for ministerial veto of an investigation, and it gives the Parliamentary Commissioner access to all departmental documents including the internal minutes. Here it is in line with the 'Justice's' second initiative in the campaign for an Ombudsman: the draft bill submitted to Ministers in 1964.[3]

It is interesting to consider the reasons for the cautious approach of the Whyatt Committee in these two aspects. The members of the Committee were very much aware of the fact that they had to persuade an administration, the Macmillan Cabinet, which had not shown itself strongly in favour of institutional reform. They also had to persuade senior Civil Servants that the adoption of an Ombudsman would not change, for the worse, the relationship between themselves and Ministers, and that it would not interfere with efficient administration in the departments. Thus we find the Whyatt Report arguing that, because of the importance of the convention of ministerial responsibility in Britain, it was advisable to give the Minister power to veto an investigation.[4]

The Committee were also aware of a distinct coolness, not to say hostility, among many M.P.s to the prospect that an Ombudsman

[1] Ibid., pp. 74–5.   [2] Ibid., pp. 70–1.
[3] See below pp. 43–6.   [4] Whyatt Report, p. 74.

might reduce their importance to the public as 'grievance chasers'. So we find the Whyatt Committee proposing that 'during an initial and testing period' (possibly five years) complaints should be channelled to the Parliamentary Commissioner only through M.P.s and peers. The 1967 Act is even more cautious in its approach. Complaints can only be made by the public to the Parliamentary Commissioner through M.P.s. Peers are not given a look in and there is no mention in the Act that confining access through M.P.s is intended as a temporary provision.[1]

Finally, it was a cautious approach on behalf of the Whyatt Committee to make a rigid distinction between discretionary decisions and maladministration, and to say that only the latter should be the concern of the Parliamentary Commissioner. The effect of this approach was to be most far-reaching. The key phrase in the 1967 Act says that the Parliamentary Commissioner may investigate a complaint that a member of the public has 'sustained injustice in consequence of maladministration'.[2]

The Wilson Government therefore closely followed the Whyatt Committee's proposals, and in so doing placed itself open to the criticism, particularly in 1967 and in the first half of 1968, that it was severely curtailing the activities of the Parliamentary Commissioner. To be fair to the Whyatt Committee, however, it must be remembered that they proposed that appeal against discretionary decisions should be a matter for administrative tribunals and that, accordingly, the tribunal sector should be greatly strengthened and improved. In particular, they recommended that the Council on Tribunals should be given power to recommend the creation of new tribunals, where it found a gap in the system of tribunals. Some of the most valuable sections of the Whyatt Report point to certain of these gaps; for example, the absence of a system of statutory tribunals to consider complaints in the national hospital service.[3]

They also recommended that a general tribunal should be set up to hear appeals from discretionary decisions on subjects where there were not sufficient appeals to justify the creation of a specialized tribunal. The Whyatt Committee gave as an example, here, appeals against discretionary decisions refusing permits for vivisection.[4]

The Wilson Government did not implement this part of the

[1] See below espec. pp. 54–5 and 102–11.
[2] Parliamentary Commissioner Act 1967, Section 5–(1) (a).
[3] Whyatt Report, pp. 12–26.　　　　[4] Ibid., pp. 31–3.

Whyatt Report during its term of office from 1964 to 1970. It did not give the Council on Tribunals power to recommend the creation of new tribunals, and it did not set up a general tribunal. The only reforming measure, in the field of administrative tribunals and inquiries, which it did bring in was the Tribunals and Inquiries Act, 1966. This modest reform enabled the Lord Chancellor to bring within the scrutiny of the Council on Tribunals certain types of inquiry which were not included under the 1958 Act.[1] It could, therefore, be argued that the Wilson Government only implemented half of the Whyatt Committee Report and did not give their approach a fair trial.

Even so, it does seem unfortunate that the Whyatt Committee decided to recommend that the Parliamentary Commissioner should be confined to cases of maladministration. In so doing, Sir John Whyatt understood that he was following the Danish practice. He said on page 55 of the Report:

It is, however, important to note that, where the administrative decisions involve the exercise of discretion, the [Danish] Ombudsman will not investigate complaints that the discretion has been exercised in an unsuitable manner or, to put the matter another way, he will not take up a complaint against administrative discretions merely because he would or might have exercised the discretion differently if he had been sitting in the administrator's chair.

This turn of phrase gives a misleading impression of the way in which the Danish Ombudsman functions. The directives for the Danish Ombudsman, adopted by the Folketing in February 1962, state at Article 3, Section 1: 'The Parliamentary Commissioner shall keep himself informed as to whether any person comprised by his jurisdiction pursues unlawful ends, takes arbitrary or unreasonable decisions or otherwise commits mistakes or acts of negligence in the discharge of his or her duties.'

The Ombudsman, Professor Stephan Hurwitz, himself describing the range of his functions, stated, also in 1962, that there are 'certain groups of discretionary administrative decisions . . . where as a rule experience has proved that the Commissioner is not able to criticise' the decision and therefore would not begin an investigation.[2] He

[1] See below Chapter XVI, pp. 321–2.
[2] Stephan Hurwitz, *The Ombudsman. Denmark's Parliamentary Commissioner for Civil and Military Administration* (Det Danske Selskab, Copenhagen, 1962), p. 18.

instanced as examples of such discretionary administrative decisions: refusal of a petition for free legal aid in law suits against private persons, refusal of an application for reduction of a tax assessment and decisions about the degree of disablement fixed in workmen's compensation cases. There is, however, a whole range of discretionary administrative decisions where he is able to criticize the action of an administrator, whether or not maladministration has been involved.[1]

We may, indeed, conclude about the Danish Ombudsman that he is free to consider the exercise of administrative discretion, whether or not maladministration is involved, except in fields where certain kinds of expertise, or special knowledge, are desirable in assessing the quality of the decision made. This is a very different picture from the position which Sir John Whyatt described as one in which the Ombudsman did not normally consider the exercise of administrative discretion unless maladministration was involved.

To be fair, it should be remembered that the statements of the powers of the Danish Ombudsman, quoted above, appeared only in 1962, after the Whyatt Report had been published. The same is true of the New Zealand Parliamentary Commissioner (Ombudsman) Act. This Act became law in 1962. A copy of the bill reached the 'Justice' offices in 1961, too late to be considered by the Whyatt Committee. It was, however, printed as an appendix to the Report.

The New Zealand Act in no way confines the Parliamentary Commissioner (Ombudsman) to cases involving maladministration. Section 19 of the Act allows the Commissioner to report on an administrative decision, recommendation, act, or omission, which is in his opinion 'unreasonable, unjust or improperly discriminatory'.[2] The committee of 'Justice' which produced a draft bill in 1964 closely followed the wording in the New Zealand Act and abandoned the Whyatt Committee's distinction between those discretionary actions which do, and those which do not, involve maladministration.[3] But, by then, the Whyatt Committee's approach had made too deep an impact on official thinking and was, as we have seen, carried over into the 1967 Parliamentary Commissioner Act.

Certain other features of the Whyatt Report deserve to be noted.

[1] See also on the powers of the Danish Ombudsman. W. Gellhorn, *Ombudsmen and Others. Citizens' Protectors in Nine Countries* (Harvard University Press, Oxford University Press, 1967), pp. 5–47.

[2] Parliamentary Commissioner (Ombudsman) Act, 1962, Section 19.

[3] See below pp. 45–6.

The sections which present the case for a Parliamentary Commissioner as a supplement to, rather than a rival of, parliamentary scrutiny of administration were particularly well done. Sir John Whyatt argued that question time and adjournment debates were valuable but that they needed to be supplemented by impartial investigation of complaints. He pointed out that the contest between a backbencher and a Minister was often an uneven one in the sense that 'the Minister has access to documents and information which are denied to his opponent.'[1] A Parliamentary Commissioner would have access to documents which the M.P. would not see and would be able to make an impartial investigation. This was an argument whose force M.P.s could readily appreciate. Experience since 1967 has shown that it was not overstated.

The Whyatt Committee's advocacy of the relationship which the Parliamentary Commissioner should have with the House of Commons was also influential. They argued that he should have the same status as the Comptroller and Auditor-General and should be answerable only to Parliament.[2] This recommendation was followed in the 1967 Act.

It is interesting to note the Whyatt Committee's attitude to the *Conseil d'État*. They rested their decision not to recommend developments in Britain along the lines of the *Conseil d'État* on two grounds. First, the Franks Committee had not recommended reconstruction of the British system of administrative tribunals in this direction and had rejected the idea of an Administrative Appeal Court. Second, the Whyatt Report argued that the successful working of the *Conseil d'État* depended 'on the corporate unity of its judicial and advisory sections', for which there is no parallel in Britain.[3]

Finally, the Whyatt Committee recommended that the Parliamentary Commissioner should not be empowered to hear complaints against local authorities. Here, again, the 1967 Act was to follow their recommendation. However, in an Appendix, they examined some of the many areas in which there was not adequate machinery for appeal against the decisions of local authorities. They suggested that local authorities should examine the possibility of appointing complaints officers who would receive and investigate complaints of maladministration on behalf of each Council.[4]

To sum up, we may say that the Whyatt Report had great in-

[1] Whyatt Report, p. 41.   [2] Ibid., p. 68.
[3] Ibid., pp. 7–8.   [4] Ibid., p. 89.

fluence over the form in which an Ombudsman type institution was eventually established in Britain. The role of the Parliamentary Commissioner and his relationship to Parliament bear a strong resemblance to the proposals set out in the Report. On balance, his powers under the 1967 Act are greater than the Whyatt Committee envisaged. But the Committee did not have the advantage of being able to consider the wider powers conferred upon the New Zealand Ombudsman. They were also seeking to frame proposals which would be acceptable to a Conservative administration which seemed to be none too eager for reform. The reception of their proposals by the Macmillan Government will be one of the themes of the next chapter.

III

THE MACMILLAN GOVERNMENT TURNS DOWN THE WHYATT REPORT

'JUSTICE' has been the most prominent and influential of the pressure groups to campaign for an Ombudsman in Britain. We must not overlook, however, the activities of another group: 'The Society for Individual Freedom'.

THE SOCIETY FOR INDIVIDUAL FREEDOM

This Society was founded in 1942 by Sir Ernest John Pickstone Benn. Sir Ernest Benn was a lifelong defender of individual rights, from a somewhat idiosyncratic position, as evidenced by the titles of a few of the many books he wrote and published: *The Confessions of a Capitalist* (1925), *Letters of an Individualist* (1929), *This Soft Age* (1933).[1] This society emerged in 1942 from a group of Conservative back-benchers who called themselves the League of Freedom. Sir Ernest Benn's organization was at first called 'The Society of Individualists'. Later it changed its name to 'The Society for Individual Freedom'. It has always been a society of right-wing individualists. Their attitude to State ownership of industry is indicated by the fourth of the 'Objects of the Society', printed on the first page of their magazine *Freedom First*: '4. Free Enterprise. We hold that the case for State intervention must at all times be clearly established.'

The first three Objects of the Society indicate support for individual liberty, parliamentary sovereignty, and the rule of law. These objects are non-partisan and the Society maintains that membership is open to everyone irrespective of party. However, the Conservative M.P.s who are associated with the Society are gener-

---

[1] Sir Ernest Benn was born in 1875 and died in 1954. He was a publisher and businessman. From 1924 to 1945 he was chairman of his own publishing firm, Ernest Benn Ltd. From 1934 to 1949 he was chairman of the United Kingdom Provident Institution.

ally thought to be on the right wing of the Conservative Party. Thus, Antony Lambton M.P. was President of the Society, over a long period, until August 1970 when he resigned after being appointed Under-Secretary of State at the Ministry of Defence, soon after the formation of the Heath Government. He was succeeded as President of the Society by Sir John Rodgers, the Conservative M.P. for Sevenoaks. Another prominent member of the Executive Committee of the Society was Victor Montagu, who, as Viscount Hinchingbrooke, had represented South Dorset in Parliament and was well known for his right-wing position on many topics.[1]

From time to time, also, some of the policies of the Society for Individual Freedom have had strong right-wing connotations. Thus, in April 1968, the Chairman of the Society, George K. Young, at a meeting of the Society in Birmingham, advocated repatriation of coloured immigrants.[2] He was reported by *The Times*, on 19 April 1968, as saying: 'If in five years we have immigrants moving out at least as fast as they came in, we may at least save the situation.' *The Times* columnist said that these were 'astonishing views'. This was some months before Enoch Powell first advocated the repatriation of immigrants.

Similarly, in October 1968, Ronald Bell, the Conservative M.P. for South Buckinghamshire, speaking at a Society for Individual Freedom Meeting, at Oxford, attacked the Race Relations Bill, then before Parliament, as an attempt to secure integration of the races 'at the point of the dagger—a legal dagger'.[3] George K. Young has defended this position with the argument that a multi-racial society necessitates authoritarian controls and is incompatible with

[1] Antony Lambton has been Conservative M.P. for Berwick-upon-Tweed since 1951. He relinquished the peerage on succeeding his father, the Earl of Durham, in 1970. He is a landowner and journalist.

Sir John Rodgers has been Conservative M.P. for Sevenoaks since 1950. He was Parliamentary Secretary at the Board of Trade from 1958 to 1960. He is a company director and author.

Victor Montagu was, as Viscount Hinchingbrooke, Conservative M.P. for South Dorset from 1941 to 1962. He succeeded to the earldom of Sandwich in 1962 but renounced the title in 1964. He was leader of the 'Suez group' of Conservative M.P.s who resigned the Whip in May 1957 in protest against the Macmillan Government's decision to allow British shipping to use the Suez Canal.

[2] George Kennedy Young has been with Kleinwort Benson's, the merchant bankers, since 1961. From 1946 to 1953 he was a member of the British Foreign Service. From 1953 to 1961 he was in the Ministry of Defence, attaining the rank of Under-Secretary in 1960. His publications include: *Masters of Indecision* (1962), *Merchant Banking* (1966), *Finance and World Power* (1968), and *Who Goes Home?* (1969).

[3] Report in the *Guardian*, 8 October 1968.

individual freedom. Therefore Britain must be prevented from becoming a multi-racial society.

This sort of attitude puts the Society for Individual Freedom a long way to the right of 'Justice' in the political spectrum, since as we have seen, 'Justice' has given help to opponents of the apartheid policies of the Government of South Africa. But 'Justice' and the Society for Individual Freedom have made common cause in the campaign for an Ombudsman or, if that is too strong a way of putting it, have worked along broadly parallel lines.

Before assessing its efforts in this direction, it is appropriate to say a little about the organization of the Society for Individual Freedom. Membership of the Society is open to anyone for an annual subscription of £1·50. In fact, many individual members contribute much more than this. The Society publishes a quarterly journal called *Freedom First* which is sent to all members. Some of its meetings every year are held in the Palace of Westminster. They usually take the form of luncheon meetings. Arrangements for the meetings are made by Conservative M.P.s who are members of the Society. These are usually the less controversial meetings of the Society. Speakers at such meetings in 1968, for example, included Sir Henry Wells, Chairman of the Land Commission and Professor John Vaizey, Professor of Economics at Brunel University.

The Society also undertakes a certain amount of case work on behalf of its members, and others, who are in dispute with nationalized industries, government departments, or local authorities. The Honorary Secretary and Organizer of the Society from 1959 to 1968 was Mrs. Lilian Hardern who had previously worked for the National Council of Women as Legal and Parliamentary Secretary and Chairman of its Housing Committee.

The Society for Individual Freedom's part in the campaign for an Ombudsman began in 1960. Early in that year, the Society commissioned T. E. Utley to write a book examining the possible relevance for Britain of the Danish institution of Ombudsman. The resulting book was called *Occasion for Ombudsman* and appeared in 1961.[1] The Society for Individual Freedom, and Dudley Glanfield, provided finance for the writing and the book was published by Dr. Donald Johnson's publishing house.[2] In fact, Dr. Johnson

---

[1] T. E. Utley, *Occasion for Ombudsman* (Christopher Johnson, 1961).

[2] Dudley Glanfield's dispute with the Central Electricity Authority is one of the cases described in *Occasion for Ombudsman*. Glanfield had contested the Electricity Authority's right to erect a pylon and cables on his land at Windlesham, Surrey.

provides one of the few links between 'Justice' and the Society for Individual Freedom. As we have seen, it was Dr. Johnson's question to the Prime Minister in 1959 which enabled 'Justice' to find the Funds for the Whyatt inquiry. Dr. Johnson is also a member both of 'Justice' and of the Society for Individual Freedom. He gave detailed help and advice to T. E. Utley in the writing of *Occasion for Ombudsman*.

The interests of the Society for Individual Freedom are reflected in the approach taken in Utley's book. The book begins with short chapters on the Danish Ombudsman, the Franks Report, and the limitations of parliamentary redress in Britain. The main part of the book consists of a description of a series of actual cases in which individuals have tried to secure the redress of grievances. Of these, three cases were concerned with nationalized industries, three with the Health Service, two concerned disputes with local authorities, one was a complaint against the police, and one was an Army personnel matter. Finally, a number of cases of certification under the Mental Health Acts were considered.

It is interesting to note that nearly all these cases fall within spheres which are excluded from the terms of reference of the Parliamentary Commissioner under the 1967 Act: nationalized industries, the National Health Service, local authorities, the police, and personnel matters in the armed forces. This is not to say that these subjects are rightly excluded from his terms of reference: the Ombudsmen in Sweden, for example, are concerned with all such matters.

The final chapter of Utley's book has the title: 'Do we need a British Ombudsman?' His answer is in the affirmative. He argues that the conception of the Ombudsman is far more consistent with British practice than is the *Conseil d'État*. He avers that 'any attempt to superimpose a *Conseil d'État* on the British civil service would be strongly and reasonably resisted'.[1] But he is not greatly enamoured of the Scandinavian practice of giving the investigating function to one man, helped by a small staff. He suggests that in the British context a committee of the House of Commons might take the place of the Ombudsman.

The Society for Individual Freedom bought 630 copies of *Occason for Ombudsman* and sent one to each Member of Parliament. Mrs. Hardern also sent a copy to Conservative Central Office before

[1] Utley, op. cit., p. 138.

the Annual Conference in 1961. But the Conservative leadership was to prove a disappointment to her.

SOME HOPEFUL SIGNS

There had been some encouraging signs in 1960 and 1961. 'Justice' brought over Professor Stephan Hurwitz, the Danish Ombudsman, for a second visit to Britain in April 1960, and this visit was a much greater success than his first one had been in 1958. On 10 April 1960 the *Observer* printed a highly favourable profile of Professor Hurwitz and explanation of his role as Ombudsman. On 12 May the *Listener* printed the text of a discussion between Professor Hurwitz and two English academic lawyers, H. W. R. Wade and J. A. G. Griffith. The discussion had been broadcast on the Third Programme under the title 'The Danish Ombudsman and His Office'. They discussed the applicability of the Danish Ombudsman system to Britain. H. W. R. Wade concluded: 'Perhaps we shall come round to your way of thinking, Professor Hurwitz. At any rate, if we do, it will not be the first time that Denmark will have conquered England.'[1]

On 19 May 1961, Dr. Donald Johnson succeeded in getting an adjournment debate on a motion asking the Government to move the appointment of a select committee to consider the institution of a Parliamentary Commissioner 'to investigate and report publicly on all cases in which an individual can claim to have suffered serious damage to his reputation, his livelihood, or his welfare, consequent on administrative or executive action by public authorities'.[2]

Dr. Johnson said that he had had this motion on the order paper for almost two years. Eventually, the Speaker came to his support by selecting it as the first motion to be debated on the day preceding the Whitsun recess.

Dr. Johnson had had to wait a long time for his debate but when it did come he had good value. The debate lasted from 11.05 a.m. to 2.16 p.m. and showed a fair measure of support for the idea of a Parliamentary Commissioner. Perhaps Members were influenced by the copies of Utley's *Occasion for Ombudsman* which they had received. Dr. Johnson noted with satisfaction during the debate that he could see one Member holding his copy.

Only one Member who spoke in the debate categorically opposed

---

[1] The *Listener*, 12 May 1960, p. 838.
[2] H.C. Deb. Vol. 640, Col. 1693.

the appointment of a Parliamentary Commissioner; this was Dudley Williams, Conservative Member for Exeter.[1] Some members, for example, Hugh Delargy, Labour Member for Thurrock, and David Weitzman, Labour Member for Stoke Newington, urged that, instead of an Ombudsman, there should be a select committee of the Commons charged with the duty of looking into individual grievances, but many Members who spoke, both Conservative and Labour, were obviously thinking of an Ombudsman on the Scandinavian pattern.

The Solicitor-General, Sir Jocelyn Simon, winding up for the Government emphasized that he was not committing the Government when he said: 'I am personally attracted by the suggestion put forward, I think originally in an article in *The Times* of 12th December last year, that a Parliamentary Commissioner might be fitted into the institution of the Committee on Public Petitions.'[2] He envisaged the relationship of the Parliamentary Commissioner to that Committee being similar to the relationship of the Comptroller and Auditor-General to the Public Accounts Committee. He ended the debate by informing the House that the Government was alive to the problem of the rights of the individual as against the State and 'in the light of this debate and the investigations by Sir John Whyatt, they will continue to study the best way of meeting the views which have been put forward today.'[3]

In October 1961, the Whyatt Report was published. In the words of the 'Justice' Annual Report for 1962, the Whyatt Report 'received wide publicity and editorial comment in national and provincial newspapers and in weekly journals'.[4] It was favourably received in two key journals in the first half of 1962. Professor S. A. de Smith, writing in the January 1962 number of the *Political Quarterly*, argued that the proposals for a Parliamentary Commissioner could be criticized on the grounds that they were too timid but that although 'The Report does not provide a blueprint; it

---

[1] Sir Rolf Dudley-Williams was M.P. for Exeter from 1951 to 1966. He founded Power Jets Limited in 1936, with Sir Frank Whittle, to develop jet propulsion. In 1959 he was Parliamentary Private Secretary to the Minister of Agriculture.

[2] H.C. Deb. Vol. 640, Col. 1756.

[4] Sir Jocelyn Simon had been Solicitor-General since 1959. He had previously been Financial Secretary to the Treasury from 1958 to 1959. He represented Middlesbrough West as a Conservative from 1951 to 1962. He has been President of the Probate and Divorce Division of the High Court since 1962. He was nominated to a life peerage in the New Year Honours List for 1971.

[4] 'Justice', Fifth Annual Report, June 1962, p. 15.

points unequivocally towards the need for constitutional reform.'[1] K. C. Wheare, Rector of Exeter College, Oxford, and a member of the Franks Committee, commented in the summer number of *Public Administration* that the obvious and justifiable criticism of the proposals was that they did not go far enough but they were 'practical, sensible and worth trying'.[2]

Yet, despite the widespread interest in the Whyatt Report, the Macmillan Government, when it eventually pronounced on the question, turned down flatly all the proposals in the Report. On 8 November 1962, Dr. Donald Johnson asked the Attorney General whether it was Her Majesty's Government's intention to appoint a Parliamentary Commissioner. The Attorney General, Sir John Hobson, replied that he was circulating in the Official Report a statement of the Government's conclusions after consideration of the Report of a Committee of 'Justice'.[3]

The Government statement rejected the 'Justice' Committee's proposals for an extension of the system of administrative tribunals and for the appointment of a Parliamentary Commissioner in the following terms:

The Government consider that there are serious objections in principle to both proposals and that it would not be possible to reconcile them with the principle of Ministerial responsibility to Parliament. They believe that any substantial extension of the system of reference to tribunals would lead to inflexibility and delays in administration, and that the appointment of a Parliamentary Commissioner would seriously interfere with the prompt and efficient despatch of public business. In the Government's view there is already adequate provision under our constitutional and Parliamentary practice for the redress of any genuine complaint of maladministration, in particular by means of the citizen's right of access to Members of Parliament.[4]

[1] S. A. de Smith, 'Anglo Saxon Ombudsman', *Political Quarterly* (1962), p. 19.

[2] K.[C. Wheare, 'The Redress of Grievances', *Public Administration* (1962), p. 127. Sir Kenneth Clinton Wheare was Gladstone Professor of Government and Public Administration at Oxford University from 1944 to 1957. He has been Rector of Exeter College, Oxford, since 1956. From 1964 to 1966 he was Vice-Chancellor of the University. His publications include *The Statute of Westminster and Dominion Status* (5th edn. 1953), *Federal Government* (4th edn. 1963), *Modern Constitutions* (1951), *Government by Committee* (1955), *Legislatures* (1963).

[3] Sir John Hobson was Attorney General from 1962 to 1964. He was first elected as Conservative M.P. for Warwick and Leamington at the by-election in March 1957 on the retirement of Sir Anthony Eden. He held the seat until his death in December 1967. He was called to the Bar in 1938 and was Recorder of Northampton from 1958 to 1962.

[4] H.C. Deb. Vol. 666, Col. 1124.

This reply was a setback to 'Justice', the more so in that no opportunity was given for a debate in the Commons on the government statement. 'Justice' commented in its Annual Report for 1963:

In anticipation of Parliamentary discussion the Council of Justice had prepared and addressed a letter and memorandum to every member of Parliament, in which various criticisms and misunderstandings of the Report had been dealt with, in particular the whole question of ministerial responsibility. It was by accident and not by foresight that this memorandum was posted on the day the Government made its statement, and provided an effective answer to it.[1]

But this answer went unheard.

It was surprising that the Macmillan Government should reject the Whyatt Report so completely particularly in view of the Solicitor-General's personal support, in May 1961, for the idea of a Parliamentary Commissioner standing in the same relation to Parliament as the Comptroller and Auditor-General. The explanation cannot be found on the basis of concerted opposition by senior Civil Servants. Indeed, we have seen that several Permanent Secretaries and Deputy Secretaries were very co-operative to Sir John Whyatt when he was preparing his report.[2] The explanation must lie chiefly in opposition to the proposals from within the Cabinet.

The fact is that the Macmillan Government was not notable for its reforming zeal in home affairs. Abroad it was another matter: 'the wind of change in Africa', the attempt to get into the European Economic Community, and Macmillan's own endeavours to bring about summit talks between the four great powers. These were the pre-occupations of the Government in the years from 1959 to 1962. The record of reform in home affairs was meagre if not negligible. The National Economic Development Council was set up by Selwyn Lloyd as Chancellor of the Exchequer in 1962. This was one of the few innovations in the lifetime of an administration which showed little interest in ideas for institutional reform.

Another factor should be borne in mind. The Society for Individual Freedom was very much a peripheral pressure group from the point of view of the leading members of the Conservative

---

[1] 'Justice', Sixth Annual Report, June 1963, p. 13.   [2] See above p. 20.

Government. Dr. Donald Johnson felt himself to be *persona non grata* with the Conservative leadership.[1] The ethos too of the Society for Individual Freedom, with its attachment to free enterprise and its hostility to state intervention, stood in contrast with Macmillan's paternalism and 'Welfare' Conservatism. Utley commented shrewdly at the end of *Occasion for Ombudsman*: 'Paradoxically, at the moment when the Labour Party is most anxious to resume its liberal tradition, the Conservative Party shows leanings towards policies that put a greater emphasis on welfare and the provision of prosperity than on the need for maintaining proper restraints on government.'[2] Utley hoped that the interest shown in the idea of an Ombudsman, among the Conservative rank and file, would overcome the indifference which he correctly forecast from the leadership on this question. However, it was not to be.

The Labour Party, on the other hand, was nearly, but not quite, ready 'to resume its liberal tradition' and take up the campaign. How and when it did will be recounted in the next chapter.

[1] See Donald Johnson, *A Cassandra at Westminster* (Johnson, 1967).
[2] T. E. Utley, op. cit., p. 144.

IV

THE LABOUR OPPOSITION TAKES UP THE SCHEME FOR A PARLIAMENTARY COMMISSIONER

THERE is no necessary connection between left of centre political attitudes and support for the idea of an Ombudsman. Indeed, in New Zealand it was the National Party, broadly equivalent to the British Conservative Party, which campaigned in 1960 for an Ombudsman. Labour, which was then in office, showed no enthusiasm for the reform. When the National Party came to power it was not slow to redeem its election pledges and get the Parliamentary Commissioner (Ombudsman) Act on to the statute book.

Can we say then that a campaign for an Ombudsman is likely to be given impetus by an opposition party and brought to fruition when there is a change of government: that, in this way, the conservatism and resistance to change among administrators can be overcome? This hypothesis also is not wholly satisfactory since the introduction of the Ombudsman in Denmark, in 1954, was a reform which was agreed by elements in the major parties.

The explanation for the Labour Party in Britain championing the campaign for an Ombudsman, while the Conservative leadership remained cold toward it, lies in two principal directions. First, individual Conservatives who were active in the campaign for an Ombudsman, in 'Justice' and in the Society for Individual Freedom, were remote from the Conservative leadership. On the other hand, some of the Labour lawyers in 'Justice', notably Gerald Gardiner and Elwyn Jones were influential with the Labour leadership. Second, the interest of the Leader of the Party can be a decisive factor in the adoption of party policies, and a change of Labour leader was important here.

The Macmillan Government publicly closed its file on the Whyatt Report on 8 November 1962 with the Attorney General's statement that the Report would not be implemented. Only just over a month later, on 14 December, the Leader of the Labour Party, Hugh Gaitskell, was taken ill. He died on 18 January 1963. The Parliamentary Labour Party then elected Harold Wilson its new leader.

Gaitskell had indicated his support for the Whyatt Report, but he had made no major move on the Ombudsman question. During 1962 he had, like the Prime Minister, Harold Macmillan, been preoccupied with the debate on entry into the Common Market. Indeed his exertions in this question, his many trips to the Continent, his consultations with Commonwealth leaders, and his major speech at the Labour Party Conference had all greatly tired him and made him more vulnerable to the illness which brought his tragic and premature death at the age of fifty-six.

It is impossible to tell just what initiative he might have taken, had he survived, towards making the establishment of an Ombudsman part of the Labour programme. What we can say is that his successor had political associates who would be particularly receptive to the idea and Wilson was himself to choose legal advisers who were already some of its strongest advocates.

The most prominent of such associates was Richard Crossman. Crossman had been a member of the constituency section of the National Executive Committee of the Labour Party since 1952. He had been associated with Harold Wilson in the contest with Gaitskell over the role of the Party Conference in 1960 and 1961. He had long been one of the most effective publicists in the Labour Party and someone who had always emphasized the need for enhancing democratic control of the machinery of administration.[1] In 1956 he wrote an important pamphlet entitled *Socialism and the New Despotism*. This was a plea to members of the Labour Party not to concentrate entirely on bringing about changes in economic structure and in the distribution of the national wealth. He summed up his argument with this statement[2]: 'The modern State, with its

[1] Richard Crossman was born in 1907. He was a tutor in Philosophy at New College Oxford from 1930 to 1937. During the Second World War he was assistant chief in psychological warfare at General Eisenhower's headquarters, from 1943 to 1945. He has been Member of Parliament for Coventry East since 1945. Before the 1964 General Election he was active as a political journalist, particularly on the *New Statesman* and the *Daily Mirror*. He was Minister of Housing and Local Government from 1964 to 1966, Lord President of the Council, and Leader of the House of Commons, from 1966 to 1968, and Secretary of State for Social Services from 1968 to 1970. After the 1970 General Election he became editor of the *New Statesman*.

[2] R. H. S. Crossman, *Socialism and the New Despotism* (Fabian Tract No. 298, Fabian Society, 1956), p. 24.

huge units of organization, is inherently totalitarian, and its natural tendency is towards despotism. These tendencies can only be held in check if we are determined to build the constitutional safeguards of freedom—and personal responsibility'. In 1956 the Ombudsman was not known about in Britain and could not be cited as one of these safeguards. But by 1963 Crossman's basic attitude had not changed. It logically made him a strong advocate of the need for an Ombudsman.

The significant accession to Harold Wilson's team of legal personalities in the Shadow Cabinet came in December 1963. On 23 December it was announced from 10 Downing Street that Gerald Gardiner was to be made a Life Peer and that his name had been recommended after consultation with the Leader of the Opposition, Harold Wilson. Gerald Gardiner was a leading barrister and had been Chairman of the General Council of the Bar in 1958 and 1959.[1] It was an open secret that Harold Wilson had chosen him to be Shadow Lord Chancellor. *The Times* commented, on 24 December 1963: 'Mr. Gardiner, for instance, is not only an outstanding lawyer but an active campaigner for several causes that stir Mr. Wilson's sympathies, law reform and opposition to apartheid among them. He is also joint chairman of the National Campaign for the Abolition of Capital Punishment.'

Most important, from the point of view of the campaign for an Ombudsman, was the fact that Gerald Gardiner was a founder member of 'Justice' and had been Chairman of its Executive Committee since June 1962. On being nominated a Life Peer, he relinquished this position but remained a member of the Council of 'Justice'.

British politics in the summer months of 1963 were dominated by the Profumo affair and the trial of Stephen Ward. These events may have helped the campaign for an Ombudsman in that, for one thing, some of the activities of the Metropolitan Police appeared in a very curious light and, for another, that the Government ultimately decided to give to Lord Denning, Master of the Rolls, the task of drawing up an impartial report on the conduct of all the main parties in the affair and of attempting to sort out fact from rumour. As 'Justice' commented in its Annual Report for 1964: 'In the Profumo affair, although this would not necessarily have been an appropriate field of enquiry for the permanent Commissioner

[1] See above p. 10 for biographical footnote on Lord Gardiner.

envisaged by Justice, it is worthy of note that Lord Denning was ultimately called upon by the Government to carry out an enquiry which had many of the essential characteristics of the Ombudsman technique.'[1]

In October 1963, Macmillan decided, because of ill health, to give up the Premiership. He was succeeded as Conservative Prime Minister by Sir Alec Douglas-Home. From then on, political interest was concentrated on the run up to the General Election which, under the Parliament Act, had to be held at the latest in December 1964.

The National Executive Committee of the Labour Party already had its prospectus for the election, as regards home policy, in the document *Signposts for the Sixties*, adopted by the Annual Conference in 1961. The Home Policy Subcommittee of the N.E.C. under its chairman George Brown now set about, in the words of the Labour Party's Annual Report for 1964, 'the firming up of policies agreed in *Signposts for the Sixties*' and the investigation of social reform.[2] The Home Policy Subcommittee set up a number of study groups to consider such reforms. One of these, which was a joint working party of the Subcommittee and of the Parliamentary Labour Party, had the task of looking into the proposal for a Parliamentary Commissioner. Its chairman was Arthur Skeffington, a member of the Home Policy Subcommittee and the representative on the N.E.C. of the Socialist, Co-operative, and Professional Organizations.[3]

One of the members of this study group was Douglas Houghton, who has described to the author how, when the group was still considering the advisability of introducing an Ombudsman, the Leader of the Party 'sprung it on them' by coming out publicly in favour of a Parliamentary Commissioner. Harold Wilson, in a

---

[1] 'Justice', Seventh Annual Report, p. 6.

[2] The Labour Party, *Report of the 63rd Annual Conference of the Labour Party* (Brighton, 1964), p. 36. The Home Policy Subcommittee of the N.E.C. included among its membership, the Leader of the Labour Party, Harold Wilson, as well as Richard Crossman, James Callaghan, and ten other Labour M.P.s.

[3] Arthur Skeffington was Labour M.P. for Hayes and Harlington from 1953 until his death in 1971. He had also been a member of the National Executive Committee of the Labour Party since 1953. He had been a barrister and teacher and a member of the London County Council from 1951 to 1958. He was Parliamentary Secretary to the Ministry of Land and Natural Resources from 1964 to 1967 and to the Ministry of Housing and Local Government from 1967 to 1970. He was, during this period, Chairman of the Committee on Public Participation in Planning which in 1969 produced the report: *People and Planning* (The Skeffington Report).

speech to the Society of Labour Lawyers at Niblett Hall, in the Temple, on 20 April 1964 said:

For some time we have been examining suggestions for a parliamentary commissioner, on the lines of the Comptroller and Auditor-General, reporting to and through a Committee on the lines of the Public Accounts Committee. Some of us, with experience of that Committee, had thought of this as a possibility even before these ideas were publicly canvassed. There are difficulties, but I am hopeful we may have proposals to put forward.[1]

Some of the difficulties were the objections raised by certain members of the study group. For example, Douglas Houghton was not, at this time, in favour of a Parliamentary Commissioner because he considered that, in general, the high standards of the Civil Service ensured that complaints were adequately looked into and that, where redress was needed, it was provided by existing administrative tribunals. Houghton had been Secretary of the Inland Revenue Staff Federation for thirty-eight years and had an understandable pride in his profession.[2] His attitude can be paralleled in Denmark and New Zealand. In both these countries, officers of the Civil Service associations resisted the introduction of the Ombudsman on the grounds that it was unnecessary and a slight on their profession. In both countries, this attitude was forgotten when the staff associations found that the Ombudsman did not criticize administrators unfairly.[3] Houghton too was to change his views about the proposal for a Parliamentary Commissioner and later became one of the principal architects of the Parliamentary Commissioner Bill in the Wilson Government.[4]

There were also objections to an Ombudsman from some Labour M.P.s on the grounds that constituents' grievances were best handled by M.P.s, but Harold Wilson effectively committed the

[1] Harold Wilson, *The New Britain: Labour's Plan Outlined by Harold Wilson. Selected Speeches, 1964* (Penguin, 1964), p. 87.

[2] Douglas Houghton has been Labour Member of Parliament for Sowerby since 1949. He was Secretary of the Inland Revenue Staff Federation from 1922 to 1960, and Chairman of the Staff Side of the Civil Service National Whitley Council from 1955 to 1957. Since 1967 he has been Chairman of the Parliamentary Labour Party. His success as a conciliator between the Parliamentary Party and the Wilson Cabinet, in 1969, was widely recognized.

[3] See Walter Gellhorn, *Ombudsman and Others*, pp. 25–7 and 91–2.

[4] See below pp. 51–60.

Labour Party to the Parliamentary Commissioner idea by his speech to the Society of Labour Lawyers. From then on it was not a question of 'whether' but of 'how' for the N.E.C. study group.

When Harold Wilson next spoke in public on the subject, he was able to put forward a much more detailed and precise proposal. This is what he said to a public meeting at Stowmarket on 3 July 1964:

For some months we have been working on proposals to ensure the right of an independent investigation in all cases of suspected injustice [to citizens]. Ministers and M.P.s of course are the first line of defence. But more will be needed in order to make their work more effective. We propose, therefore, that a Parliamentary Commissioner or Civil Rights Commissioner—the title will need further thought—be appointed to investigate, on behalf of the public, administrative decisions which can affect the rights and welfare of individuals.

What we propose is that the Commissioner be appointed by Letters Patent, wholly independent of the Government and administrative machine, and responsible only to Parliament. It would be his duty to investigate complaints and to report both on individual cases where an injustice may appear to have been involved, or on defects in the system which have the effect of creating injustice or of failing to provide adequate rights of reconsideration or appeal. The Commissioner's report would be to Parliament and would, of course, be debatable by Parliament. But, in addition, there should be a high-powered Select Committee of the House who would make it their business to go through the periodic reports of the Commissioner and report to Parliament on them.[1]

Harold Wilson went on to say that such a committee would be closely analogous to the Public Accounts Committee and its relationship to the Parliamentary Commissioner would be similar to the Public Accounts Committee's relationship to the Comptroller and Auditor-General. This observation was not new. It had been made, as we have seen, by the Whyatt Committee.[2] But it gained added force from the fact that Harold Wilson had himself been Chairman of the Public Accounts Committee from 1959 to 1963. This was a more than usually vigorous period in the Committee's history during which its reports received major publicity for their highlighting of the size of Government expenditure on missiles, and for their campaign against the large profits being earned by drug firms pro-

[1] Labour Party News Release of Harold Wilson's speech at Stowmarket, 3 July 1964, pp. 1 and 2.
[2] See above p. 26.

viding medicines for the National Health Service.[1] During this period, Harold Wilson as Chairman of the Public Accounts Committee, worked closely with the Comptroller and Auditor-General, Sir Edmund Compton, whom he was later to choose as Britain's first Parliamentary Commissioner.

Two further points which Harold Wilson made in his speech at Stowmarket are also of interest. He said that in order to prevent the Parliamentary Commissioner and the Select Committee from being swamped by too many cases 'it might be necessary, for example, in the first year or two, to limit their sphere of activities to actions taken by the Government machine. Later, their powers could be extended, into the field of other public bodies and local authorities, though there is, of course, a very strong case for providing at least the larger local authorities with their own Ombudsman'.[2]

He also said that it might be right 'to provide that access to the Commissioner should be through a Member of Parliament' since 'nothing should be done which could even marginally diminish the great and valuable work done by M.P.s on behalf of their constituents and the public generally.'[3] This represented a concession to the views of many Labour back-benchers on this question.

Meanwhile, 'Justice' had been made aware both through Harold Wilson's speech to the Society of Labour Lawyers in April, and through Gerald Gardiner, that the time was ripe for a renewed initiative in the campaign for an Ombudsman. In June 1964, the Council of 'Justice' reported to the Annual General Meeting: 'In the hope that the next government, of whatever complexion it may be, will look more favourably at the 'Justice' proposals, the members of Sir John Whyatt's Advisory Committee have been asked to reappraise them in the light of some criticisms that have been made, and to put them into a practical legislative framework.'[4]

Norman Marsh was again asked to be Chairman of the Advisory Committee. Other members of the original Advisory Committee who served again were Sir Sydney Caine and Professor H. W. R. Wade. Sir John Whyatt could not be a member since he was now Judge of the Chief Court for the Persian Gulf. The new member who came in was Geoffrey Marshall, tutor and praelector in politics

---

[1] See F. Stacey, *The Government of Modern Britain* (Clarendon Press, 1968), pp. 134–135.
[2] Labour Party News Release, 3 July 1964, p. 3.
[3] Ibid., p. 3.   [4] 'Justice', Seventh Annual Report, 1964, p. 6.

at the Queen's College, Oxford. Geoffrey Marshall was a member of 'Justice' and was invited to join the Committee because of his well informed articles on the Ombudsman in *The Times*, *Public Law*, and *The Lawyer*.[1] Tom Sargant, the Secretary of 'Justice', helped the Committee as he had helped the Whyatt Committee.

The new factors which the Committee had to consider were the New Zealand Parliamentary Commissioner (Ombudsman) Act, 1962, and the criticisms which had been made in Britain of the Whyatt Report. Members of the Committee sent their ideas to Marsh, who prepared a draft bill. This was criticized by the Committee and Marsh then prepared a revised draft which the Committee agreed. There were four meetings of the Committee in the summer of 1964, but some of the discussion also went on by correspondence.

The members of the Committee agreed on two major changes from the recommendations in the Whyatt Report. They were all agreed that the proposal to give a Minister the right to veto an investigation had been a mistake. It had been put in to meet the susceptibilities of Ministers in the Macmillan Government who objected to the infringement of Ministerial responsibility. The provision had not achieved its purpose, it had been widely criticized in Britain, and was not found in the New Zealand Act. The Ministerial veto therefore went out altogether from the 'Justice' draft.

The Committee were also agreed that the Parliamentary Commissioner should be able to see the internal departmental minutes in a case and not merely the internal and external correspondence as the Whyatt Report had recommended. Here again, the Committee were able to draw upon the New Zealand Act and New Zealand experience which showed that it was feasible for the Parliamentary Commissioner to have access to the internal minutes. On these two points, access to minutes and absence of a veto, the bill introduced by the Wilson Government was to concur.

On the question of whether the public should have direct access to the Parliamentary Commissioner, the members of the Committee were not all agreed. Geoffrey Marshall argued for direct access, as in

---

[1] G. Marshall, 'A Critique of the Ombudsman Report', *The Lawyer* (1961), pp. 29–32; 'The New Zealand Parliamentary Commissioner (Ombudsman) Act, 1962', *Public Law* (1963); 'Should Britain Have an Ombudsman', *The Times*, 23 April 1963. Works by Geoffrey Marshall include: *Parliamentary Sovereignty and the Commonwealth* (Clarendon Press, 1957), *Police and Government* (Methuen, 1965), *Some Problems of the Constitution*, with G. C. Moodie (Hutchinson University Library, 4th edn., 1967).

New Zealand, Sweden, Denmark, Norway, and Finland. The majority of the Committee, however, favoured limiting access through M.P.s, at least for an initial period as the Whyatt Report had recommended. The draft bill, as finally agreed, provided, at Section 6, that access to the Parliamentary Commissioner should only be through M.P.s. This approach, of course, fitted in well with Harold Wilson's since, as we have seen, he had indicated in his Stowmarket speech that access might have to be only through M.P.s.

Another suggestion of Geoffrey Marshall's was accepted by the Committee. This was that the Parliamentary Commissioner should be a member of the Council on Tribunals in order to improve liaison between his office and the tribunal sector. This idea was approved by the Committee and incorporated in their draft bill. It was taken up by the Wilson Government and implemented in the 1967 Act.

One major change which the Committee recommended was not, however, to be accepted by the Wilson Government. The Committee were agreed that instead of limiting the Parliamentary Commissioner to investigating cases where maladministration was alleged, as the Whyatt Report recommended, the Commissioner should be empowered to examine the use of administrative discretion with wide terms of reference, similar to those employed in the New Zealand Act.

Thus the New Zealand Act empowers the Parliamentary Commissioner to report upon any 'decision, recommendation, act or omission' which, in his opinion:

(a) Appears to have been contrary to law; or
(b) Was unreasonable, unjust, oppressive, or improperly discriminatory, or was in accordance with a rule of law or a provision of any enactment or a practice that is or may be unreasonable, unjust, oppressive or improperly discriminatory; or
(c) Was based wholly or partly on a mistake of law or fact; or
(d) Was wrong.[1]

The 'Justice' draft bill reproduced these provisions exactly in their Section 10 except that they substituted for the New Zealand sub-

[1] The New Zealand Statutes 1962, No. 10, The Parliamentary Commissioner (Ombudsman) Act, Section 19.

section '(d) Was wrong' their own subsection (d) which read as follows: 'shows a failure to conform with a proper standard of conduct on the part of an officer, employee or member of the Department or organization concerned'. This was a major widening of the terms of reference of the Parliamentary Commissioner, compared with the proposals in the Whyatt Report, but it was not to prove acceptable to the Wilson Government.

When the 'Justice' draft bill had been approved by the Committee, a copy was sent to Lord Gardiner, as Shadow Lord Chancellor. The Committee decided not to publish the draft as they were all conscious of the fact that none of them were skilled parliamentary draftsmen and that, in Britain, the craft of parliamentary draftsmen is as much a 'mystery' as that of any medieval guild. It was thought better that they should not lay themselves open to expert criticism from this direction.

The time for the General Election was now fast approaching. In August 1964, Peter Shore, the Research Secretary of the Labour Party and Secretary of the Home Policy Subcommittee of the N.E.C., went on holiday to France. He took with him the necessary papers for drafting the Election Manifesto and wrote the draft while he was on holiday. When he returned to Britain, in September, the draft manifesto was discussed first by the Home Policy Subcommittee of the N.E.C. and then by a joint meeting of the N.E.C. and the Parliamentary Labour Party which finally approved it.[1]

The manifesto gave great prominence to the pledge to establish a Parliamentary Commissioner. The Preface, headed 'The New Britain', contained a second paragraph which read as follows:

Here is the Case for Planning, and the details of how a Labour Cabinet will formulate the national economic plan with both sides of industry operating in partnership with the Government.

And here, in this manifesto, is the answer to the Tory gibe that Planning could involve a loss of individual liberty. Labour has resolved to humanise the whole administration of the state *and to set up the new office of Parliamentary Commissioner with the right and duty to investigate and expose any misuse of government power as it affects the citizen.*[2]

[1] Peter Shore has been Labour M.P. for Stepney since 1964. He was Secretary of State for Economic Affairs from 1967 to 1969 and Minister without Portfolio and Deputy Leader of the House of Commons from 1969 to 1970. From 1959 to 1964 he was head of the Labour Party research department.

[2] Labour Party, *Let's Go With Labour for a New Britain. Manifesto for the 1964 General Election*, p. 3.

The last part of the paragraph was set in heavy type. In the final section of the manifesto the undertaking was renewed in slightly greater detail:

At the same time new ways must be found to ensure that the growth of government activity does not infringe the liberties of the subject. This is why we attach so much importance to humanising the whole administration of the state and that is why we shall set up the new office of Parliamentary Commissioner with the right to investigate the grievances of the citizen and report to a Select Committee of the House.[1]

This more detailed statement accurately conveyed the gist of Harold Wilson's speech at Stowmarket in June. The undertaking given in the Preface, on the other hand, was wider. To say that the Parliamentary Commissioner would have 'the right and duty to investigate and expose any misuse of government power as it affects the citizen' was to imply that the Commissioner would be able to take up complaints against local authorities as well as against all central government services. Harold Wilson, as we have seen, had said at Stowmarket that it might be necessary to exclude local authorities at least for the first year or two. In the event, the Parliamentary Commissioner Act was to exclude also a large number of central government services. Was the manifesto unwise to make such a wide commitment which was not to be fully realized? Something must be allowed for rhetoric, something also for the difficulties of translating the pledge in the manifesto into legislation. It is to the difficulties of drafting the bill that we can now turn.

[1] Ibid., p. 24.

Part Two

THE DRAFTING OF THE PARLIAMENTARY COMMISSIONER BILL AND ITS PASSAGE THROUGH PARLIAMENT

V

DRAFTING THE BILL

AT the General Election in October 1964 Labour was returned to power with a majority of four over all other parties. It was barely a working majority, but Harold Wilson, as Premier, made it clear from the outset that his Government was fully determined to implement the Labour Election Manifesto. Prominent in this manifesto, we have seen, was the pledge to establish a Parliamentary Commissioner.

Douglas Houghton was Chairman of the Home Affairs Committee of the Cabinet. A subcommittee of this Committee, with Houghton as Chairman, was set up to plan the Parliamentary Commissioner Bill. Its membership included the new Lord Chancellor, Lord Gardiner, Sir Eric Fletcher, a Minister without Portfolio and spokesman in the Commons for the Lord Chancellor's office, and Niall MacDermot, the Financial Secretary to the Treasury.[1] MacDermot was included because the Cabinet decided that since the Treasury had responsibility for the machinery of government, it should be the department to take charge of the bill.

This Cabinet Subcommittee initially had a large additional membership which was constantly changing. Since almost every department could be affected by the bill, twenty-six departments were, at the outset, represented on the Subcommittee. Departments sometimes sent a Minister of State to represent them, sometimes a Parliamentary Secretary. Thus there was a marked lack of continuity in representation. Parallel to the Cabinet subcommittee, a

---

[1] Sir Eric Fletcher represented Islington East for Labour from 1945 to 1970. He was Minister without Portfolio from 1964 to 1966. He was a solicitor and had been a member of the London County Council from 1934 to 1949.

Niall MacDermot Q.C. was Labour M.P. for Derby North from 1962 to 1970. He was called to the Bar in 1946 and was Recorder of Newark from 1963 to 1964. He was Financial Secretary to the Treasury from 1964 to 1967 and Minister of State at the Ministry of Housing and Local Government from 1967 to 1968. Since October 1968 he has been Honorary Treasurer of 'Justice'.

Committee of Permanent Officials on the Bill was chaired by Sir Philip Allen, a Second Secretary at the Treasury.[1] The fact that a Treasury official occupied the chair of this committee further indicated the key role accorded to this department.

Houghton's Subcommittee at first made heavy weather of its task. A great many departments argued that they should be excluded from the purview of the Parliamentary Commissioner and many voices were raised against the scheme, as a whole, or against individual aspects of it. The situation was worsened by the fact that the composition of the Subcommittee was always changing.

Houghton could see that little progress was being made and he feared that the whole project would sink through the floor. He therefore decided to deliver an ultimatum. He told the Subcommittee that the Government was committed to the reform and it must go through. To make progress possible he would propose that the Subcommittee should be drastically reduced in size from thirty-eight to twelve members: the normal size of the Home Affairs Committee of the Cabinet. This recommendation was accepted and from then on the Subcommittee began to rough out the scheme for a Parliamentary Commissioner more effectively.

The committee of permanent officials, of course, depended on the lead given to it by the Subcommittee of the Home Affairs Committee and by the Cabinet as a whole. It was fortunate, however, that this committee was chaired by Sir Philip Allen since he proved to be a firm advocate with his colleagues of the need for a Parliamentary Commissioner. He was later, as a member of the Fulton Committee on the Civil Service, to support that Committee's recommendation in favour of a greater degree of openness between the Higher Civil Service and the community.[2]

The Subcommittee of the Home Affairs Committee of the Cabinet had three documents, prepared from outside the Civil Service, to consider. The first two of these were the Whyatt Report of 1961, and the 'Justice' draft bill drawn up in the summer of 1964. Both of these we have examined in some detail. The third document was a memorandum from the Legal and Judicial Group of the

---

[1] Sir Philip Allen had been Assistant Under Secretary of State at the Home Office from 1952 to 1955, Deputy Secretary at the Ministry of Housing and Local Government from 1955 to 1960, and Deputy Under Secretary of State at the Home Office from 1960 to 1962. He was Second Secretary at the Treasury from 1963 to 1966 and has been Permanent Under Secretary of State at the Home Office since 1966.

[2] Cmnd. 3638, The Civil Service Vol. I, Report of the Committee 1966-68, pp. 91-9.

Parliamentary Labour Party. It is to this document and its preparation that we now turn.

The Legal and Judicial Group of the Parliamentary Labour
Party is one of the many subject groups which are set up by the
Party in each session. Like the other subject groups it is open to all
Labour M.P.s, but attendance is normally confined to those who
are specially interested. The Chairman of the Group in the session
1964–5 was William Wells, a barrister and Queen's Counsel and
Member of Parliament for Walsall North.[1]

The Group held three meetings in February 1965 to consider
the 'proposal for the appointment of an Ombudsman'. It met on
1, 17, and 22 February, the number of Labour Members attending
varying between eleven and seven. This may seem a very small
attendance for so important a topic. In fact, it is normal for the
attendance at subject groups to be of this order except when a
highly controversial and topical subject is under consideration. The
demands on the time of Labour M.P.s are quite great. For example,
on one not exceptional Wednesday (19 February 1969) in the session
1968–9, no less than five subject groups were meeting in the latter
part of the afternoon as well as the Scottish and Welsh Area Groups.

The average attendance of these groups tends to be small, but
they are none the less influential since a number of those who attend
are likely to take a keen interest in the topic when it comes to the
House of Commons in debate. The memorandum prepared in this
instance by the Legal and Judicial Group was certainly given careful
consideration by the Subcommittee of the Home Affairs Committee
of the Cabinet.

The memorandum, which was sent to Sir Eric Fletcher and
communicated by him to the Cabinet Subcommittee, began by
saying that the members of the group 'had been unanimous in
thinking that the appointment of an Ombudsman was an urgent
public need and that the Government would have the enthusiastic
support of the Group in introducing the necessary legislation'. The
memorandum then went on to record five conclusions which the
group had reached on what they felt were some of the most difficult
decisions which would have to be made in planning the bill.

First, they concluded that: 'Complaints should normally be

---

[1] William T. Wells Q.C. was M.P. for Walsall from 1945 to 1955. Since 1955 he has
represented Walsall North. He was called to the Bar in 1932 and has been Recorder of
King's Lynn since 1965. He is a member of the Council of 'Justice'.

sent to the Ombudsman by a Member of Parliament, but the Ombudsman should have the right to take up any points raised by a complainant who said that he had already approached a named M.P. about the matter.' This would meet the case of an individual who could not persuade the M.P. to forward his complaint.

Second, the memorandum proposed that: 'The Ombudsman should have the right to inspect all Departmental Minutes and Records. Where documents of a very high degree of security classification were involved and the Department thought it inappropriate for security reasons for the Ombudsman to see them the Minister concerned should personally issue a certificate to that effect'.

Third: 'At present the duties of the Ombudsman should not extend to dealing with complaints against the police'.

Fourth: 'The Ombudsman should be appointed by the Queen on the recommendation of the Prime Minister. The majority view was that he should report to a Select Committee of the House, analogous to the Public Accounts Committee, and that he should be answerable to Parliament.'

Fifth: 'The Ombudsman should have the right to enquire into what were (a) prima facie cases of misconduct, (b) cases where prima facie the decision reached by a Department appeared so contrary to the evidence adduced to the Department as to suggest that it had been unfairly arrived at.'

These were some of the key questions which were extensively discussed by the Subcommittee of the Cabinet. For example, it was a crucial decision as to whether citizens should have direct access to the Parliamentary Commissioner, as in the Scandinavian countries and New Zealand, or whether access should be only through M.P.s. The Legal and Judicial Group of the Parliamentary Labour Party thought that access should only be through an M.P. but that as a safeguard a member of the public should be allowed direct access if he had already approached an M.P. without success. The Whyatt Committee had proposed that access should be only through M.P.s during an initial, possibly five-year period.

The Subcommittee of the Cabinet took a long time to decide this question. Eventually, they were influenced by the view that opinion amongst M.P.s was generally opposed to allowing members of the public direct access to the Parliamentary Commissioner. They were also concerned by the possibility that allowing direct access to the Commissioner would cause him to be swamped by the volume of complaints. The Subcommittee therefore concluded that access should be only through M.P.s, and without any qualification that this would be an interim limitation as the Whyatt Report had proposed. To meet the problem of the unhelpful Member, however, it was decided that a citizen would be able to ask any Member to take up his complaint, he would not be limited to interceding with the Member for his own constituency.

The Subcommittee also had to consider whether peers as well as M.P.s should be empowered to forward complaints to the Parliamentary Commissioner. The Whyatt Report had recommended that access should be through peers as well as M.P.s but Labour Ministers were divided on the question. This was one of the issues which had to be referred to the Cabinet where the decision was made not to include peers.

Another question which had to be decided at the highest level was whether the Parliamentary Commissioner should be given full access to the departmental files in a case. The Whyatt Report had said, cautiously, that he should normally be able only to see the inward and outward correspondence and not the internal minutes. The 'Justice' draft bill had provided for full access to the files and the Legal and Judicial Group of the P.L.P. had recommended full access with the proviso that, on security grounds, a Minister could, by personal certificate, prevent access to a document by the Commissioner.

Douglas Houghton was convinced that if the Parliamentary Commissioner was to be really effective he would have to have power to look at all the documents. He wrote a memorandum to the Cabinet to this effect and the Cabinet adopted his view. The Act gave the Parliamentary Commissioner access to all the documents but allowed a Minister to prevent disclosure by the Commissioner of documents or information where this, in the Minister's opinion, 'would be prejudicial to the safety of the State or otherwise contrary to the public interest'.[1]

The Whyatt Report also recommended that a Minister should be able to veto an investigation by the Parliamentary Commissioner. This suggestion had been widely criticized. It was dropped from the 'Justice' draft bill and had not been advocated by the Subject Group of Labour M.P.s. Houghton himself was convinced that the attitude in the Whyatt Report had been much too cautious here.

---

[1] Parliamentary Commissioner Act, 1967, Section 11, Subsection (3).

3—B.O.

When the bill appeared, it made no provision for a ministerial veto.

On the question of whether the Parliamentary Commissioner should look only at maladministration, however, the Government returned to the attitude put forward in the Whyatt Report. The White Paper summarized the Cabinet's conclusions as follows: 'The Commissioner will be concerned with faults in administration. It will not be for him to criticise policy, or to examine a decision on the exercise of discretionary powers, unless it appears to him that the decision has been affected by a fault in administration.'[1] This intention, as we shall see, was followed in the Parliamentary Commissioner Act.

In taking this decision, the Cabinet Subcommittee was rejecting the example of the New Zealand statute which allows the Ombudsman to look at any decision which seems to him to be unreasonable and on the basis of which the 'Justice' draft bill had been drawn up. The Cabinet's decision may perhaps be said to have been nearer the view of the Labour Party Legal and Judicial Group here. We have seen that they recommended that the Parliamentary Commissioner should look at prima facie cases of misconduct and at decisions which prima facie had been unfairly arrived at.

We may say perhaps then that the Subcommittee had two sources in favour of limiting the Parliamentary Commissioner to maladministration (the Whyatt Report and the Legal and Judicial Group Memorandum) and one in favour of allowing him to look at any discretionary decision (the 'Justice' draft bill). What, however, seems to have been decisive was the view, once more, that if the Parliamentary Commissioner was not limited to maladministration he would be overwhelmed by the volume of complaints. The point was often made in Government circles that Britain was the first country with a really large population to have an Ombudsman type institution. Of the other countries with an Ombudsman, the largest, Sweden, has a population of only seven and a half million.

The Cabinet Subcommittee spent a lot of time considering which services should be included and which excluded from the Parliamentary Commissioner's purview. One sector which needed careful consideration was the police. On the one hand, there had been recent reforms in the administration of the police following on a Royal Commission Report and improvements had been made in the

[1] Cmnd. 2767, The Parliamentary Commissioner for Administration, October 1965.

method of making a complaint against the police.[1] A system had been instituted under which the Chief Constable of another force could be brought in to examine a complaint, so that there would be a greater degree of impartiality than under the old system under which a Chief Constable heard complaints against members of his own force.[2] On the other hand, there continued to be disquiet about methods of securing redress against the police and a minority report of the Royal Commission had recommended an Ombudsman for the police. Eventually, it was decided to give the new system an extended trial and not to allow the Parliamentary Commissioner to look at complaints against the police.

If Scandinavian experience had been followed the police would have been brought within the purview of the Parliamentary Commissioner. The same observation could be made of the decision to exclude personnel matters in the Civil Service. Here, the Cabinet Subcommittee was influenced by the opinion of the Civil Service unions who were consulted on the question. Their view was that the existing Whitley machinery was felt to be satisfactory by Civil Servants, and that allowing complaints to go to the Parliamentary Commissioner would be inimical to unionism in the Civil Service since Civil Servants who were not members of unions would have access to him, while the Whitley machinery, on its staff side, is articulated to the unions. Douglas Houghton as a former Secretary, for twenty-eight years, of the Inland Revenue Staff Federation, clearly had sympathy with this view.

The position of local authorities was given careful consideration. We have seen that the Whyatt Report had not favoured allowing complaints to the Parliamentary Commissioner from local authorities, while recognizing that there was a need for better methods of redress against local authorities. Harold Wilson had taken a similar line in his speech at Stowmarket. This was also the view of Ministers on the Cabinet Subcommittee. It was thought that to allow complaints against local authorities would introduce too much central control of local government. Many felt that local authorities should have their own Ombudsman but that these could best be instituted after the reform of the structure of local government which, it was anticipated, would follow the report of the Maud Royal Commission on Local Government.

[1] Cmnd. 1728, Report of the Royal Commission on the Police, 1962.
[2] Provision for this reform was made by the Police Act, 1964.

As regards hospitals, it seems that Kenneth Robinson, the Minister of Health, and his advisers, were always opposed to the inclusion of the hospitals. Some Ministers, Richard Crossman for example, were strongly convinced that the hospitals should be included. Crossman was not, however, closely concerned with planning the Parliamentary Commissioner Bill.

Ministers, like Crossman, who wanted a Parliamentary Commissioner with wide powers viewed the exclusion of the hospitals as temporary and took a similar attitude to the exclusion of personnel matters in the armed forces, another sector which is in the purview of Scandinavian Ombudsmen. They could at least take comfort from the thought that while the range of services with which the Parliamentary Commissioner would deal would be restricted, certainly when compared with the undertaking in the 1964 Election Manifesto, his investigatory powers within this limited range of services would be considerable. The decision to allow him to see all the departmental files and not to allow a Ministerial veto would make him an effective means of redress within his limited frame of reference.

With the general lines of the Parliamentary Commissioner reform now roughed out, the Cabinet decided that it would be advisable to present the scheme for reform to Parliament in a White Paper, before introducing legislation. In October 1965, a White Paper entitled *The Parliamentary Commissioner for Administration* was presented to Parliament.[1]

The White Paper stated that the Government had decided to introduce legislation for the appointment of a Parliamentary Commissioner for Administration. It went on to explain that the Government had examined the arrangements made for the scrutiny of individual grievances in Sweden, Finland, Denmark, Norway, and New Zealand. But it immediately pointed out that these examples would not be closely followed in Britain.

In Britain, Parliament is the place for ventilating the grievances of the citizen—by history, tradition and past and present practice. It is one of the functions of the elected Member of Parliament to try to secure that his constituents do not suffer injustice at the hand of the Government. The procedures of Parliamentary Questions, Adjournment Debates and Debates on Supply have developed for this purpose under the British

[1] Cmnd. 2767, The Parliamentary Commissioner for Administration.

pattern of parliamentary government; and Members are continually taking up constituents' complaints in correspondence with Ministers, and bringing citizens' grievances, great or small to Parliament, where Ministers individually and Her Majesty's Government collectively are accountable. We do not want to create any new institution which would erode the functions of Members of Parliament in this respect, nor to replace remedies which the British Constitution already provides. Our proposal is to develop those remedies still further. We shall give Members of Parliament a better instrument which they can use to protect the citizen, namely, the services of a Parliamentary Commissioner for Administration.[1]

Having thus clearly stated their intention of creating a Parliamentary Commissioner who would be a complement to Members of Parliament, and not in any sense a rival to them, the White Paper went on to explain how the public would only have access to him through M.P.s. The White Paper then listed the government departments which would be subject to investigation by the Commissioner. Forty-seven departments were listed including all the principal Departments of State, such as the Treasury, Foreign Office, Home Office, Ministry of Defence, etc. As regards the Post Office, it was stated that its functions in relation to national savings and the control of broadcasting and wireless telegraphy would be included. The postal service was not therefore, by implication, included.

Although the whole range of central departments was to be subject to scrutiny by the Parliamentary Commissioner there were some sectors from which he was to be excluded. These were: 'the exercise of powers to preserve the safety of the State; matters which Ministers certify as affecting relations with other countries; matters relating to the administration of colonial territories; and the exercise of powers in relation to investigating crime or determining whether a matter shall go to the courts'.[2] Also to be excluded were the exercise of the Prerogative of Mercy, the conferring of honours by the Sovereign, and the making of appointments by the Crown or by Ministers. Personnel matters in the Civil Service and personnel and disciplinary matters in the Armed Forces were also to be excluded as were the purely commercial relationships of departments with customers or suppliers.

The Parliamentary Commissioner would have discretion as to

[1] Cmnd. 2767, p. 3, para. 4.
[1] Cmnd. 2767, p. 5, para. 8.

whether he would take up a matter which was within the competence of a court of law. The White Paper said that where the Commissioner considered that a complainant could not reasonably be expected to use his remedy in the courts, the Commissioner could take up such a case. Normally, however, he would not do so. He would not, however, have such a discretion as regards administrative tribunals. He would be excluded from dealing with cases which could go to such tribunals, but he would himself be a member of the Council on Tribunals and its Scottish Committee. This last proposal was taken from the 'Justice' draft bill and, we have seen, was originally put forward by Geoffrey Marshall.

Two other points are particularly interesting in the White Paper. It stated that the list of departments subject to the Commissioner would be amended from time to time as the structure of government machinery itself changed. The Government would seek power to do this by subordinate instrument. Finally, it should be noted that although the Ministry of Health was listed among the departments included, this was meant to refer only to the Ministry itself. The Subcommittee of the Cabinet had not intended to include the Hospital Boards. In fact we have seen that a decision had been made to exclude them. The White Paper did not, however, make this clear and this was one respect in which it did not accurately convey the character of the later bill. It is to the reception of the White Paper and to the introduction of the Parliamentary Commissioner Bill that we now turn.

VI

THE FIRST TEXT OF THE BILL AND A CONSERVATIVE COUNTER-PROPOSAL

THE TIMES and the *Guardian* gave a moderately warm welcome to the White Paper on the Parliamentary Commissioner. A *Times* editorial on 13 October 1965 commented that limiting access through M.P.s 'may have been necessary in order to overcome the suspicion of MPs lest they should be left out of the act'. It pointed out that the Parliamentary Commissioner could not inquire into the police, public corporations, and local government which were three fertile sources of grievance. The editor's attitude, in general, can be conveyed by the following passage:

The Government have produced a minimal edition of the innovation. It is not necessarily the worse for that. The institution stands a better chance of becoming established if it does not rove too widely at first. Tall oaks from little acorns grow, and if this one is nurtured properly it may come in time to occupy an important place in the administrative arrangements of the country.

The editor of the *Guardian*, on the same day, said: 'The Government intends to give Britain's first Ombudsman (or Parliamentary Commissioner) a good chance to do his job effectively.' The *Guardian* praised the proposal in the White Paper to empower the Parliamentary Commissioner to examine a department's internal minutes when investigating a case. It pointed out that this went further than the proposal in the Whyatt Report to allow the Commissioner only to look at the correspondence in the case.

There was no debate in the Commons on the White Paper but a former Conservative Attorney General, Sir Lionel Heald, used the opportunity of the debate on the Address, following the Queen's Speech, to present his views on the Government's proposals.[1] In

[1] Sir Lionel Heald Q.C. had been Attorney General in the Churchill Government

his speech, on 10 November 1965, he welcomed the publication of the White Paper and said it should be a vehicle for full and free discussion. He spoke with approval of the operation of Ombudsmen in Scandinavia and New Zealand but argued that the position would be very different in Britain. In this country, with its much larger population, it would be necessary to have 6, or possibly 12, assistant Ombudsmen all over the country, each with his own staff and office. Thus we would lose the feature of the system which had proved valuable in Scandinavia and New Zealand, of having one Ombudsman who applied his own methods and worked out his own principles.

Sir Lionel Heald thought that the proposals in the White Paper would decrease the power of M.P.s to assist their constituents because a constituent would be able to take his case to another Member and ask him to take it up with the Ombudsman. He argued, also, that there were 'no teeth' in the Government's proposals since the Parliamentary Commissioner could only recommend, he could not require redress. At this point, he referred to the proposals of a 'group of which I am not actually a member, but with which I am associated through the Inns of Court Conservative Society'.[1]

Their proposal was for 'an administrative commission, something on the lines which exist in countries like France', instead of an Ombudsman. This scheme was put forward by a committee of the Inns of Court Conservative and Unionist Society in their pamphlet *Let Right Be Done* published by the Conservative Political Centre in January 1966.[2] This committee had begun work in January 1965 before the White Paper appeared. It was not intended, initially, that their pamphlet should be a counterblast to the White Paper but this was what in fact it proved to be. The authors of the pamphlet described the Government's scheme as a proposal for 'a "toothless Ombudsman" operating in a form which does not lend itself to expansion'.[3]

They criticized the exclusion of local authorities, of personnel matters in the Civil Service and the Armed Forces, of the com-

---

from 1951 to 1954. He represented Chertsey from 1950 to 1970. From 1964 to 1966 he was Vice-Chairman of the Conservative Parliamentary Legal Committee. He is a Director of British Lion Films, Ltd.

[1] H.C. Deb. Vol. 720, Col. 268.

[2] Inns of Court Conservative and Unionist Society, *Let Right be Done* (Conservative Political Centre, 1966).

[3] Ibid., p. 15.

mercial relations of departments, and the limitation of the Commissioner to cases involving maladministration. They also criticized the idea that an Ombudsman, or Parliamentary Commissioner, could work in a country with a population of over fifty million. Only in a country with a population around that of New Zealand, which has only two and a half million people could the Ombudsman be seen by the citizen 'as his or her *personal* champion'.[1] Finally, they were critical of the fact that an Ombudsman cannot, like the *Conseil d'État*, require redress for the citizen, or the payment of compensation; he can only recommend redress.

Having rejected the idea of an Ombudsman, the authors argued that the real solution to the problem of providing some system for protecting the individual against the State lay in the establishment of an Administrative Commission. This Commission, which they suggested should be grafted on to the Privy Council, would consist of a Judicial Division and an Investigating Division. The membership of the Judicial Division would be drawn from the higher judiciary, from the higher ranks of the Civil Service, from industry and commerce, from the trade unions, the professions, and the universities. A complaint would first of all be examined by the Investigating Division. This Division, if it thought there was some substance in the complaint, would ask the department concerned to provide information, but it would not be able to require the production of the departmental files. If the Investigating Division did not secure a satisfactory reply from the department it could refer the matter to the Judicial Division. If the Judicial Division then found for the complainant it could require the department to provide redress or pay compensation.

In essence, this proposal was an adaptation of the sort of machinery provided by the *Conseil d'État*. It should be noted however that it had a number of defects which are not found in the *Conseil d'État*. First, the Investigating Division would not be able to require the production of files, whereas a member of the *Conseil d'État*, when investigating a case, can require production of all the relevant documents. Second, a complainant might have to pay the costs of a hearing before the Judicial Division, if he insisted on a hearing, against the opinion of the Investigating Division, and the final decision went against him. In the *Conseil d'État* the complainant is not required to pay costs although he can employ counsel in

[1] Ibid., p. 8.

certain types of case. Finally, the amorphous composition of the proposed Judicial Division compares very unfavourably with the composition of the *Conseil d'État* whose members have a knowledge of administration and the law. They are senior or middle rank administrators assisted by some of the brightest young entrants from the *École Nationale d'Administration*. They all share a common ethos and tradition in the service of the *Conseil d'État*.

Whatever the defects of the proposals put forward in *Let Right be Done*, they are of great interest for two reasons in particular. First they were the only developed proposals for a *Conseil d'État* type innovation to be put forward since the proposals made to the Franks Commission in 1957. From the time that the Franks Report turned down the idea of such reforms, only one leading academic campaigned in favour of a *Conseil d'État* type reform in place of an Ombudsman. This was J. D. B. Mitchell, Professor of Constitutional Law at the University of Edinburgh. Writing in *Public Law*, in 1962, and in the symposium on the Ombudsman edited by D. C. Rowat, in 1965, he had attacked 'The Ombudsman Fallacy' and 'The Irrelevance of the Ombudsman Proposals'.[1]

In part, his arguments against an Ombudsman were similar to those put forward in *Let Right be Done*. In particular he, too, maintained that an Ombudsman would not work well in a country as large as Britain with a population of fifty million. His objection was really more fundamental, however, in that he argued that the whole relationship between law and government in Britain needed reform. He considered that the establishment of machinery on the lines of the *Conseil d'État* would enable such a reform to be made; while setting up an Ombudsman would only conceal the necessity for reform.

The second point of interest about *Let Right be Done* was that one of the Joint Chairmen of the Committee of the Inns of Court Conservative and Unionist Society which prepared the pamphlet was William L. Roots Q.C., M.P.[2] William Roots had been a mem-

---

[1] See J. D. B. Mitchell, 'The Ombudsman Fallacy', *Public Law* (1962), pp. 24–33, and 'The Irrelevance of the Ombudsman Proposals', in D. C. Rowat (ed.) *The Ombudsman. Citizen's Defender* (Allen and Unwin, 1965), pp. 273–81.

[2] William L. Roots Q.C. was Conservative M.P. for Kensington South from 1959 to 1967. He was called to the Bar in 1933. He had been active in local government and had at one time been leader of the Conservative Party on Kensington Borough Council. From 1952 to 1955 he was Chairman of Fulham and Kensington Hospital Management Committee. In the session 1965–6 he was joint Vice-Chairman of the Conservative Parliamentary Committee on Home Affairs. He is a director of a brewery company.

ber of the Council of 'Justice' since 1963. In this capacity he was
therefore, in a sense, committed to supporting the Ombudsman
solution. He was also later to be the chief Conservative spokesman
in the House of Commons Standing Committee on the Parliamentary Commissioner Bill. In this role he was largely to put forward
the view that the powers of the Parliamentary Commissioner should
be increased.

His personal position with, as it were, a foot in two camps illustrates the dilemma in which the Conservative Party stood at this time.
Was it to oppose the Government's proposal for a Parliamentary
Commissioner root and branch, was it to propose a *Conseil d'État*
as an alternative, or was it to say that the Government's proposals did
not go far enough?

Meanwhile, work had been going on, within the Government, in
drafting the Parliamentary Commissioner Bill. When the Home
Affairs Committee of the Cabinet, under Houghton's chairmanship,
had approved the draft of the White Paper, the task of drafting the
bill was entrusted to Niall MacDermot, the Financial Secretary to
the Treasury, assisted by Treasury officials and the parliamentary
draftsman. The choice of Niall MacDermot to take charge of the bill
followed logically from the Cabinet's earlier decision that the
Treasury should have responsibility for the bill. It was not altogether a welcome choice from the point of view of some members of
the Subcommittee of the Cabinet. The Lord Chancellor, Lord
Gardiner, had hoped that his office would have responsibility for the
bill and that it would be introduced in the Commons jointly by the
Home Secretary and by Sir Eric Fletcher, the spokesman for the
Lord Chancellor there. Douglas Houghton similarly had hoped
that he would be in charge of the bill in the Commons, since he had
played a major part as Chairman of the Subcommittee of the Cabinet in getting the project off the ground.

Would the bill have given greater powers to the Parliamentary
Commissioner if either Lord Gardiner and Sir Eric Fletcher or
Douglas Houghton had been in charge of it? Certainly all three of
them were more fully committed to the reform than Niall Mac-
Dermot was. MacDermot's role was that of the able advocate
keeping closely to the compromise brief which the Cabinet had
given him. He was not an ardent reformer as Gardiner was, but
Gardiner was to play his part in the passage of the bill. He was to be
in charge of the bill in the House of Lords and was to be responsible

for introducing an amendment there which strengthened the position of the Commissioner.[1]

In drafting the Parliamentary Commissioner Bill, MacDermot and his team kept closely to the outlines which had been provided by the White Paper. When the Bill was published on 14 February 1966 it contained only one major surprise. Schedule 3, at the very end of the Bill, listed matters which would not be subject to investigation by the Parliamentary Commissioner. These comprised a number of matters which had been foreshadowed in the White Paper: relations with other countries, the exercise of powers in investigating crime or protecting the security of the State, the contractual or commercial transactions of departments, the prerogative of mercy, and personnel matters in the Armed Forces and the Civil Service. In addition, Subsection 8 listed as matters not subject to investigation: 'Action taken on behalf of the Minister of Health or the Secretary of State by a Regional Hospital Board, Board of Governors of a Teaching Hospital, Hospital Management Committee or Board of Management, or by the Public Health Laboratory Service Board'.[2] So the National Hospital Service would be excluded from the Parliamentary Commissioner's purview. We have seen that this had been intended by the Cabinet Subcommittee but this had not been spelled out in the White Paper.

On 28 February 1966, a fortnight after the first reading in the Commons of the Parliamentary Commissioner Bill, the Prime Minister announced that he had asked the Queen for a dissolution and that a General Election would be held at the end of March. The Government had lived dangerously with its tiny majority since October 1964. Now that the Gallup Poll and the National Opinion Poll showed a comfortable lead for the Government (varying from 9 to 14 per cent at the end of February), Harold Wilson took the opportunity of trying to improve his majority. This he was able to do with conspicuous success. At the General Election Labour was returned to power with a majority of 97 over all other parties.

The Labour Manifesto for the 1966 General Election pointed out, under the heading 'Wider Democracy in the New Britain', that a start had been made on a number of reforms including 'the proposal for a Parliamentary Commissioner (or 'Ombudsman') to investigate

---

[1] See below pp. 216-8 and 225.
[2] Parliamentary Commissioner Bill, 1966, Schedule 3, Subsection 8.

complaints by the citizen against the Administration'.[1] The Government soon reintroduced the Parliamentary Commissioner Bill. On 20 July 1966 a new bill received its first reading. This bill differed little from the bill introduced in February. There had been some tidying up in the drafting and one important omission was made good. The new bill contained a provision that the Parliamentary Commissioner would hold office during good behaviour and a further, related, provision that he could only be removed from office 'by Her Majesty in consequence of an Address from the House of Commons'.[2] These additions would bring the status of the Parliamentary Commissioner closer to that of the Comptroller and Auditor-General. Indeed, an amendment to be made to the bill in the Commons which provided for his removal only as a consequence of Addresses from both Houses of Parliament was to bring it closer still.[3]

The day after the Parliamentary Commissioner Bill was published, on 21 July 1966, Sir Lionel Heald sent a copy of the bill to Mrs. Lilian Hardern, the Secretary of the Society for Individual Freedom, and asked for the comments of her Society. The Society's letter in reply to Sir Lionel was published in the autumn 1966 number of *Freedom First*.[4] Their reply began as follows:

Dear Sir Lionel,

We now have had an opportunity to study in detail the Parliamentary Commissioner Bill of which you kindly sent a copy with your letter of 21st July. As you know, our Society was not widely enthusiastic about the Parliamentary Commissioner concept since grievances and abuses arise— in our opinion—mainly out of local authority questions and the Bill as proposed concerns itself solely with central government departments. We remain fundamentally unhappy about this although accepting that it is at least the first step to a true 'Ombudsman'.[5]

The letter then went on to make a list of detailed criticisms of the Bill and suggestions for amendments. They can be summarized as follows. The Society considered that Scotland and Wales should at least have Assistant Commissioners and that Northern Ireland

---

[1] Manifesto of the Labour Party, General Election 1966, *Time for a Decision*, p. 19.
[2] Parliamentary Commissioner Bill, July 1966, Section 1, Subsections (2) and (3).
[3] See below pp. 169–70.
[4] *Freedom First*, Autumn 1966, pp. 9–11.
[5] Ibid. p. 9.

should have its own Parliamentary Commissioner. They did not consider the concept of 'maladministration' was satisfactory since the issue, in their opinion,

is less one of faulty administration than of abuse of executive powers and immunities, or of failure to give due consideration to special circumstances which might arise in an individual case. This is not the same as 'fault' since the administrative process is such that an 'abuse' could be excellently administered. Nor is this a semantic quibble but a real issue which France, Europe's most administered state, recognizes and attempts to solve by the concept of administrative law.[1]

They disagreed with all the following exclusions from the Parliamentary Commissioner's field of oversight: local authorities, public corporations, the excluded matters in the Post Office, action taken on passports in relation to the security of the state, the activities of British embassies abroad, and personnel matters in the Armed Forces. They were particularly emphatic that the hospitals should not be excluded. Their comment here was pithy: 'This is definitely not acceptable. These are the sort of bodies which do want watching.'[2]

There were a number of other features of the Bill which they wished to see elucidated or changed. They wanted to know what the exclusion of 'contractual or other commercial transactions' would mean. They were not happy about the total exclusion of actions taken in the Colonies by British officials. They considered that while Cabinet documents should be exempt from examination by the Parliamentary Commissioner, 'Cabinet Committee' documents should not, since 'Some Cabinet Committees as you know are simply inter-departmental working groups and the Cabinet Committee classification is a matter of registry convenience.'[3]

This all amounted, without any doubt, to an argument for greatly strengthening the powers of the Parliamentary Commissioner and widening his terms of reference. Sir Lionel Heald was faced, therefore, on the one hand with the views of a pressure group which favoured the establishment of an Ombudsman and wanted a great strengthening of the Parliamentary Commissioner Bill, and on the other hand with a group of Conservative lawyers, with which he was himself associated, the Inns of Court Conservative and Unionist Society, who opposed the very concept of an Ombudsman.

[1] Ibid., p. 9.   [2] Ibid., p. 10.   [3] Ibid., p. 9.

How to reconcile, if possible, these differing trends of opinion was a problem the Conservative leadership would have to face at the second reading debate. In the meantime, the Conservative front bench could react strongly against the Prime Minister's announcement, on 4 August 1966, that the Parliamentary Commissioner had been appointed before the Bill setting up his office had received a second reading.

The Prime Minister announced in the Commons on 4 August 1966 that Sir Edmund Compton had been appointed Parliamentary Commissioner designate. He would take up his duties on 1 September 1966 but, until the Parliamentary Commissioner Bill became law, he would not be able to receive or consider complaints. In the meantime, he would be organizing his office. Edward Heath as Conservative Leader of the Opposition criticized this statement. He asked the Prime Minister whether he would return to the normal constitutional practice of saying something would happen 'if' a bill passed the House and not 'when'.[1]

The Liberal Leader, Jo Grimond, reacted even more strongly. He argued that this was an interference with the freedom of Parliament. There were many different views about the nature and functions of the Ombudsman, and if the House decided to make a change it would put Sir Edmund Compton in a most difficult position. To this the Prime Minister replied that if the House decided, during passage of the Bill, that some other form of parliamentary commissioner was more suitable, perhaps a judicial appointment, then obviously the arrangement would have to be reconsidered.[2]

It is interesting to consider why the Wilson Government thought it desirable to make this early appointment. The procedure clearly had disadvantages in that it was felt by many to be high-handed. Even the all-party Select Committee on Estimates, with its Labour majority, was to criticize the Government for putting down a supplementary estimate to meet the salaries of the Parliamentary Commissioner designate and his staff, before the passage of the Bill.[3] On the other hand, there were advantages in the early appointment since Sir Edmund Compton was able to get his office

---

[1] H.C. Deb. Vol. 733, Col. 696.
[2] H.C. Deb. Vol. 733, Col. 698.
[3] H.C. 257 of 1966–7, Report of the Select Committee on Estimates, Winter Supplementary Estimates.

fully organized and ready for an immediate start after the passage of the Bill. All stages of the Bill were completed on 15 March 1967 and the Parliamentary Commissioner began to investigate complaints forwarded to him on 1 April. There would have been a much greater period of delay in bringing the Act into operation if the appointment had not been made until the end of March.

There was also a personal conundrum which faced the Government. Sir Edmund Compton had been Comptroller and Auditor-General since 1958 and was in his sixtieth year. At the same time, Sir Bruce Fraser who had been Permanent Secretary at the Ministry of Land and Natural Resources was without a post since that Ministry had just been absorbed into the Ministry of Housing and Local Government. He was 55 and was considered a good candidate for the post of Comptroller and Auditor-General. The answer to the conundrum therefore was to make Sir Edmund Compton Parliamentary Commissioner designate and put Sir Bruce Fraser in the office he vacated as Comptroller and Auditor-General. This in fact was done, the appointment of Sir Bruce Fraser being announced on 5 August 1966, the day after Sir Edmund Compton's appointment. It can be argued that in this way the Government service retained in its employ two very able men whom it might otherwise have lost to private employment.

The Liberals, besides being critical of what was, in their view, the premature appointment of the Parliamentary Commissioner, were, at this time, canvassing an alternative approach to the establishment of an Ombudsman. On 4 May 1966 Lord Wade, the deputy Liberal Whip in the Lords, had announced his intention of introducing a private member's bill in which one of the chief proposals would be the introduction of a system of regional Ombudsmen.[1] On 9 August 1966, Dr. Michael Winstanley, the Liberal Member for Cheadle, wrote to the *Guardian* explaining the Liberal view on the appointment of Sir Edmund Compton as Parliamentary Commissioner.[2] He argued that an 'ombudsman-like type of official' was needed in the field of local government, but what was needed in central govern-

---

[1] Donald William Wade was made a life peer in 1964. He was Liberal M.P. for Huddersfield West from 1950 to 1964. From 1962 to 1964 he was Deputy Leader of the Liberal Party in the Commons.

[2] Dr. Michael Winstanley was Liberal Member for Cheadle from 1966 to 1970. He is a medical practitioner, radio and television broadcaster, and journalist. He has been a member of the Liberal Party Council since 1961. He was a member of the Select Committee on the Parliamentary Commissioner from 1967 to 1970.

ment was the strengthening of Parliament to enable M.P.s to perform their duty of protecting the citizen from ministerial injustice. Liberals, he concluded, looked upon the proposal to appoint a Parliamentary Commissioner 'as a method of resisting necessary reform of Parliament'.

Lord Wade's Local Government (Rights of the Public) Bill was not discussed in the Lords until 18 October 1966 when a debate took place on the motion that the Bill be read a second time. Part I of his Bill provided that an Ombudsman would be set up for each of the economic planning regions in order to investigate complaints against local authorities. Other provisions in the Bill would have altered the law in relation to declaration of interest by members of local authorities and would have given the public the right of admittance to meetings of all committees of local authorities, unless they were specifically excluded by resolution of the authority.

Lord Kennet, Parliamentary Secretary to the Ministry of Housing and Local Government, speaking for the Government, did not oppose the Bill in principle but argued against its timing. The first thing to do, he maintained, was to get the Parliamentary Commissioner off the ground and running, to find out how to fit an Ombudsman into a nation such as Britain, before going on to the question whether there should be more Ombudsmen at regional or local level. It would also be better to wait for the Report of the Royal Commission on Local Government before deciding what form such Ombudsmen would take. He advised the House to reject the second reading of the Bill.[1]

The same day that Lord Wade's Bill was being discussed and rejected in the Lords, 18 October 1966, the Government's Parliamentary Commissioner Bill was being debated in the Commons and received its second reading. It is to the second reading of the Bill that we now turn.

[1] H.L. Deb. Vol. 277, Cols. 42–4. Lord Kennet was Parliamentary Secretary to the Ministry of Housing and Local Government from 1966 to 1970. He is, perhaps, better known as Wayland Young (his name before succeeding to the title) and is the author of many books including *The Profumo Affair* (1963), *Eros Denied* (1965), and *Existing Mechanisms of Arms Control* (1965).

VII

THE SECOND READING IN THE COMMONS

ON the day allotted for the second reading of the Parliamentary Commissioner Bill, 18 October 1966, it was hard to forecast what the attitude of the Conservative Opposition would be to the Bill. As we have seen, only one leading Conservative, Sir Lionel Heald, had spoken in the House on the subject and his attitude had been equivocal.[1] A group of Conservative lawyers, the Inns of Court Conservative and Unionist Society, had roundly condemned the proposal for a Parliamentary Commissioner, but the Leader of the Party, Edward Heath, had not indicated whether he shared their views. Operating on the flanks of the Conservative Party, the Society for Individual Freedom had made it clear that they wanted a Parliamentary Commissioner with greatly strengthened powers.

The attitude of the Liberals was also in doubt. As we have seen, Michael Winstanley had argued that an Ombudsman was needed for local government but that in central government the need was for improving the effectiveness of M.P.s by parliamentary reform.[2] On the other hand, another Liberal M.P., Eric Lubbock introduced a petition at the start of business in the Commons on 18 October which asked for the Parliamentary Commissioner Bill to be extended to Northern Ireland. The petition had been signed by the members of the Opposition of all political parties in the Northern Ireland Parliament. The fact that Eric Lubbock presented this petition invited the presumption that he, personally, was in favour of the Parliamentary Commissioner Bill. This presumption was to be confirmed by his subsequent interventions later in the day on the second reading of the Bill.[3]

---

[1] On the debate on the Address on 10 November 1965, H.C. Deb. 720, Cols. 262–9, see above pp. 61–2.

[2] In a letter to the *Guardian* on 9 August 1966. See above pp. 70–1.

[3] Eric Lubbock was Liberal Member for Orpington from 1962 to 1970. He was

On the Labour side, there were many Members who wanted to see the powers of the Parliamentary Commissioner greatly extended. Their point of view had been eloquently stated that morning by Mrs. Lena Jeger in her political column in the *Guardian*. For these Members, the question was whether the Government would be willing to accept amendments strengthening the powers of the Commissioner, or whether it would stick closely to the compromise worked out in the Cabinet Subcommittee.

The stage was set, therefore, for a second reading debate of more than usual interest. The Minister who came to the dispatch box at 3.43 p.m. to open the debate was the Lord President of the Council and Leader of the House, Richard Crossman. As a speaker he is always worth hearing and his speech was brilliant even by his own standards. Yet it was not an impeccable performance since the speech included one misleading statement on a key issue.[1] For this he had some excuse. He had only become Leader of the House in August 1966. Until then he had been fully immersed in his former department as Minister of Housing. He had not therefore been involved in the long preparation of the Parliamentary Commissioner Bill. Nor, as Lord President of the Council, did he have his own staff of Civil Service advisers. He was dependent upon the briefs prepared by the Civil Service team from the Treasury who were working with Niall MacDermot. In the circumstances, Crossman's speech was really a *tour de force*.

He began by saying that 'as a long standing advocate of Parliamentary reform, I am pleased and proud that the privilege has fallen to me to move the Second Reading of the Parliamentary Commissioner Bill.' He emphasized that, in introducing this reform, the Government was not proposing to establish an Ombudsman on the Scandinavian pattern. The Swedish Ombudsman, for example, he argued, 'though ultimately responsible to Parliament is an independent investigator and judge'.[2] The British Parliamentary Commissioner, by contrast, would be an adjunct to existing methods of Parliamentary scrutiny of the executive. He would be able to carry out impartial investigations into cases of alleged maladministration, but he would act only in response to complaints from Members. He would enhance, but would not replace, the existing methods of

---

Secretary in 1966 of the Parliamentary Civil Liberties Group. He is a chartered engineer and is heir to the Avebury barony.

[1] See below pp. 78–9.　　[2] H.C. Deb. Vol. 734, Col. 42.

checking and challenging administration by parliamentary question and Members' letters to Ministers.

Crossman traced the ancestry of the Bill to 'Justice' and the Whyatt Report. He recalled the rejection of the Whyatt recommendations by the Macmillan Government in November 1962. He then described the way in which the Labour Party had taken up the idea and quoted from Harold Wilson's Stowmarket speech in July 1964 in which he had committed the Party to establishing a Parliamentary Commissioner if returned to office.

Crossman pointed out that the Bill he was introducing went much further than the Whyatt Report had recommended in a number of ways. It did not give a Minister the right to veto an investigation. Indeed, the Minister's own actions and observations would be subject to investigation by the Parliamentary Commissioner.

Again, while the Whyatt Report proposed that the Commissioner should not have access to the internal minutes of departments, the Bill gave him access to all departmental papers. Only Cabinet papers would be excluded from his scrutiny. Ministers would not be able to withhold documents from the Commissioner by claiming Crown Privilege as they can do in the courts.

The Liberal Leader, Jeremy Thorpe, intervened at this stage to ask Crossman to explain what would be the effect of Clause 11 (3) which appeared to give a Minister complete veto of publication.[1] Crossman replied that it did not give the Minister the right to veto an investigation. But after an investigation was completed he could forbid disclosure of information which (to quote Clause 11 (3)) 'would be prejudicial to the safety of the State or otherwise contrary to the public interest'. He defended this provision against criticisms of it which had been advanced in an editorial of *The Times* that morning.

He then went on to discuss the concept of maladministration. Clause 5 of the Bill provided that the Commissioner might investigate a complaint about personal injustice caused by maladminstration. 'What about the definition of maladministration?' he asked rhetorically.[2] In the first place he could define it negatively. It did not extend to policy which remained a matter for Parliament. It did not include discretionary decisions where complainants disliked the decisions but could not fault the manner in which they were taken.

---

[1] H.C. Deb. Vol. 734, Col. 49.
[2] Ibid., Col. 51.

He said that a positive definition of maladministration would be far more difficult to achieve. 'We might have made an attempt in this Clause to define, by catalogue, all of the qualities which make up maladministration, which might count for maladministration by a Civil Servant. It would be a wonderful exercise—bias, neglect, inattention, delay, incompetence, inaptitude, perversity, turpitude, arbitrariness and so on. It would be a long and interesting list.'[1]

This was perhaps the most memorable section of Crossman's speech. The author knows one senior Civil Servant, who deals with Parliamentary Commissioner cases, who keeps a copy of the Crossman catalogue of sins on a card, tucked in with the pencils, in front of him on his desk. The Parliamentary Commissioner has himself referred to the 'Crossman Catalogue' in one of his reports.

Crossman then went on to defend the Government's choice of Parliamentary Commissioner arguing that, whereas a judge was appropriate to the Scandinavian situation, in Britain a Parliamentary officer was what was wanted 'and Sir Edmund Compton is a most distinguished Parliamentary officer already', having served the House very ably for eight years as Comptroller and Auditor-General.

The Parliamentary Commissioner would report to each individual Member who lodged a complaint with him, he would make an annual report to the whole House, and would be able to make a special report to the House when he thought that the maladministration or injustice had not been, or would not be, remedied.[2] He said he had been asked whether this would involve the setting up of a new Select Committee. He said that the Government were anxious for the House to take its own decision, 'but clearly there is a strong case for a special Select Committee to handle the Commissioner's special reports as well as his annual report.'[3]

There then followed several interventions from back-benchers who wanted to know more about the relationship between the Parliamentary Commissioner, Members of Parliament, and the public. Crossman was able to clear up a number of points; for example he confirmed, in answer to Mrs. Anne Kerr and Sydney Silverman, that while a member of the public would be able to ask any M.P. to take up his complaint with the Parliamentary Commissioner, an M.P. who was approached by someone who was not one of his constituents would normally be expected to consult with

[1] Ibid., Col. 51. [2] Ibid., Col. 53. [3] Ibid., Col. 54.

the M.P. for the constituency concerned before taking up the case.[1]

He next turned to the fields from which the Parliamentary Commissioner would be excluded. On local government, he said:

it seems to me right that our parliamentary Ombudsman should deal only with the area of ministerial and therefore of parliamentary control, leaving it to elected local authorities to work out their own way of equipping their councillors with an Office designed to remedy individual grievances of ratepayers by means of a searching investigation. I hope that big authorities will make the experiment as soon as possible.[2]

On Civil Servants, he commented that their own representatives did not want them included. It was better to rely on the well-tried system of Whitley Councils 'through which all manner of complaints are satisfactorily pursued'.

He argued that, as regards the serving soldier, those countries which provided for complaints to the Ombudsman from service men had all instituted a separate military commissioner. 'If my hon. Friends want a military commissioner, that is a separate institution which should be thought of separately and, if necessary, organized separately.'[3]

At this point, William Baxter, Labour M.P. for West Stirlingshire, intervened to ask whether it would not be better to give the Parliamentary Commissioner a broader field of inquiry since many complaints would overlap the functions of a Minister on the one hand and of a local authority or nationalized industry on the other.[4] He was supported by Sydney Silverman and Sir Tatton Brinton, Conservative M.P. for Kidderminster. Sir Tatton Brinton wanted to know what would be the position as regards planning where the citizen has a right of appeal to the Minister from the decision of the local planning authority.

Crossman replied to the first point that a Minister was careful not to intervene in a complaint against a local authority where there was no provision for appeal to him. In the case of planning, where there was such a provision for appeal, the Minister's inspectors were subject to the oversight of the Council on Tribunals. However, if it was possible to show that there had been maladministra-

---

[1] Ibid., Cols. 55–6. [2] Ibid., Col. 57.
[3] Ibid., Cols. 57–8. [4] Ibid., Col. 58.

tion at the appeal stage then the matter could go to the Parliamentary Commissioner.

He began the final part of his speech by claiming that 'Through the office of Parliamentary Commissioner, we put at the disposal of the back bench Member an extremely sharp and piercing instrument of investigation.' Ministers, he said had a very clear choice. 'In framing the Bill, we could have created a blunt instrument which could be used over a relatively wide field with comparatively small risk.' Alternatively, they could fashion a very sharp instrument, but in this case it was necessary that the limits of operation should 'be extremely carefully and narrowly defined in this first period'.[1]

At this late stage, Leo Abse, the Labour Member for Pontypool, intervened to ask whether the Minister did not agree that although the Parliamentary Commissioner might be useful 'for the slothful and indolent Member of Parliament' many Members believed that they could be their own Ombudsman in the Commons. Crossman replied that he thought the whole of his speech was an answer to the argument put forward by the Member for Pontypool. The Parliamentary Commissioner could help the Member to be much more effective in securing redress for his constituents.

He concluded:

How often in the past have we all shared the sense of impotence with which a frustrated back-bencher rises and says, 'In view of the unsatisfactory nature of the reply, I give notice that I will raise the matter on the Adjournment.' Now he has something else to rise for. Instead of merely threatening a half-hour Adjournment debate, he can tell the Minister with whose action he is not satisfied that he intends to raise the issue with the Parliamentary Commissioner.[2]

His speech had taken forty-four minutes which, in view of the many interventions by other Members, was an astonishingly short time for such a full and lucid exposition of the subject. It had been an able speech in which he had defended the Government's Bill from many points of view and had yet allowed the percipient listener to observe that he, personally, was in favour of a considerable extension of the reform which was now being proposed. For example, he had spoken of the need to define the limits within which the Parliamentary Commissioner would operate, carefully and narrowly 'in this first period'. He had not argued against allowing complaints

[1] Ibid., Col. 60.   [1] Ibid., Col. 61.

from members of the Armed Forces to a Parliamentary Commissioner, but had said there should be a separate Commissioner for this purpose. Similarly he had argued that local authorities should set up their own offices for the redress of grievances.

Yet, despite the many good features of Crossman's speech it contained one misleading statement which was not in fact directly challenged during the second reading debate, but was to be noticed later. He had pointed out correctly that the Whyatt Report had recommended that the Parliamentary Commissioner should investigate complaints of maladministration against government departments, but that complaints against the exercise of discretionary powers, which did not involve maladministration, should be a matter for administrative tribunals. 'As regards exercise of discretion powers, they suggested this should normally be subject to appeal to an independent authority, and recommended extending the powers of the Council on Tribunals for this purpose. The Tribunals and Inquiries Bill, which was given a Second Reading in this House in August, is addressed to this part of their report.'[1]

The clear implication of this statement, although it was not precisely spelled out, was that the Council on Tribunals was being given the power, as the Whyatt Report recommended, to propose the creation of new administrative tribunals where it found a gap in the system of tribunals. In fact, the Tribunals and Inquiries Bill gave the Council on Tribunals no such power. It was a modest measure, introduced originally in the House of Lords in April 1966, which extended the jurisdiction of the Council on Tribunals to a category of inquiry (inquiries held by Ministers under discretionary powers) which had not been covered by the Tribunals and Inquiries Act, 1958. It could in no way be said to implement the recommendations in the Whyatt Report.

How then do we explain the misleading character of the Minister's statement? Was it a sleight of hand or was he not fully informed about the character of the Tribunals and Inquiries Bill? The latter explanation seems the more likely. It is to be noted also that his full and clear exposition of the subject laid him open to revealing any inconsistency in the Government's position. It could well be maintained that it was inconsistent to confine the Parliamentary Commissioner to maladministration while failing to extend the range of scope of administrative tribunals to deal with complaints

[1] Ibid., Col. 45.

against discretionary powers which did not involve maladministration.

The Opposition spokesman who followed Crossman in the second reading debate did not make this criticism of the Bill. It was Quintin Hogg who opened for the Opposition and his role was difficult enough in all conscience.[1] He had been a Member of the Macmillan Government which turned down the Whyatt Committee's proposal for a Parliamentary Commissioner. He was himself highly sceptical of the value of having such a Commissioner, but he knew that many Conservative M.P.s were in favour, at least in principle, of this reform.

He began by arguing that 'The number of interruptions to which the Lord President of the Council courteously gave way during the course of his speech illustrates that this measure is both more difficult and more controversial than the right hon. Gentleman was prepared at least at the outset to concede.'[2] Speaking personally, he believed that the decision of the Macmillan administration to turn down the Whyatt Committee's proposal for a Parliamentary Commissioner had been right. He made it clear, however, that there had been Ministers at the time who did not share this majority view of the Cabinet.[3] His own objections to the present Bill were various.

In the first place he argued that the Bill was an attempt to import an institution into this country which had grown up in much smaller unitary states—in fact, Sweden, Norway, Denmark, and New Zealand. Its success in those countries derived partly from the fact that the population of each country is much smaller than that of Britain. 'In his natural habitat of a country with a maximum population of about 7 million,' he argued, 'the Ombudsman or the Parliamentary Commissioner is a sort of uncle figure.'[4]

Another point was that those countries had different parliamentary institutions, for example in the Scandinavian countries there

---

[1] Quintin Hogg Q.C. was, at this time, Conservative M.P. for St. Marylebone. He represented Oxford for the Conservatives from 1938 to 1950. In 1950 he succeeded to the peerage as Lord Hailsham. In 1963 he renounced his peerage when he was a candidate for leadership of the Conservative Party. He was then elected M.P. for St. Marylebone which he represented until 1970. On the formation of the Heath Government, in June 1970, he was appointed Lord Chancellor and made a life peer. He was First Lord of the Admiralty from 1955 to 1956, Minister of Education in 1957, and from 1959 to 1964 was Minister for Science, while also holding the office of either Lord Privy Seal or Lord President of the Council. He was Conservative spokesman in the Commons on Home Office affairs from 1966 to 1970.

[2] H.C. Deb. Vol. 734, Col. 61.   [3] Ibid., Col. 63.   [4] Ibid., Col. 66.

was 'an almost complete absence of parliamentary question time.'[1]
He argued that in Britain there was no need for a Parliamentary
Commissioner since the individual Member had many opportunities
to influence Ministers not only at question time, but through making
personal representations, and through intervening in debates on the
floor of the House, in debates on Money Bills and on Supply Days
as well as in Adjournment Debates.[2]

In fact, the proposal for a Parliamentary Commissioner brought
with it various anomalies and disadvantages. For one thing, the Bill
'carves up the areas of possible grievance in what must ultimately
be an arbitrary way'. He argued that 'A grievance machinery which
carves up the machinery of government in such an arbitrary way
will render that machinery largely ineffective to do what it is designed to do.'[3] The confusion in the minds of members of the public
about the terms of reference of the Parliamentary Commissioner
would, in his view, create many problems for M.P.s.

However, since he realized that the Bill would become law, he
did not want to make a purely negative contribution to the debate.
He would make a constructive suggestion which was that the House
should set up a Grievance Committee which would control the work
of the Parliamentary Commissioner. This Committee would refer to
the Commissioner for investigation either individual complaints or
generalized complaints which it felt had not been adequately ventilated. It would see to it that the individual back-bencher had
already exhausted, so far as was reasonable, the existing grievance
machinery.[4]

The advantage which Hogg claimed for his proposal over the
system proposed in the Bill was that the constituent would not be
able to say to an M.P. that his complaint should go, in the first
instance, to the Ombudsman. His proposal would give an additional
weapon to the Member, as against the Executive, but it would not
undermine the existing position of Members as, he claimed, the
proposal in the Bill would.

There had earlier been an amusing exchange between Hogg and
the Lord President. Crossman had intervened to point out that
Hogg was referring in his speech to 'the Ombudsman'. Crossman
said that this was not fair since 'We have explained that the Parliamentary Commissioner differs from the Swedish model. I wish the

[1] Ibid., Col. 65.   [2] Ibid., Col. 66.
[3] Ibid., Col. 67.   [4] Ibid., Col. 73.

right hon. and learned Gentleman would describe the proposal in the Bill as it is.'[1] The ironic thing about this was that, as we have seen, Crossman had himself, in his speech, referred to 'our parliamentary Ombudsman'.[2]

Hogg's speech had lasted forty-three minutes, one minute less than Crossman's speech. There then followed sixteen speeches from all parts of the House before the debate was concluded from the Opposition side by Sir John Hobson who was followed by the second Ministerial speaker, Niall MacDermot. Out of these sixteen speeches, six were by Conservatives, eight by Labour Members, one was from a Liberal, and one from the Plaid Cymru (Welsh Nationalist) Member. Of the six Conservative speakers none was as critical of the Bill as Hogg had been. One of them, Harold Gurden, the Member for Birmingham, Selly Oak, said he, in common with many other Conservative M.P.s, had consistently supported the idea of a Parliamentary Commissioner for Administration. He recalled that he had taken part in the debate which Dr. Donald Johnson had initiated in 1961.

His criticism of the Bill was that it did not go far enough. He criticized the exclusion of the police, of the hospitals, and of nationalized industries from investigation by the Parliamentary Commissioner. On local authorities, he took the view that it would be wrong for local authorities to have their own commissioners. 'All sorts of conflicting decisions would be made by local authorities, sometimes within a few miles of each other.'[3] He welcomed the Bill but the Government must not think it is the last word. 'They ought to accept Amendments in Committee.'[4]

Among the other Conservative speakers, Miss J. M. Quennell, the Member for Petersfield welcomed the Bill with 'very modified rapture.'[5] She pointed to the anomaly noticed by the Council on Tribunals in their Annual Report for 1965 that members of the public can complain directly to the Council on Tribunals about tribunals but, under the present Bill, could only approach the Parliamentary Commissioner through an M.P. She thought that personnel matters in the Armed Forces and the Civil Service should be brought within the ambit of the Commissioner.

---

[1] Ibid., Col. 70.   [2] Ibid., Col. 57, See above p. 76.
[3] Ibid., Col. 140.   [4] Ibid., Col. 141.
[5] Ibid., Col. 114. Miss J. M. Quennell has represented Petersfield since 1960. She has been a farm manager and is now a company director.

Charles Fletcher-Cooke, the Conservative Member for Darwen, welcomed whole-heartedly the principle behind the Bill.[1] He particularly welcomed the Government's decision not to allow a Minister to veto an investigation by the Commissioner and to give the Commissioner access to internal minutes. This made the Commissioner very strong indeed and did give rise to reasonable fears, like those voiced by Quintin Hogg, about the future relations of Members with the Commissioner and with members of the public. He thought it would be very difficult for M.P.s to act as a screen or sieve in deciding which cases they should forward to the Commissioner.[2]

He criticized the exclusion of contractual and commercial transactions from investigation by the Commissioner. He also criticized the distinction in the Bill beween maladministration and the exercise of discretionary powers without maladministration. He thought that it would mean that almost every complaint of injustice could be defeated under the Bill by the plea that it was an exercise of discretion. He thought that there were 'logical fallacies in the framework of the Bill which will have to be put right and which will have to be analysed at length in what promises to be a most interesting Committee.'[3]

These three Conservative speakers were all therefore in favour of the principle of the Bill but wanted the position of the Parliamentary Commissioner to be clarified and strengthened. This was also the attitude of two well-known Conservative former Ministers who took part in the debate: Sir Lionel Heald and Sir Hugh Munro-Lucas-Tooth.

Sir Lionel Heald was, as we have seen, the only M.P. to make a speech in the House on the White Paper on the Parliamentary Commissioner. He had also been in close touch with the Society for Individual Freedom and knew of their desire to see the terms of reference of the Commissioner greatly widened.[4] In his speech in this debate, he said that he was glad to agree with Richard Crossman about the general desirability of the Bill. 'I shall certainly

---

[1] Charles Fletcher-Cooke, Q.C. has represented Darwen as a Conservative since 1951. He was Under-Secretary at the Home Office from 1961 to 1963. He contested East Dorset as a Labour candidate in 1945. He has been Vice-Chairman of the Conservative Parliamentary Committee on Trade and Industry since 1965.

[2] H.C. Deb. Vol. 734, Col. 147.

[3] Ibid., Col. 151.

[4] See above pp. 67–8.

not oppose it. I did not oppose the idea when it was introduced some years ago. I have always been interested in it.'[1]

He thought, however, that the House had not been properly treated over the Bill. Since it was such a complex matter he considered, as he had pointed out to the House in 1965, that there should have been a debate on the White Paper. Failing that, he thought that the Government should have adopted the suggestion of the Study of Parliament Group that the Bill should go to a Select Committee 'where the sort of difficult subjects we have been discussing today, and about which we still do not know much, could be gone into.'[2]

One of these difficult subjects was the question of maladministration. When he recalled the many cases of grievance which he had dealt with since he had become a Member of the House, he considered that more than half of these cases would be excluded from scrutiny by the Parliamentary Commissioner if 'maladministration' was going to be interpreted in the way which he thought it would be interpreted. He pointed out that a very senior member of the Cabinet, Michael Stewart, the First Secretary of State and Secretary of State for Economic Affairs, had written an article in the *New Statesman* on 25 September 1964, forecasting the role of the Parliamentary Commissioner. Stewart had written that—'The Commissioner will be concerned with those episodes . . . where all the authorities have behaved correctly, yet the result is absurd or unjust.' This was exactly what the Commissioner, according to the Bill, would not be able to do. He would not be able to consider such cases because they would not be maladministration.

He also criticized some of the various exclusions from the Commissioner's terms of reference, for example the Armed Services, the postal services, nationalized industries, police, and hospitals. He hoped that the Government would accept constructive amendments in committee and that all such amendments would not be voted down on party lines. He concluded: 'I am sure that there could be genuine co-operation between the parties and that we want to try to forge a useful instrument. However, at the moment I can only reinforce the views of the Society of Individual Freedom, which has described the Bill as "half-baked".'[3]

The views of Sir Hugh Munro-Lucas-Tooth take on special interest, with hindsight, since he was to become the first Chairman

[1] H.C. Deb. Vol. 734, Col. 79.   [2] Ibid., Col. 80.   [3] Ibid., Col. 83.

of the House of Commons Select Committee on the Parliamentary Commissioner.[1] Like Sir Lionel Heald, he welcomed the Bill in general terms. Unlike Quintin Hogg, he did not think that the M.P. could readily get complaints against government departments investigated. He pointed to the delay involved in getting an oral answer to a question 'and getting an Adjournment debate is something which some of us think is almost an impossibility.'[2] They had moved a very long way from the situation he first knew as a young Member forty years ago when it was relatively easy to raise something on the Adjournment.

Like Sir Lionel Heald, he was concerned about the concept of maladministration but from a rather different point of view. He argued that if maladministration was held to include 'ineptitude', as Crossman had indicated, a very large proportion of cases could be investigated by the Commissioner. But it would be very difficult for the M.P. to say of any specific case whether misfeasance or ineptitude was involved. He would therefore be 'under the strongest possible pressure and temptation to pass the papers at once to the Commissioner.'[3] One of two possible results might then occur: either there would be disappointment since the Commissioner would be able to look at so few of the cases sent to him, or the Commissioner and his staff would be swamped by the volume of cases.

Sir Hugh Lucas-Tooth then asked some specific questions about details of the Bill. For example, Clause 4 (2) limited the scope of the Bill to functions exercised on behalf of the Crown. Did this mean that it applied to agents of the Crown or was it only concerned with servants of the Crown? Again did Clause 5 (3) prohibit inquiry into questions of naturalization and deportation orders? How far would the Bill be retrospective in effect?

It will be seen from this résumé that five of the six Conservative speakers in the main body of the debate were in favour of the Bill and wanted to strengthen its provisions. The sixth Conservative, Bryant Godman Irvine, the Member for Rye, also said that he hoped the Bill would be accepted.[4]

---

[1] Sir Hugh Munro-Lucas-Tooth of Teananich was Under-Secretary at the Home Office from 1952 to 1955. He was Member for the Isle of Ely from 1924 to 1929. Re-elected to the Commons in 1945, he represented Hendon South as a Conservative until 1970. He was born in 1903 and was called to the Bar in 1933.

[2] H.C. Deb. Vol. 734, Col. 88.   [3] Ibid., Col. 91.

[4] Bryant Godman Irvine was first elected in 1955. He is a farmer and was Vice-Chairman of the Conservative Parliamentary Agriculture Committee from 1964 to 1970. He was born in 1909 and was called to the Bar in 1932.

On the Labour side, seven of the back-benchers who contributed to the debate were strongly in favour of the Bill while one, A. J. Irvine, had misgivings about it and made a counter-proposal.[1] He considered that the establishment of a Parliamentary Commissioner, as proposed in the Bill, would be detrimental to the role of the M.P. in taking up injustices suffered by constituents. He argued that the Parliamentary Commissioner ought to be a Member of the House. 'This is the contention which I have pressed within my party whilst consideration of this matter has proceeded.'[2] He did not specify where this consideration had gone on, but he had been a member of the Legal and Judicial Group of the Parliamentary Labour Party which had discussed the proposal for an Ombudsman in 1965 and had sent a memorandum to the Government.[3]

He thought that the Parliamentary Commissioner should be a senior Member of the House, a member of the Opposition, and should be chosen for the duration of a Parliament. However, the question had been prejudged and the Parliamentary Commissioner designate had been appointed. 'The whole thing has been decided. This is as startling an instance of this House being used as a rubber stamp as I have ever come across in the whole of my experience.'[4]

The seven other Labour back-benchers who spoke in the debate all warmly supported the Bill. They can be subdivided into those who said the Bill made a good beginning and wanted the Ombudsman principle extended but did not press for specific amendments, and those who argued for specific amendments to the Bill. In the first category was Norman Haseldine, the Member for Bradford West, who, in a maiden speech welcomed the Bill but argued that there would be a growing demand for bringing in local authorities once the system was established.[5] He also hoped that 'experience will quickly enable us to grant powers to the Commissioner to initiate inquiries on his own initiative—such matters as may be revealed in the Press, and which may be considered by a Select Committee as suitable for investigation.'[6]

[1] A. J. Irvine Q.C. has been Member for Liverpool, Edge Hill, since 1947. He was called to the Bar in 1935 and took silk in 1958. He was Solicitor-General from 1967 to 1970. He had been Chairman of the Select Committee on Procedure from 1964 to 1965.
[2] H.C. Deb. Vol. 734, Col. 94.
[3] See above pp. 52–4.
[4] H.C. Deb. Vol. 734, Col. 95.
[5] Norman Haseldine was Labour Member for Bradford West from 1966 to 1970. He is a public relations officer.
[6] H.C. Deb. Vol. 734, Col. 78.

Sydney Silverman spoke warmly about the principle behind the Bill.[1] 'What we are doing here is making a hesitant, tentative and perhaps not quite adequate approach towards the greatest constitutional amendment that this House of Commons has ever approached since the days when universal suffrage became applicable to our electoral system.'[2] We are endeavouring 'to make the individual House of Commons back-bench Member's defence of his constituents against the Executive more effective than it has ever been'.[3]

Members would no longer be dependent, if dissatisfied, 'on a half-hour Adjournment debate, taking place under impossible circumstances', nor would they be dependent, when a case was tested on a vote in the House, 'on a Division conducted on purely party political considerations'. Members would no longer be deprived of access to the documentation on which a Minister's case rested. He reserved his right to put forward amendments in Committee but he thought the House should give a very warm welcome to the Bill.

Hugh Delargy was one of the veteran campaigners for an Ombudsman.[4] He had, with Dr. Donald Johnson, initiated the debate in May 1961. He had also, as he told the House, written a newspaper column seven years and eight months ago, advocating 'an Ombudsmand'.

The Bill had been very well presented by Crossman but it was not perfect. Many of the questions raised in this debate would have to be raised in Committee. He pointed to the fact that the Parliamentary Commissioner would not be able to initiate his own inquiries and that local authorities, the Armed Forces, and the police would not come within his jurisdiction. Anyway they were making a start.

He concluded by commenting that 'Everyone is delighted—or at least nearly everyone—that the man appointed to the post is not a

---

[1] Sydney Silverman represented Nelson and Colne for Labour from 1935 until his death in 1968. He was born in 1895. He promoted a private member's bill to abolish capital punishment which led to the passage of the Conservative Government's Homicide Act 1957. He later sponsored, as a private member, a bill which became law as the Murder (Abolition of Death Penalty) Act, 1965.

[2] H.C. Deb. Vol. 734, Col. 78.

[3] Ibid., Col. 124.

[4] Hugh Delargy, Labour Member for Thurrock, was elected in 1950. He had previously represented the Platting division of Manchester from 1945 to 1950. He was born in 1908. He had been a teacher, journalist, labourer, and insurance official.

lawyer or a judge. It could, with great profit, be written into the Bill that all lawyers will forever be ineligible for this post.'[1]

We come now to the category of Labour back-benchers who advocated specific changes in the Bill. Their speeches were similar to the speeches by Haseldine, Silverman, and Delargy in that they welcomed the Bill and supported the system which it introduced, but they differed in that they all argued for specific amendments to the Bill. Thus Denis Coe advocated the provision of legal aid for people appearing before the Parliamentary Commissioner on occasions when he allowed legal representation for a hearing.[2] He said that he needed to be convinced that it was right to exclude the hospitals from supervision by the Commissioner.

In general terms, he advocated the extension of the Ombudsman system to local authorities but he disagreed with Crossman's suggestion that the solution might be in 'a great number of local Ombudsmen appointed by leading local authorities'.[3] He thought that something should be done about the police and the nationalized industries. He thought that it would be wrong 'to assume that by appointing a Parliamentary Commissioner we have finally solved all the problems af maladministration. As the Whyatt Committee pointed out, perhaps new tribunals are required.'[4]

Mrs. Lena Jeger welcomed the Bill but said 'I very much hope that during the Committee stage there will be some very radical alterations to it if it is to be as effective as I believe is necessary.'[5] The police should be brought in. She pointed out that the Minority Report of the Royal Commission on the Police had advocated a Commissioner of Rights for police questions. The three members who signed the minority report had also suggested that 'If the Government were at any time to decide to institute an Ombudsman for the whole field of public administration then he could absorb the police complaints as well.'

As far as local authorities were concerned she did not think it would be sufficient to have commissioners appointed by local authorities. She thought they should look into the question of having regional commissioners to investigate complaints against

---

[1] H.C. Deb. Vol. 734, Col. 87.
[2] Dennis Coe was Labour Member for Middleton and Prestwich from 1966 to 1970. He was born in 1929 and had been a lecturer in government at Manchester College of Commerce.
[3] H.C. Deb. Vol. 734, Col. 108.   [4] Ibid., Col. 109.   [5] Ibid., Col. 114.

local authorities. They should look into this at Committee stage.[1]

She very much agreed with the criticism that the hospitals should be brought in. She also asked about the position where local authorities were carrying out functions for which a central government department held ultimate responsibility. For example, what would be the position where local authorities ran various institutions through their children's departments? Were not these institutions ultimately the responsibility of the Home Secretary? She suggested that in Committee they 'should extend the Bill to cover cases where local authorities are carrying out statutory duties and where there has been some failure'.[2]

She thought that personnel matters in the Armed Forces should be included and if it was necessary to have a separate military commissioner, then an amendment to this effect should be tabled at Committee stage.[3] This was a lively speech, well informed, and downright.[4]

David Weitzman was to have the satisfaction of himself moving and carrying at Committee stage an amendment which he now proposed.[5] He suggested that the Parliamentary Commissioner should be given a discretion to investigate cases where the person aggrieved has, or had, the right of appeal to an administrative tribunal. Clause 5 (2a) of the Bill denied the Commissioner any such discretion while the following subsection, 5 (2b), gave him discretion to look at cases which could have been taken to a court of law. Weitzman suggested that the Bill should be amended to give the Commissioner discretion to look at either type of case.

He went on to argue that the hospitals should be brought in, that contractual or other commercial transactions by government departments should not be excluded, and that personnel matters in the Armed Forces and the Civil Service should be brought within the Commissioner's sphere of investigation. He also urged that Clause 11 (3), which empowered the Minister to prevent the Commissioner disclosing the contents of a document, which he had

---

[1] Ibid., Col. 117.   [2] Ibid., Col. 118.   [3] Ibid., Col. 120.

[4] Mrs. Lena Jeger, Labour Member for Holborn and St. Pancras South, since 1964, had previously represented the constituency from 1953 to 1959. She is a journalist and was born in 1915.

[5] David Weitzman Q.C., Member for Stoke Newington and Hackney North since 1950, had previously represented Stoke Newington from 1945 to 1950. He was born in 1898 and was called to the Bar in 1922.

seen during an investigation, on the ground that it would be 'prejudicial to the safety of the State or otherwise contrary to the public interest', be amended. He urged that the words 'or otherwise contrary to the public interest' should be deleted.[1]

Finally, John Lee, while welcoming the Bill very warmly as 'a very remarkable and, indeed, a most exciting and imaginative legislative innovation', also argued for a major change in the Bill.[2] He proposed that Schedule III, which lists the spheres from which the Parliamentary Commissioner is excluded, should be taken out. He thought that the simple criterion should be accepted that 'anything on which it is permissible to ask a Parliamentary Question on the Floor of the House ought to be the subject of investigation by the Commissioner.'[3]

To meet the objection that the Commissioner might receive a flood of complaints, he proposed that in cases where the Commissioner doubted whether the complaint justified the expense of a full investigation, the complainant could 'be called upon to forward some sort of financial security'.[4] He also urged that the Commissioner should be given power to initiate investigations.

Jeremy Thorpe, was the only Liberal to speak in the debate.[5] His position on the Bill was similar to the position taken by the great majority of Labour back-bench speakers, although he did support Sir Lionel Heald's suggestion that the Bill should be considered by a Select Committee after the second reading.

He was critical of the fact that local authorities had been excluded. He would like a Select Committee to consider the possibility of having 'regional commissioners or Ombudsmen to deal with parliamentary and local government complaints'.[6] He thought that the hospital boards and nationalized industries should be brought within the system.

The new office could be an extremely useful weapon for back-bench Members, but it did not remove the necessity for giving

[1] H.C. Deb. Vol. 734, Col. 138.
[2] John Lee was Labour Member for Reading from 1966 to 1970. He was born in 1927. He is a barrister. He was a member of the Colonial Service in Ghana from 1951 to 1958 and on the staff of the B.B.C. from 1959 to 1965.
[3] H.C. Deb. Vol. 734, Col. 144.
[4] Ibid., Col. 145.
[5] Jeremy Thorpe has been Liberal Member for Devon North since 1959. He was elected Leader of the Liberal Party in the Commons in 1967 on the resignation of Jo Grimond. He was born in 1929 and was called to the Bar in 1954.
[6] H.C. Deb. Vol. 734, Col. 129.

Members additional power to cross-examine the Executive and it should not be allowed to push even further into the background the possibility of parliamentary reform. He ended by saying that he knew that the House would agree 'that we are extremely fortunate in the personality of the Parliamentary Commissioner selected and I know that, certainly from this bench, we would like to wish him well in his task.'

Gwynfor Evans, the one Plaid Cymru Member, welcomed the Bill.[1] 'I support the Bill warmly. I think it has an excellent purpose. I think it can be a means whereby Parliament and the public can more effectively control the Executive. I do not share the fears of hon. Members on this side of the House in that matter, but we must ensure that this purpose is achieved fully.'[2]

His main contribution to the debate was to advocate a separate Parliamentary Commissioner for Wales who would also look into complaints against local authorities in Wales. John Rankin, the Labour Member for Glasgow, Govan, then intervened to say that he wanted to advocate a separate Parliamentary Commissioner for Scotland.

Sir John Hobson concluded the debate for the Conservative Opposition. He said that a notable feature of the debate was 'the general welcome which had been given to the Bill coupled with the expression of widespread anxiety about its exact nature, its likely effect, and the powers, status and functions of the Parliamentary Commissioner whom it proposes to establish'.[3] He was very sorry that the Member for Kensington South (William Roots), who sat on the Conservative Front Bench, had not been called to speak in the debate. Had he been called he would have put forward the alternative to a Parliamentary Commissioner proposed in their pamphlet by the Inns of Court Conservative and Unionist Association.[4]

Sir John touched on the limitations in the Bill on the position and powers of the Parliamentary Commissioner. He agreed with

---

[1] Gwynfor Evans was elected Plaid Cymru Member for Carmarthen at a by-election in 1966. He lost the seat to Labour at the General Election of 1970. He has been President of Plaid Cymru since 1945.

[2] H.C. Deb. Vol. 724, Col. 123.

[3] Ibid., Col. 152.

[4] It was a surprising feature of the debate that no Conservative advocated this suggestion for Judicial and Investigating Commissions broadly modelled on the French *Conseil d'État*. See above pp. 62–5.

those Members who had said that Crossman's proposal that it should be left to individual local authorities to set up their own commissioners was not an adequate answer. In his own view either nothing must be done about complaints against local authorities 'or this matter must be done on a national basis, either with regional commissioners or some other form of central organisation'.[1]

He thought that the Parliamentary Commissioner should be able to consider the contractual and commercial transactions of government departments. He criticized the fact that the Parliamentary Commissioner could not award compensation. He could only make a report and there could be publicity. 'While it may be that on many occasions the publicity may result in something being done to put the matter right, I am prepared to lay a large amount of money that public money will never be the method by which it is put right.'[2] If, indeed, Sir John did lay a bet on this subject, he will have lost his wager. For example, after the Parliamentary Commissioner's report on the Sachsenhausen case, in 1967, the complainants were all paid compensation by the Foreign Office which they had been previously denied.[3] Similarly, in 1968, the Ministry of Transport paid nearly £8,000 in compensation to one complainant after an investigation by the Parliamentary Commissioner.[4]

One of the most interesting features of Sir John Hobson's speech was his observation that, whereas the White Paper had said (at paragraph 11) that the Parliamentary Commissioner would not be able to examine decisions taken in the exercise of discretionary powers, he could not find a single word about this in the Bill. This comment, reinforced by the views of Sir Hugh Lucas-Tooth in Comittee, was to give rise to a reappraisal of the text of the Bill by the Treasury team and to the amendment which the Government put in at Report stage. This amendment was later taken out in the Lords after strong criticisms in the Press and from peers of all parties, and a new clause drafted by Lord Gardiner was put in.[5]

Finally, Sir John said he hoped that the Parliamentary Commissioner would be made a parliamentary official, in the true sense, in that he should be removed only by an address of both Houses of Parliament and not of one. The Conservatives moved an amendment to this effect in Standing Committee but it was defeated. Their amendment was however carried at Report stage.

[1] H.C. Deb. Vol. 734, Col. 156.   [2] Ibid., Cols. 157–8.
[3] See below p. 257.   [4] See below p. 288.   [5] See below pp. 216–8 and 225.

Sir John Hobson concluded by saying that he thought that there should have been a debate on the White Paper before they had the Bill 'because there is a great deal more to be said about the Bill and the shape of it, but at any rate we will have the opportunity in Committee of seeing how we can improve it.'[1]

Niall MacDermot, the Financial Secretary to the Treasury, had to reply to a wide-ranging debate. He was faced with a war on two fronts since he had to reply to those who claimed that the Parliamentary Commissioner was unnecessary, or would have undesirable consequences, on the one hand, and those who said that the Bill did not go far enough, on the other. We have seen that the weight of speeches in the debate had been in the second category. Only Quintin Hogg, A. J. Irvine, and Leo Abse (in his brief intervention) had clearly indicated that they were in the first category. Some of the other Conservative speeches had included misgivings about the new system, but, on balance, they were all in favour of extending the powers of the Commissioner.

Nevertheless, MacDermot dealt first with some of the objections which Hogg had raised. In particular, he sought to meet the objection that the Bill would undermine the authority of Members of Parliament. He argued that the fact that the Commissioner was to be a parliamentary officer was in itself a safeguard against this happening.

He took up the question which Miss Quennell had asked as to why they were not allowing the public direct access to the Commissioner. This sprang from the Government's whole conception of him as an officer of Parliament. 'We envisage his supplementing rather than supplanting hon. Members as protectors of the rights of individuals.'[2]

Turning to the arguments of those who wanted an extension of the Parliamentary Commissioner's powers, he took up the question as to whether the Commissioner should be able to look at discretionary decisions where maladministration was not involved. If we did this we would be substituting the decision of the Commissioner for the decision of the Minister. 'Do we want government by Government or do we want government by Commissioner?' he asked.[3]

He had been asked, he said, to define more positively what we envisage by maladministration. 'I do not want to be limited to any

---

[1] H.C. Deb. Vol. 734, Col. 162.   [2] Ibid., Col. 166.   [3] Ibid., Col. 167.

definition, but I have found very helpful the phrase which Lord Denning used in the debate on the Franks Committee Report.' Lord Denning had spoken of occasions when there was 'abuse or misuse of power in the interests of the Department at the expense of the individual'.[1]

He said that the decision not to include local authorities stemmed from the decision that it was a Parliamentary Commissioner they were providing for. Following the report of the Local Government Commission there would be reorganization in the structure of local government and 'in that context and in the light of experience we will have gained from the Commissioner, it may be possible to devise a similar procedure for local authorities.'[2]

As to the police, the same consideration applied: 'the police are not controlled by the central Government and this is the reason for their exclusion.' As regards the Home Secretary's responsibility for the Metropolitan Police, he was not responsible for individual complaints about the Metropolitan Police. As to instituting a new system of complaints against the police, 'We have agreed under the Police Act, 1964, to set up a new complaints procedure, and I suggest that we should first see how that works out.'[3]

His reply to the Members who had referred to bringing in the National Health Service was: 'This is a difficult one which we will want to consider carefully.'[4] He pointed out that three hospitals— Broadmoor, Rampton and Moss Side—would be within the scope of the Commissioner since they were the direct responsibility of the Minister of Health. He argued that to include other hospitals would be going beyond the sphere of government departments.

On the question of contracts and commercial transactions, he put forward the argument that the principle behind the Bill was that the Parliamentary Commissioner would be dealing with relations between the Government and the governed. 'When dealing with commercial and contractual relationships between Government Departments and outside bodies we are not dealing with that relationship.'[5] He put forward the same argument against allowing the Commissioner to consider personnel matters in the Forces. Here again, he argued, internal relationships within the Armed Forces were not matters of the relationship between Government and the

---

[1] Ibid., Col. 168. [2] Ibid., Col. 170. [3] Ibid. Col. 170.
[4] Ibid., Col. 170. [5] Ibid., Col. 171.

governed. This was a somewhat curious argument whose implication was that the service man was not also a citizen.

In general, MacDermot's speech was capable, but, in cricketing terms, it was a skilful defensive innings. He gave nothing away and did not chance his arm at any stage. Nevertheless, no one wanted to oppose the second reading. The Bill was read a second time without a division and the debate ended just before 10.00 p.m.

There followed a very short debate lasting only a few minutes on the Money Resolution for the Parliamentary Commissioner Bill. Sir John Hobson asked Niall MacDermot if he could give a breakdown of the total staff likely to be employed in the Parliamentary Commissioner's Office. He also wanted to know whether the Money Resolution would cover the payment of expenses involved for people who made complaints.

MacDermot replied that 'The total staff whom we have in mind, including not only the officers, but all the clerical staff, typists and messengers totals, I think, 63.'[1] As to his other question, the £200,000 voted in the Money Resolution would cover not only all the salaries involved but also the expenses of witnesses and other persons attending such inquiries as the Parliamentary Commissioner might call.

[1] Ibid., Col. 174.

VIII

THE COMMITTEE STAGE IN THE COMMONS—THE FIRST TO FIFTH SITTINGS OF THE STANDING COMMITTEE

THE committee stage of the Bill opened on Thursday, 27 October 1966, nine days after the second reading debate. The committee stage was taken in Standing Committee B consisting of twenty-one Members drawn from the two main political parties. Since 1960 it has become the normal practice of the House of Commons to send all important Bills to standing committee, unless they have constitutional significance, in which case they are still taken in Committee of the whole House.[1] It could have been argued that the Parliamentary Commissioner Bill did have constitutional importance but this contention was not advanced. In practice, the convention that Bills of constitutional importance are taken in standing committee is held usually to apply to Bills which concern electoral changes (Representation of the People Bills), or, for example, the powers of the Upper House (Parliament Bills) or the attainment of independence by former colonies (e.g. the Jamaica Independence Bill, 1962).

The advantages of sending important Bills to standing committee are very considerable. It is a great time-saving device. Committee stage is the most time-consuming stage of legislation. If all important Bills are taken in committee of the whole House a bottleneck is created which is avoided when several bills are being taken at the same time in a series of standing committees.

But the saving of time is not the only advantage of taking a Bill in standing committee. The atmosphere in standing committee is less formal than in committee of the whole House and attitudes tend to be less partisan.

The physical surroundings differ a great deal from those in the full Chamber. Standing committees meet in the committee rooms

[1] See F. Stacey, op. cit., pp. 92–102.

which open onto a long corridor on an upper floor of the Palace of Westminster. Each committee room is rectangular in shape. The Members on the Government side sit in rows of chairs on one side, Opposition Members sit facing them.

At one end there are a few seats for the Press and public. At the other end there is a long table on a slightly raised platform. The chairman of the committee sits at the middle of this table flanked by the committee clerks and the Minister's advisers. The seats of all the members of the committee, and of the Press and public, are all on the same level. Only in the larger committee room, where the Scottish Grand Committee meets, are the seats tiered.

In these surroundings, speeches tend to be even more conversational than they are in the full House. The committee also develops a certain *esprit de corps* even though, since 1960, each committee is formed *ad hoc* for the Bill which it is considering and disperses when the committee stage has ended. The members are all cooped up together for the duration of the committee stage and 'cooped up' is not an inappropriate phrase. Members often go out into the corridor during the proceedings. There a Member may chat, quietly dictate a letter to his secretary (if he has one), or buy a cup of coffee from the trolley when it comes round. But Members are pretty well tied to the committee room when the standing committee is in session, or to the corridor just outside.

There are no division bells to summon them to votes as in the whole House. Divisions are called by the policeman in attendance who goes to the door of the committee room and shouts 'Division' down the corridor. The Member who wants to record his vote must then be on hand in the corridor so that he can hurry into the committee room to vote.

Membership of a standing committee is therefore an exacting task if it is conscientiously performed. In addition, the times at which standing committees meet make membership none too popular. They normally sit from 10.30 a.m. to 1.0 p.m. on two mornings a week. When a Bill is a long and controversial one, the standing committee concerned may be in almost continuous session taking up afternoons and evenings as well and, exceptionally, going on into the night.

The fact that work on a standing committee inevitably takes up many mornings makes it unpopular with those M.P.s who combine service in the House with working at another occupation as barrister, company director, merchant banker, etc. It can therefore be difficult to recruit members for standing committees. On the other hand, with a Bill like the Parliamentary Commissioner Bill there are many M.P.s who are keenly interested in the Bill and are anxious to secure a place on the standing committee.

The members of a standing committee are chosen by the Committee of Selection. This is a committee of fairly senior Members of the House and is nominated by the whole House. Representatives of the Party Whips' Offices also sit on the Committee. The Committee of Selection tries to choose members for the standing committee on a Bill from among those who have a special interest or knowledge of the subject matter of the Bill. Members who speak on the second reading of a Bill have clearly indicated an interest. Eight of the twenty-one members of Standing Committee B, on this occasion, had spoken in the second reading debate on the Parliamentary Commissioner Bill. These were, on the Labour side, Denis Coe, Norman Haseldine, John Lee, Sydney Silverman, and David Weitzman to name back-benchers only. In addition, the Minister in charge of the Bill in Standing Committee, Niall MacDermot, had replied to the debate at second reading.

On the Conservative side, two members of the standing committee had spoken in the second reading debate. These were Charles Fletcher-Cooke and Sir Hugh Munro-Lucas-Tooth. The Opposition leader on the standing committee, William Roots, had not spoken in the second reading debate but he had been expecting to be called.[1] One further Labour back-bencher had not been called in the debate but, in an intervention, had shown his interest in the Bill. This was John Rankin, the Labour Member for the Govan division of Glasgow, who had intervened in the debate to say that he wanted to propose that a Parliamentary Commissioner for Scotland be appointed.[2]

Of the members of the standing committee who had not spoken at second reading, one had long been associated with the campaign for an Ombudsman. This was Sir John Foster, the Conservative Member for Northwich, who had been Chairman of the Executive Committee of 'Justice' in 1961 and 1962 and Vice-Chairman from 1958 to 1960.[3] Another member who had declared his interest in the reform

[1] See above p. 90.   [2] See above p. 90.

[3] Sir John Foster Q.C. was first elected to the Commons in 1945. He was Under-Secretary for Commonwealth Relations in the Churchill Government from 1951 to 1954. He was born in 1904 and was called to the Bar in 1927. From 1934 to 1939 he was Lecturer in Private International Law at Oxford. From 1938 to 1964 he was Recorder of Oxford. He is a Director of investment, property, and other companies.

was Paul Rose, the Labour Member for the Blackley division of Manchester.[1] He had written an article for *Tribune* contrasting the powers of the Parliamentary Commissioner with those exercised by Ombudsmen abroad.

Several other members of the standing committee were lawyers. Alexander Lyon, the Labour Member for York, was a barrister who was also keenly interested in the introduction of a Parliamentary Commissioner and was later to be an active member of the Select Committee on the Parliamentary Commissioner.[2] Antony Buck, the Conservative Member for Colchester, was also a barrister.[3] He had been joint secretary of the Conservative Parliamentary Committee on Home Affairs from 1964 to 1966. He had also been secretary of the Bow Group for two years. Another Conservative, Anthony Grant, was a solicitor.[4] He had been secretary of the Conservative Parliamentary Legal Committee from 1965 to 1966.

Of the non-lawyers, Cranley Onslow, the Conservative Member for Woking, was a journalist who had been a member of the Foreign Service for nine years.[5] Michael English, the Labour Member for Nottingham West, was a departmental manager who had been active in local government for many years.[6] Dame Joan Vickers, the Conservative Member for Plymouth, Devonport, also had considerable local government experience. She had been a member of the London County Council from 1937 to 1945. She is a campaigner for many causes, not the least of which is womens' rights. From 1962 to 1963 she was the British delegate to the Status of Women Commission at the United Nations.[7] Sitting on the committee as Labour whip was Ioan Evans, the Member for the Yardley Division of Birmingham.[8]

[1] Paul B. Rose was elected in 1964. He was born in 1935 and was called to the Bar in 1958.

[2] Alexander Lyon was first elected in 1966. He was born in 1931 and called to the Bar in 1954.

[3] Antony Buck was first elected in 1961. He was born in 1928 and was called to the Bar in 1954.

[4] Anthony Grant, Conservative Member for Harrow Central, was first elected in 1964.

[5] Cranley Onslow was first elected in 1964. He was born in 1926. He was a member of the Foreign Service from 1951 to 1960. He was secretary of the Conservative Parliamentary Aviation Committee from 1965 to 1966.

[6] Michael English was first elected in 1964. He was born in 1930 and was educated at Liverpool University. He was a member of Rochdale Borough Council from 1953 to 1965. He was Vice-Chairman in 1966 of the Labour Parliamentary Public Works and Accomodation Committee.

[7] Dame Joan Vickers was first elected in 1955. She was born in 1907.

[8] Ioan Evans was first elected in 1964. He lost the seat to a Conservative in 1970. He was born in 1927 and was educated at Swansea University College. He had been a member of West Bromwich Education Committee.

Finally, Hugh Jenkins, the Labour Member for Putney, Wandsworth, had served on the London County Council. He had been assistant general secretary of British Actors' Equity Association from 1957 to 1964.[1]

This was, then, a strong committee to consider the Bill. Of its twenty-one members, twelve were lawyers and four had local government experience. Two of the Conservatives were former Ministers and several members, on both sides of the committee, were officers of Conservative or Labour parliamentary specialist groups. Most important, a very high proportion of the members of the standing committee were to be active in the committee in attempting to improve the Bill.

The committee met on ten occasions sitting every Tuesday and Thursday morning, from 10.30 a.m. to 1.0 p.m., from Thursday, 27 October to Tuesday, 29 November. During these sittings the whole Bill was considered without recourse to the closure or to any guillotine procedure.

The Chairman throughout was Wing Commander Robert Grant-Ferris, the Conservative Member for Nantwich.[2] The Chairmen of standing committees are all members of the Commons Chairmen's panel. They are drawn from all parties but must be back-benchers. They follow the rules of procedure which have been established over the centuries by Speakers of the House of Commons, and the Standing Orders determined by the Commons.[3]

The first amendment to be discussed at the opening of the committee's business on 27 October 1966 was moved by the leading Conservative spokesman on the committee, William Roots. Subsection (3) of clause 1 of the Bill provided that the Parliamentary Commissioner 'may be removed from office by Her Majesty in consequence of an Address from the House of Commons'. The Conservatives proposed to change this to 'Addresses from both Houses of Parliament'. The Financial Secretary to the Treasury, Niall MacDermot, approved of the amendment and said he hoped the committee would accept it since it would make the Parliamentary

---

[1] Hugh Jenkins was first elected in 1964. He was born in 1908.

[2] Robert Grant-Ferris was elected in 1955. Born in 1907 he was called to the Bar in 1937. He was created a Knight Bachelor in June 1969. He is a landowner. After the General Election of 1970 he was elected Deputy Speaker and Chairman of Ways and Means.

[3] See Erskine May, *The Law, Privileges, Proceedings and Usages of Parliament* (17th edn., Butterworth, 1964), and Standing Orders of the House of Commons, Public Business.

Commissioner more independent of the Government of the day, and would make his position analogous to that of the Comptroller and Auditor-General.

The Labour members of the committee were not willing to support their Minister here. Sidney Silverman argued that the Parliamentary Commissioner would be a servant of the House of Commons, therefore only the Commons should be concerned in his removal. They should not give 'an added power, an unnecessary power which they could not very responsibly perform, to the House of Lords.'[1]

David Weitzman took a similar view and, in the division, nine Labour Members voted against the amendment. Seven Conservatives voted for it and were joined by the Minister and the Labour Whip. The result therefore was a 9–9 tie and the Chairman exercised his casting vote against the amendment. Here he was following the convention that where there is a tie the Chairman uses his vote in favour of the Bill as introduced. In fact, this Conservative amendment was to be reintroduced, and was to succeed, at report stage.[2]

Clause 2 which dealt with the salary and pension of the Commissioner was then quickly approved. But on Clause 3, 'Administrative Provisions,' John Rankin moved an amendment to provide for a 'Parliamentary Commissioner for Scottish matters'. Rankin pointed out that many of the functions of central government which would be the concern of the Parliamentary Commissioner, such as Agriculture, Education, Health, Housing, and Land, were now the responsibility of the Scottish Office. It was therefore appropriate that someone in the Parliamentary Commissioner's office should be designated Parliamentary Commissioner for Scottish matters.

David Weitzman, from the Labour benches, supported the amendment as did Sir John Foster from the Conservative side of the committee. Sir John Foster thought the same considerations applied to Northern Ireland 'and to a certain extent to Wales'.[3] Paul Rose, in supporting the amendment from the Labour side, pointed out that he had an amendment down for later discussion dealing with Northern Ireland. He also said that 'if pressed' he would like to see

---

[1] Official Report of Standing Committee B, 1966–7. The Parliamentary Commissioner Bill, Col. 10.

[2] See below pp. 169–70.

[3] The Parliamentary Commissioner Bill, Col. 24.

Parliamentary Commissioners for the English regions as well as for Scotland, Northern Ireland, and Wales. This would be in conformity with the general tendency toward regional government, it would bring the office of Parliamentary Commissioner nearer to the people, and would make the volume of work for each Commissioner comparable to that experienced in Scandinavia and New Zealand.

Niall MacDermot, opposing the amendment, told the committee that he understood that 'already thought has been given to this matter by the P.C.A. designate and that it is contemplated, for the reasons that have been expressed, that it will be necessary to have an office of the Parliamentary Commissioner in Scotland'.[1] There would not however be a separate, independent, officer dealing with Scotland. On the question of regional Commissioners, he said that, 'It may be that at a later stage, in the years to come, when we have seen how it works, there will be a case for regional Commissioners, perhaps concerned either wholly or partly with local government matters but we are not at that stage at the moment.'[2] John Rankin then thanked the Minister 'for his potential support' and asked leave to withdraw his amendment.

On Clause 4, 'Departments and Authorities Subject to Investigation', the Chairman first ruled that three amendments which sought to bring local authorities within the purview of the Parliamentary Commissioner were all out of order. This was because they did not come within the ambit of the Bill since it was concerned with central government.

The Chairman did, however, rule in order an amendment which proposed to give the Parliamentary Commissioner power to look at the actions of a Minister of the Crown where he is acting in default of a local authority, or other public body which is not part of the central government. William Roots moved this amendment and there followed a long discussion which continued until 1.0 p.m., when the Chairman adjourned the committee without putting the amendment as provided in Standing Orders. During the discussion, certain fascinating sidelights were thrown on authorities which would be subject to investigation. For example, Charles Fletcher-Cooke ascertained from the Minister that the Bank of England would be subject to investigation by the Parliamentary Commissioner when it was exercising, as agent of the Treasury, functions of exchange control.[3] In general, the Minister's attitude was that the amendment was

[1] Ibid., Col. 26.   [2] Ibid., Col. 31.   [1] Ibid., Col. 40.

unnecessary since action by a central department, in default of an action by an outside body, was already covered by the Bill.

When the committee met for its second sitting on Tuesday, 1 November at 10.30 a.m., the first business was to put William Roots's amendment to the vote. In the division it was lost by 7 votes to 10. This was a straight party vote with only Conservatives voting for the amendment and only Labour members against.

William Roots then moved a further amendment to Clause 4 which sought to make 'servants' or 'agents' of the Crown subject to investigation by the Commissioner as well as 'officers' of departments or other bodies exercising functions on behalf of the Crown. It will be recalled that Sir Hugh Lucas-Tooth at second reading had raised the question of whether 'servants or agents' of the Crown would be included under the Bill.[1]

Niall MacDermot replied that the amendment was unnecessary since servants or agents of the Crown would be included under the Bill. The ordinary rules of vicarious responsibility applied.[2] A local authority acting as an agent for the Minister of Transport in connection with work on a trunk road would be liable to investigation by the Parliamentary Commissioner in respect of that work.[3] Conservative members were not altogether satisfied with the Minister's reply and pressed him to accept the amendments to include agents and servants in order to give greater certainty. The Minister agreed to do this and the amendment was by leave withdrawn.[4] Clause 4 was then approved.

Discussion then opened on Clause 5, 'Matters Subject to Investigation.' Clause 5 was not to be voted until part-way through the fifth sitting of the committee on 10 November 1966. Discussion on it, then, took most of the second sitting, the whole of the third and fourth sittings, and part of the fifth sitting. It was the clause which took by far the largest part of the committee's time.

This did not indicate any lack of balance since Clause 5 was the very nub of the Bill. The first part of Clause 5 read as follows:

5—(1) Subject to the provisions of this section, the Commissioner may investigate any action taken by a government department or other

---

[1] See above p. 84.
[2] The Parliamentary Commissioner Bill, Col. 53.   [3] Ibid., Col. 56.
[4] At report stage the Minister, in fact, introduced a series of amendments to make clear that 'servants' or 'agents' would be subject to investigation by the Commissioner. See below p. 170.

authority to which this Act applies, being action taken in the exercise of administrative functions of that department or authority, in any case where:

(a) a written complaint is duly made to a member of the House of Commons by a member of the public who claims to have sustained injustice in consequence of maladministration in connection with the action so taken; and

(b) the complaint is referred to the Commissioner, with the consent of the person who made it, by a member of that House with a request to conduct an investigation thereon.

The leader of the Conservative members, William Roots, was called first by the Chairman to put Amendment No. 13 which sought to include 'any exercise of discretionary powers' among action taken by a government department which the Commissioner could investigate. At the same time, the Chairman ruled the committee would discuss Amendment No. 14, also put down by the Conservatives, which would have the effect of excluding consideration by the Commissioner of the exercise of discretionary powers.

The Conservatives therefore sought by these two amendments to try to test out the exact nature of the powers which would be given to the Commissioner by the phrase in Clause 5 which allowed him to look into a complaint that someone had 'sustained injustice in consequence of maladministration'. William Roots opened the discussion by arguing that: 'If the Parliamentary Commissioner is to be effective, we should make it quite clear that he has the power to examine the discretionary decisions.'[1] This did not mean, however, that he would simply form a fresh opinion. His function should be to consider whether the person making the decision had before him 'the proper facts, and only the proper facts, to exercise that discretion'.

Sir Hugh Lucas-Tooth moved an amendment which sought to leave out the word 'maladministration' from the Clause and to insert instead 'misfeasance of negligence'. He argued, as he had done on second reading, that the reference to maladministration in the Bill would be 'applicable to hundreds of thousands of cases which come in every year to Members of Parliament complaining simply about bad decisions'.[2] He thought that the Commissioner should not be 'a court of appeal for every ministerial act'.[3] If we allowed this to happen, 'We shall simply put a burden on the Commissioner which

---

[1] Parliamentary Commissioner Bill, Col. 59.
[2] Ibid., Col. 61.   [3] Ibid., Col. 62.

he will be quite incapable of discharging. We shall have a Government and, so to speak, a counter-Government, operating in the same building.'[1] Therefore he wanted to see the powers given to the Commissioner narrowed. He wanted the Bill to cover a very large range of Government, but to be very narrow in its application.[2]

Sir John Foster presented a very different point of view from the Conservative benches. He was in favour of leaving in the phrase 'injustice in consequence of maladministration'. But he hoped that, in practice, the Parliamentary Commissioner would give a broad interpretation to the word 'maladministration'. Whenever the Commissioner thought that an injustice had been suffered, he should say so, even if he found that regulations in the department had been followed. He should be able to say, 'I think that these regulations ought to be changed.'[3] He thought that Britain should follow the Danish practice, under which, for the Danish Commissioner, 'maladministration means that in this matter the country is badly administered.'[4]

On the Labour side, Sidney Silverman took a similar view. So did David Weitzman who said he took a directly opposite view to that of Sir Hugh Lucas-Tooth. He would like to see the powers of the Commissioner widened rather than narrowed. If he thought that the Financial Secretary would accept it he would support Amendment 13 (giving the Commissioner power to consider discretionary decisions) but he would definitely oppose Amendment 14 (excluding discretionary decisions). John Rankin also hoped that the scope of the Bill would widen and that in time we would 'simply say to ourselves that any injustice from any quarter is something that we must deal with and also something that will ultimately go up to the Comissioner'.[5]

The Financial Secretary, Niall MacDermot, had a difficult task in dealing on three fronts with the arguments which had been put forward. He had to meet the probing amendments put down by William Roots and to attempt to define what was involved in the concept of 'injustice in consequence of maladministration'. He had to resist the narrowing amendment put down by Lucas-Tooth, while at the same time discouraging the more generous interpretations put on the Clause by Sir John Foster and the Labour members.

He emphasized that: 'It is not our intention when setting up a

[1] Ibid., Col. 63.   [2] Ibid., Col. 64.   [3] Ibid., Col. 79.
[4] Ibid., Col. 78.   [5] Ibid., Col. 66.

Parliamentary Commissioner for Administration, that he shall suddenly become a court of appeal for that whole host of administrative decisions which Parliament has decided shall not be the subject of an appeal.'[1] Discretionary decisions by the Minister would not be looked at unless they involved a fault in administration, that is where they involved a degree of bias, or prejudice, or irrelevant matters had been taken into consideration.[2]

He was therefore opposed to Amendment 13 which would widen the powers of the Commissioner, but he was also opposed to Amendment 14 which would be too restrictive. They did not want to exclude from consideration all exercise of discretionary powers, since the exercise of such powers, when there was an element of maladministration, should be capable of investigation by the Commissioner.

He opposed Lucas-Tooth's amendment to substitute 'misfeasance of negligence' for 'maladministration' on the ground that this too would make the scope of the Commissioner's powers too narrow. After a long and involved debate, William Roots's Amendment 13 to give the Commissioner power to consider discretionary decisions was put to the vote. The amendment was defeated, only five Conservative members voting for it and ten Labour members against. Sir Hugh Lucas-Tooth had announced that he would abstain on the vote since he did not want to see the scope of the Commissioner's powers widened, but he would not move his own amendment.

After the division, William Roots announced that in the light of the debate he would not move Amendment 14. The debate had thrown some additional light on what the Government intended by the concept of 'injustice in consequence of maladministration'. But it had also left a number of key questions unanswered, or imperfectly answered. In particular, it had left in the minds of the Minister's advisers the lingering doubt as to whether there was force in the arguments put forward by Sir John Hobson on second reading that the Bill, as drafted, gave the Commissioner wider scope to look at discretionary decisions than had originally been intended. It was this doubt which led to the introduction of the much criticized Government amendment to Clause 5 at report stage.[3]

The committee then went on to discuss another highly controversial feature of Clause 5, the provision that a written complaint had to be made by a member of the public to a member of the House of Commons who would then refer it to the Parliamentary

[1] Ibid., Col. 68.   [2] Ibid., Col. 73.   [3] See below pp. 174–8.

Commissioner. A long list of amendments put down by members of the committee sought to alter this provision.

The first to be taken was Cranley Onslow's amendment which sought to provide that a member of the public could complain directly to the Parliamentary Commissioner, but that the Commissioner would only take up the complaint if the M.P. for the constituency in which the aggrieved person resided supported the investigation, or if it was supported by another M.P. whom the person aggrieved designated.

Onslow argued that this would remove one of the undesirable features of the Bill: the right given to members of the public to take their complaints to any M.P. This would, in his opinion,

encourage the development within the House of what I might call 'grievance collectors'—hon. Members who, because a complaint could be referred to any Member, would tend to set themselves up as prepared to act as champions of liberty in this context, prepared always to take a case and pass it to the Parliamentary Commissioner, prepared to devote their resources to equip themselves with a staff almost to 'go out and beat the hedges', to have cases referred to them which they could then champion with the Parliamentary Commissioner.[1]

Michael English, who followed Cranley Onslow thought that Onslow's amendment would not have the effect that he intended. If a member of the public could designate an M.P. to support his complaint, several thousand people would, for example, designate the Member for Orpington who would be flooded with complaints. (Eric Lubbock, at that time Liberal Member for Orpington, was famous for the care and energy which he devoted to cases brought to him by constituents.)

English then went on to speak to his own amendment which sought to delete paragraph 1a in Clause 5. One of the features which he most objected to in this paragraph was the provision that complaints must be written. He thought this biased the system towards the highly literate sections of the population. Complaints should be capable of being received orally.

[1] The Parliamentary Commissioner Bill, Col. 93. Onslow's fear that some Members would become grievance collectors has proved unfounded. Sir Edmund Compton told the Select Committee on the Parliamentary Commissioner, in December 1967, that he had 'no evidence of any Member setting himself up as Ombudsman Member, as a channel on which the public in general can rely and to whom the public should go'. See below pp. 269–70.

Niall MacDermot, in speaking to both amendments, opposed Onslow's amendment on the grounds that it would introduce a more circuitous procedure. It was also intrinsically undesirable since it would give the designated M.P. a veto over a complaint going to the Commissioner, unless the member of the public would be empowered to write again to the Commissioner designating another M.P.

He also resisted Michael English's amendment on the ground that 'the minimum degree of formality that is required is that the complaint should be put down on a piece of paper.'[1]

Sidney Silverman then rose to say that he thought that the procedure laid down in the Bill was satisfactory but hardly had time to develop his argument when one o'clock arrived and the Chairman adjourned the committee.

When the committee resumed for its third sitting on 3 November at 10.30 a.m., Onslow's amendment was still before the committee. Dame Joan Vickers said that she partially supported Onslow's amendment. She thought that the system provided for in the Bill would worsen the relationship between M.P.s and their constituents. When an M.P. turned down the request by a constituent to submit his case to the Commissioner, the constituent could then take his case to another M.P. If the second M.P. forwarded the case to the Commissioner, the constituent would lose confidence in his own M.P. The answer, she thought, was to allow direct access to the Commissioner by members of the public as is provided for in every other country which has a Parliamentary Commissioner or Ombudsman.[2]

William Roots then spoke in favour of two amendments which would permit such direct access to the Commissioner. He also moved a third amendment which would allow peers as well as M.P.s to send cases to the Commissioner. The committee then got into some confusion due to the fact that they were discussing eleven amendments at one and the same time. Some members said that they could not understand the effect of some of the amendments. John Rankin intervened to say that he could not even find all the amendments but was told by the Chairman that this perhaps was because he was not in the room when the relevant page numbers were read out.

Eventually, Paul Rose spoke to one of the grouped amendments. He referred first to the issues concerning access to the Commissioner

---

[1] The Parliamentary Commissioner Bill, Col. 101.   [2] Ibid., Cols. 107–8.

which had already been discussed. He personally would have favoured direct access to the Commissioner, but since this might have caused too great a volume of work he thought it was right to provide that a member of the public could choose which M.P. he would ask to take up his case. A constituent's Member might be a member of the Government or he might be opposed to the constituent's point of view in a matter which was politically delicate. In such a case the constituent would be able to go to another Member.[1]

His own amendment would give the Commissioner discretion to investigate a whole area of administration where his own specific investigations, or complaints of a general nature, had indicated to him that there might be some general malfeasance or maladministration in a Department. This power was based on the precedent of the Swedish and Danish Ombudsmen who have power to take up cases on their own initiative.[2]

Sir Hugh Lucas-Tooth addressed himself to the question of whether direct access should be allowed to the Commissioner. He was entirely against direct access. 'The Parliamentary Commissioner, as I see it, is being created in order to help Members of Parliament to do their job; that is the purpose as I see it. If that is so, then I think that access to him must come through Members of Parliament.'[3]

On the question of access through peers he was opposed to this, and therefore differed from the Conservative leader's view. He thought that it would extend the scope of the Bill and that, therefore, it was, on the whole, undesirable at this stage. It might be desirable later on.[4]

David Weitzman supported Sir Hugh's point of view. He thought they should provide for access only through M.P.s while 'this great experiment' is in its initial stages.[5] Denis Coe took a similar view emphasizing the need to limit the number of cases going to the Commissioner. He pointed out that no country which has an Ombudsman has a population, like that of Britain, of about 50 million. Both Coe and Weitzman argued that the Parliamentary Commissioner was being established in order to assist Members of Parliament.[6]

Sir John Foster took the opposite view and spoke in favour of the amendment which would give direct access to the Commissioner by members of the public. He disagreed with the argument put forward

[1] Ibid., Col. 113.   [2] Ibid. Cols. 114–15.   [3] Ibid., Col. 118.
[4] Ibid., Cols. 118–19.   [5] Ibid., Cols. 119–20.   [6] Ibid., Cols. 120–1.

by Sir Hugh Lucas-Tooth. 'He conceives the Bill as setting up the Parliamentary Commissioner to help Members of Parliament. I regard the Parliamentary Commissioner as being set up to remedy injustice.'[1] He did not think that the Commissioner would be swamped by the volume of complaints if direct access were permitted. If, however, the committee voted against direct access, he was in favour of allowing access through peers.

The other three members who spoke on this topic were all opposed to allowing direct access to the Commissioner. They were Alexander Lyon, John Rankin, and Hugh Jenkins: all Labour members. Niall MacDermot argued against direct access on the grounds that in Denmark and Sweden conditions were different. In Denmark, he claimed, Members of Parliament do not have the right to take up individual grievances; in Sweden there is no doctrine of Ministerial responsibility for the acts of Civil Servants. It was therefore appropriate for those countries to allow direct access to their Ombudsmen, while it was not appropriate in Britain to allow direct access to the Parliamentary Commissioner.[2] He did not mention that in New Zealand M.P.s can take up individual grievances, there is Ministerial responsibility, and the public has direct access to the Parliamentary Commissioner. It was, perhaps, fortunate for him that none of the members who favoured direct access pointed this out in the debate.

MacDermot argued that it was on grounds of principle that the Government was against direct access to the Commissioner. 'Surely this is one of the most important aspects of the long constitutional tradition that the Executive in this country is answerable to Parliament, and Parliament is the body which is there to probe and control the Executive. I would say therefore that it is on a high constitutional principle that we propose that access shall be through Members of Parliament.'[3]

He was opposed to peers being a channel for complaints to the Commissioner. He did not think that peers took up many individual grievances, and bringing them in would complicate the conventions which would need to develop when a constituent did not go to his own M.P. with a complaint. As to Paul Rose's amendment, he thought there were dangers in allowing the Parliamentary Commissioner or individual Members to initiate investigations. If this were done there would be much more likelihood of the Commissioner

[1] Ibid., Col. 123.   [2] Ibid., Col. 130.   [3] Ibid., Col. 131.

becoming a political shuttlecock. 'Members would seek to drag him into what in effect were political controversies, to invoke his aid and assistance.'[1]

By the time that Cransley Onslow rose to defend his amendment which had opened the debate, he could see that most of his colleagues on the Conservative side of the committee were in favour of allowing direct access to the Commissioner. He therefore announced that he would vote for direct access and would withdraw his own amendment. On a procedural rule he was not able to do this but his amendment was negatived without a division.

The next amendment due to be taken was the amendment moved by Michael English to allow consideration of oral complaints to the Commissioner. Since Michael English was not present and no other member wanted to move the amendment it was not taken. Several members had argued in the debate that it was essential that all complaints to the Commissioner should be written.

The Committee then moved at once to vote on the amendment which would allow direct access to the Commissioner. The amendment was defeated by nine votes to six. All those who voted against changing the Bill in this respect were Labour members, those who wanted direct access were Conservatives. But Sir Hugh Lucas-Tooth abstained in this division.

Dame Joan Vickers then moved an amendment which would have the effect of requiring a member of the public to submit his complaint to the Commissioner only through 'the Member of the House of Commons in whose constituency he resides'.[2] If this were not done she could foresee some Members being flooded with complaints to the Commissioner. Her amendment would prevent a member of the public 'from circularizing all Members of Parliament until he finds one—he is practically bound to find one, I think,—who will take up his complaint'.[3] Niall MacDermot opposed this amendment on the grounds, already advanced by Paul Rose, that a member of the public should be able to go to a Member, other than the Member for the constituency where he lived, in case his own Member was, perhaps, the Minister against whose decision he was complaining or because, for reason of differing political views, he did not have confidence in his own Member. The amendment was negatived without a division.

William Roots then put his amendment to make peers a channel

---

[1] Ibid., Col. 133.   [2] Ibid., Col. 143.   [3] Ibid., Col. 145.

for complaint to the Commissioner. The amendment was defeated by eight votes to five. Dame Joan Vickers voted with the majority here. The other seven in the majority were Labour members. She had indicated in the debate that she opposed peers being brought in since she felt that certain peers who are in the public eye, such as Lord Arran and Lord Montgomery, would receive a great volume of complaints. One Labour member, Hugh Jenkins, who had said that he thought peers should be a channel, did not vote. All those who voted for the inclusion of peers were Conservatives.

Finally, Paul Rose's amendment to allow the Commissioner to undertake an investigation on his own initiative was put to the vote. Paul Rose said that he now wished to withdraw his amendment but Conservative members pressed for a vote. In the division it was defeated by eight votes to five. Only Conservatives voted for the amendment and only Labour members against. Paul Rose abstained as did another Labour member, John Rankin, who had spoken in the debate in favour of the Commissioner starting an investigation on his own initiative.

David Weitzman then moved an amendment which was to result in one of the main changes in the Bill during its passage through Parliament. Section (2) of Clause 5 in the Bill, as introduced, provided that the Commissioner should not conduct an investigation of:

'(a) any action in respect of which the person aggrieved has or had a right of appeal, reference or review' to an administrative tribunal; and
'(b) any action in respect of which the person aggrieved has or had a remedy by way of proceedings in any court of law.'

There then followed a proviso that the Commissioner might conduct an investigation although an aggrieved person had a remedy in a court of law, if he was satisfied that, in the particular circumstances, it was not reasonable to expect him to take, or have taken, proceedings in a law court.

The object of David Weitzman's amendment was to give the Commissioner a similar discretion in relation to administrative tribunals. He moved to insert the words 'save at his discretion' into the phrase introducing Section (2) of Clause 5. This would have amended Section (2) so that the Commissioner would be empowered, at his discretion, to look at cases which could go, or could have gone, either to administrative tribunals or to the courts of law.

The debate which followed was of great interest for several reasons. First, it elicited from the Minister a clear statement of the grounds upon which the Government thought it desirable to give the Commissioner discretion to look at a case which could go, or could have gone, to a court of law. There were substantially two grounds. In the first place, MacDermot said:

there are some remedies in the courts which are so wide and so general that almost any complaint could or might be the subject of proceedings involving them in the ordinary courts. One knows, for example, that the remedy of a declaration in the Chancery Division is a very wide one indeed. It clearly would be wrong, and we would be frustrating our own intentions if we were to hamstring the Parliamentary Commissioner by not enabling him to investigate any claim where one of these rather peripheral remedies —if that is the right word to use—might have been invoked by the complainant.[1]

The second main ground was that there would be cases 'where the cost and expense of legal proceedings would be quite disproportionate to the complaint which the complainant has'.[2]

Another very interesting feature of the Minister's statement was the account which he gave of the Commissioner's powers, under the Bill as introduced, in relation to cases which could go to administrative tribunals. MacDermot explained that the Commissioner could investigate administrative action by a department prior to the tribunal proceedings. He could investigate an allegation that evidence had been withheld improperly from a tribunal, or that there had been neglect or misrepresentation in the preparation of evidence.[3] But the Commissioner would not be able to consider whether the tribunal proceedings had been fairly conducted.

If Weitzman's amendment was accepted, the Commissioner would be given such a power. This would enable him to become, in effect, a court of appeal from a tribunal which, MacDermot argued, would be clearly wrong. Where there was a complaint against a tribunal this should lie, as at present, to the courts or to the Council on Tribunals.

Not one of the members of the standing committee who spoke in this debate was satisfied with the Minister's attitude on this question. On the Conservative side, Dame Joan Vickers, Antony Buck, Sir John Foster, and William Roots all spoke in favour of Weitzman's

[1] Ibid., Col. 155.   [2] Ibid., Col. 156.   [3] Ibid., Col. 158.

amendment. Sir Hugh Lucas-Tooth gave qualified support to the amendment. He did not think that the clause, as drafted, gave enough scope to the Commissioner. On the other hand, he thought Weitzman's amendment went a little too far in the other direction, but he would prefer to see the amendment accepted than to see the clause as it was.[1]

On the Labour side, Sydney Silverman, John Rankin, and Alexander Lyon all supported Weitzman. Their view could well be summarized in Lyon's statement that they did not want the Commissioner to become a Court of Appeal from administrative tribunals, but they were also conscious that borderline cases were often the very cases in which there was real injustice. They wanted an M.P. to be able to refer a case which involved tribunal proceedings, or could have involved such proceedings, to the Commissioner where the Member thought there had been maladministration. The Commissioner should then decide 'at his discretion' whether to take up the case.

Michael English was one Labour member who expressed his dissatisfaction with the clause but considered that Weitzman's amendment was too wide. He suggested that the Minister might accept a less far-reaching amendment.

Niall MacDermot was therefore faced on this question by a potential coalition of some of his own supporters and the whole of the Conservative opposition on the committee. In his winding-up speech he made a conciliatory gesture. He would be prepared to look again at the question of whether there might be an area where, although an individual had the right to go to a tribunal, it would be much more satisfactory to have the matter dealt with by the Commissioner. He was not himself personally persuaded that there was such an area, but he was open to argument and would gladly look at it again.

This was not, however, a sufficient concession to satisfy David Weitzman and the members, both Labour and Conservative, who had supported him. The amendment was carried by twelve votes to seven. David Weitzman, Alexander Lyon, John Rankin, and Sydney Silverman were the Labour members who voted with eight Conservatives in the majority. The minority consisted of the Minister, his Whip, and five other Labour members.

This was one of the most important amendments made in the Bill

[1] Ibid., Col. 177.

during its passage through Parliament. Although carried against the Minister in standing committee, it was not to be reversed at report stage. The wording of the clause was then modified but the principle of the amendment, introduced by Weitzman, was not abandoned. The Act, as eventually passed, provided that the Commissioner would in general, not investigate an action where there was a right of appeal by the aggrieved person to an administrative tribunal or a law court. But he could make an investigation, in either case, if he was satisfied that it was not reasonable, in the particular circumstances, to expect the aggrieved person to take his case to an administrative tribunal or a court of law.[1]

This gave the British Parliamentary Commissioner a discretion which is not possessed by the New Zealand Ombudsman. The New Zealand Parliamentary Commissioner (Ombudsman) Act, 1962 excludes the Ombudsman from investigating any actions 'in respect of which there is, under the provisions of any enactment, a right of appeal or objection, or a right to apply for a review, on the merits of the case, to any Court, or to any tribunal constituted by or under any enactment'.[2] This exclusion is complete. The New Zealand Ombudsman has apparently no discretion to waive it in any circumstances.

The standing committee next went on to discuss Subsection (3) of Clause 5 which provided that the Parliamentary Commissioner could not investigate any of the matters described in Schedule 3 of the Act. This Schedule listed eleven areas which were not subject to investigation. These included such matters as relations with foreign powers, actions taken with respect to passports, the hospitals, contractual and commercial transactions of government departments, and personnel matters in the Armed Forces and in the Civil Service.

Alexander Lyon introduced an amendment which would delete this subsection and thereby remove all basis for Schedule 3 which could then, in its turn, be deleted. Lyon said: 'I am trying to give to the Parliamentary Commissioner the power to investigate a whole area of maladministration which the Financial Secretary, by means of Schedule 3, is trying to exclude.' He argued that the Parliamentary Commissioner should himself decide the limits of his own powers within the field of central government. 'We should have

---

[1] Parliamentary Commissioner Act, 1967, Clause 5, Subsection 2.
[2] The Parliamentary Commissioner (Ombudsman) Act, 1962, Section II, Subsection (5) (a).

enough confidence in the man whom we appoint to be able to say that he will use his discretion wisely.' There would be, too, a Select Committee of the Commons which could place 'a controlling rein on the way in which he exercises his discretion'.[1]

Lyon found there was no support for this view on the standing committee. David Weitzman and Sir John Foster said that they would be arguing against certain of the specific exclusions in Schedule 3, but they were not in favour of removing Schedule 3 altogether. Niall MacDermot, therefore, had little difficulty in arguing against the amendment and putting forward the view that if the Parliamentary Commissioner could decide the limits of his own powers he 'would be subject to political pressures on the one side to investigate, and on behalf of the Government not to, and this would weaken his whole standing and office'.[2]

William Roots, on the Conservative side, asked his honourable friends to vote against the amendment. Alexander Lyon then, seeing that there was no support for his amendment, asked for leave to withdraw it, which was granted by the committee.

The committee then went on to discuss an amendment proposed by William Roots and other Conservative members which gave power to the House of Commons to instruct the Parliamentary Commissioner, by resolution, to investigate a particular case under one of the headings from which he was excluded by Schedule 3. This amendment was supported by speeches, on the Conservative side, from Sir Hugh-Lucas-Tooth, Sir John Foster, and Cranley Onslow. On the Labour side, those who spoke in favour of the amendment, at the fourth sitting, were Michael English, Hugh Jenkins, and David Weitzman.

One of the arguments used was that this would be a much less cumbersome machinery for authorizing an inquiry, into something about which Members of Parliament were concerned, than the procedure for setting up an inquiry under the Tribunals of Inquiry (Evidence) Act, 1921. Under this Act, inquiries can be set up by resolution of both Houses of Parliament. Such inquiries have power to compel the attendance of witnesses and the production of documents. They are usually presided over by a High Court judge assisted by two or more persons having qualifications relevant to the

[1] Official Report of Standing Committee B, 1966–7, The Parliamentary Commissioner Bill, Col. 190.
[2] Ibid., Col. 193.

subject matter of the complaint. Since these inquiries are elaborate and expensive it is often difficult to induce a Government to agree to their appointment.[1]

Sir Hugh-Lucas-Tooth and Sir John Foster both argued that to instruct the Parliamentary Commissioner, by resolution of the Commons, to undertake an inquiry into one of the normally exempted spheres, would be a much simpler procedure.[2] William Roots and Michael English argued that the resolution procedure would allow the House to authorize an inquiry, in a particular case which was excluded by Schedule 3, on the grounds that there were special, and perhaps unforeseen, reasons for making such an inquiry. The resolution would lessen the rigidity of Schedule 3.[3]

The Minister therefore found the weight of opinion against him when he sought to resist the amendment. He argued, as he had done against the previous amendment, that, 'Surely, it would be running a great risk of making the Parliamentary Commissioner the subject matter of ordinary political battle and political conflict, if we said that a Resolution of the House could overrule any such exclusion.' (That is, any exclusion under Schedule 3.)[4] He argued that the House should determine the jurisdiction of the Parliamentary Commissioner; it should try to get the statutory exclusions right, 'and then must stand by them as statutory exclusions'.[5]

The committee did not find the Minister's arguments convincing. When the committee adjourned at one o'clock on 8 November, only one member had indicated that he did not support the amendment. This was Alexander Lyon and he did not share the Minister's views. He was sympathetic to the object of the amendment but preferred his own amendment to the subsection. His amendment proposed that a Select Committee of the House could ask the Commissioner to investigate a subject which was otherwise excluded under Schedule 3.

When the committee met again, two days later, for its fifth sitting, it was soon apparent that the Minister, Niall MacDermot, had changed his ground in one important respect. On rising to re-open the debate on William Roots's amendment, he said: 'If I have the sense of the Committee, I think that there is a general anxiety whether the provisions relating to Schedule 3 at the moment are too

[1] See, especially, the comments on Inquiries under the 1921 Act in 'Justice', *The Citizen and the Administration*, pp. 42–3.

[2] Official Report of Standing Committee B. 1966–7, The Parliamentary Commissioner Bill, Cols. 195–7.

[3] Ibid., Cols. 203–4.   [4] Ibid., Col. 200.   [5] Ibid., Col. 201.

rigid.' One of the proposals for providing greater flexibility was the proposal in the Roots amendment to allow the House, by resolution, to waive one of the exclusions in order to allow investigation by the Commissioner in a particular instance.

Another suggestion had been made by Michael English at the previous sitting. MacDermot thought that this suggestion merited consideration. 'It is that we should provide power to amend Schedule 3 by Order, which would be subject to either affirmative or negative Resolution on the Floor of the House.'[1] Indeed, he preferred this suggestion to the proposal that exceptions to the Schedule could be made in individual cases. He undertook to look at the matter again before the report stage of the Bill.

What had caused the Minister to produce this concession? There had been a private discussion between the Labour members on the standing committee and the Minister. It was apparent that all the Labour members were in favour of providing greater flexibility in relation to Schedule 3. It was also apparent that many of them were prepared to vote with the Conservatives to bring about changes in the Bill, as they had done on Weitzman's important amendment to Clause 5.

MacDermot, on his side, pointed out that he was in some difficulty since the Bill had been approved by a committee of the Cabinet. It was not open to him to make concessions without reference to the Cabinet committee. One of the Labour back-benchers then told him that he must get concessions approved or they would amend every section of Schedule 3 in standing committee and 'they had the votes'.

MacDermot then came up with the concession that Schedule 3 could be amended by Order. The Labour members of the standing committee insisted that the Bill should provide that Orders could only be laid to take out some of the exclusions in Schedule 3, not to add further exclusions. This was the formula which was, in fact, embodied in the amendment introduced by the Minister at report stage. It was potentially of great importance since it would enable the jurisdiction of the Parliamentary Commissioner to be widened very easily, without the need for the passage of a new statute in each instance.

The agreement he had reached with his back-benchers now therefore eased the position for the Minister in the resumed debate on 10 November. The Conservatives continued to argue for their amend-

[1] Ibid., Col. 211.

ment but Weitzman spoke for the majority of the Labour members when he said that he thought it would be best, as the Minister had suggested, to look at the question again at report stage.

When the amendment was put to the vote it was defeated by nine votes to eight. Most of the Labour members voted against the amendment but one of them was evidently not satisfied with the Minister's promised concession. This was Sydney Silverman who voted, with the Conservatives, for the amendment. It was an omen of the continued independence of outlook, on his own side of the committee, which the Minister was to encounter in later sessions.

On the next amendment, however, the Minister had less difficulty. Alexander Lyon now moved his amendment which proposed to give a Select Committee of the Commons power to refer to the Commissioner for investigation a case which otherwise would be excluded by the provisions of Schedule 3.

Lyon argued that one of the arguments advanced by the Financial Secretary to the Treasury against the previous amendment would not apply to this amendment. MacDermot had suggested that to allow the House by resolution to instruct the Parliamentary Commissioner to investigate one of the excluded subjects would possibly make the Commissioner 'into a kind of political football'.[1] This would be less likely to happen if a Select Committee were given this power since a Select Committee would, like the Public Accounts Committee, strive to get a non-partisan approach right from the beginning. The Select Committee would be a much easier procedure for looking at individual cases than the procedure by resolution of the whole House.

Lyon's arguments did not, however, procure much support for the amendment. Sydney Silverman preferred the procedure by resolution of the whole House which seemed to him to be simple, quick, and straightforward.[2]

William Roots also preferred resolution by the whole House, although he saw some virtue in Lyon's amendment. He did not propose to press for the amendment, however, since the Minister had promised to look at the whole question again. Lyon's amendment was then negatived without a division.

The committee then approved Clause 5, as amended, and moved on to discuss Clause 6 which dealt with 'Provisions Relating to Complaints'. The first subsection of Clause 6 stated that: 'A com-

[1] Ibid., Col. 217.   [2] Ibid., Col. 219.

plaint under this Act may be made by any individual, or by any body of persons whether incorporated or not, not being,'—a local authority or a nationalized industry or any other authority whose members are appointed by Her Majesty, by a Minister of the Crown, or by a government department.

William Roots moved an amendment to delete mention of local authorities. This would then allow them to make complaints to the Parliamentary Commissioner. Roots argued that, 'Where a local authority has suffered, or feels that it has suffered, by maladministration, it should have a right to complain.'[1] He instanced a case with which he was currently dealing in which 'certain premises in a local authority's area are being put to a use by a private body, at the instance and the instigation of a Government Department, quite contrary to the plans and wishes of the local authority.' In such a case, the local authority should be able to complain to the Parliamentary Commissioner against what it conceived to be maladministration on the part of the government department.

Michael English supported Roots's amendment. Indeed, he told the committee he had himself put down amendments to allow local authorities to complain to the Commissioner before he knew of the Conservative amendment to this effect. English argued that, since the Parliamentary Commissioner was only 'to investigate complaints affecting branches of the central Government', it was illogical to say that a local authority should not be able to make a complaint. 'If a local authority is not part of the Government, in the sense that it is not to be investigated by the Parliamentary Commissioner—with which I agree—then it seems to me that the logic leads to the conclusion that for this purpose it is on the other side of the fence and can be a member of the public for the purpose of raising a complaint of maladministration against the central Government.'[2]

He did not, however, think that a nationalized industry should be able to complain to the Parliamentary Commissioner. He saw 'good reason for precluding the nationalized industries from complaining against what is, in effect, their principal shareholder'.[3]

The Minister's main argument against giving local authorities the right to complain was that local authorities and nationalized industries 'already have well-recognised and perfectly adequate means for raising their complaints with the central Government. They have, of course, direct access to Departments, and to Ministers

[1] Ibid., Col. 228.   [2] Ibid., Cols. 229–30.   [3] Ibid., Col. 231.

if they wish to carry the matter to Ministerial level, and if they are not satisfied with the decision, they have many people who are ready to speak on their behalf in the House.'[1]

This reply did not satisfy Sir Hugh Lucas-Tooth, for the Conservatives, nor William Roots, and, on the Labour benches, Michael English and David Weitzman also voiced their dissatisfaction. David Weitzman pointed out that, as things stood, a local authority could put forward its case to the Government but it did not have the opportunity to ask for 'an independent inquiry by an independent person, the Parliamentary Commissioner'.[2] In a similar vein, Michael English commented, ironically: 'I have yet to find a local authority which has access to all the papers of Government, except Cabinet papers.'[3]

Three Labour members who intervened, however, did not support the amendment. John Lee asked whether it was 'not true to say that most of the complaints that a local authority will make will be of a kind that in the last analysis amounts to a conflict of policy between a local authority and a Government'. There would be conflict over such things as compulsory purchase orders, reversal of planning decisions. He envisaged 'political football being played between, for example, Conservative local authorities and a Labour Government and *vice-versa*'.[4] The Commissioner's work would be vitiated by political conflict.

Paul Rose and Sydney Silverman took a similar view. When the amendment was put to the vote, it was defeated by ten votes to eight. But it was not a straight party division. All those who opposed the amendment were Labour members, but one Labour member, Michael English, voted with the Conservatives for the amendment.

There were two interesting exchanges during the debate on this amendment. William Roots commented that, as he understood it, without the passage of the amendment, a local authority would sometimes be able, in effect, to make a complaint to the Commissioner, by asking a resident in the area to make a complaint on its behalf. The Financial Secretary did not deny that this was so and since the passage of the Act some complaints have been made by local authorities in this way. The opportunities for a complaint by a local authority by this indirect means are, of course, fewer than if they had been specifically given power to complain in the Act. A local

---

[1] Ibid., Col. 232.   [2] Ibid., Col. 234.
[3] Ibid., Col. 236.   [4] Ibid., Col. 235.

authority must find someone who is willing to complain on its behalf and who must be able to show that he is personally suffering injustice through the maladministration alleged.

The second interesting side issue which emerged in the debate was
raised by Michael English. The subsection spoke of a 'local authority
or other authority or body constituted for purposes of . . . local
government', not being empowered to complain to the Parliamentary Commissioner. English asked what these words implied. The
Minister answered that they included not only joint boards which
exercise functions on behalf of two or more local authorities, but
also local authority associations. They did not include, however,
professional associations and trade unions in local government: such
bodies as the National and Local Government Officers' Association.

The first subsection of Clause 6 had, then, given rise to a keen
debate about the rights of local authorities in relation to the Parliamentary Commissioner. Subsections 2, 3, and 4 were much less
controversial but they were the subject of a series of amendments
from the Conservative side of the committee, some of which were
intended to elicit the effect of the subsection and some of which
proposed material changes.

Subsection 2 of Clause 6 provided that where a person by whom
a complaint might have been made under the Act had died or for any
reason was unable to act for himself, the complaint might be made
'by his personal representative or by a member of his family or
other individual suitable to represent him'. Antony Buck, for the
Conservatives, moved an amendment which would give to a County
Court Judge or Sheriff the task of deciding whether an individual
was suitable to represent the complainant. Niall MacDermot told
the committee that, under the Act, the Parliamentary Commissioner
would himself decide whether an individual was a suitable person
to represent a complainant who could not submit his own complaint.
The committee were clearly satisfied that the Parliamentary Commissioner should have this discretion and the amendment was, by
leave, withdrawn.

Antony Buck then moved an amendment to subsection 3 which
would extend from twelve months to three years the time limit
during which the Parliamentary Commissioner would take up a case.
The Financial Secretary pointed out that although the Bill provided
that a complaint had to be 'sent to a Member of the House of Commons not later than twelve months from the day on which the person

aggrieved first had notice of the matters alleged in the complaint', the subsection also provided that the Commissioner could investigate a complaint not sent in within the twelve month period, 'if he considers that there are special circumstances which make it proper so to do'.

MacDermot argued that this provision made better sense than the three-year period which Antony Buck's amendment proposed. As a normal rule it was better to keep the delay a short one. 'We all know', he said, 'how investigations suffer if they are allowed to go too stale—recollections are at fault and become hazy and so one cannot secure a satisfactory investigation.' [1] At the same time, it was desirable to give the Parliamentary Commissioner discretion to look at a case after the twelve months had gone by. For example, the person making the complaint might have been ill or incapacitated in some way and therefore have been unable to submit his complaint during the twelve-month period.

Antony Buck then told the committee that he still felt the twelve-month period was a little too short. He was, however, reassured by the Minister's account of the discretion which the Bill gave to the Commissioner to ignore the time limit. He asked leave to withdraw his amendment.

Subsection 4 of Clause 6 provided that a complaint could not be entertained under the Act unless the aggrieved person was resident in the United Kingdom or the complaint related to action taken in relation to him while he was present in the United Kingdom, 'or in relation to rights or obligations which accrued or arose in the United Kingdom'. Antony Buck moved an amendment to insert the word 'normally' before 'resident'. Anyone who was normally resident in the United Kingdom would then be able to complain to the Parliamentary Commissioner.

MacDermot resisted this amendment on the grounds that the phrase 'normally resident' was not precise. He thought that the provisions of the subsection were 'pretty wide'. A complainant could qualify in one of three ways: he could be resident in the United Kingdom, he could be non-resident but be complaining about the action of a government department relating to him while he was in the United Kingdom, he could be non-resident but be complaining about actions which affected his rights or obligations accruing in the United Kingdom.

[1] Ibid., Col. 246.

After some discussion of hypothetical cases which might arise under these provisions it was apparent that the committee supported the Minister's view and the amendment was negatived without a division. At this point the fifth sitting of the committee came to an end.

IX

THE COMMITTEE STAGE
CONTINUED—THE SIXTH TO
TENTH SITTINGS OF THE
STANDING COMMITTEE

THE committee resumed for its sixth sitting at 10.30 a.m. on Tuesday, 15 November. Its first business was to consider further amendments to Subsection 4 of Clause 6 which defined the residential or other qualifications which were necessary for a complaint to be validly made to the Commissioner. The Financial Secretary pointed out that the amendments on the Order Paper, in fact, made two proposals. 'The first is to extend the jurisdiction of the Commissioner to cases arising on a British ship or aircraft. The second is to extend it to areas within the British limits of the Continental Shelf.' He indicated that he was sympathetic to both proposals but that they would need some care in drafting. If William Roots would withdraw his amendments he would undertake to look further at the question and bring forward a suitable amendment on report. The amendments were then by leave withdrawn. The Minister was as good as his word since amendments extending the Parliamentary Commissioner's jurisdiction to ships and aircraft, registered in the United Kingdom, and to 'an installation in a designated area within the meaning of the Continental Shelf Act 1964' were introduced on report.

It is noticeable that all the amendments to Subsections 2 to 4 of Clause 6 were made by Conservatives. Their amendments to Subsections 2 and 3 were not successful but produced some elucidation of the provisions of the Bill. Their amendments to Subsection 4 were, in effect, accepted by the Minister.

Clause 6 was then approved as a whole by the committee which then went on to consider Clause 7 which dealt with 'Procedure In Respect of Investigations'. The Clause provided in Subsection 1 that where the Commissioner proposes to conduct an investigation under the Act he shall give to 'the principal officer of the department or authority concerned, and to any other person who is alleged in the complaint to have taken or authorised the action complained of, an opportunity to comment on any allegations contained in the complaint'. No amendment was offered to this subsection and it was embodied without change in the Act in its final form.

Subsection 2 provided that every investigation by the Parliamentary Commissioner should be private, that the procedure for investigation should be determined by the Commissioner, as he 'considers appropriate in the circumstances of the case', and that he may decide whether any person from whom he obtains information, in an inquiry, may be represented by a counsel or solicitor.

Antony Buck (Conservative) moved to add the words 'provided that it is in accordance with the rules of natural justice' after the phrase in which the subsection stated that 'the procedure for conducting an investigation shall be such as the Commissioner considers appropriate in the circumstances of the case.' To define the rules of natural justice he quoted from Earl Jowitt's *Dictionary of English Law*: 'to act fairly, in good faith, without bias, and in a judicial temper, and to give each party an opportunity of adequately stating his case.'

Niall MacDermot, opposing this amendment, put forward a number of arguments against it. He thought it was unnecessary, particularly since Subsection 1 of the clause provided that the Commissioner must give the person complained against an opportunity to reply to any allegations made. It would be entirely without precedent. 'Many tribunals are set up which have to act in accordance with the rules of natural justice but that provision is never written into the Bill concerning them.'[1]

Furthermore, when the Commissioner was investigating a case he would not in fact be exercising a judicial function. Also, the Government had deliberately tried not to tie down the Commissioner in considering what procedures he might use. They were impressed by the argument in the Whyatt Report in favour of the Commissioner following as informal a procedure as possible. The Whyatt Committee had pointed out that Parliamentary Commissioners in other countries find enormous advantages in informality. The Government anticipated that the Parliamentary Commissioner would

[1] The Parliamentary Commissioner Bill, Col. 269.

in some cases be able to investigate a case entirely, or almost entirely, by correspondence, by looking at documents and calling for reports. At other times, he will want to see witnesses. Sometimes it will be proper and natural to give the right to one party to a dispute the opportunity to question and cross-examine witnesses; in others it will not be proper and natural. We must give a very free hand to this officer in deciding what his procedure should be in any particular case.[1]

Antony Buck then announced he would withdraw the amendment. On his side of the committee (the Conservative side), he said that they had 'great confidence in the person who has already been designated as the Parliamentary Commissioner'. He went on adding a slight partisan barb to what had been a non-partisan intervention, 'and we have great confidence that future appointments will be made from our own side of the Committee and by those who represent this party.'

There were no further amendments to Clause 7 but, on the debate 'that the Clause stand part of the Bill', Paul Rose (Labour) raised the question of legal aid being made available to the parties involved in a complaint to the Commissioner. It was not possible to put down amendments providing for the granting of legal aid since this would have involved extra expenditure which was not covered by the Financial Resolution. Rose argued, however, that provision should be made for legal aid. This was particularly important since the clause provided that, in certain circumstances, legal representation might be allowed. When legal representation, but not legal aid, is allowed, the more powerful of the parties to a dispute is given an extra advantage.

David Weitzman (Labour) and John Rankin (Labour) supported this argument and were joined by Dame Joan Vickers (Conservative). Cranley Onslow (Conservative), who had himself been a Civil Servant, put the case for the Civil Servants and suggested that the Civil Servant, involved in the administrative act which was the subject of the complaint, should also be entitled to legal aid.

Niall MacDermot replied that, as he had already told the committee, cases in which the Commissioner decided on a formal procedure, in which legal representation would be necessary, would be infrequent. He then went on to make the following points: it would be illogical to extend legal aid to proceedings before the

[1] Ibid., Col. 270.

Parliamentary Commissioner when there was no provision for legal aid before administrative tribunals; if a Civil Servant required legal protection beyond that afforded him by his department, he imagined that legal representation would be found for him through his staff association.

This reply did not give much satisfaction to David Weitzman who commented that the fact that legal aid was not granted before administrative tribunals was no argument for saying that it should not be granted before the Parliamentary Commissioner. The Minister then pointed out that Subsection 3 of the Clause provided that the Commissioner could pay the complainant or any other person involved in an investigation 'sums in respect of expenses properly incurred by them'. He thought that this would include legal expenses incurred by a person appearing before the Commissioner. He would look further into the matter and 'give a clearer and firmer indication to the House at the Report Stage'.[1] Clause 7 was then approved by the committee.

Clause 8 of the Bill dealt with 'Evidence'. No amendment was put down to the first three subsections and they were embodied unchanged in the Act. Subsection (1) provides that: 'For the purposes of an investigation under this Act the Commissioner may require any Minister, officer or member of the department concerned' to furnish information or produce documents relevant to the investigation. This provision was of great importance and had been, as we have seen, universally welcomed when the Act was published. It gave the Commissioner access to all departmental documents and went much further than the Whyatt proposals which would only have allowed the Commissioner to see the correspondence in the case and not the internal minutes.

Subsection (2) gives the Commissioner the same powers as a court of law in respect of the attendance and examination of witnesses. Subsection (3) is also of great importance. It provides that the Commissioner shall not be denied access to any document, either on the grounds of the need to maintain secrecy, or on the grounds of Crown Privilege. This also was a widely welcomed feature of the Bill.

To Subsection (4), however, the Conservatives did put down an amendment. This subsection exempted Cabinet proceedings and Cabinet documents from the general access to governmental

[1] Ibid., Col. 277.

information which the Commissioner was given. The Conservatives did not oppose exempting Cabinet proceedings but they were concerned about the phrase in the subsection which provided that no person should be required to 'produce any document relating to proceedings of the Cabinet or of any committee of the Cabinet'.

William Roots explained to the committee that they considered these words might result in the Commissioner being refused access to a document which had been before the Cabinet, even if the document gave no indication of what had been discussed in Cabinet. He, therefore, proposed a modification of the phrase so that no person would be required to produce any document for the Commissioner 'so far as it involves a disclosure of any proceedings of the Cabinet'.

David Weitzman (Labour) agreed that the words in the subsection were unsatisfactory but he was not happy about the amendment. Charles Fletcher-Cooke (Conservative) and Sir John Foster (Conservative) both supported William Roots's view that the subsection, as drafted, might prevent the Commissioner from seeing an important document merely because there was a note on it saying that it had been considered by the Cabinet.

Niall MacDermot, replying, indicated that he saw the force of the criticism made of the subsection. He thought that the Conservative amendment including the phrase 'so far as it involves' was a vague one in other respects. He thought the procedure they would follow in practice would be to blank out those parts of a document which referred to Cabinet discussions in making a photostat for the Parliamentary Commissioner. He thought that they would have power to do this with the existing wording but he would see if the procedure could be spelled out more specifically and more clearly.[1]

The Minister was as good as his word. The final text of Subsection (4) of Clause 8, as it appears in the Act, states that no person shall be required to produce to the Commissioner 'so much of any document as relates to such proceedings', that is proceedings in Cabinet or in Cabinet committees.

The Minister having given his assurance, William Roots withdrew his amendment and Clause 8 was approved. Clause 9 was then voted without any debate. This Clause, which is titled 'Obstruction and Contempt' provides that any one who 'without lawful excuse obstructs the Commissioner or any officer of the Commissioner in

[1] Ibid., Col. 282.

the performance of his functions', under the Act, can be held guilty of contempt of court and can be dealt with by a court of law as if the offence had been committed in that court.

The committee then went on to consider Clause 10—'Reports by Commissioner'. A lengthy amendment had been put down by William Roots, for the Conservatives, to Subsection (1) of this Clause. Subsection (1) provided that when the Commissioner had carried out an investigation under the Act he should send to the Member of Parliament, who had forwarded a complaint to him, a report of the results of the investigation. Similarly, where the Commissioner decided not to make an investigation, he would send the Member of Parliament a statement of his reasons for not conducting an investigation.

William Roots moved that the Commissioner should send a copy of his report on an investigation to:

(a) the person who made the complaint,
(b) any Member of the House whom he considers to be concerned,
(c) any person or persons against whom the complaint was made,
(d) any person mentioned in his report.

Niall MacDermot resisted this amendment. In general, he thought they should not lay down procedures too rigidly in the Bill, but should allow the Commissioner to work things out in practice 'and with the assistance of a Select Committee of the House'.[1]

Referring to specific proposals in the amendment, he thought that it would not be right for the Commissioner to send his report directly to the complainant. The Member of Parliament was surely the right person to receive the report and pass it on to the complainant. 'He may well have comments that he wants to make to the complainant at the time that he passes on the report—comments as to whether he accepts it, and as to what further action he would propose to take in the matter'.[2]

He was critical of the proposal in the amendment that the report should be sent 'to any Member of the House of Commons whom he considers to be concerned'. This was vague, it would often be difficult to say which Members would be concerned. On the sending of the report to the person complained against, this would be the responsibility of the department, which, under the Act would have to see the Commissioner's report.

---

[1] Ibid., Col. 287.   [2] Ibid., Col. 287.

David Weitzman agreed with the Minister that it was better for the Commissioner to report back to the Member of Parliament who had forwarded the complaint. Cranley Onslow was inclined to agree that the amendment as drafted was not perfect, but he did not see why the procedures which the House wanted the Commissioner to follow should not be indicated in the Act. He also asked what provision there would be for releasing reports to the Press.

McDermot replied that where the Commissioner's reports were laid before Parliament (in the case of his Annual or Special Reports) they would be immediately available to the Press. As for individual reports, once they were received by a Member of Parliament he would be free to hand them to the Press. He imagined that the Member would, of course, obtain the consent of the complainant before releasing a report to the Press. On the general question of defining the procedures which the Commissioner would follow, he reiterated that he thought it best that a Select Committee of the House should recommend procedures to the Commissioner when they had gained some practical experience of the working of the Act.[1]

The amendment was then negatived.

Subsection (2) of Clause 10 provided that if, after conducting an investigation, it appeared to the Commissioner that an injustice had been caused in consequence of maladministration and 'that the injustice has not been, or will not be, remedied, he may, if he thinks fit, lay before the House of Commons a special report upon the case'.

William Roots, for the Conservatives, moved an amendment which would add to the subsection a requirement for the Commissioner to 'report monthly to any Select Committee specially appointed to receive his reports the complaints upon which he decided not to conduct an investigation and the reasons for his decisions but these reports shall not be published without the authority of the Select Committee'. William Roots argued that it was very important that the Select Committee should see the pattern of the Commissioner's decisions whether to investigate or not to investigate. A frequent report of this type would enable the House to tell 'whether the Commissioner was taking too narrow a view of the powers which the Bill will have given him'.[2] The House would also be able to tell whether the Bill was proving more limiting than it would have wished.

Two Labour members criticized the amendment. Michael

---

[1] Ibid., Col. 291.   [2] Ibid., Col. 294.

English thought it was unnecessary since an appropriate Select Committee of the House would be any way able to call for such evidence from the Commissioner. Alexander Lyon thought the amendment was too narrow for what it was trying to achieve. The Select Committee should have a continuing interest in what the Parliamentary Commissioner was doing. He should not be required to give frequent reports only on the cases which he did not take up. 'Surely', he said, 'what is intended is that it (the Select Committee) should be meeting constantly and that the Parliamentary Commissioner should refer to it any difficulties which he found in the application of his statutory powers and also any general issues arising out of the cases with which he had been dealing where he felt that the Select Committee, because of its influence, would be able to bring the Government's attention to bear upon the need for future legislation.'[1] He asked the Minister if he could give further information on the way in which the Select Committee would work.

Niall MacDermot replied that he envisaged that it would be a Committee like the Public Accounts Committee. He hoped that the tradition would be established from the start that it would not operate on party lines. 'We also envisage that the Chairman of the Committee, like the Chairman of the Public Accounts Committee, should be an Opposition back-bench Member.'[2] This was to prove a very important commitment which the Government had to recognize as binding when the time came to elect the first Chairman of the Select Committee.[3]

William Roots welcomed the Minister's statement. In fact he said he was delighted with it. 'I regard it as absolutely vital in spelling out exactly how the Government expect that this office will work.'[4] He then withdrew his amendment with the consent of the Committee.

William Roots then moved an amendment to insert a new subsection which would empower the Commissioner in his report of an investigation 'to state what remedy he considers appropriate to right the injustice to the complainant including the payment of compensation'. This new subsection would, he argued, fill one of the gaps in the Commissioner's powers.[5]

Niall MacDermot resisted the amendment. He thought the Bill, as drafted, would allow the Commissioner to say that he thought the

[1] Ibid., Col. 297.   [2] Ibid., Col. 301.   [3] See below pp. 259–60.
[4] The Parliamentary Commissioner Bill, Col. 301.   [5] Ibid. Col., 302.

department should make an *ex gratia* payment by way of compensation and that if the department indicated that it was not prepared to make one, the Commissioner would be entitled to say so in his special report to the House. It would, however, change the whole character of the Commissioner 'if we were to set him up as a tribunal to assess compensation and neither do we want to confer on him the burden of deciding what shall be done in detail' by the department.[1]

David Weitzman (Labour) was not satisfied by this answer. In his opinion, the Parliamentary Commissioner would be the best person to decide what remedy ought to be put forward. 'He has gone into the facts in great detail, he has examined the files, he has seen what the position is, and he is the person who, if an injustice has been perpetrated, will know what is a remedy for the injustice. If it is a question of assessing an amount of compensation, surely he is the best person to put forward the amount of money that should be given.'[2] He thought there was a real gap in the Bill and something on the lines of the amendment was necessary.

When the amendment was put to the vote it was lost by nine votes to five. Only Conservatives voted for the amendment and only Labours members against, but David Weitzman did not vote.

The committee then went on to consider an amendment put down by Paul Rose to Subsection (3) of Clause 10. This subsection provided that: 'The Commissioner shall annually lay before the House of Commons a general report on the performance of his functions under this Act.' Rose moved to add 'in which he may at his discretion make such recommendations based upon his investigation of complaints as he may think fit in respect of future legislation'.[3]

This amendment, he said, was based on 'the Swedish model where the Ombudsman makes recommendations on legislation based on his findings in dealing with certain cases. As a result, the Ombudsman there has been responsible for a great deal of useful social legislation.'[4] He did not expect that the British Parliamentary Commissioner would use this power to 'suggest legislation which has a political connotation. I should expect him to deal with legislation which already exists where there is an obvious loophole or an obvious failure to implement what Parliament intended.'

Niall MacDermot replied that the amendment was unnecessary:

[1] Ibid., Col. 305.   [2] Ibid., Col. 306.
[3] Ibid., Col. 307.   [4] Ibid., Cols. 308–9.

'the Commissioner is entitled under the Bill as it stands, to make recommendations of this kind, if he wants to, and I must, therefore, advise the Committee that I do not think it is necessary or desirable to spell the matter out in these terms.'[1] Paul Rose said that he was delighted with this assurance and he withdrew his amendment.

In general, Niall MacDermot was remarkably accurate in predicting the ways in which the provisions in the Bill would operate. Here, however, his prediction was not accurate. The Parliamentary Commissioner, in practice, has not felt himself empowered to propose changes in legislation. Indeed, at first, he did not consider that he was able to criticize a departmental rule, even when he found that it was inequitable in its effects, as in the Sachsenhausen case. The Select Committee then recommended that where the Parliamentary Commissioner found that a departmental rule was harsh in its effect, he should consider whether the department had taken action to revise the rule. The Parliamentary Commissioner accepted this recommendation in November 1968.[2]

The standing committee next considered an amendment put down by William Roots to Subsection (4) of Clause 10. Subsection (4) provided that: 'For the purposes of the law of defamation, any report made by the Commissioner to the House of Commons, and any words contained in a communication made for the purposes of this Act by or to the Commissioner or his officers to or by a Member of that House, shall be entitled to absolute privilege.'

William Roots moved an amendment which sought to make communications from the complainant in presenting his complaint absolutely privileged in a similar way. MacDermot replied that the subsection extended the application of the doctrine of Parliamentary privilege to communications between the Commissioner and Members of Parliament. It would be wrong to extend it outside Parliament to communications from a complainant.

No one then spoke in support of the amendment and, indeed, a Member on each side of the Committee proceeded to criticize the wording of the subsection as going too far in extending the application of parliamentary privilege. Michael English (Labour) pointed out that Clause 10 (4), as worded in the Bill, would give absolute privilege to communications between Members of Parliament and the Commissioner whereas communications between Members of Parliament and Ministers were not similarly privileged. Sir John

---

[1] Ibid., Col. 311.   [2] See below pp. 281–2.

Foster (Conservative) argued that the subsection, as worded, would mean that if the report was used at any time afterwards by anybody it would be absolutely privileged. If someone, twenty years later, published a report of the Commissioner in order to ruin someone's reputation, the report would still be absolutely privileged. This was unfair. The clause should be reworded to make it clear that the report was only absolutely privileged at the time of publication.

Niall MacDermot acknowledged the force of the criticisms which had been made. He would gladly look further into the points which had been made. The amendment was then negatived and Clause 10, as a whole, was approved.

The Minister did keep his promise to look at the provisions on defamation again. At report stage he introduced an amendment which defined more precisely the categories of publication or communication which would be absolutely privileged.[1]

The discussion on Subsection (4) of Clause 10 had run on from the sixth to the seventh sittings of the committee. It was concluded early in the seventh sitting which took place in the morning of Thursday, 17 November. The committee then moved on to consider Clause 11—'Provision for Secrecy of Information'. This clause provided in Subsection (1) that 'the Commissioner, his officers and his servants hold office under her Majesty within the meaning of the Official Secrets Act of 1911.' No amendment was put down to this subsection and it was eventually embodied without change in the Act.

Subsection (2) of Clause 11 provided that information obtained by the Commissioner or his officers should not be disclosed except:

(a) for the purposes of the investigation and of any report to be made thereon under this Act;

(b) for the purposes of any proceedings for any offence under the Official Secrets Acts of 1911 to 1939, or an offence of perjury; or

(c) for the purposes of any proceedings under section 9 of this Act (that is proceedings taken against someone who obstructs the Commissioner, or one of his officers, in the performance of his functions under the Act).

Antony Buck, for the Conservatives, moved an amendment to add a new subheading as follows:

'(a) for the purposes of the investigation and at the request of

[1] See below pp. 180-2.

any Tribunal set up under the Tribunals of Inquiry (Evidence) Act 1921.'

He said that the Conservative members of the committee felt that 'there is considerable force in the argument that the Commissioner should also have been empowered to be, and be made, a competent and compellable witness in any proceedings which might be brought under a Tribunal set up under the Tribunals of Inquiry Evidence Act, 1921.'[1] Examples of inquiries under this Act were the 1948 inquiry into the alleged bribery of Ministers (Lynskey Tribunal), an inquiry in 1957 into allegations of improper disclosure of information about the raising of the Bank Rate (Parker Tribunal), and an inquiry in 1959 into allegations that policemen had assaulted a boy (the Thurso case).

In cases of this type, Buck argued, 'the Parliamentary Commissioner may have investigated certain matters which are on the fringes of those which are specifically being dealt with by the Tribunal.'[2] Lord Justice Salmon in his recent report on the procedure used in Tribunals of Inquiry under the 1921 Act had recommended that power should exist to compel people to give evidence to the Tribunal. The Conservatives saw no reason why the Parliamentary Commissioner and his staff should be exempted from giving evidence to such a Tribunal.

Niall MacDermot's reply to this argument took two principal lines. First, he thought the occasion would rarely arise. One of the reasons why they were setting up the Parliamentary Commissioner was that there was a widespread feeling that the 1921 Act tribunals procedure was too heavy a sledge-hammer to crack a nut, like the Thurso boy case. They hoped that the Commissioner might deal with such cases. (He omitted to mention that the Commissioner was excluded from considering complaints against the police in the Bill under discussion.)

His second main argument was that it was right to exclude the Commissioner from being required to give evidence in the courts except under subheadings (b) and (c) in the clause (proceedings under the Official Secrets Act which affected him or his staff, proceedings in a case where there had been obstruction of the Commissioner in his work). It was important that people should feel free to give evidence to the Commissioner without being liable to be

---

[1] The Parliamentary Commissioner Bill, Col. 321.   [2] Ibid., Col. 322.

brought before the courts at a later date on account of that evidence. If, however, the Commissioner used the formal procedure, which was open to him, to take evidence on oath, then it should be possible for proceedings to be taken in the courts against alleged perjury committed in giving evidence on oath. Subsection (b) also provided for this. In general, however, it was expected that the Commissioner would keep to informal procedures in making his investigations and it was important that people involved in these investigations should be protected from being subsequently brought before the courts, or before a Tribunal of Inquiry on account of evidence given to the Commissioner.

Discussion in the committee ranged widely on this amendment. For example, Michael English wanted to know whether the clause would prevent the Commissioner from giving adequate evidence to a Select Committee on the Parliamentary Commissioner. But on the specific proposal in the amendment, to make the Commissioner liable to be called to give evidence to a Tribunal of Inquiry, it was clear that the weight of opinion did not support Anthony Buck's view. He withdrew the amendment.

Subsection (3) of Clause 11 provided that a Minister might give notice to the Commissioner, in writing, that disclosure of a document which he had seen in his investigation, or of specific information he had gained, would 'be prejudicial to the safety of the State or otherwise contrary to the public interest'. In such a case, the Commissioner would not be able to reveal the nature of the document, or information concerned, to the Member of Parliament who had sent him the complaint, or to the complainant.

Paul Rose (Labour) moved an amendment to this subsection which sought to delete the words 'or otherwise contrary to the public interest'. Rose commented that in his opinion the wording in the subsection provided 'a remarkably broad shield for any Minister, a shield so broad that if Harold had had it at the battle of Hastings he might have won and the Common Market would now be applying for entry into Britain'.[1]

He accepted the need for security and for documents involving security not to be disclosed. But the question of matters which were not in the public interest required some further definition. He wanted to know 'what is not in the public interest and what matters are envisaged by my honourable and learned Friend as coming

[1] Ibid., Col. 332.

within that category. I also want to know who is to decide what is not in the public interest. Is it the Parliamentary Commissioner or is it the Minister concerned?'[1]

MacDermot replied that the term 'public interest' had been considered by the courts in a number of cases and in particular was defined by Lord Simon in the Thetis case in 1942 when he had interpreted it as meaning 'the proper functioning of the public service'. Thus a Minister might not allow the Parliamentary Commissioner to disclose documents concerned with tax returns. In such a case, the safety of the State would not be in danger but the proper functioning of the service would, since it was important to preserve the rule of confidentiality in income tax returns.

David Weitzman (Labour) was not altogether satisfied with the Minister's reply. MacDermot had said that it was for the Minister to say when a document should not be disclosed. Weitzman thought that the decision should be made jointly by the Minister and the Parliamentary Commissioner. If the Commissioner 'agreed that it should not be disclosed, well and good. If he did not agree, then it ought to be published.'[2]

Rose, in speaking again to his amendment, took a similar view. But he said he was somewhat reassured by the Minister's statement in the debate that the Commissioner would be able in his report to comment on the fact that a Minister had not allowed him to disclose a document he had seen. He thought this would be a very valuable protection since the Commissioner would be able to say 'that certain matters were unjustifiably kept away from the public by the Minister'.

He also acknowledged that his amendment went too far since there were documents of a confidential nature which should not be disclosed, even though they did not concern the safety of the State. Finally, he would like to hear what the Minister had to say about the next amendment before he made up his mind about the subsection. He therefore, asked leave to withdraw his own amendment.

Before considering the next amendment it is appropriate, at this stage, to consider the use which has been made by Ministers of the power to instruct the Commissioner not to disclose a document which he has seen in the course of an investigation. In the first seventeen months of operation of the Parliamentary Commissioner's office this power had not been used on a single occasion.

---

[1] Ibid., Col. 332.   [2] Ibid., Col. 339.

The next amendment, which was moved by Antony Buck for the Conservatives, proposed to add to Subsection (3) 'but the Commissioner shall not thereby be prevented from condemning any maladministration without disclosing such documents or information'. Buck told the committee that the Conservatives were moving this amendment because they thought that it should be made crystal clear that in cases where a Minister prevented a document from being disclosed, it would still be possible for the Commissioner to make a report saying that maladministration had occurred.[1]

Niall MacDermot, in his reply, said that he could give an unqualified assurance that, under the Bill as drafted, the Commissioner would not be debarred from condemning maladministration in a case where he was not able to disclose all the documents. In view of this assurance, Buck withdrew his amendment, but he asked the Minister whether he would draw the attention of the distinguished judge, currently conducting an inquiry into Crown Privilege, to the provisions in Clause 11 relating to the public interest.

MacDermot replied that he would certainly call the attention of the Lord Chancellor to Antony Buck's point, since it was the Lord Chancellor who had appointed Lord Pearson to conduct an inquiry into Crown Privilege. This matter was of some potential importance since it was anticipated by many that Lord Pearson might recommend a narrower interpretation of the term 'public interest' in the application of Crown Privilege and clearly Buck hoped that a narrow interpretation might then also be given to the words 'to the public interest' in so far as it affected the ability of Ministers to prohibit the Parliamentary Commissioner from disclosing documents he had seen.

In the debate on the motion that Clause 11 stand part of the Bill, the Minister told Michael English (Labour) that he would look into the question of whether there would be any difficulty under the Bill as drafted in the Parliamentary Commissioner giving necessary information to the Select Committee about the cases he had investigated. He thought this was covered by the phrase in Subsection (2) which allowed the Commissioner to disclose information '(a) for the purposes of the investigation and of any report to be made thereon under this Act'.

No subsequent change was made in this phrasing, so a further look must have satisfied the Minister. A considerable change was

[1] Ibid., Cols. 342–3.

made, however, under subheading (b) of Subsection (2). The original phrasing allowed the Commissioner to disclose information '(b) for the purposes of any proceedings for an offence under the Official Secrets Acts 1911 to 1939, or an offence of perjury'. Sir John Foster (Conservative) had pointed out that the phrase was widely worded and implied that the Commissioner could give information about any breach of the Official Secrets Act, or perjury, which he discovered during the course of his investigations.

The Minister promised to look at this point and was as good as his word. In the Act, as finally approved, the wording was extended to make clear that the Commissioner could only give information in proceedings for an alleged offence under the Official Secrets Act, or for an alleged perjury, if these proceedings related to himself or his officers or to someone who had given evidence under oath to the Commissioner.

The committee then approved Clause 11 as a whole. The committee had not carried any amendment to the Clause, but debate on the amendments which were withdrawn had made possible a valuable probing of the effect of the provisions in the Clause. It also prompted the Minister to introduce clarifying amendments himself at a later stage.

The committee then approved Clause 12 of the Bill without any debate. This Clause which was titled 'Interpretation' merely defined the meaning of certain expressions in the Act. For example, it made clear that the word 'action' included failure to act; therefore, failure to act on the part of a government department could be maladministration.

While Clause 12 was uncontroversial, Clause 13 was the occasion of a more heated debate than on any other part of the Bill. The Clause was entitled 'Application to Northern Ireland'. Its effect was to extend the Act to Northern Ireland into those spheres in which the United Kingdom Government has authority in Northern Ireland and also where a Northern Ireland department acts as an agent of a United Kingdom department. In all other spheres, however, departments of the Northern Ireland Government would not be subject to investigation by the Parliamentary Commissioner.

Paul Rose (Labour) moved an amendment which would give the Parliamentary Commissioner authority to investigate complaints against all departments of the Northern Ireland Government. He recalled that about eighteen months before on the Floor of the House, I was unwise enough to speak in the debate on Northern Ireland. As a result, the mantle of unofficial Ombudsman or Parliamentary Commissioner for Northern Ireland fell upon my unwilling shoulders. During that time and until the election of my honourable Friend the Member for Belfast West (Gerard Fitt, Republican Labour, was elected in 1966) who has now taken up that mantle, I learned a great deal about the maladministration which occurs in that part of the United Kingdom and about the need for the extension of the Parliamentary Commissioner's duties to cover those Ministries upon whom power has devolved under the Government of Ireland Acts.[1]

Examples of this maladministration which he then enlarged upon were bias in making appointments by Northern Ireland Ministries to bodies like the Health Service Board, misfeasance in the arrangements for elections to Stormont, discrimination against Catholic areas in economic development, the misuse of power under the Northern Ireland Special Powers Act, and discrimination against Catholics in the allocation of houses. On appointments, he said that of twenty-four members of the Health Service Board 'not one is a Roman Catholic, not one a trade unionist, not one a member of the Labour Party'.[2]

The Parliamentary Commissioner should be able to examine this discrimination in appointments to the Health Service Board and to other organizations such as the Tourist Board and the Housing Trust where similar discrimination existed. He should be able to examine allegations of deliberate neglect by the Northern Ireland Government of the economic development of areas west of the Bann. He should be able to investigate the exercise of power by the Home Office in Northern Ireland under the Special Powers Act of which he understood 'Dr. Vorster in South Africa once said that he was particularly jealous'.[3]

He should be able to examine allegations of discrimination in housing. There were constant examples of these instanced in the Northern Ireland Press and the Northern Ireland Parliament.

Paul Rose recalled that he and the honourable Member for Orpington (Eric Lubbock) had recently delivered a petition to the House from all the Opposition Members of the Stormont Parliament asking for the powers of the Parliamentary Commissioner to be extended to Northern Ireland. The Opposition Members included the representatives of the Labour Party, the Liberal Party, the

[1] Ibid., Col. 349.   [2] Ibid., Col. 352.   [3] Ibid., Col. 354.

Nationalist Party, and the Republican Labour Party at Stormont. At Westminster, a motion on the Order Paper supporting his amendment already had the support of 125 Members. Since members of the Government are not allowed to sign motions, this meant that fifty per cent of the back-bench members of the Parliamentary Labour Party were already supporting the motion.

In the debate which followed, Paul Rose received full support from one Labour member of the committee, John Lee. Two other Labour members, Michael English and Alexander Lyon, agreed, in general, with the criticisms which he had made of administration in Northern Ireland, but did not support the amendment. Michael English thought that the issues in Northern Ireland were of too great political importance to be brought within the purview of the Parliamentary Commissioner. Since, he said, 'I want the Parliamentary Commissioner to succeed in his endeavours, I do not wish to bring into his job an enormous political dispute of this character in the initial stages'.[1]

Alexander Lyon told the committee that he would vote against the amendment if it were put to the vote, but this did not mean that he was out of sympathy with the objects of the amendment. His feeling was that this standing committee was not 'the appropriate forum at which to decide such a major Constitutional question'.[2]

On the Conservative side there were two speeches from members of the committee. Dame Joan Vickers dissented in a measured way from the picture of conditions in Northern Ireland which Paul Rose had drawn. Northern Ireland was not a totalitarian state, it could not be compared with South Africa. Constituencies were smaller than English constituencies and there was greater opportunity for citizens in Northern Ireland to get their grievances redressed. There was accordingly less need for a Parliamentary Commissioner in Northern Irish affairs. Antony Buck spoke with less moderation. He said

we on this side of the Committee much regret the terms in which the Amendment has sought to be moved. We utterly refute the allegations which have been made and, in my submission to the Committee, this was certainly not the place to attempt to air them. They will not help responsible people of whatever opinion in Northern Ireland in the exercise in which they are indulging at the moment which is to try and lower the temperature and to smooth out affairs between the main contenders, the Roman Catholics and the Protestants there.[3]

[1] Ibid., Col. 366.   [2] Ibid., Col. 367.   [3] Ibid., Col. 365.

This speech brought a hot response from Michael English, Alexander Lyon, and Paul Rose himself. Rose thought that people of goodwill in Northern Ireland would welcome anything which 'would help to take the lid off some of the more unpleasant practices' there.

The Minister's chief contribution to the debate was to point out in a factual manner the spheres within which the Parliamentary Commissioner would have competence in Northern Ireland under the Bill. First, there would be powers which are exercised by United Kingdom departments in Northern Ireland. For example, against the activities of the Customs and Excise Department and the Defence Department in Northern Ireland, there could be complaint to the Parliamentary Commissioner. Second, there were functions in which Northern Ireland departments were acting as agents for United Kingdom departments. For example, agricultural deficiency payments were made by the Northern Ireland Ministry of Agriculture on behalf of the United Kingdom Ministry of Agriculture, Fisheries, and Food. Passports are issued in Northern Ireland on behalf of the London Passport Office. The Northern Ireland Ministry of Health and Social Services repays income tax to unemployed persons on behalf of the United Kingdom. In all these cases complaint could be made to the Parliamentary Commissioner.[1]

Where, however, a matter was purely the responsibility of Northern Ireland Ministers, it would not be appropriate for the United Kingdom Parliamentary Commissioner to have competence. The same principle applied as in relation to local government in Britain. Where 'there was no responsibility by Ministers here in Whitehall, and no responsibility and no answerability to our Parliament' the Parliamentary Commissioner should not have any competence.

Consequently, if there is to be a Parliamentary Commissioner responsible in the field which is covered by the Amendment, it must be a Parliamentary Commissioner of the Northern Ireland Government responsible to the Northern Ireland Parliament. It would be quite improper for me to comment upon the question whether such a Commissioner should or should not be set up. It is a matter for the Northern Ireland Government and I note that the honourable Lady the Member for Devonport [Dame Joan Vickers] has quoted a message from the Prime Minister of Northern Ireland indicating that if we decide to set up a Commissioner that is a matter which they would consider.[2]

[1] Ibid., Col. 363.   [2] Ibid., Col. 365.

Paul Rose was not impressed by this reply from the Minister. 'The fact that the Prime Minister of Northern Ireland said that he would consider it leaves me a little cold, because, as I have said, when I visited Northern Ireland the then Home Secretary made it clear that a Parliamentary Commissioner would not be considered. "Consider it" in any event does not go very far. It can be considered and turned down.'[1]

He was, however, impressed by the argument put forward by the Financial Secretary and by some of his honourable Friends that a standing committee of twenty members was not the place to make such an important constitutional change, particularly when those twenty members were not unanimous about it. He would, therefore, withdraw his amendment.

This debate in standing committee was little noticed in British newspapers but it was given a good coverage in the Northern Irish Press. Two years later, the campaign for civil rights in Northern Ireland had made the rights of minorities there a major issue in British politics. In the summer of 1969 it became an issue which attracted world-wide attention when severe fighting broke out in parts of Londonderry and Belfast between members of the Catholic community and the Royal Ulster Constabulary. The British Government acceded to the request from the Northern Ireland Government that it should send in troops to maintain law and order.

Paul Rose continued to act as a spokesman at Westminster for the civil rights campaign in Northern Ireland. On 22 April 1969 he opened an emergency debate in the Commons on events which had occurred during the preceding weekend in Londonderry.[2] At the beginning of the day's business he had introduced into the Commons, with Gerard Fitt, the newly elected Member for Mid-Ulster, Miss Bernadette Devlin, who had been elected at a by-election at Mid-Ulster on a civil rights platform.

The Government of Northern Ireland did act upon its pledge to give serious consideration to the demand for a Parliamentary Commissioner for Northern Ireland. The Northern Ireland Government introduced a Bill into the Stormont Parliament which became law in 1969. Under the Parliamentary Commissioner (Northern Ireland) Act, of that year, Sir Edmund Compton was appointed Parliamentary Commissioner for Northern Ireland, with power to investigate complaints against departments of the Northern Ireland Govern-

[1] Ibid., Col. 372.   [2] H.C. Deb. Vol. 782, Cols. 262–71.

ment. He established an office in Belfast with a staff of eight which he visited once a week. The Northern Ireland Government also set up, in December 1969, a Commissioner of Complaints to investigate complaints against local authorities, hospitals, and other health authorities.[1]

After Paul Rose had withdrawn his amendment to Clause 13, the Clause was approved as a whole. Clause 14 was then approved without debate. This clause was uncontroversial, providing, for example, that the Act would 'come into force on such date as Her Majesty may by Order in Council appoint'.

All the clauses in the Bill had now been approved by the standing committee which had now reached its eighth sitting. There remained to discuss three Schedules to the Bill. Schedule 1 was uncontroversial. It was concerned with 'Pensions and other Benefits' payable to the Parliamentary Commissioner. This Schedule was approved without discussion.

Schedules 2 and 3 were much more controversial. Schedule 2 listed the 'Departments and Authorities Subject to Investigation', Schedule 3 listed 'Matters Not Subject to Investigation'.

Schedule 2 listed forty-three government departments including not only all the great departments such as the Treasury, the Foreign Office, the Home Office, and the Board of Trade, but also many lesser known authorities such as the National Debt Office, the Land Registry, and the Public Trustee. William Roots, for the Conservatives, moved an amendment to include sixteen other departments or authorities.

Niall MacDermot spoke to each of these sixteen in turn. The Crown Agents for Overseas Governments had not been included because they act on behalf of overseas Governments and do so in commercial and contractual matters.

The Colonial Office and the Commonwealth Relations Office were not included because they had ceased to exist as departments and their functions had been transferred to the Commonwealth Office. The Government had it in mind that a complaint against the Colonial Office or the Commonwealth Relations Office could be investigated by the Parliamentary Commissioner and that he would deal with the Commonwealth Office in investigating it. But he thanked honourable Members for drawing his attention to the point. He thought 'that it would be an improvement to the Bill if we were to

[1] See below Chapter XVI, pp. 333-4.

move, on Report, a general Amendment making it quite clear, in respect of any Department, that matters within the scope of the Department would include matters within the scope of any predecessor Department from which functions had been transferred. That would cover this case and one or two other cases'.[1] The Minister was as good as his word. In the final text of the Act, note 8 of Schedule 2 embodies this provision.

The next department which the Roots amendment proposed to add was the Exchequer and Audit Department. MacDermot thought it would be wrong to include it since it 'is in effect, the staff of the Comptroller and Auditor General, who is not an officer of the Government but is another officer of the House, and I suggest to the Committee that it would be wrong to ask one officer of the House to investigate complaints against the staff of another officer of the House and that it is quite unnecessary to do so' since the Comptroller and Auditor-General already reports to the Public Accounts Committee.[2]

It was proposed to add to the list the Government Hospitality Fund. This in fact was already included since it was a subordinate department of the Treasury and note 5 to the Schedule mentioned that subordinate departments of the Treasury were in.

The Roots amendment next proposed that the Heralds College should be included. He did not think that this was a Government Department which acted on behalf of the Crown. It was a private body established by Charter. The Law Commission did not have any administrative functions in relation to the public. 'It is an advisory body which is set up to review the law and to make recommendations about law reform to the Lord Chancellor or other Ministers. It does not, therefore, have any functions which, I suggest to the Committee, could be a proper subject of inquiry by the P.C.A.'[3]

He criticized the proposal to include the 'Department of the Lord President of the Council'. This, he said, was not a very apt description of the Lord President's staff which was in fact divided into two parts. On the one hand there was the staff of the Privy Council Office for which he was responsible and on the other hand the personal staff of the private office of the Lord President. It would be wrong to include the Privy Council Office since this performed

---

[1] The Parliamentary Commissioner Bill, Col. 378.
[2] Ibid., Col. 378.   [3] Ibid., Col. 379.

judicial, quasi-judicial, and prerogative functions. Examples of each were its function as an appellate tribunal for appeals from Colonies, its quasi-judicial function in considering appeals made against the striking-off of a medical practitioner, and such prerogative functions as the granting of Royal Charters and procedure on the appointment of Ministers and the dissolution of Parliament.

On the other hand, he could see that it would be logical to include the private office of the Lord President since the private office of the Lord Privy Seal and the Minister without Portfolio were included within the provisions of the Bill. He undertook to put down an amendment, therefore, to achieve this effect and in the final Act the Lord President of the Council's Office is listed in Schedule 2.

Roots's amendment proposed that the National Board for Prices and Incomes should be included. The Minister opposed this on the ground that it was 'an advisory body and, generally speaking, we have excluded advisory bodies from the scope of the Bill'.[1]

He criticized, in a similar way, the proposal to include the National Parks Commission. This was an overwhelmingly advisory body. It could designate national parks, but any such designation required Ministerial confirmation.

On the proposal to include the Registrar of Restrictive Trading Agreements, he maintained that the Registrar was an officer of the Restrictive Practices Court rather than an administrative Civil Servant. An appeal to the High Court would lie against any failure by him to discharge his duties properly.

Finally, he said that it was unnecessary to list the Scottish Development Department. 'In effect, it is a Department of the Scottish Office and is, therefore, already within the scope of the Bill.'[2]

In the debate which followed, a number of Conservative members of the committee indicated dissatisfaction with some of the arguments which the Minister had used for excluding some types of authority. For example, Sir Hugh Lucas-Tooth said 'I can well imagine that an advisory body might make a decision on improper grounds; it might be affected by either malice or vengeance. Such a decision, although not directly affecting a particular citizen, might indirectly affect him very much indeed'.[3]

He was not in favour of the broad functions of advisory bodies being open to investigation by the Commissioner, but he was in

[1] Ibid., Col. 381.   [2] Ibid., Col. 383.   [3] Ibid., Col. 385.

favour of their being open to investigation within a limited field. William Roots in his summing up, supported him. He thought, for example, that the Commissioner should be able to look into the question of whether there had been maladministration in arriving at advice given by the National Board for Prices and Incomes.[1]

The Minister did not concede anything here. The function of the Commissioner was to investigate actions of a Minister or of those acting on behalf of a Minister. An advisory body does not take decisions. The decisions are taken by the Minister and such decisions would be open to investigation by the Commissioner.

If a complaint was made about the functioning of an advisory body, such as the National Board for Prices and Incomes, complaint should be in the first instance to the Chairman of the Board. 'If satisfaction were not received then, the complaint would be made to my right honourable Friend the Secretary of State for the Department of Economic Affairs. If he refused to investigate the complaint, that would be an administrative decision on his part which could then be the subject of an investigation, if he thought fit, by the Parliamentary Commissioner.'[2]

Another line of criticism was advanced by Conservative members. Two Conservatives, Charles Fletcher-Cooke and Sir John Foster, argued that authorities which had judicial or quasi-judicial functions should not necessarily be exempt from investigation by the Parliamentary Commissioner. Sir John Foster asked the Committee to envisage a case before the Privy Council in which 'either negligently or maliciously the client, the litigant, has been misinformed as to the date of the hearing, or some notice has not been sent out properly to him'.[3] The Parliamentary Commissioner should be able to investigate such maladministration by the staff of a court.

The Minister's answer to this argument was that it was up to the courts themselves to deal with complaints about their internal administration. In the Queen's Bench Division, for example, it is the Lord Chief Justice who would investigate any such complaint. 'I feel that it would be almost an insult to the Lord Chief Justice to suggest that that function should be duplicated by it being possible for complaints to be made to the Parliamentary Commissioner.'[4]

Although individual Conservatives were not wholly satisfied on these matters, the Minister's replies, in general, were adequate for

[1] Ibid., Col. 394.   [2] Ibid., Col. 395.
[3] Ibid., Col. 387.   [4] Ibid., Col. 390.

William Roots who withdrew the amendment. He then moved an amendment to add the Land Commission to the authorities subject to investigation. The Minister replied that the Land Commission was not included simply because it did not yet exist. He agreed that it was a proper body to be included within the scope of the Bill. 'If it exists in time for it to be included within the Bill, then we shall move an Amendment at the appropriate stage.' [1]

William Roots then withdrew his amendment and the committee approved Schedule 2. The Land Commission did, in fact, come into existence before the Bill had completed all its stages and it was included in Schedule 2 of the Act.

Schedule 3 of the Bill listed 'Matters not Subject to Investigation'. Since much of the criticism of the Bill had been directed to the areas of central government which were exempt from investigation by the Commissioner, it was to be expected that discussion of this Schedule would be extensive. In fact, it was discussed for the remaining, and longer, part of the eighth sitting and for the whole of the ninth and tenth sittings.

Paragraph 1 of Schedule 3 provided that 'Action taken in matters certified by a Secretary of State or other Minister of the Crown to affect relations or dealings between the Government of the United Kingdom and any other government or any international organisation of States or Governments' should be exempt from investigation. Alexander Lyon (Labour) moved an amendment to delete this paragraph.

The Minister explained that the paragraph did not have the effect of removing all dealings between the United Kingdom with other governments, or with international organizations, from the ambit of the Commissioner. Such relations, or dealings, would only be exempt from investigation if a Minister issued a certificate to make them exempt. Such a certificate would be issued in cases of a sensitive political nature in which the Foreign Office considered that investigation might prejudice relations with a foreign government or be contrary to international law or practice. Having received this explanation, Alexander Lyon withdrew his amendment.

Paragraph 2 exempted 'Action taken, in any country or territory outside the United Kingdom by or on behalf of any officer representing or acting under the authority of Her Majesty, in respect of the United Kingdom, or any other officer of the Government of the

[1] Ibid., Col. 396.

United Kingdom'. Antony Buck, for the Conservatives, moved an amendment to delete this paragraph. The committee also considered, at the same time, an amendment to add to the paragraph the words 'except in so far as these relate to consular matters'.

This, in fact, was the main question under discussion. Buck criticized the paragraph on the ground that 'Action taken' by Civil Servants abroad was too wide a category. It could cover such things as export credit guarantees 'besides a whole range of consular activities in which there could well be matters of maladministration which should be investigated by the Parliamentary Commissioner'.[1]

Cranley Onslow (Conservative) supported the amendments. He told the committee: 'I have to declare an interest of sorts in that I once held the post of British Consul, in North Burma, of all places, where, I hasten to add, I was never caught in any indiscretions.'[2] Niall MacDermot replied that the principal reason for not including actions taken by consular representatives abroad was purely a practical one. There would be an obvious difficulty 'in the Parliamentary Commissioner and his staff investigating a case which arose on the other side of the world. We want him to be able to go along many fruitful paths, but we had not considered that the Road to Mandalay was one of them.'[3]

He agreed, however, that the paragraph was very widely worded. If it was the wish of the committee that the Commissioner should be able to investigate at least some of the consular activities which acutely affect private citizens and their rights, he would gladly undertake to look further at this question. On the basis of this undertaking, Antony Buck withdrew his amendment. But the Minister's second thoughts did not produce any concession and the paragraph was embodied unchanged in the Act.

Paragraph 3 exempted 'Action taken in connection with the administration of the government of any country or territory outside the United Kingdom which forms part of Her Majesty's dominions or in which Her Majesty has jurisdiction'. Alexander Lyon (Labour) moved an amendment to delete this paragraph. He was particularly concerned that the paragraph would exclude investigation of maladministration in British colonies. He did not think there was much force in the Minister's objection to the Parliamentary Commissioner making investigations abroad. 'After all this is not the age of the slow boat to China. There are jets now which take one to the furthest

<hr />

[1] Ibid., Col. 400.   [2] Ibid., Col. 401.   [3] Ibid., Col. 400.

corners of the earth in the time that it takes some people to get to London Airport.'[1] Cost might be a factor, but if there was a serious case of maladministration it would be a small matter to pay a little extra cost for the Commissioner to investigate and find a just solution.

Two Conservatives, Charles Fletcher-Cooke and William Roots, supported the amendment but the Minister would not make any concession. He thought that it would be very much resented in British colonies if the actions of governments in the colonies were subject to investigation by the British Parliamentary Commissioner. Alexander Lyon did not agree. He thought that experience would prove him to be right and the Minister wrong. But since the Minister had already given an undertaking to consider an amendment on Report giving a power by Order in Council to delete some of the exclusions in Schedule 3, he would withdraw his amendment. If then experience showed the need to make administration in the colonies subject to investigation by the Commissioner, the change could be easily made.

Paragraph 4 exempted 'Action taken by the Secretary of State under the Extradition Act 1870 or the Fugitive Offenders Act 1881'. Michael English (Labour) moved an amendment to delete this paragraph, but he described it as a probing amendment designed 'to find out the Government's exact intention in making this exclusion'.[2]

MacDermot explained that this was discretionary action taken by the Secretary of State after the person concerned had exercised all his rights of appeal in the courts against proposed extradition (or return under the Fugitive Offenders Act). In some cases appeal could go right up to the House of Lords. After all these rights of appeal had been exercised, a discretionary power remained with the Secretary of State whether or not to make an Order. Michael English then told the committee that in the light of this explanation, he was quite happy about the paragraph and would withdraw his amendment.

Paragraph 5 exempted 'Action taken by or with the authority of the Secretary of State for the purposes of investigating crime or of protecting the security of the State, including action taken with respect to passports'. Michael English moved a similar probing amendment to this paragraph. The Minister explained that the

---

[1] Ibid., Col. 409.
[2] Ibid., Col. 415.

paragraph covered cases 'where action is taken on the authority of a personal warrant of the Home Secretary'.[1]

The Home Secretary has authority to intercept communications, for example, by tapping a telephone line, for the purpose of investigating serious crime or matters relating to the security of the State. He also has power to withhold or withdraw passport facilities to assist the investigation of crime. These powers are only used in exceptional cases.

The paragraph dealt only with the use of such powers. It did not cover any other police action. The Minister was closely questioned on this point by Sir Hugh Lucas-Tooth. Sir Hugh suggested that the paragraph, as phrased, would exempt any action taken by the Metropolitan Police from investigation since technically any action of the Metropolitan Police was taken on the authority of the Secretary of State.

The Minister replied that this was to misconceive the relationship between the Secretary of State and the Metropolitan Police. He has power only to give them direction on policy questions. He does not have power to give them directions or instructions on how they shall, or shall not, conduct any particular case. Therefore, this kind of activity by the Metropolitan Police would not anyway be subject to investigation by the Parliamentary Commissioner.

MacDermot thought that another point raised by Sir Hugh Lucas-Tooth had greater force. Sir Hugh had argued that the words in the paragraph 'including action taken with respect to passports' were too wide. To make sure that the administration of passports should not be generally exempt from investigation the phrase should be re-worded. The Minister undertook to look at this point and was as good as his word. In the final Act the word 'so' is introduced in this phrase and it reads 'including action so taken with respect to passports'. This makes clear that it is action taken in connection with the Minister's use of extraordinary powers for investigating crime or protecting the security of the State.

After this discussion on the role of the Home Secretary in relation to the paragraph, and the Minister's exposition of it, Michael English told the committee that he would withdraw his amendment.

Paragraph 6 exempted from investigation 'The commencement or conduct of civil or criminal proceedings before any court of law in the United Kingdom, of proceedings at any place under the Naval

[1] Ibid., Col. 417.

Discipline Act 1957, the Army Act 1955, or the Air Force Act 1955, or of proceedings before any international court or tribunal'. Alexander Lyon moved an amendment to delete this paragraph. He thought it was right to exempt from investigation the conduct of civil or criminal proceedings before a court of law but he did not think it right to exempt their 'commencement'. There was a possibility of maladministration in a decision taken by a government official, for example in the Ministry of Social Service, or the Ministry of Labour, whether or not to prosecute in a particular case. Bias, for example, might enter in the decision to prosecute, when it had previously been the policy of the Ministry not to prosecute in similar cases.

Lyon raised this point at the end of the eighth sitting. When the ninth sitting began, the Minister told the committee that he had thought about the point carefully. He saw the force of Lyon's argument but, in practice, he told the committee, 'in virtually all the cases where a prosecution is not by the police but by a Government Department, it is carried out on the advice of the legal officers of the Department who consider it carefully and decide on legal grounds, whether they think there is proper evidence. I do not feel that this would prove a very fruitful source of investigation by the Parliamentary Commissioner.'[1]

Alexander Lyon had not, in fact, arrived in time for the beginning of the morning's proceedings and was not there to say whether or not he was satisfied by the Minister's answer. In the absence of any statement from him as to whether he would withdraw or persist in the amendment, the committee negatived the amendment without a division.

He arrived immediately afterwards apologizing for his late arrival and need to recover his breath, but in time to move an amendment to paragraph 7. This paragraph exempted 'Any exercise of the prerogative of mercy or of the power of a Secretary of State to make a reference in respect of any person to the Court of Criminal Appeal, the High Court of Justiciary or the Courts-Martial Appeal Court'.

Alexander Lyon said that he merely wanted an explanation from the Financial Secretary to justify this exclusion. Michael English (Labour), however, intervened to put a point which he said had been made to him by the National Council for Civil Liberties. In their

[1] Ibid., Col. 426.

experience it was much more difficult to persuade the Secretary of State to make a reference to the Court of Criminal Appeal than to persuade him to exercise, in appropriate cases, the prerogative of mercy. Nobody, he thought, objected to the use of the prerogative of mercy being excluded from investigation, but he would like the Minister to comment on the other exclusion.

The Minister replied that the Secretary of State's power to refer a point, or a whole case, to the Court of Appeal was ancillary to his power to recommend the exercise of the prerogative of mercy. He thought that it involved 'peculiarly a discretionary power and a discretionary decision by the Home Secretary personally which would not on other grounds be the kind of matter which the Parliamentary Commissioner would investigate'.[1] This was a reference, by implication, to his earlier comments on Clause 5 on the need to exclude the Commissioner from considering the exercise of discretionary power by Ministers.

Alexander Lyon then told the Committee that in view of the Minister's lucid explanation of the paragraph, he would withdraw his amendment.

Paragraph 8 of Schedule 3 excluded 'Action taken on behalf of the Minister of Health or the Secretary of State by a Regional Hospital Board, Board of Governors of a Teaching Hospital, Hospital Management Committee or Board of Management, or by the Public Health Laboratory Service Board'. This exclusion had been widely criticized and it was certain that William Roots's amendment to delete the paragraph, moved on behalf of the Conservatives, would be keenly debated.

William Roots argued that the case for excluding the hospital service from scrutiny by the Parliamentary Commissioner was a very weak one. It had been suggested that the test of whether or not a topic should be excluded could be found in the answer to the question: 'Is this a matter on which the Minister could be questioned in the Commons?'

Thus local authorities and nationalized industries were excluded on the grounds that no Minister could be questioned about the internal administration of either types of authority. But a Minister was responsible for and could be questioned about the activities of regional hospital boards, teaching hospitals, or hospital management committees. He thought that the paragraph would 'deprive the

[1] Ibid., Col. 429.

subject of a most valuable facility which the Parliamentary Commissioner might give him'.[1]

The Minister defended exclusion of the hospitals on the following grounds. First, he argued that the hospital service was in a special and unique position. The hospital authorities are not like the local offices of government departments. The Minister is answerable and responsible for the hospitals but, in practice, they have a degree of independence which does not apply to the local offices of the Ministry of Labour or the Ministry of Social Security. The hospital authorities are also, he argued, very much local bodies. They are not democratically elected but 'the people who serve them are known locally and can be approached locally in the way that a local councillor can be and is'.[2]

His second line of argument was that the hospital service was only part of the National Health Service. There was also the general practitioner service which is organized by the Executive Councils who do not act on behalf of the Minister and would, therefore, be outside the scope of the Bill. Again, there were 'the welfare services within the Health Service' which are administered by the local authorities and would similarly be outside the Bill. If the hospital service were brought within the scrutiny of the Parliamentary Commissioner, cases could arise in which the Commissioner could look at part of the complaint by a patient, but could not look at his complaint against the general practitioner in a case in which the hospital service and the general practitioner were involved.

His third line of argument was that the vast majority of complaints related to matters in which clinical judgement was involved. The Parliamentary Commissioner would not be equipped to decide this kind of question in which technical and medical considerations would be important.

His fourth argument was that the procedure for investigating complaints in the hospital service had recently been reformed. On 7 March 1966, the Minister of Health had issued a circular to all hospital authorities making recommendations about the ways in which complaints should be handled.[3] In particular, he quoted from the circular the recommendation that inquiries into the most serious type of complaints should be headed by an independent lawyer, or other competent person from outside the hospital service, and should

---

[1] Ibid., Col. 431.   [2] Ibid., Col. 432.
[3] H.M.(66) 15. 'Methods of Dealing with Complaints by Patients.'

include persons to advise on any professional or technical matters. The complainant, and the person complained against, should have the right to attend throughout the hearing and to cross-examine witnesses. They should also be allowed legal representation at the hearing if they wished to arrange for it. The Minister suggested to the committee 'that it is better, since this procedure has recently been overhauled and revised that we should let this be tried in the first instance'.[1]

His final argument was that they should take care not to overload the Commissioner. To include the hospital service would make a very large extension to his functions. He, therefore, asked the committee 'to agree that at the outset, and in the first instance in any event, we should not seek to include this field within the scope of the Commissioner's activities'.[2]

He reminded the committee that he had, on an earlier amendment, undertaken to consider the suggestion put forward by Michael English that the Bill should give power to Ministers to amend Schedule 3 by Order. He could now tell the committee that he intended to move an amendment to this effect at report stage and, in reply to a question from Antony Buck, he gave an assurance that this would give power only to delete matters from the Schedule, not to provide for the addition of further excluded areas.

In the debate which followed, the Minister's arguments, in favour of excluding the hospital service, were strongly attacked from both the Conservative and Labour sides of the committee. Antony Buck (Conservative) said that, in his view, the Minister's statement about the complaints procedure in the hospital service strengthened the case for giving some supervision to the Parliamentary Commissioner. The procedure which the Minister described did not have statutory authority, it was not mandatory on the hospital authorities. 'If there has been a breakdown in the procedure, which is not mandatory, that should be at once an ideal matter for the Parliamentary Commissioner to investigate.'[3]

David Weitzman (Labour) took a similar view. Suppose the 'hospital board has adopted the procedure put forward by the Minister but there have been mistakes by its officials with regard to it and there has been some form of maladministration. Why should not the Commissioner have a right to inquire into that?'[4]

---

[1] The Parliamentary Commissioner Bill, Col. 436.
[2] Ibid., Col. 436. [3] Ibid., Col. 437. [4] Ibid., Col. 439.

Charles Fletcher-Cooke (Conservative) thought that it was not a good argument to say that the Parliamentary Commissioner would be overloaded with complaints. He believed that the hospital service was an area where there would be many complaints. Was that not a reason why the Commissioner should, rather than should not, be able to investigate? He also criticized the argument that the Commissioner would not be equipped to consider clinical matters. He did not think that such matters were any more esoteric than questions with which the Commissioner might have to deal from the Ministry of Technology involving perhaps nuclear fission, automation, or cybernetics.

Alexander Lyon (Labour) did not agree with this view. He thought that it would not be sensible to ask the Commissioner to look at clinical matters. If this were done, he would need his own staff of consultants to advise him in evaluating clinical questions. Lyon proposed, however, that while areas of clinical judgement should be outside the Parliamentary Commissioner's ambit, he should be able to investigate in the hospital service 'all those areas of administrative judgement which are in no sense different from administrative action or judgement in any other department of Government'.[1]

Lyon criticized two other arguments which the Minister had used. Lyon thought that a regional hospital board could in no way be compared with a local authority. It is not answerable to a local electorate. Indeed, it is an area of government which is answerable to nobody and, therefore, should be open to investigation by an independent authority.

On the argument that there would be overlapping areas between the general practitioner, the local authority welfare service, and the hospital board, he thought that this need in no way debar investigation by the Commissioner. If he found, in a case, that the real burden of a complaint was against a general practitioner and not a hospital authority, then he could discontinue that case.

Sir Hugh Lucas-Tooth (Conservative) said that he entirely agreed with every word spoken by Alexander Lyon. After many years' experience as a member of the board of a teaching hospital, he could assure the committee that there was no sort of parallel between a hospital board and a local authority. He also agreed with Lyon that clinical matters should not be subject to investigation by the Com-

[1] Ibid., Col. 442.

missioner, but that the administration of hospitals could and should be subject to investigation.

Michael English (Labour) told the committee that he thought administrators in the hospital service should be subject to investigation by the Commissioner because they were the Minister's agents and, like all other agents of the Minister under the Bill, they should be brought in. Since the Minister had made a concession by promising to introduce an amendment on report stage allowing the Schedule to be altered by Order, he would not now vote for the amendment to delete paragraph 8. He would abstain.[1]

Dame Joan Vickers (Conservative) supported the amendment. She pointed to the position in large country areas such as the southwest where 'it is practically impossible for the individual concerned to get in touch with the Hospital boards' when they want to make complaints.[2]

Denis Coe (Labour) indicated that he too was in favour, in principle, of making the hospital service subject to investigation by the Commissioner but his speech brought the only crumb of comfort to the Minister from the whole debate. He said that he was impressed by the Minister's argument that for the time being the hospitals should be left out since they could not accurately judge the volume of work that the Commissioner would have to handle in other fields. He accepted the Minister's assurance that it would be made possible, by Order, to take out the paragraph excluding the hospitals at a later date.

Of those who spoke in the debate, therefore, not one speaker, apart from the Minister himself, was in favour of excluding the hospital service on grounds of principle. One member of the Committee was prepared to accept its exclusion for the time being. Niall MacDermot must have felt like saying to himself at the end of the debate in the words which Bagehot attributed to an old Secretary of the Treasury: 'This is a bad case, an indefensible case. We must apply our *majority* to this question.'

Niall MacDermot's majority, however, was not reliable. When the vote was taken on the motion 'That the words proposed to be left out stand part of the Schedule', only seven Labour members voted for the motion and eight Conservatives voted against it. This meant that paragraph 8 was deleted from the Bill and that the hospital service was brought within the Commissioner's sphere of

[1] Ibid., Col. 448.   [2] Ibid., Col. 450.

investigation. The Government defeat occurred because three Labour members abstained. Michael English, we have seen, had already announced his intention of abstaining. David Weitzman and Hugh Jenkins were also recorded as being present at the committee, but did not vote in this division.

The victory for those who wanted the hospital service included was, however, shortlived. At report stage, the Minister was able to use his majority to greater effect and paragraph 8 was restored. It is worth considering why the Government felt unable to bow to parliamentary opinion on this question. Niall MacDermot told the committee in his winding-up speech in the standing committee debate that the Minister of Health (Kenneth Robinson) 'is firmly of the view at present that it would not be desirable, for the reasons that I have been indicating, to make these complaints the subject of investigation by the Parliamentary Commissioner. He would much prefer to devise and have within the service the effective kind of procedure which he is seeking to achieve.'[1]

It is clear that the Minister of Health's view was the decisive factor on this question. Not every Cabinet Minister, it seems, agreed with him but nothing was said, at the time, to indicate any difference of opinion within the Government on this issue. Not quite two years later, in July 1968, Kenneth Robinson himself put forward the suggestion that either the Parliamentary Commissioner should be given authority to investigate complaints against the health authorities, including the hospitals, or that there should be a separate Commissioner, or Commissioners, for the Health Service. This suggestion was made in the Minister's Green Paper on reorganization of the Health Service.[2]

Richard Crossman, as Secretary of State for the Social Services, issued a second Green Paper in February 1970, which proposed a different structure for a reorganized and unified Health Service, in an attempt to meet criticisms that the structure proposed by Robinson was too bureaucratic and remote. Crossman's Green Paper reiterated the proposal for a Health Commissioner and announced that consultations were taking place about it with professional and other interests.[3] With the change of government, following the general election of 1970, plans for reorganization of the Health Service came to a halt. By the spring of 1971, the Hospital Service in Britain still had not secured a Commissioner to investigate com-

[1] Ibid., Col. 457.   [2] See below Chapter XV, pp. 294–5.   [3] See below p. 295.

plaints, neither had it been brought within the ambit of the Parliamentary Commissioner, although the Select Committee on the Parliamentary Commissioner had reported in July 1968 that, in their view, the reasons advanced for not including the hospitals were unsound.[1]

The debate in standing committee on the paragraph of the Bill which proposed to exclude the hospitals had seen the Minister, in effect, facing a coalition of Opposition members on the committee and his own back-benchers. On the next excluded sphere, the Conservatives were not supported in their criticism by any Labour member of the committee.

Paragraph 9 excluded 'Action taken in matters relating to contractual or other commercial transactions whether within the United Kingdom or elsewhere'. William Roots, for the Conservatives, moved an amendment to delete this paragraph and was supported in the debate by five other Conservatives: Sir John Foster, Sir Hugh Lucas-Tooth, Charles Fletcher-Cooke, Cranley Onslow, and Antony Buck. Their argument ran as follows. A government department is often in a monopoly position when it negotiates contracts with private firms. The government is 'virtually the only customer and the company's existence may turn on the fair allocation of work—whether there is grave bias within a Department for example'.[2]

Such bias, Sir John Foster suggested, might take the form of contracts in a certain area being 'allotted only to Labour sympathisers and Labour supporters'.[3] The Government might also discriminate by awarding licences to provide airline services to the nationalized corporations and not private firms. Again, the Government might say 'We shall not give contracts to any firms which have contributed to the Conservative Party'.[4] All these forms of discrimination should be capable of investigation by the Parliamentary Commissioner, who should be able to say in his report that the government department, in awarding a contract, had 'exercised discrimination which was not commercial in its character. It was non-commercial discrimination.'[5]

These arguments received no favourable response on the Labour side of the committee. Niall MacDermot said that he saw no reason

---

[1] See below p. 294.
[2] William Roots, The Parliamentary Commissioner Bill, Col. 461.
[3] Ibid., Col. 464.   [4] Ibid., Col. 465.   [5] Ibid., Col. 466.

'why the Government as a contractor should be placed in a worse position than that of a large private firm. If the Parliamentary Commissioner is not to be able to investigate complaints between private firms, should he be able to do so between a private firm and the Government in a contractual field?'[1]

Charles Fletcher-Cooke (Conservative) had asked whether it would not be appropriate for the Commissioner to inquire into complaints from small contractors that they had been unfairly kept off the Ministry of Works' list of contractors and builders. The Minister's reply to this was that he did not think the Parliamentary Commissioner was the person to decide the competence of a particular painter or craftsman, and whether or not he ought to be on the list. He emphasized also that there was no right to appear on government departments' lists. Departments should have the same commercial freedom as other bodies have to decide which tenders they should accept from contractors.

On the question of 'non-commercial discrimination' raised by Sir John Foster, the Minister answered that the right person to investigate this was the Comptroller and Auditor-General. His officers are placed permanently in the departments to exercise surveillance over contract procedures. One of their functions is to see that the commercial interests of the Government, and therefore of the taxpayers, are not prejudiced by discrimination, of the wrong kind, in the making of contracts.

The Minister received strong support from two Labour backbenchers in resisting the amendment. Hugh Jenkins and Michael English had helped to bring about a Government defeat by abstaining in the division on the hospitals but Hugh Jenkins now told the committee: 'I rise to assure my honourable and learned Friend that my support for him on this occasion is not merely there, but enthusiastically there.'[2] Those who supported the amendment were apparently suggesting that contractors, in relation to the Government, needed 'some special looking after, and I suggest that, looking back over the past few years, the true facts seem to indicate the reverse—that the Government have been taken for a ride'. On the question of contributions by private firms to Conservative Party funds he said to the chairman of the committee: 'Perhaps you will permit me to say in passing that it causes me some grief that every time I drink half a pint of bitter in the House, I automatically and

[1] Ibid., Col. 794.   [2] Ibid., Col. 468.

inadvertently make a small contribution towards the Conservative Party Fund through Messrs. Whitbread. I little care for that.'[1]

When the division took place on the question 'That the words proposed to be left out stand part of the Schedule', nine Labour members voted for the motion and seven Conservatives against. The division had taken place entirely on party lines. The Conservatives, in championing the cause of the contractors, both large and small, were speaking for a section of the population in which Conservative affiliations are widespread. While, however, the Minister made no concession to the main argument advanced by the Conservatives in this debate, he did promise to consider a point raised by Sir Hugh Lucas-Tooth. Sir Hugh had argued that the phrase 'Action in matters relating to contractual or other commercial transactions' was too wide. He suggested that this could prevent the Parliamentary Commissioner from looking into cases like Crichel Down where there had been compulsory acquisition of land by the Government, but where there had also been contractual and commercial transactions at some stage in the case. He also mentioned, in this connection, his own experience when a public authority had told him that they could acquire a house of his compulsorily but they were prepared to bargain with him. He did so bargain and sold the house in the ordinary way. Was this then a commercial transaction? Where was the line to be drawn?

The Minister promised to look at these points and see if any amendment of the paragraph would be desirable. He was as good as his word. In the Act, as finally approved, the wording of paragraph 9 was extended to make clear that while contractual or other commercial transactions were excluded from investigation by the Parliamentary Commissioner, this did not apply to:

'(a) the acquisition of land compulsorily or in circumstances in which it could be acquired compulsorily;

(b) the disposal as surplus of land acquired compulsorily or in such circumstances as aforesaid.'

This covered the Crichel Down type of case. In this case, it will be recalled, land had been compulsorily acquired by one government department and another government department later refused to return it to its former owner.[2] It would have been a telling indictment of the Act if it could have been said that it did not allow the

---

[1] Ibid., Cols. 468–9.   [2] See above p. 4.

Parliamentary Commissioner to look at a Crichel Down type of case. The Government was wise to make a concession on this issue.

The division on paragraph 9 was taken at the very end of the ninth sitting of the standing committee. The tenth and final sitting which took place on Tuesday morning, 29 November 1966, was given over entirely to discussion of paragraph 10 of Schedule 3. This paragraph excluded:

Action taken in respect of appointments or removals, pay, discipline, superannuation, or other personnel matters in relation to:

(a) service in any of the armed forces of the Crown, including reserve and auxiliary and cadet forces;

(b) service in any office or employment under the Crown or under any authority listed in Schedule 2 to this Act; or

(c) service in any office or employment, or under any contract for services, in respect of which power to take action, or to approve the action to be taken, in such matters is vested in Her Majesty, any Minister of the Crown or any such authority as aforesaid.

Alexander Lyon (Labour) had put down an amendment to delete this whole paragraph. He was again, however, a little late in arriving at the committee and Antony Buck (Conservative) moved the Amendment in Lyon's absence. Buck explained that procedurally he needed to do this although the amendments which the Conservatives favoured were not quite so wide. They considered that it would be an embarrassment to the Parliamentary Commissioner if he were to be called upon to investigate disciplinary matters in the Armed Forces. They, therefore, favoured retaining this exclusion alone in paragraph 10. Otherwise they thought that the Parliamentary Commissioner should be able to look at personnel matters in the Armed Forces and in the Civil Service.

When Alexander Lyon arrived, he told the committee that he, too, favoured excluding discipline in the Armed Forces from the Parliamentary Commissioner's scrutiny. He said that his interest in bringing personnel matters in the Civil Service in 'came about because I have a constituent who, for thirty years, has been waiting for justice in relation to the reason why he was dismissed from the Civil Service'.[1] This man had been employed as a messenger in a defence establishment. He was dismissed, allegedly on medical grounds, and he always maintained that the real reason was political

[1] Ibid., Col. 480.

victimization because he was organizing union activities in his department of the Civil Service.

Lyon told the committee that he had looked into the case as closely as possible and so had three of the previous Members who had represented York. The man concerned had been waiting for years 'since the first mooting, for an Ombudsman who would look into the matter on his behalf. I have now pointed out to him that this paragraph in the Schedule would exclude the case which he alleges. He wrote to me only yesterday to ask me to see if I could have the paragraph revised.'[1]

Taking the argument to a wider plane, he said that he could not accept the argument that the paragraph was basically on the same footing as paragraph 9. While it was, in his opinion, reasonably argued that the Government, as contractor, should not be in a different position from any other contractor, it was not reasonable to say that the Government, as an employer, should not be in the same position as any other employer.

A member of the Armed Forces, for example, had to sign a contract but he could not 'break the contract and come out of the Army without the permission of the Government, otherwise he is liable to be prosecuted for a military quasi-criminal offence'.[2] Even within the Civil Service the normal rights of an employee are limited in many ways.

All the members of the committee who followed him in the debate, except of course the Minister, took a similar view supporting deletion of the whole of paragraph 10 except for the provision excluding discipline in the Armed Forces. These members were, on the Conservative side, Anthony Grant, Sir Hugh Lucas-Tooth, Dame Joan Vickers, Cranley Onslow, Sir John Foster, and William Roots. On the Labour side, David Weitzman supported Alexander Lyon.

Dame Joan Vickers told the committee that there were about 22,000 people in the city of Plymouth, for which she is a Member, who would be affected by the paragraph since they were Civil Servants. At least 18,000 of these were industrial Civil Servants, earning in many cases quite low wages. She had taken up numerous cases of grievance from such constituents and thought the need for the Parliamentary Commissioner to be able to investigate their grievances was plain.

Niall MacDermot told the committee that the Staff Side of the

---

[1] Ibid., Col. 480.   [2] Ibid., Col. 482.

Civil Service National Whitley Council had been consulted on the question of whether they thought the Parliamentary Commissioner should be able to investigate personnel matters in the Civil Service. They had said they did not think it would be appropriate and that they wished to maintain the existing procedures for negotiation and appeal within the Civil Service.

The Minister greatly surprised members of the committee when he then read from *Estacode*, the volume which brings together all rules affecting the Civil Service. He quoted from a rule which he said had been in existence since 1922. This rule stated that a Civil Servant 'must not attempt to bring political or other outside influence to support or advance his individual claims as a civil servant'. This meant that a Civil Servant should not raise his individual grievance with a Member of Parliament but that he could raise matters 'affecting the Service as a whole or affecting a particular group in the Service'.[1]

It was at once apparent that this rule was honoured much more in the breach than in the observance. David Weitzman told the committee that he had taken up at least half a dozen cases for Civil Servants and that reference had never been made to the rule. Dame Joan Vickers said that she had never been prevented in the past from taking up such cases and said she hoped she would not be prevented in future. Cranley Onslow told the committee that not only did he think it essential that it should be possible for a Civil Servant to take his case to an M.P. if he was dissatisfied with the treatment he had received from the internal review procedure, but if he was approached about such cases he would continue to take them up with Ministers, whether or not he was told it was wrong to do so.[2]

The Minister's argument was that since Civil Servants were prevented by the rule in *Estacode* from approaching Members of Parliament with their individual grievances about their treatment in the Service, they could not be allowed to complain to the Parliamentary Commissioner for whom the only approach permissible was through a Member of Parliament. This brought an interesting side issue into the debate. Sir John Foster pointed out that if the Bill had permitted citizens to approach the Parliamentary Commissioner directly as happened in Denmark, then Niall MacDermot's argument would have no force. He mentioned that the Danish Parliamentary Commissioner was at that moment sitting in the room listening to

[1] Ibid., Col. 491.   [2] Ibid., Col. 508.

the debate, although he could not, of course, take part in the debate and confirm what Sir John had said.

Sir John Foster commented that he personally thought 'the House made a mistake in restricting the Parliamentary Commissioner to being a servant of the House', but he thought that in this matter he was in a minority on both sides of the House, and on both sides of the committee.[1] Dame Joan Vickers then commented drily that she was sorry then that Sir John Foster had not supported her amendment to allow complaints to be made directly to the Parliamentary Commissioner by members of the public. Later in the debate, Cranley Onslow told the committee that he had been powerfully influenced by Sir John Foster's analysis and indicated that he too saw the value of providing for direct access to the Parliamentary Commissioner.[2]

Two further issues were clarified during the debate. The Minister was asked by Antony Buck to explain why the Civil Service Commission was included among the departments which could be investigated by the Commissioner while appointments and other personnel matters in the Civil Service were excluded by paragraph 10. MacDermot explained that complaints against the Civil Service Commission could be investigated in so far as they related to the process of selecting people for entry into the Civil Service. This fitted in with the Government's conception that complaints which arose out of the relationship between Government and the governed should be capable of investigation by the Parliamentary Commissioner, but complaints which arose out of any employer-employee relationship should not.

The Minister was asked by David Weitzman to explain the obscure wording of Subsection (c) of paragraph 10.[3] MacDermot explained that the reference here to 'service in any office or employment—in respect of which power to take action—is vested in Her Majesty, any Minister of the Crown, etc.' applied to such matters as complaints about police pensions in the Metropolitan Police and teachers' pensions. These matters could be subject to investigation by the Commissioner if they were not expressly excluded in the paragraph, because of the general powers possessed by the Home Secretary in Metropolitan Police affairs and by the Minister of Education in the question of teachers' superannuation. If these matters were not excluded there would be an anomalous situation in

---

[1] Ibid., Col. 498.   [2] Ibid., Col. 507.   [3] See above p. 162.

which pension questions in the Metropolitan Police could be considered by the Parliamentary Commissioner, and teachers' pensions could be considered, but not those of Civil Servants.

These explanations, and the debate as a whole, helped to enlighten the critics of paragraph 10 but did nothing to convince them of its necessity. The Minister's arguments for excluding personnel matters in the Civil Service made no impression on his critics. On the question of excluding non-disciplinary matters in the Armed Forces, MacDermot's arguments were that the Parliamentary Commissioner in New Zealand could not consider this field, and that it would be difficult to separate personnel matters which did not have a disciplinary content from those which did.

Alexander Lyon told the committee that he did not find these arguments convincing. Neither did any other member of the committee who spoke in the debate. When the issue was put to the committee in a division, there was a tie. The seven Conservative members present voted against leaving paragraph 10 unchanged, seven Labour members voted in favour. Alexander Lyon and David Weitzman, on the Labour side, abstained.

The chairman of the committee, Grant Ferris, then announced, as stated in the Report, 'that he would vote for the original form of the Schedule, in order that the Amendment might be further considered at a later stage by the House, and that accordingly he declared himself with the Ayes'.[1] This is the normal practice for chairmen when there is a tie. By dint, therefore, of his casting vote paragraph 10 was approved. It was not amended at a subsequent stage and was eventually incorporated in the Act without change. The decision was, therefore, maintained to exclude the Parliamentary Commissioner from looking into personnel matters in the Civil Service and in the Armed Forces.

When the Select Committee on the Parliamentary Commissioner came to look at these exclusions, discussion centred on much the same issues as were raised in standing committee. As with exclusion of the hospitals, the Select Committee reported, in January 1970, that exclusion of personnel matters in the Civil Service and the Armed Forces from investigation by the Parliamentary Commissioner was unsound.[2] No decision came from the Government until May 1971. A White Paper then announced that the Heath Government had decided not to allow the Parliamentary Commissioner

[1] Ibid., Col. 513.   [2] See below pp. 301–2.

to look at personnel matters in the Civil Service and the Armed Forces.

When paragraph 10 had been approved by the committee, by dint of the chairman's casting vote, there remained to consider only paragraph 11 which excluded from consideration by the Commissioner 'The grant of honours, awards or privileges within the gift of the Crown, including the grant of Royal Charters'. Alexander Lyon had an amendment down to delete this paragraph, but he now announced that he would not move his amendment. But since its subject matter was the grant of honours, he thought it would be appropriate for him to say how much the committee had enjoyed the conduct of the case for the Government by the Financial Secretary and that they ought to pay due honour to him for the charm and courtesy he had shown.

Niall MacDermot then thanked the chairman for the way in which he had conducted the proceedings of the committee and was supported in this by the Conservative leader, William Roots. The chairman, in his reply, said that it had been for him 'a most agreeable experience to preside over a Committee of which one can say that it has represented Parliament working absolutely at its best'.[1]

An evaluation of the whole legislative process in the passage of this Bill will be made in Chapter XVI.[2] At this point, we can sum up briefly on the work of the standing committee. We can say first of all that the Bill had been very fully discussed. Two important amendments had been carried against the Minister: David Weitzman's amendment to Clause 5 which allowed the Commissioner to look at something which could go to a tribunal, and the Conservative amendment which brought the Hospital Service within the Commissioner's purview. This amendment was to be reversed at report stage, but Weitzman's amendment was to stand with only minor modification. An important change in the Bill had been suggested by Michael English. This was the introduction of power to take out by Order in Council, any of the spheres, listed in Schedule 3, from which the Parliamentary Commissioner was excluded. The Minister had been persuaded to accept this change under pressure, in particular from his own back-benchers, and was to carry out his promise to introduce the necessary amendment on Report.

He had also been induced, during the course of close scrutiny of the provisions in the Bill, to accept the need in principle for a great

[1] The Parliamentary Commissioner Bill, Col. 514. [2] See below pp. 340-2.

many minor changes advocated, in some cases by Conservative, and, in some cases by Labour members of the committee. The great majority of these promised changes were to be effected either at report stage in the Commons or in the Lords.

The chairman of the standing committee was, indeed, not exaggerating when he said that he had seen, in the consideration of this Bill, 'Parliament working absolutely at its best'. The members of standing committee B had been, over the ten sittings working co-operatively, probing the intentions of the Bill, working out its implications, and trying, often successfully, to persuade the Minister to modify provisions in the Bill.

X

THE REPORT STAGE AND THIRD READING IN THE COMMONS

THE Parliamentary Commissioner Bill was considered on report in the House of Commons on Tuesday, 24 January 1967, nearly two months after the Bill had been completed in standing committee. The report stage did not begin until 7.8 p.m. on that day, because discussion of the report stage of the Iron and Steel Bill, which had begun on 18 January and had extended over four Parliamentary days, had only just been completed. This illustrates the difference in the time taken, on report, on highly controversial measures such as the Iron and Steel Bill which proposed to renationalize large sectors of the iron and steel industry and a Bill such as the Parliamentary Commissioner Bill. The report stage of this Bill was completed in one evening, the debate extending over 4 hours 42 minutes from 7.8 p.m. to 11.50 p.m.

The procedure on report stage in the Commons differs from the procedure at the committee stage in that while in committee every clause and schedule of the Bill must be considered, at report stage only those clauses and schedules are considered to which new amendments have been put down. The first amendment which had been put down to the Parliamentary Commissioner Bill related to Subsection (3) of Clause 1. This proposed to make the Parliamentary Commissioner removable by Addresses from both Houses of Parliament instead of by an Address from the House of Commons as proposed in the Bill.

Quintin Hogg moved this amendment, for the Conservatives, pointing out that he was doing so in place of William Roots who was present in the House but, due to a temporary illness, did not feel able to move the amendment himself. Hogg recalled that, in the standing committee, there had been a tie when this amendment had been proposed. The chairman had then exercised his casting vote against the amendment, according to established procedure, in order to give a further opportunity for the question to be considered on report. He also recalled that in the division in standing committee, the Minister, Niall MacDermot, had voted with the Conservatives in favour of the amendment. He hoped that the Ministers would join them again in supporting the amendment.

The chief argument he advanced in favour of the amendment was that 'If the Parliamentary Commissioner is, in truth and in fact, to be independent of the Executive, his appointment should be not merely subject to the will of the Executive, his appointment should be not merely subject to the will of the majority of this House but to the will of Parliament.'[1] His position should be comparable to that of the judges of the High Court and of the Comptroller and Auditor-General, all of whom could only be removed by Addresses from both Houses of Parliament.

Richard Crossman, Lord President of the Council and Leader of the House, in replying, said that he agreed with this argument and advised the House to accept the amendment. Only short speeches were made by Sydney Silverman and David Weitzman in support of the view that removal should be by an Address from the House of Commons alone. The amendment was then accepted without a division.

No new amendment was put down to Clause 2. On Clause 3 (Administrative Provisions), the Financial Secretary to the Treasury moved a number of amendments whose object it was to make clear that the scope of investigations by the Parliamentary Commissioner would extend not only to the acts of officers themselves and of departments but to anyone acting 'as a statutory agent of the Department'.[2] Thus a local authority acting in any agency capacity for the Minister of Transport in doing trunk road work would be subject to investigation. So would the motoring associations, the A.A. and R.A.C., when exercising certain functions concerning international driving certificates.

The amendments he moved were also to Clauses 5, 11, and 12 making this position clear. They were in response to queries raised by Conservative members in standing committee and were now welcomed by William Roots on behalf of the Conservatives. They were agreed to without opposition.

The next amendment was moved to Clause 4 (Departments and Authorities Subject to Investigation) by Sir John Hobson on behalf of the Conservatives. He proposed to add the following words:

[1] H.C. Deb. Vol. 739, Col. 1351.   [2] Ibid., Col. 1359.

'Notwithstanding the provisions of this section and of section 5 of this Act the Commissioner shall have power to carry out any investigations directed by a Resolution passed by both Houses of Parliament and shall report thereon to both Houses as soon as his investigation has been completed.'

Sir John Hobson argued that the Government had been fairly successful in seeing that the powers of the Parliamentary Commissioner were constricted. The amendment would give power to both Houses to direct the Commissioner to undertake a special inquiry which would be outside the provisions of the Act.

At present, under the Tribunals of Inquiry Act, 1921, special inquiries could be commissioned by Parliament but these were 'a very heavy-handed hammer' which the recent Royal Commission, presided over by Lord Justice Salmon, had rightly said should be used only on the rarest occasions and on occasions of great public anxiety and interest. The amendment would help to fill the gap between inquiries under the 1921 Act and the Parliamentary Commissioner's limited field of investigation in the Bill under consideration.[1]

Leslie Hale (Labour) supported the amendment. He was highly critical of inquiries under the 1921 Act. He had been a legal adviser to John Belcher under the Lynskey Tribunal, commissioned under this Act. In his opinion, the whole inquiry had been a tragedy. The rules of evidence were perverted, roving questions were asked on subjects on which there had been no prior warning, and witnesses were brought when a promise had been given that they would not be asked to testify. For example, Mrs. Belcher was brought from her kitchen to testify against her husband who was a distinguished Minister of the Crown. He thought that a special inquiry in private by a trusted and independent person, such as the Parliamentary Commissioner, would be much to be preferred when it was advisable to have an exceptional inquiry outside the scope of the Act.[2]

Sir Hugh Lucas-Tooth (Conservative) then spoke to his own amendment which proposed that the Minister responsible for the department concerned should be empowered to authorize an inquiry which would not be permissible under the Act. He told the House that he supported the amendment moved by Sir John Hobson. His amendment went less far, but he thought that both amendments would improve the Bill and he hoped both would be approved.

[1] Ibid., Cols. 1360-2.   [2] Ibid., Cols. 1362-5.

Niall MacDermot, in replying, pointed out that the official Opposition amendment was similar to one which had been discussed in standing committee.[1] He pointed out that the Government was now proposing to give power to amend Schedule 3 by Order in Council and would shortly be bringing in an amendment to this effect. This would introduce greater flexibility and enable the powers of the Parliamentary Commissioner to be widened without the need for the passage of a new Act of Parliament.

He also argued that the Opposition amendment was an extremely far-reaching one. It would enable Parliament to disregard all the limitations in the Bill. For example, Parliament would be able to instruct the Commissioner to investigate the action of local authorities, nationalized industries, or private companies. The investigation need not be limited to maladministration, the consent of the person involved in the complaint need not be secured, the Parliamentary Commissioner could review decisions of the courts, and the time limits laid down in the Bill could be ignored.[2]

On the amendment proposed by Sir Hugh Lucas-Tooth, he criticized this proposal on the ground that it would lead Members to press Ministers to consent to investigations which would not otherwise be permitted under the Act. It would be better, rather than allowing special cases to be pleaded, to adopt the procedure of amending Schedule 3 by Order to allow a whole exempted category of cases to be brought in.

Antony Buck (Conservative) then argued that the Minister had shown 'a wild mistrust of Parliament. Does the hon. and learned Gentleman really think that Parliament will behave in such an irresponsible way as to call upon the Parliamentary Commissioner to investigate matters inappropriate to him? That view would seem to be something of an insult to Parliament. It is absurd that the Parliamentary Commissioner cannot be called upon by Parliament to investigate anything that Parliament wants.'[3]

This argument however did not impress Emlyn Hooson (Liberal).[4] In his view 'Parliament must be very careful not to give power for things to be done in its name, because one never knows what the

---

[1] See above pp. 115–8.
[2] H.C. Deb. Vol. 739, Cols. 1366–8.
[3] Ibid., Col. 1370.
[4] Emlyn Hooson Q.C. has represented Montgomery for the Liberals since 1962. He was called to the Bar in 1949. He is Liberal spokesman in the Commons on Wales, law, and agriculture.

future complexion of Parliament may be. I agree that it is hardly likely that a future Parliament would resort to measures which none of us here would approve of but nevertheless it remains our duty to make its task very hard if such a Parliament came about.' He thought that the principle stated by the Financial Secretary was absolutely right.[1]

When the Opposition amendment was put to the vote it was lost by 170 votes to 88. It was a straight party vote with Conservatives voting for the amendment and Labour Members against. However, Emlyn Hooson (Liberal) voted against the amendment and Leslie Hale, the Labour Member who had supported the amendment, did not vote. Sir Hugh Lucas-Tooth's amendment was not voted on.

No further amendment had been put down to Clause 4. The House then considered an amendment moved to Clause 5 (Matters Subject to Investigation) by the Financial Secretary. His amendment followed on from the changes which had been made to Subsection (2) of the Clause by David Weitzman's amendment in standing committee. As we have seen, this amendment had been carried, against the Minister, and had the effect of allowing the Parliamentary Commissioner to look, at his discretion, at cases in which there was the right of appeal either to a court of law or to an administrative tribunal.[2]

The Minister admitted that he had 'had a somewhat rough passage' on this question in the standing committee. He explained that the Bill originally provided that the Commissioner could look at a case which could have gone to a court of law, if he did not consider it reasonable for the complainant to take his case to the courts. It did not extend the same discretion to matters which could go to administrative tribunals.

The Government now accepted, in principle, the decision of the standing committee that courts of law and administrative tribunals should be placed on all fours in this question. One of the reasons for their acceptance was that he had now had the opportunity to consult the Secretary of the Council on Tribunals on the question of matters which could go to a tribunal being subject to investigation by the Commissioner, at his discretion. The Secretary of the Council on Tribunals had said that he saw no objection to this provision.

However, the effect of the amendments passed in standing committee was altogether too wide. They gave the Commissioner power

[1] Ibid., Cols. 1371–2.   [2] See above pp. 111–4.

to look at cases which had gone to the courts of law or to administrative tribunals; in other words, he could become a court of appeal from a court of law or a tribunal. The amendment which he now proposed would restrict him to looking, at his discretion, to cases which *could have gone* or *could go* to administrative tribunals.

David Weitzman told the Committee that he was disappointed at the Minister's amendment, although he recognized there was some advance over the position which the Minister had taken in standing committee. He did not attempt to divide the House on the issue and the Minister's amendment was accepted.

The Government's amendment should not therefore be seen as a reversal of what had been achieved in standing committee. The final result still constituted an important concession to the views put forward by David Weitzman and his supporters in the standing committee.

One further matter of interest was brought up in this debate. MacDermot maintained the view, although challenged on this point by Weitzman, that, under the Bill, although the Commissioner would not be able to act as an appellate tribunal from an administrative tribunal, he would be able to investigate an administrative failure in the steps leading up to the actual tribunal proceedings. He could, for example, investigate a complaint that a department had failed to lay the proper facts before a tribunal.[1]

The next amendment to be taken also related to Clause 5. The Financial Secretary to the Treasury moved the insertion of a new Subsection (4) to Clause 5 which read as follows:

'(4) Nothing in this section shall be construed as authorising or requiring the Commissioner to review by way of appeal any decision taken by a government department or other authority in the exercise of a discretion vested in that department or authority.'

He said this amendment was 'largely a drafting matter and seeks to overcome the criticism that was made both on Second Reading and in Committee that the Bill as drafted does nowhere in terms exclude the discretionary decisions from the scope of the Parliamentary Commissioner's powers'.[2] He did not say who had made this criticism, but Sir Hugh Lucas-Tooth (Conservative) had argued that the provision in the Bill, in Clause 5, which empowered the

---

[1] H.C. Deb. Vol. 739, Col. 1382.   [2] Ibid., Col. 1383.

Commissioner to investigate complaints from members of the public (when forwarded to him by M.P.s) who claim 'to have sustained injustice in consequence of maladministration' would mean that the Commissioner would have to consider 'hundreds of thousands of cases' every year in which members of the public are complaining to M.P.s about bad decisions by Ministers.[1]

This interpretation had somewhat alarmed the Financial Secretary and his team of advisers. The Government's intention had been to distinguish clearly between maladministration which could be investigated by the Parliamentary Commissioner and discretionary decisions, taken without maladministration, which would not be subject to investigation. The intention to make this distinction had been stated in the White Paper.

The Ministerial team had now come round to the view, as a result of the discussion in standing committee, that this distinction had not been clearly made in the Bill. They genuinely saw the amendment now proposed as a drafting amendment, or as one member of the team put it to this author, as a declaratory amendment.

This was not, however, how it was seen on most of the Conservative benches where its introduction raised a veritable storm of criticism. Sir John Hobson told the House that as a result of this amendment 'the ombudsman will be almost totally excluded from the files of Government Departments'.[2] Pretty well everything in a department is disposed of on the wish of the Minister. When the Ombudsman asked him why something was done in a certain way, he would be able to say that it was done at his discretion. Then the Parliamentary Commissioner would be able to look no further into the matter.

Daniel Awdry (Conservative) said that if the amendment was accepted it would 'undermine the very purpose of the Bill . . . We will emasculate the Bill if we take away from the Parliamentary Commissioner the right to look at the exercise of a discretion by the Minister'.[3] Here Richard Crossman intervened to deny that this was so. He quoted his own statement in the second reading debate that 'Discretionary decision, properly exercised which the complainant dislikes but cannot fault the manner in which it was taken, is

---

[1] Official Report of Standing Committee B. Parliamentary Commissioner Bill, Col. 61.
[2] H.C. Deb. Vol. 739, Col. 1385.
[3] Ibid., Cols. 1387 and 1388. Daniel Awdry has represented Chippenham since 1962. He is a solicitor.

excluded by the Clause.' The present amendment did 'not alter anything but merely makes unambiguous what we candidly told hon. Members was the way we should deal with the issue'.[1] It was the approach advocated by the Whyatt Report which the Government had accepted.

Emlyn Hooson (Liberal) then argued that 'If the Financial Secretary considers that the Amendment is not really necessary, it should be left out because the view is widely held that it will circumscribe the powers of the Parliamentary Commissioner and provide a shield behind which civil servants will be able to hide for many weeks.'[2] He argued that Civil Servants would, as a delaying tactic, claim that they were exercising their discretion, in order to avoid investigation by the Commissioner.

Sir Lionel Heald (Conservative) also told the House that he felt great anxiety about acceptance of the amendment. He recalled that Michael Stewart (who at the time of this debate was Foreign Secretary) had written in the *New Statesman* in September 1964 that 'The Commissioner will be concerned with those episodes where all the authorities have behaved correctly, yet the result is absurd or unjust.' Sir Lionel Heald then went on:

The right hon. Gentleman, for whom we have the greatest respect and who takes a keen interest in the rights of the individual, did not talk about 'maladministration'. He did not use any ambiguous language of that kind. He made it clear that if there had been an injustice it would be the job of the Labour Government's great Parliamentary Commissioner to right it. Since then we have been plunging in this morass of the expression 'maladministration'.[3]

Harold Gurden (Conservative) who followed him told the House that 'The Amendment proves the critics right when they said that in the production of the Bill the Government had gone back on their promise to the electorate . . . Almost the whole of the Bill will be pretty useless if the Amendment is passed.'[4]

Quintin Hogg, winding up for the Conservatives, went even further. His school days are clearly a vivid memory for him and he now found one of the expressions he used at school most appropriate.

[1] H.C. Deb. Vol. 739, Col. 1388.   [2] Ibid., Col. 1390.
[3] Ibid., Col. 1390.   [4] Ibid., Col. 1392.

When I was at my first school, we had a rather jolly schoolboy expression for 'swindle'. We called it 'swiz'. A swiz was not something which involved any particular moral turpitude on the part of those who were guilty of the swiz but meant that those who were the victims of the swiz somehow felt with justification that they had been swindled.

As the House knows from my speech on Second Reading, I have always regarded the ombudsman as a swiz. Now we have arrived at the moment of truth.... Despite what has been said by one of my hon. Friends, I agree that it is a drafting Amendment. The Bill was always drafted to be a swiz, and now it is spelt into the Bill. I shall vote against it.[1]

His position was essentially different from that of the other Conservatives who had spoken in the debate. All of them, including, in fact, Harold Gurden had, in principle, supported the Bill and were disappointed with the shape it was now taking with the introduction of this latest amendment. Quintin Hogg, however, had always been opposed to it and now cast himself in the role of a vindicated Cassandra.

Niall MacDermot, in winding up the debate, made the best of a difficult situation. Like Crossman, he commented on the fact that the Bill was based upon the proposals in the Whyatt Report. The Macmillan Government, of which Quintin Hogg had been a member, had rejected the Whyatt Report proposals but not on the ground that they would be a 'swiz'. In fact they had dismissed them on the quite different grounds that they would seriously interfere with the prompt and efficient dispatch of public business.

It was significant that in the debate on the amendment there had not been one speech from a Labour back-bencher. Five Conservatives and one Liberal had spoken in the debate and all of them were opposed to the amendment. Only the two Ministers took part from the Government side.

When the amendment was put to the vote it was carried by 156 votes to 92. Among the Labour Members who had sat on the standing committee, there were some who abstained on this vote. David Weitzman and Sidney Silverman were two who were present in the debate but did not vote in this division. Michael English, Alexander Lyon, and Paul Rose did, however, vote for the amendment. If their intention was to support the Government at this stage but to hope for a later concession, this hope was to be realized. As we shall see, the unfavourable reception which the amendment received

[1] Ibid., Cols. 1392-3.

in the House was to be mirrored in the Press. When the Bill was under discussion in the Lords the amendment was taken out again, and a more acceptable substitute was inserted in Clause 12.[1]

Richard Crossman found himself in quite a different situation when moving the next amendment which was also to Clause 5. This amendment proposed to insert a new subsection as follows:

'(4) Her Majesty may by Order in Council amend the said Schedule 3 so as to exclude from the provisions of that Schedule such actions or matters as may be described in the Order; and any statutory instrument made by virtue of this subsection shall be subject to annulment in pursuance of a resolution of either House of Parliament.'

He was able to tell the House that this amendment changed the Bill in an important respect in that it would make it possible to extend the areas within which the Parliamentary Commissioner could investigate, by means of an Order in Council, without the passage of a new Bill. He hoped that Members of the Opposition who had been so critical of the previous amendment would applaud his efforts in this amendment to widen the extent of the Bill.

William Roots and Cranley Onslow who followed him did not, however, feel able to applaud the Minister. William Roots said that he did give him credit for bringing forward the amendment but pointed out that the absence of such a provision 'had caused great concern among the Opposition Members of the Standing Committee'.[2] He concluded 'The Amendment gives a glimmer that it may be possible to correct the overlimited ambit of the Commissioner's powers on which both sides of the Committee were thoroughly dissatisfied. To that extent the Amendment is welcome.'[3]

Cranley Onslow (Conservative) took a similar view. No one else contributed to debate on this amendment. There was no speech from a Labour member. Not even Michael English who, as we have seen, was the real author of the amendment rose to speak.[4] Back-benchers on the Government side are, of course, under some pressure from their Whips not to speak too much when business is behind the clock, as it was on this parliamentary day, and the House is likely to sit late. The amendment was agreed without a division.

The next amendment was to Clause 6 (Provisions Relating to Complaints), and was introduced by the Financial Secretary. The

---

[1] See below pp. 223 and 225.   [2] H.C. Deb. Vol. 739, Col. 1398.
[3] Ibid., Col. 1399.   [4] See above p. 117.

Minister, in fact, moved two amendments which had the effect of giving the power to investigate actions taking place on ships or aircraft, or on the part of the Continental Shelf which contains an installation or designated area within the meaning of the Continental Shelf Act, 1964. These amendments had been suggested in standing committee and were now agreed to without a division.[1]

No new amendment had been put down to Clause 7 (Procedure in Respect of Investigations). The next amendment was to Clause 8 (Evidence). This amendment was also moved by the Minister to meet a point raised in standing committee. It made it clear that a reference to Cabinet proceedings would not be used to withhold from the Commissioner the whole of documents which otherwise were not related to Cabinet proceedings. The amendment met the point raised in standing committee by William Roots (Conservative).[2] The amendment was approved without a division.

No new amendment was put down to Clause 9 (Obstruction and Contempt). On Clause 10 (Reports by Commissioner), Niall Mac-Dermot moved an amendment to insert a new section (2) worded as follows:

'(2) In any case where the Commissioner conducts an investigation under this Act, he shall also send a report of the results of the investigation to the principal officer of the department or authority concerned and to any other person who is alleged in the relevant complaint to have taken or authorized the action complained of.'

The Financial Secretary told the House that the amendment arose indirectly from a point made in standing committee. In the Bill, as drafted, the Parliamentary Commissioner was instructed to send a report of the result of his investigation to the Member who had forwarded a complaint to him, but this was all.

Niall MacDermot had told the standing committee that it was not necessary to state in the Bill that the Commissioner's report of an investigation should also be sent to the department concerned and the officer named in the complaint, although this procedure would be followed.[3] The Government, it seems, had now decided that it would be wise to require that this should be done. The amendment was agreed to.

The next amendment, moved by Niall MacDermot, was also to Clause 10. It was, he told the House, a new point which had arisen

---

[1] See above pp. 122–4.   [2] See above pp. 127–8.
[3] The Parliamentary Commissioner Bill, Col. 288.

from a suggestion made by the Parliamentary Commissioner designate (Sir Edmund Compton). The Bill as drafted allowed him to make three kinds of reports: (1) results reports in individual cases which would be sent to the M.P. and the department concerned, (2) special reports which he would lay before the House in cases where he had found an injustice but it had not been remedied, (3) an annual report which he would lay before the House.

The amendment proposed that the Commissioner should also have power, from time to time, to lay such other reports on the performance of his functions as he thinks fit. Such reports would enable the Commissioner to draw attention to the way in which the Act was working. They would play an important part in the process of working out procedural conventions for the handling of individual cases, in which the Commissioner, the Select Committee, and the House would be engaged. The amendment was agreed to.

The Parliamentary Commissioner has not made frequent use of this power. In his first four years of operation, he made only three reports of this kind. These were on Aircraft Noise, Sachsenhausen, and the Duccio Painting.[1] The Sachsenhausen report was of major importance while the other two were of interest but of less significance. While it is possible to argue that the Parliamentary Commissioner might make more use of his power to make such reports, there is no doubt that it is a very valuable power. The addition of this amendment is an instance of the advantage of already having a Commissioner designate while the Bill was passing through Parliament. In fact, his advice was often sought behind the scenes. In the case of this amendment, it was also communicated to the House.

Niall MacDermot next moved a long amendment to Clause 10 modifying the provision in the Bill which made reports by the Commissioner, and communications between the Commissioner and M.P.s (in relation to complaints), absolutely privileged. The Financial Secretary told the House that the amendment was now being introduced to meet criticisms made in standing committee that this provision was too wide. The new amendment had the effect of confining absolute privilege only to the following categories of publication or communication: (1) publication of a report by the Parliamentary Commissioner to the House, (2) communications between M.P.s and the Commissioner, or his officers, about complaints, (3) publication of a report by the M.P. by sending it to the

[1] See below pp. 247, 262–8 and 311.

complainant, (4) communication of his report by the Commissioner to the department and the Civil Servant complained against.

Percy Grieve, Conservative Member for Solihull, had put down an amendment to this amendment.[1] This sought to exclude the second category, communications between M.P.s and the Commissioner, from being absolutely privileged. In speaking to his amendment, he argued that it was wrong to make communications between M.P.s and the Commissioner absolutely privileged when communications between M.P.s and Ministers were not so privileged. When an M.P. wrote to a Minister, or to the Commissioner, it was sufficient for him to be protected by the ordinary law of qualified privilege under which the M.P.'s action in forwarding a complaint could not be impugned unless he made himself guilty of malice in so doing.[2]

Percy Grieve was supported in this view by two other Conservatives, Sir Douglas Glover and Ian Percival.[3] Sir Douglas Glover instanced a hypothetical case in which he supposed that he, as an M.P., had received a letter of complaint from a constituent about a certain insurance company. Supposing that he had then written to the Parliamentary Commissioner saying that this was one of the 'shark' companies and that he ought to investigate. Supposing that it then turned out that this 'was one of the soundest and straightest companies in the country. In that circumstance I ought not to be covered by privilege, because I am making a selective judgement on the results of the publicity which has gone out, and I am ruining the reputation of a perfectly sound firm.'[4]

Leslie Hale (Labour) took a different view and supported the Minister's amendment.[5] He received hundreds of letters from constituents and many of them concerned urgent matters. It was his duty, in common with that of other M.P.s, to pass on such complaints and it was impossible for him to check on the accuracy of allegations made. It was therefore only reasonable that his communications with the Parliamentary Commissioner should be absolutely privileged.

[1] Percival Grieve Q.C. has been Conservative M.P. for Solihull since 1964. He has been Recorder of Northampton since 1965.

[2] H.C. Deb. Vol. 739, Cols. 1406–8.

[3] Sir Douglas Glover was Conservative M.P. for Ormskirk from 1953 to 1970. He was a Director of the Anglo-Dominion Finance Company.

Ian Percival Q.C. was first elected for Southport in 1959. He is Vice-Chairman of the Conservative M.P.s' Legal Committee.

[4] H.C. Deb. Vol. 739, Cols. 1408–9.

[5] Leslie Hale was, at this time, Labour M.P. for Oldham West. He was first elected to the Commons in 1945. He resigned his seat in 1968 because of ill health. He is a solicitor.

Niall MacDermot in winding up the debate took a similar view. He pointed out that 'Not all Members of Parliament are trained lawyers and many hon. Members identify themselves strongly with constituents on whose behalf they take up cases.' They should be free to communicate with the Commissioner without running the risk of having proceedings for libel taken against them.

When the Minister's amendments were put to the House, they were carried without a division. Similarly, Percy Grieve's amendment to the amendment was defeated by a voice vote. It was evident therefore that the view put forward by the three Conservative members was not the official Opposition view. Indeed, MacDermot's amendment met the criticism put forward by the chief Conservative critic of this aspect of the Bill in standing committee, Sir John Foster.[1]

The next amendment, moved by Niall MacDermot, was to Clause 11 (Provision for Secrecy of Information). This was also an amendment which the Financial Secretary had undertaken at committee stage to introduce later. It dealt with a point which had been raised by Sir John Foster by making clear that proceedings for perjury could only be taken under the Act when it was alleged that there had been perjury in the course of an investigation by the Commissioner, or in respect of information he had obtained. The amendment was agreed to.

To Clause 12 (Interpretation) there was only one small amendment, which was consequential on amendments made earlier. This amendment indicated that the word 'officer' in the Bill includes employee. It was moved by the Financial Secretary and agreed to without debate.

There remained only the Schedules to the Bill to be considered on report. No amendment had been put down to Schedule 1, 'Pensions and Other Benefits' of the Commissioner. To Schedule 2, 'Departments and Authorities Subject to Investigation', an amendment was moved by William Roots for the Conservatives. This was to insert 'Land Commission'. MacDermot replied that this could not be done because the Land Commission Bill had not yet become an Act of Parliament. William Roots therefore withdrew his amendment.

Three further amendments were moved to this Schedule. The first, moved by the Financial Secretary, added the Lord President of the Council's Office to the Authorities subject to investigation. A

[1] See above pp. 133–4.

further amendment made clear that this did not include the Privy Council Office. These amendments gave an effect to an undertaking, made in standing committee, that the Lord President's own office would be made subject to investigation in common with those of other Ministers without Portfolio.

A third amendment, also moved by the Minister, also gave an effect to an undertaking made in standing committee. This made it clear, as MacDermot told the House, that 'where there has been a transfer of functions from a Department which has ceased to exist to a present Department, the Commissioner's powers in relation to the present Department will include those transferred functions.'[1] All three amendments were agreed to.

As in standing committee, much more attention was given at report stage to Schedule 3 (Matters not Subject to Investigation). The first amendment had been put down to paragraph 2 of the Schedule which excluded the actions of consular officials abroad from the Parliamentary Commissioner's scrutiny. Roots's amendment sought to include the activities of consuls in so far as they affect 'the legal rights or status of a citizen of the United Kingdom'.

Niall MacDermot, in replying, recalled that he had told the standing committee that he would see 'whether it would be possible to bring some of the activities of consuls within the scope of the Commissioner's investigation'.[2] But on looking further into it, he had to advise the House that 'it would not be workable, certainly at present, for us to include consular activities within the scope of the Commissioner's powers'.[3]

One reason was severely practical. There are over 400 consular posts throughout the world ranging from such places 'as Oulu in North Finland to Gallegos on the southern tip of the Argentine, from Katmandu to Tampico to Suva—in fact, to all quarters of the globe'. In view of the impracticality of having the Commissioner flying to all parts of the world to investigate complaints against consuls, he had suggested to the standing committee that it might be possible to deal with such cases by a different procedure relying largely on correspondence.

This idea had not found favour with the Foreign Office who felt it would be very unfair to their staff. They considered that a consul should have the same rights in an investigation as any other Civil

---

[1] H.C. Deb. Vol. 739, Col. 1419.
[2] Ibid., Col. 1419.   [3] Ibid., Col. 1420.

Servant: in other words that a consul should be able, in person, to answer the case brought against him.

The Parliamentary Commissioner designate also did not favour the idea. The Financial Secretary told the House that 'the Commissioner designate himself did not relish at all the prospect of a kind of second-class investigation which he would be expected to make in relation to consular activities and be expected to make a report and reach a decision without being free to investigate the matter as fully as he would in any other case'.[1] Finally, MacDermot reiterated the point which he had made in standing committee that the activities of consuls were 'to a high degree dependent on the actions of local authorities and local persons for which we are not responsible and over which we have no control and which it would not be appropriate for the Commissioner to investigate'.[2]

The four Conservatives who followed in the debate, Sir Lionel Heald, Cranley Onslow, Sir Douglas Glover, and Robert Cooke were not at all convinced by these arguments.[3] Sir Lionel Heald told the House that 'A protest should be made against probably one of the most bureaucratic speeches that has been made in the House for a long time.'[4] Administrative convenience should count for little where the legal rights of a British subject were involved. The speeches from the three other Conservatives were in a similar vein. No one else spoke to the amendment and it was negatived without a division.

No amendments had been put down to paragraphs 3 to 7 of the Schedule excluding from investigation such matters as government in the colonies, extradition, the decision to take civil or criminal proceedings and the exercise of the prerogative of mercy.[5]

The next amendment put down was moved by Richard Crossman. This sought to reinsert the paragraph which had been taken out in standing committee: this was the paragraph which excluded from investigation the regional hospitals boards, teaching hospitals, hospital management committees, etc.

---

[1] Ibid., Cols. 1420–1.

[2] Ibid., Col. 1421.

[3] Robert Cooke (Conservative) was first elected for Bristol West in 1957. He was Chairman of the Conservative M.P.s' Broadcasting and Communications Committee from 1963 to 1966. He is a landowner and horticulturist.

[4] H.C. Deb. Vol. 739, Col. 1424.

[5] See above pp. 149–53 for an account of discussion on these exclusions in standing committee.

In a brief speech, Crossman told the House that the main argument against including the hospital service was that, if it were in, one part of the Health Service would be subject to investigation by the Commissioner while the general practitioner services and the local authority health services were not. He would like to see the hospital service and local government each having their own commissioner. So he thought that it was better 'on balance that these services should be excluded now, always on the understanding that at a later date they can be put under the Commissioner by order of the House'.[1]

In the debate that followed every speaker condemned the Government's move to reverse, in this amendment, the decision taken in standing committee to include the hospitals. Those who took part in the debate were, on the Conservative side, William Roots, Sir Douglas Glover, Dame Joan Vickers, Sir Lionel Heald, and Quintin Hogg. From the Labour benches, Michael English, Dr. David Owen, Mrs. Lena Jeger, Alexander Lyon, and Laurence Pavitt were equally critical of the Government's move. The one Liberal speaker, Emlyn Hooson, took a similar view, indeed he used the same words to describe the amendment as had been used by William Roots and Michael English. It was 'a highly retrograde step'.[2]

Crossman's arguments in favour of excluding the hospitals were demolished as effectively as similar arguments had been when they were advanced in standing committee by Niall MacDermot. Michael English pointed out that there were many fields, transport was an example, where functions were divided between local authorities and the Crown. Yet this was not made an argument for saying that the Ministry of Transport should be excluded from investigation by the Parliamentary Commissioner.[3]

Mrs. Lena Jeger pointed out that the Swedish Ombudsman can investigate complaints against hospital authorities.[4] Dame Joan Vickers gave an example from the New Zealand Ombudsman's reports of complaints from hospital patients which he had investigated.[5] Dr. David Owen's contribution was of particular interest since he was the first hospital doctor to speak in the House on this subject. He had been a neurological registrar at St. Thomas's Hospital, London.[6] He thought that the case for excluding the

---

[1] H.C. Deb. Vol. 739, Col. 1428.   [2] Ibid., Col. 1432.
[3] Ibid., Col. 1430.   [4] Ibid., Col. 1435.   [5] Ibid., Col. 1436.
[6] Dr. David Owen (Labour) was first elected for Plymouth, Sutton, in 1966.

hospitals from investigation by the Parliamentary Commissioner had 'not truly been made out'.[1]

Another speaker with a special interest in the Health Service was Laurence Pavitt. He spoke as a member of a regional hospital board and, for many years, a member of a hospital management committee. He was chairman of the Labour M.P.s' health services group and had been National Organizer of the Medical Practitioners' Union from 1956 to 1959.[2] He wanted an Ombudsman for the hospital service and did not agree with those who, like Alexander Lyon, argued that the Ombudsman should be concerned only with administrative but not clinical matters. He thought both could be brought within his ambit.

This was one side issue on which there was disagreement amongst some of the speakers. William Roots argued for such a distinction and the official Opposition amendment sought to bring administrative, but not clinical matters, in the hospitals within the Commissioner's sphere of investigation. Michael English, like Laurence Pavitt, opposed the idea of making such a distinction.

In fact, the amendment to the amendment was not moved by the Opposition, neither was there any division on the Government's amendment despite the unanimous condemnation which it received from all sides of the House. Quintin Hogg told the House that the Opposition had agreed not to force divisions after a certain hour and that hour was now long past. It was then 11.30 p.m. and the House, as we have seen, had just completed several days of long-drawn-out and exhausting debates on the Iron and Steel Bill.

Hogg said, however, that it would be difficult for the Opposition to keep to its self-denying ordinance of not forcing divisions unless the Government gave them some comfort on this issue and gave an undertaking to look at the question again before the Bill reached the Lords.

Crossman, when pressed to give a precise assurance, said that he did give an assurance 'that between now and its passage through another place, in view of what has been said here, we will certainly reconsider this and discuss it with the Minister of Health'.[3] But he had also said, a little earlier, 'we will discuss it once again with the

[1] H.C. Deb. Vol. 739, Col. 1432.
[2] Laurence Pavitt (Labour and Co-operative) was first elected for Willesden West in 1959.
[3] H.C. Deb. Vol. 739, Col. 1443.

Minister of Health, who has very strong and considered views on the subject.'[1] The implication was that the Minister of Health was unlikely to change his mind. Nevertheless, the Conservatives did not force a division and the amendment was agreed to.

Niall MacDermot then moved an amendment to the paragraph which excluded from investigation actions taken in matters relating to contractual or other commercial transactions. This amendment, he told the House, met two points which had been raised in standing committee. First, it made clear that government action in relation to contracts between purely private parties could be investigated. Thus action by the Board of Trade in relation to proposed mergers could be looked at by the Parliamentary Commissioner.

Second, the acquisition of land compulsorily by a government department, or in circumstances in which it could be acquired compulsorily, was brought in. So was the disposal of land so acquired. In this way the points raised by Sir Hugh Lucas-Tooth were met and it was made clear that the Parliamentary Commissioner would be able to deal with a Crichel Down type case.[2] The amendment was agreed to.

The report stage ended with discussion of two amendments which had been put down to the paragraph which excluded from investigation personnel matters in the Civil Service and in the Armed Forces. The amendments, which were moved by Quintin Hogg, sought to bring appointments, removals, pay, superannuation, and other personnel matters in the Civil Service and the Armed Forces within the Parliamentary Commissioner's field of investigation. All that would be excluded would be matters of discipline.

Quintin Hogg told the House that if there was to be any justification for the operations of the Parliamentary Commissioner, these personnel questions were exactly the kinds of things that he should be looking into. He apologized for not developing his argument because of the lateness of the hour. When he sat down it was 11.45 p.m.

Niall MacDermot, in replying, also said he would speak briefly. As regards the Civil Service, he concentrated on the argument that the staff side of the Whitley Council was content with the existing procedures and did not want the Parliamentary Commissioner to have power to investigate in Civil Service personnel matters. As regards the Armed Forces, his experience in taking up cases on

[1] Ibid., Col. 1442.   [2] See above pp. 161–2.

behalf of service men was that he often got a better response than in taking up cases with many other departments. If Members felt that the existing procedures for investigating complaints in the Armed Forces were inadequate, they could raise the matter on the defence debates. The amendment was negatived without a division and the report stage concluded.

THE THIRD READING

The third reading of the Bill then began at once and lasted only fifteen minutes. Niall MacDermot rose to move the third reading at 11.50 p.m. and the question was put and agreed to at 12.5 a.m. MacDermot told the House that, from his own point of view, it had been 'an extraordinarily interesting Bill to pilot through the House'.[1] He hoped that the House would feel as a result of the report stage that the Government had 'met a number of valuable criticisms of the Bill during Committee'. He also paid tribute to the help which the Government had received from the Parliamentary Commissioner designate. It had been a very great help to have his advice on a number of points.

Finally, he spoke about the need to give thought, after passage of the Bill, to the establishment of a Select Committee. As he saw it, the House should not be concerned with the investigations. Its role should be to help 'to work out the procedures and, in particular, the conventions which we must devise among ourselves as hon. Members in handling complaints which are to be referred to the Commissioner and, secondly, in receiving his reports and seeing what kind of action we need to take as Members of Parliament to put right situations which are brought to light by his investigations'.[2]

Dame Joan Vickers (Conservative) told the House that she was worried about Clause 5 of the Bill and the enormous responsibility it would put on individual M.P.s. They would have to decide which complaints should be sent on to the Commissioner. If an M.P. told a constituent that a case was not suitable for the Commissioner, the constituent might take his case to another M.P. who might succeed in getting the case investigated. 'If that sort of thing happens constituents will lose confidence in their Member of Parliament.'[3] She hoped that the Government would consider issuing an instruction leaflet to the public and to M.P.s to advise them on the type of case

---

[1] H.C. Deb. Vol. 739, Col. 1448.
[2] Ibid., Col. 1449.   [3] Ibid., Cols. 1449–50.

which should be sent on to the Commissioner. There was also the problem of what should be done if a person circulated 630 Members at one time with his complaint.

Alexander Lyon (Labour) told Miss Vickers that he hoped the fears she expressed would to some extent be allayed by the way in which the Select Committee worked. He hoped that it would 'gradually work out a procedure whereby these difficulties are ironed out'.[1] As one who had consistently criticized various parts of the Bill, he thought it would be churlish 'not to pay some tribute to the very fact that this Bill has been introduced and is being passed into law, because this Commissioner is the greatest aid to the liberty of the subject, in his relationships with the State, to have been provided since 1947, when the former Labour Government introduced the Crown Proceedings Act'.[2]

Quintin Hogg had the last word in this brief third reading debate. 'I am just as agnostic about the virtues of this Bill as I was at the beginning', he told the House. The Government, in planning the office of Parliamentary Commissioner, was 'faced with the dilemma of making it either a Frankenstein or a nonentity—a Frankenstein if it has effective powers and a nonentity if it has not. The Government quite rightly, has opted for its being a nonentity.' He argued that 'A Frankenstein would, I think, have undermined the power of Ministers and would have undermined the authority of individual Members of Parliament.'[3] His ultimate conclusion was that the Bill 'is a noble facade without anything behind it'.

If the committee stage of the Bill saw, in the opinion, of the chairman of Standing Committee B, 'Parliament working absolutely at its best', the report stage did not, by contrast, see the Commons at its worst. Nevertheless, by comparison, the report stage comes out much less well.

It is true that debate on report was truncated. The House was exhausted after a series of arduous debates on the report stage of the Iron and Steel Bill. The time allotted for report on the Parliamentary Commissioner Bill had been whittled down and, as we have seen,

[1] Ibid., Col. 1451.
[2] Ibid., Col. 1451.
[3] Ibid., Col. 1452. Hogg was using the term 'Frankenstein' incorrectly since in Mary Shelley's novel Frankenstein was the creator of the monster and not the monster itself. However, common usage may have legitimized this transference to the monster of the creator's own name: witness *Bride of Frankenstein*, *Frankenstein Must Be Killed*, and other box-office successes.

the Opposition agreed not to force divisions during the later proceedings on report.

If this self-denying ordinance, as Quintin Hogg called it, had not been made, would there have been any Government defeats on report? In particular would the Government have been defeated on its amendment to restore the hospitals to the excluded categories in Schedule 3? It seems highly unlikely. One of the significant features of the main division which took place in the earlier stages on report was that there were no Labour rebels. On the Government amendment which prevented the Commissioner from reviewing the exercise of a discretion in a government department, no Labour votes were cast with the Conservatives against the amendment.

For one Civil Servant who watched all the proceedings in standing committee and on report, the great difference which he noted between the stages was the impact of party discipline on the Labour benches at report, contrasted with a lack of impact in standing committee. Labour back-benchers made much of the running in trying to amend the Bill in standing committee, and on occasion they voted against the Government or abstained in crucial divisions.

On report, Labour criticisms of provisions in the Bill, or of Government amendments, were few and far between. Only on the hospitals issue did several Labour back-benchers make their criticisms known. On many amendments, only Conservatives spoke. If more time had been given for report it is likely that there would have been more criticisms of Government amendments from the Labour side and more Labour speeches in favour of provisions in the Bill as a counter to Conservative criticisms. As we have noted, one of the functions of a Government back-bencher, when time is pressing (as it often is), is to keep his mouth shut and let the majority vote carry the day.

We may say, however, that despite the truncated nature of the report stage it still played an important part in the legislative process. Some M.P.s who were not members of the standing committee, but were knowledgeable on the subject of the Bill, like Sir Lionel Heald and Sir John Hobson, took a prominent part in the debate on report. This is one of the functions of report stage.

The Government used report stage to introduce a whole string of amendments which they had promised to draft after the intensive discussion of the Bill in standing committee. One amendment, to give the House of Lords a part in any move to dismiss the Parliamentary Commissioner, was introduced by the Conservatives and accepted by the Government. More controversially, the Government used report stage to carry two amendments which were to be widely criticized: they reversed the decision of the standing committee to include the hospitals within the Commissioner's sphere of investigation and they introduced an amendment excluding the Commissioner from reviewing, by way of appeal, any exercise of discretionary authority by a government department. These two amendments were given a lot of publicity in the Press. In the period before the Bill reached the Lords, and during proceedings in the Lords, much of the discussion of the Bill centred round these amendments.

XI

THE SECOND READING IN THE LORDS

THE Press had taken little interest in the progress of the Parliamentary Commissioner Bill when it was in standing committee. There had been a few brief reports in the more serious papers. For example, on 9 November 1966, the *Guardian* had printed a short account of David Weitzman's success in carrying his amendment to allow the Commissioner to look at questions which could go to an administrative tribunal. On 25 November, the *Guardian* gave a little more space to a report of the decision in the standing committee, by a majority of one, to include the hospitals within the Commissioner's sphere of investigation. But these were small reports tucked away in the inside pages.

The debate on report stage, and particularly the Government's amendment to prevent the Commissioner from reviewing the discretionary acts of government departments, received much more coverage, and comment in the Press was overwhelmingly unfavourable. There is no doubt that the Ministers in charge of the Bill were surprised and taken aback by this reaction.

When the Lord Chancellor, Lord Gardiner, opened the second reading debate in the Lords, on Wednesday, 8 February 1967, fifteen days after the report stage and third reading in the Commons, he began by referring to the comment in the Press. He told the House that

during the last fortnight (I do not know whether or not these things are catching) there have been several newspaper articles suggesting—partly I think because of a misapprehension by the newspapers of the effect of a subsection recently inserted in the Bill in another place—that this Bill is a shadow of its former self and will not achieve the object it was intended to achieve. This really came to a head in a remarkably silly article in a paper for which I ordinarily have regard, namely *The Economist*. The article was headed:

'Stop it. The Lords should throw out the Ombudsman Bill and insist on a better one.'

A little later Lord Gardiner commented: 'If I did not think this was a good Bill I should not be moving its Second Reading.'[1] He gave the House a full and clear account of the background to the Bill, of the Franks Committee, the Whyatt Report and its rejection by the Macmillan Government, and of the Labour decision to set up a Parliamentary Commissioner. He then outlined the main provisions of the Bill.

Here, the main point of interest was his discussion of Subsection (4) of Clause 5, added on report, which prevented the Commissioner from reviewing by way of appeal any discretionary decision taken by a government department. He said that this subsection 'was put in only as a suggestion to make the thing clear. . . . It was never intended that a Parliamentary Commissioner or Ombudsman should be a one-man court of appeal against every policy decision or discretionary decision of a Minister. From the Whyatt Report on, that has always been the case.'[2]

He then went on to fall into the same error which Crossman had made in the second reading debate in the Commons. He told the House: 'In regard to discretionary decisions, the Whyatt Report recommended an extension of the powers of the Council on Tribunals to a wider class of case, and that your Lordships did only a few months ago.' The inaccuracy of this statement was to be pointed out later in the debate, by Lord Reay. At the end of the debate, Lord Shackleton, for the Government, acknowledged that the Tribunals and Inquiries Act, 1966, to which the Lord Chancellor was referring in his speech had not implemented the Whyatt Committee proposals on tribunals.[3]

Lord Gardiner went on to explain to the House the distinction between discretionary decisions by a Minister which the Commissioner could not look at, and cases of maladministration with which he would be concerned. He took, as an example, the power given to the Board of Trade to decide whether or not someone was to be allowed to start an insurance business. The Minister's decision on this question was a discretionary decision for which he was responsible to Parliament, and the Commissioner would not be able to review that decision by way of appeal. But the Comissioner would

[1] H.L. Deb. Vol. 279, Col. 1365.   [2] Ibid., Col. 1376.   [3] See below p. 202.

'be able to cross-examine the President of the Board of Trade and his officials, and look at all the documents and report that the Minister had only one source of information, and that a rather doubtful one; that he made no attempt to check the information outside; that there were, in fact, relevant documents in the Department at the time and that he did not have them in front of him when he came to make his decision.'[1] In other words, the Commissioner would not be able to review a discretionary decision properly arrived at, but if such a decision was improperly arrived at, this could be maladministration and would be subject to investigation.

The Lord Chancellor also touched upon those spheres from which the Parliamentary Commissioner was excluded. He thought that 'to suggest that the Parliamentary Commissioner should take under his wing local authorities would be quite contrary to the whole conception of the Parliamentary Commissioner.'[2] He was really an extension of the powers of Members of the House of Commons to deal with grievances against government departments.

As regards other excluded matters like personnel questions in the Armed Forces and the Civil Service, these could always be included later by simple Order in Council. He urged upon his fellow peers 'the view that it is wise not to try to do too much at first'.[3] No country with an Ombudsman has a population of more than 6 million, 'and here we are trying to apply the same idea to a population of 50 million.' He thought it was 'a sensible English habit to start things on a reasonable scale, and if they work they can always be extended'.[4]

Finally, he took up a subject which would be of obvious interest to his fellow peers: the provision in the Bill that an approach to the Parliamentary Commissioner could only be made through a member of the House of Commons. The reason for this was that M.P.s dealt with an enormous number of constituency problems while peers received very few letters asking them to take up individual grievances.

The speeches in the subsequent debate can be divided into a number of fairly clear categories. First, there were two speeches by Conservative peers who were critical of the Bill. Lord Harlech, the Deputy Leader of the Opposition in the Lords, was gently critical.[5]

[1] H.L. Deb. Vol. 279, Col. 1377.   [2] Ibid., Col. 1378.
[3] Ibid., Col. 1380.   [4] Ibid., Col. 1379-80.
[5] William David Ormsby Gore, 5th Baron Harlech, was born in 1918. From 1950 to

He was not opposed in principle to the establishment of a Parliamentary Commissioner although he thought it was still open to argument whether it would do more harm than good.

The Government had 'somewhat emasculated' the Bill in the Commons. Subsection (4) added to Clause 5 seemed to him 'to give the Bureaucracy a loophole as large as the Round Tower of Windsor'.[1] He thought it was 'a rather feeble and tepid Bill, and therefore it deserves a rather tepid welcome in your Lordships' House'.[2]

Lord Redmayne was more strongly critical of the Bill. He thought that, if it achieved its purpose at all, it would 'lead to a further deterioration in the position and reputation of the elected Member of Parliament'.[3] The function of the M.P. was to raise the grievances of his constituents at Question Time, on Adjournment Debates, and on Supply. The establishment of a Parliamentary Commissioner would detract from these opportunities 'by debasing the currency'. M.P.s would be blackmailed into taking cases to the Parliamentary Commissioner under the implied threat that if they did not do so, cases would be taken to another Member.[4]

His speech, to some extent, resembled Quintin Hogg's speech on second reading in the Commons. Like Quintin Hogg, he thought it would be better if the Select Committee sifted all the cases before they went to the Commissioner to see whether all the proper Parliamentary means—'Question, letter, Adjournment Debate, all the rest of it'—had been used first. Like Quintin Hogg, he had been a member of the Macmillan Government which had turned down the Whyatt proposals. He had indeed been Chief Whip in that Government.[5]

Another category was provided by the two Liberal peers, Lords Wade and Reay who welcomed the Bill, but were in favour of extending its scope. Lord Wade told the House that it was clear to him 'that the right attitude to this Bill should be one of endeavour to amend it and improve it, so that we create in this new office a really

---

1961 he was Conservative M.P. for Oswestry. He was a Minister of State for Foreign Affairs from 1957 to 1961 and British Ambassador in Washington from 1961 to 1965. He is Chairman of Harlech Television.

[1] H.L. Deb. Vol. 279, Col. 1388.
[2] Ibid., Col. 1389.   [3] Ibid., Col. 1402.   [4] Ibid., Col. 1403.
[5] Martin Redmayne was created Baron Redmayne in 1966, a life peer. He was Conservative M.P. for Rushcliffe, Nottingham, from 1950 to 1966. From 1959 to 1964 he was Conservative Chief Whip.

important Parliamentary reform and a reform in the realm of the protection of the individual'.

Lord Wade was particularly concerned about the exclusion of local authorities under the Bill. He reminded the House that he had introduced a Bill on 18 October 1966 with the object of setting up separate machinery for dealing with local complaints at regional level. This Bill had been defeated on second reading by 'a formidable Labour-Conservative coalition'.[1] He was considering whether to table an amendment to the Parliamentary Commissioner Bill to enable some of the large number of complaints against local authorities to be investigated.

On the question of discretionary actions of government departments, he would certainly advocate deleting Subsection (4) of Clause 5. He thought it would be used as a protection by government departments against any awkward investigations. He told the House that his 'noble and learned friend Lord McNair, whose views I always listen to with great respect, has sent me this comment: that he regards this particular proviso as most dangerous'.[2] Two other improvements which he advocated were making peers a channel for communication of complaints to the Parliamentary Commissioner, and including superannuation questions in the Civil Service within his sphere of investigation.

Lord Reay spoke in similar vein.[3] The Parliamentary Commissioner would 'provide a remedy for certain cases of injustice, although unquestionably only for a very small minority of such cases, which do result from maladministration.'[4] He also emphasized the need to provide for machinery for investigating complaints against local authorities. He said there was 'no disagreement that it is in this area in which most complaints are made and felt by ordinary people.'[5]

On the question of maladministration and discretionary decisions, he was not satisfied with the approach that the first should be a matter for the Parliamentary Commissioner and the second for administrative tribunals. He knew that the Whyatt Committee had made this recommendation, but he was not convinced that the

[1] H.L. Deb. Vol. 279, Col. 1392. See also above p. 71.

[2] Ibid., Col. 1394. Arnold Duncan McNair was created 1st Baron McNair in 1955. He was born in 1885. He was President of the International Court of Justice from 1952 to 1955 and President of the European Court of Human Rights from 1959 to 1965.

[3] Hugh William Mackay, 14th Baron Reay, was born in 1937. He is Chief of the Clan Mackay.

[4] H.L. Deb. Vol. 279. Col. 1428.   [5] Ibid., Col. 1429.

recent Act amending the Tribunals and Inquiries Act of 1958 had substantially changed the position. Tribunals were rare. He would like to know from the Lord Chancellor whether the Government would be proposing to create more administrative tribunals. He supported the view that peers should be a channel of communication to the Commissioner.

A third category can be found in the speeches of two Labour peers who adopted a broadly 'ministerial' point of view: Lords Silkin and Mitchison. Lord Silkin told the House that he welcomed the Bill without qualification.[1] He did not see any difficulty in distinguishing maladministration from questions of discretion. He did, however, mention three ways in which he would like to see the Bill extended. He would like to see peers made a channel of communication to the Commissioner; he would like the Commissioner to have power to initiate his own inquiries (a power possessed by the New Zealand Ombudsman) and he agreed with Lord Wade that it would be desirable, if practicable, to amend the Bill so that local authorities could be brought in. In his own experience 'the vast majority of cases of maladministration arise in respect of local authorities.'[2]

Lord Mitchison also saw no difficulty in understanding what was meant by maladministration.[3] He thought that it would be not only utterly impracticable but completely illogical to bring local government matters within the scope of the Bill. He thought that the alternative approach, used in France, of having 'a system of administrative law which runs down from the *conseil d'état* to local tribunals' might well be considered for examining complaints against local authorities.[4]

A fourth category is provided by the speeches of Lady Burton and Lady Elliot. Both these ladies have party allegiances, respectively Labour and Conservative, but both spoke in their capacities as public watch-dogs in a specialized sphere. Baroness Burton of Coventry is Chairman of the Council on Tribunals. Baroness Elliot of Harwood

---

[1] Lewis Silkin was created 1st Baron Silkin in 1950. He was Labour M.P. for Peckham from 1936 to 1950. He was Minister of Town and Country Planning from 1945 to 1950 and Deputy Leader of the Official Opposition in the Lords from 1955 to 1964. He had been Chairman of the Town Planning Committee of the L.C.C. from 1940 to 1945.

[2] H. L. Deb. Vol. 279, Col. 1399.

[3] Gilbert Richard Mitchison was created Baron Mitchison, a life peer, in 1964. He is a barrister and was Labour M.P. for Kettering from 1945 to 1964. He was Joint Parliamentary Secretary to the Ministry of Land and Natural Resources from 1964 to 1966.

[4] H.L. Deb. Vol. 279, Col. 1427.

was, at that time, Chairman of the Consumer Council. Both gave a general welcome to the Bill but wanted to see its scope extended.

Lady Burton argued for Ombudsmen, or Commissioners, at local level.[1] She had read that Bristol Corporation had set up a Consumer Advisory Service which would deal with queries and complaints from members of the public against government bodies and the Corporation. Complaints to this Service were being dealt with by the city public relations officer. She asked if this experiment had been successful and how many other local authorities were making similar arrangements.

She was worried about Subsection (4) Clause 5 with its exclusion of the discretionary decisions of government departments. She was not happy either about the exclusion of the hospitals. Finally, she said she was glad that the Parliamentary Commissioner was to be an *ex officio* member of the Council on Tribunals. She wished the Parliamentary Commissioner well, and thought that 'we could have had no better appointment than Sir Edmund Compton.'[2]

Lady Elliot told the House that she was interested in the Bill in the first instance 'because I look upon it as one of the protections for the consumer, and I am, as I need not remind your Lordships, responsible at the moment for an organisation which protects consumers.'[3] She was very sorry that the hospital service had been excluded from investigation by the Parliamentary Commissioner. She thought it was a matter which affected a great many of the citizens of this country. 'Indeed in the priority of candidates for the Ombudsman's protection, I would put the National Health Service very high in the list.'[4] She was not impressed by the arguments put forward at report stage by Government spokesmen in favour of excluding the hospitals.

She was also not happy about the exclusion of the Consular Service. She told the House that the ordinary traveller abroad was 'sometimes let down very badly by tour operators and bogus travel agents'.[5] He could also suffer much inconvenience when abroad and

---

[1] Elaine Frances Burton was created Baroness Burton of Coventry in 1962. She is a life peeress. She was born in 1904 and was Labour M.P. for Coventry South from 1950 to 1959. She has been Chairman of the Council on Tribunals since 1967.

[2] H.L. Deb. Vol. 279, Col. 1417.

[3] Ibid., Col. 1418. Katherine Elliot, who was born in 1903, was created Baroness Elliot of Harwood in 1958. She was one of the first life peers. She is the widow of Colonel Walter Elliot, the Conservative Minister of Health from 1938 to 1940.

From 1956 to 1957 she was Chairman of the National Union of Conservative and Unionist Associations. She was Chairman of the Consumer Council from 1963 to 1968.

[4] Ibid., Col. 1418.   [5] Ibid., Col. 1420.

the only person to whom he could go was the Consular representative.

The Government spokesman in the Commons had said 'that there are 400 Consuls and that it would be impossible for the Parliamentary Commissioner to control them without having to fly around visiting them'. She did not anticipate that this would be necessary. There were, after all, airmail posts all over the world and there were not likely to be complaints against all 400 Consuls.

She raised the question of complaints about the police not being included and commented that 'the standing criticism of the present manner of investigation of complaints by the police authorities is left untouched.'[1] She noted that 'the Swedish Ombudsman is able to exonerate, as well as to investigate the powers of the police' and she thought that was certainly welcome. She thought that the local authority sphere should be brought under the Parliamentary Commissioner since 'many of the gravest decisions affecting individuals emanate from local government—and I speak with some authority, having been for thirty years a member of a local authority.'[2]

Finally, she raised the same point that Michael English had raised, without success, in the Commons standing committee. Under Clause 5(1) (a), all complaints must be written complaints to the Parliamentary Commissioner. She knew 'through working closely with the Citizens Advice Bureau, that the greater proportion of all the complaints they get come to them from people who would be quite incapable of making written application on these points'.[3] Shackleton at this point intervened to say that her fears on this question were groundless. He did not expand on this point and it is a little mysterious to know what he had in mind since subsection (5) (1) (a) was incorporated in the final Act.

In many ways the most interesting speech in the debate, containing the most penetrating criticism of the Bill, was made by Lord Lloyd of Hampstead who is an authority on comparative law. He is Quain Professor of Jurisprudence at University College, London.[4] Lord Lloyd said that the general idea underlying the Bill deserved support, but he was doubtful whether the Parliamentary Commissioner

---

[1] Ibid., Col. 1422.   [2] Ibid., Col. 1422.   [3] Ibid., Col. 1423.

[4] Dennis Lloyd was made a life peer in 1965. He was born in 1915 and called to the Bar in 1956. His publications include *Rent Control* (2nd edn. 1955), *Public Policy: A Comparative Study in English and French Law* (1953) and *United Kingdom: Development of its Laws and Constitution* (1955).

would have the 'real cutting edge' which Crossman had claimed in the
Commons he would.

He thought that the distinction in the Bill 'between discretion and
maladministration, which undoubtedly stems from the Whyatt
Report itself, is, in my respectful view, an unsound and undesirable
distinction'.[1] As he understood it, the effect of the Bill would be that
if a department followed the right procedure, the Parliamentary
Commissioner would be powerless, even if the result was 'demon-
strably wrong, unfair or absurd'. He thought that it would be much
better to adopt the approach followed in New Zealand where their
Ombudsman, in the words of the New Zealand Act, could 'review
any decision which was unreasonable, unjust, oppressive, improperly
discriminatory or wrong'. In his opinion, this approach 'would give
the public a much greater sense of having a genuine protector
against faulty administration'.[2]

At this stage in his speech, Lord Shackleton intervened to point
out that the New Zealand Ombudsman did not have the right to
review the decisions of Ministers. This was a fair comment and was
one which had been made in private in discussions in the Treasury
team which was responsible for the Bill. There was, however, no
subsequent development of this point in the debate or discussion of
the issue whether it is better to have the New Zealand pattern under
which all decisions made by Civil Servants are subject to review but
the decisions of Ministers are excluded, or to have the decisions of
Ministers, as well as of Civil Servants, subject to investigation but
only where they involve maladministration.[3]

Lord Lloyd then went on to say that he did not agree

> with the argument that we must not let the Commissioner deal with dis-
> cretion because we want government by Government and not by Com-
> missioner. This again, I suggest, is a false point because administrative
> decisions are sometimes foolish, unwise or ill-considered, and that is why
> we have tribunals to deal with these matters. If there is not a tribunal to
> deal with every matter, which would be very difficult, it is extremely
> desirable, it seems to me, to have an Ombudsman who can listen to com-
> plaints.[4]

Lord Lloyd concluded by saying that 'the concept of an Ombuds-

---

[1] H.L. Deb. Vol. 279, Col. 1438.   [2] Ibid., Col. 1440.
[3] For discussion of this question, see below Chapter XVI.
[4] H.L. Deb. Vol. 279, Cols. 1442–3.

man seems to be a very fruitful one as providing a valuable supplement to the rather limited resources of our whole piecemeal administrative law.'[1] For his part he would have wished for a rather bolder measure. He thought that the public might be rather disappointed when it became apparent to them how limited the sphere of activity of the Commissioner was.

After Lord Lloyd had sat down, there followed an unintentionally comic exchange between Lord Airedale and the Marquess of Exeter. Lord Airedale sought to illustrate the argument for an Ombudsman for local government questions by giving the House an illustration of his own dealings with the Rural District Council where he lives.[2] He described the extensive delays which had incurred in correspondence with the Council, because of the difficulty of getting replies to his letters and the irrelevance of some of the replies when they arrived. The correspondence had concerned two cottages which he owned and about which the Council had incorrectly, he said, written to inform him that they had no refrigerators or ventilated food storage.

The Marquess of Exeter then rose to tell the House that he was 'the chief ogre in this particular little story that we have just heard from the noble Lord, Lord Airedale' since he was the Chairman of the Rural District Council concerned. He assured the House that this Council were 'second to none in their public spiritedness' and that 'they have an extremely efficient body of officers who serve them.'[3] He also instanced a case in which he said Lord Airedale had taken five months to complete a form which the Council needed in connection with his intention to convert part of his house into flats.

Viscount Colville of Culross then made the winding-up speech for the Conservative peers.[4] His speech was, on the whole, more friendly to the Bill than the speeches of the earlier Conservative spokesmen, Lords Harlech and Redmayne, had been. His attitude was that the Bill did not give wide powers to the Commissioner but

[1] Ibid.
[2] Oliver James Vandeleur Kitson, 4th Baron Airedale, was born in 1915. He has been Deputy Speaker of the House of Lords since 1962.
[3] H.L. Deb. Vol. 279, Col. 1446–7. David George Brownlow Cecil, 6th Marquess of Exeter, was born in 1905. He was Conservative M.P. for Peterborough from 1931 to 1943.
[4] John Mark Alexander Colville, 4th Viscount Colville of Culross, was born in 1933. He is a barrister.

'we should in this matter start slowly, and in doing so we should recognize that we are starting slowly and are starting in a purely limited sphere.' [1]

He said that he very much disagreed with Lord Lloyd who wanted to allow the Commissioner to look at the policy decisions of government departments, or Ministers, straightaway. He thought it better that the Parliamentary Commissioner should be limited for the time being to looking at maladministration.

He said that the noble Lords behind him looked upon the Bill as an experiment. In those terms he was sure they would support it 'and we will do our level best to improve it as it goes through this House.' One of the improvements he had mentioned in his speech was the possibility that the power to modify the Bill by Order in Council might be extended so that not only the excluded sectors in Schedule 3, like the hospitals, but other excluded sectors, such as local authority matters, might be brought in.

One of the difficulties which he saw in the Bill was that the Parliamentary Commissioner would report to the Commons, but the report would in some cases relate to departments whose Ministerial heads would be in the Lords. Would it not be better therefore if the Commissioner's reports were to Parliament so that they could be debated in the Lords? There was much less pressure of time too in the Lords than in the Commons, so it would be easier to have debates on the Commissioner's reports.

Lord Shackleton, replying to the debate, said that it was 'one of the most difficult debates to which to reply that it has ever been my lot to suffer'. [2] He began by correcting the statement made by the Lord Chancellor, at the beginning of the debate, about the effect of the recent Tribunal and Inquiries Act. He was afraid that the statement was not accurate. All that that Act did was to bring within the jurisdiction of the Council on Tribunals 'discretionary inquiries which a Minister has power, but is under no duty to hold'. [3] He told the House that he must apologize on behalf of the Lord Chancellor, who was anxious to put the matter right.

[1] H.L. Deb. Vol. 279, Col. 1455.
[2] Ibid., Col. 1456. Edward Arthur Shackleton was made Baron Shackleton, a life peer, in 1958. He was born in 1911 and is the son of Sir Arthur Shackleton, the Antarctic Explorer. He was Labour M.P. for Preston from 1946 to 1950 and for Preston South from 1950 to 1955. He was a Minister without Portfolio in the Wilson Government and Deputy Leader of the House of Lords from 1967 to 1968.
[3] Ibid., Col. 1456.

Of the numerous points which Lord Shackleton then touched on in his speech the following were of most interest. He had been asked in the debate whether the provision in Clause 5 meant that a government department might prevent the Parliamentary Commissioner from investigating a case by saying that it had been an exercise of Ministerial discretion. Lord Shackleton said that such a statement could not prevent an investigation. The Parliamentary Commissioner 'is a highly independent figure, and will be answerable only to himself in judging whether or not a matter should be investigated'.[1]

On the question of extending the Parliamentary Commissioner's jurisdiction to include local authority matters, he told Lords Reay and Wade that, in his opinion, it would be quite improper to amend the Bill in this way, since the Bill was 'intended to investigate administrative action taken on behalf of the Crown'.[2] Finally, in speaking against making peers a channel for complaints, he introduced one new argument. This was that over the years M.P.s 'acquire experience and are able to judge those matters which should go to the Parliamentary Commissioner'.[3] Peers, on the other hand, raise very few citizen grievances with Ministers and therefore do not acquire much experience in 'constituency' problems. They would be able to undertake the task of screening complaints, and deciding which should go forward to the Commissioner, much less well. In general, his speech covered familiar ground and gave little or no indication that the Government would be willing to make concessions in the fields in which individual peers had been advocating amendments.

He concluded by saying that he was grateful 'that your Lordships are not going to oppose the Second Reading of this Bill. I hope that when we come to the Amendments we shall be able to discuss them fully and freely.'[4] The Bill was then read a second time and committed to a Committee of the whole House.

The second reading debate in the Lords had gone on for five hours as against the six hours seventeen minutes given to second reading in the Commons. It had been a good debate, with a generally high level of contribution. There had been a concentration on certain issues. Not surprisingly, a large part of the discussion was given over to the modification made to Clause 5 on report in the Commons and to the likely effect of excluding the Commissioner

---

[1] Ibid., Col. 1459. [2] Ibid., Col. 1462.
[3] Ibid., Col. 1466. [4] Ibid., Col. 1467.

from reviewing, by way of appeal, discretionary decisions by government departments.

More surprisingly, perhaps, there was a great deal of discussion in the debate about whether local authorities could be brought in. Excluding the Ministers (Lords Gardiner and Shackleton), who opened and closed the debate, twelve peers spoke. Of these, no less than seven (Lords Wade, Reay, Silkin, Airedale, Viscount Colville, and Ladies Burton and Elliot) made clear their sympathy with the view that local authorities should be subject to investigation by the Commissioner, or through some later extension of the system set up by the Bill. On reflection, this is not so surprising in view of the experience of local government which many of these peers possessed (for example Lord Silkin had five years as Chairman of the L.C.C. Town Planning Committee and Lady Elliot thirty years as a local councillor). Considerable, although relatively less interest, was also shown in the debate in the issue of whether or not peers should be made a channel of complaint to the Commissioner.

In view of the interest taken in the question of who are the active peers in the Lords nowadays, it is worthwhile to analyse the background of the peers who spoke in this debate. Of the fourteen peers who took part, seven were life peers and two were hereditary peers of first creation. Only five were hereditary peers who had inherited their titles: Lords Harlech, Reay, Airedale, the Marquess of Exeter, and Viscount Colville.

Three of these hereditary peers, Lords Harlech and Reay and Viscount Colville, made important contributions to this debate. But the life peers, on their side, included a number of distinguished people with specialized knowledge which was particularly appropriate to the Bill. These were Lady Burton with her experience in social service and as Chairman of the Council on Tribunals, Lady Elliot as Chairman of the Consumer Council, and Lord Lloyd as an eminent comparative lawyer.

Eight of those who spoke in the debate (six life peers and two hereditary peers) also had long experience as M.P.s. This debate therefore illustrates the generalization that many of the peers who are active in the Lords are former M.P.s. It also weakens the force of Lord Shackleton's argument that peers should not be a channel to the Parliamentary Commissioner because they do not have experience of constituency problems.

XII

THE COMMITTEE STAGE IN THE LORDS

THE Government had given no indication in the second reading debate in the Lords that it intended to accept any major amendment to the Bill. Critics in the Press of the Bill, as it had emerged from the Commons, were, therefore, in no way assuaged. For example, on the Sunday after the second reading debate the *Sunday Times* printed an article by Hugo Young, on its editorial page, under the heading 'The Vanishing Ombudsman'.[1] The theme of the article was that the Government had beaten a steady retreat from their election manifesto promise to set up a Parliamentary Commissioner in order 'to humanize the administration'. All the most fertile grounds of grievance had been eliminated one by one: local authority matters, the Health Service, personnel questions in Government employment. Finally, a blanket prohibition had been imposed on the Parliamentary Commissioner investigating the discretionary decisions of government departments. Now, only the Lords remained 'to save the public from disillusionment on one of the most serious issues of the moment'.

Such criticisms were pointed up by the Parkes case which hit the headlines in the week following. The case had been taken up by Jack Ashley, Labour M.P. for Stoke on Trent.[2] Leslie Parkes was one of his constituents. Parkes was accused of desertion from the army. He had been arrested by the civil police in June 1966 and brought before a magistrate who had discharged him. More than seven months later, during the night of 9 to 10 February, he was arrested by the military police and charged with desertion. It was alleged that Parkes had been 'lured' to a police station by the civil police, on this occasion, and then handed over to the military

---

[1] *Sunday Times*, 12 February 1967.
[2] Jack Ashley has been Labour M.P. for Stoke on Trent South since 1966. He is chairman of the all-party Lords and Commons group on disablement.

police. A further questionable, and highly sensational feature, of the case was that photographs in the press showed Parkes handcuffed to one military policeman while another military policeman stood guard over him with a pick-handle. After two interchanges on the subject in the Commons and a furore in the Press, Denis Healey, the Secretary of State for Defence, announced on 15 February, that he had ordered the release of Parkes from custody and the dropping of the charge against him. Columnists were not slow to point out that, as the Parliamentary Commissioner Bill now stood, the Ombudsman would be excluded from taking up any comparable case.

At the end of the week in which the storm over the arrest of Leslie Parkes had blown up, the *Sunday Mirror* pitched into the discussion in a characteristic way. In its issue of 19 February, a full-page article on page 3 was headed 'Ombudsboob—£8,600 for the Swordless Crusader'. A photograph of Parkes handcuffed to a military policeman was captioned 'Parkes—now the handcuffs are off.' Juxtaposed to this was a photograph of the Parliamentary Commissioner designate captioned 'Sir Edmund—the shackles are on.'

The article contained such phrases as:

Leslie Parkes has had the handcuffs struck from his wrists. The pick-handles have been put away. . . . Today, the *Sunday Mirror*'s concern is for another man in shackles—handcuffs, ball and chain, gag, the lot. He is Sir Edmund Gerald Compton KCB formerly the distinguished watchdog of public spending as Comptroller and Auditor General, now preparing to start his new job as Britain's first Ombudsman.

. . . The Government has just inserted a clause in the Bill banning the Ombudsman from commenting on any decision taken by a Government department which involves the department's own discretion.

. . . Mr. Quinton Hogg has called the Government's version of the Ombudsman a swizz.

. . . The *Sunday Mirror* suggests that while the Bill is still before Parliament, every Minister and Labour M.P. should read again the role of the Ombudsman as it was defined in Labour's 1964 Election Manifesto.

'Labour has resolved to humanize the whole administration of the State and to set up the new office of Parliamentary Commissioner with the right and duty to investigate and expose any misuse of Government power as it affects the citizen.'

At the time it sounded like a good idea.

Whatever Happened to It?

The *Daily Mirror* and the *Sunday Mirror* can be said to provide 'discriminating support' to the Labour Party. When they decide to criticize Labour policies or actions, they often hit hard, as in this case. Through this article the *Sunday Mirror* attempted to serve notice on Labour Ministers that if they did not make some changes in the Bill at committee or report stage in the Lords, they would lose support from the paper altogether for the Parliamentary Commissioner reform.

Less powerful interests were also trying to prod the Government at this time. The *Guardian* reported on Saturday, 18 February 1967 that: 'The Patients' Association is lobbying party spokesmen in the House of Lords in an effort to get hospital matters put back within the scope of the ombudsman.' It also reported that the Consumer Council was 'opposed to the exclusion of hospitals from the ombudsman's domain'.

When the Lords met on Tuesday, 21 February to consider the Parliamentary Commissioner Bill in Committee of the whole House, peers could then hardly fail to be aware of the interest being taken in their proceedings. Clauses 1 to 3 of the Bill were agreed to without debate. The first amendment was moved by Lord Somers to Clause 4 of the Bill.[1]

Clause 4 was entitled 'Departments and Authorities Subject to Investigation'. Lord Somers's amendment proposed to add a new subsection providing that the Act would apply to any authority taking action under the Town and Country Planning Acts, to any authority taking action for the compulsory acquisition of land, and to any authority developing or disposing of land compulsorily acquired. In speaking to this amendment, Lord Somers said that the action of local authorities in the field of planning and demolition of property could often give rise to a strong sense of injustice by the people affected. The amendment was designed to enable the Parliamentary Commissioner to investigate such cases.

Lord Shackleton replied that, under the Bill, the Parliamentary Commissioner would have considerable powers to investigate many of these cases. 'Virtually all compulsory acquisitions to which objection is taken require Ministerial approval. Therefore every opposed case of compulsory acquisition must be considered on its

---

[1] John Patrick Somers Cocks, 8th Baron Somers, was born in 1907. He was Director of Music at Epsom College from 1949 to 1953. He has been Professor of Composition and Theory at the Royal College of Music since 1967.

merits by the central Government and any maladministration will enter into that consideration.'[1] It was the same with the development of land: if the local authority wanted to change the development of land which had been compulsorily acquired, Ministerial approval was again required.

Lord Somers then said that in view of this assurance he would withdraw his amendment, but he asked to know what would be done to inform the general public that such cases could be taken to the Commissioner where maladministration was alleged. Lord Shackleton replied that one of the advantages of having M.P.s as the channel to the Commissioner was that through M.P.s the general public would, in time, get to know in which fields the Ombudsman could help and in which he could not. It was interesting to note that the Minister himself in this exchange fell into the established usage in referring to 'the Ombudsman'.[2]

Lord Somers's amendment having been withdrawn, Lord Wade then moved an amendment which would make it possible for the Parliamentary Commissioner to investigate complaints against local authorities. The amendment merely proposed to leave out the words in Subsection (2) of Clause 4 which said that Her Majesty was not empowered by Order in Council to add to the list of authorities subject to investigation 'any body or authority' whose functions were not exercised on behalf of the Crown.

Lord Wade told the House that the amendment would involve an amendment to the title of the Bill and a later amendment had been tabled with this intention. The object of his amendment was to give power by Order in Council to widen the scope of the Bill to provide for the investigation of complaints against local authorities. He envisaged three ways in which this might be done. The first was 'by a local Ombudsman appointed by the local authority; the second is by some kind of Regional Ombudsman; and the third is by a deputy of the Parliamentary Commissioner giving special attention to complaints affecting local authorities.'[3]

The disadvantage of the first method would be that, in some types of case, an employee of the council could not really be expected to carry out the investigation. An example of such cases which he gave was an occasion when the finance committee had approved the sale of land without putting out to public tender, although under standing orders it was required to do so, and when it was alleged

[1] H.L. Deb. Vol. 280, Col. 611.   [2] Ibid., Col. 612.   [3] Ibid., Col. 614.

that the chairman of the committee was under a personal obligation to the purchaser. He therefore favoured having either a regional Ombudsman or having an assistant or deputy to the Parliamentary Ombudsman who would deal with local authority matters. Another advantage of either of these two methods was that it would then be possible to deal with the border line between the responsibility of government departments and the responsibility of local authorities. An example here was when a local authority was acting in accordance with a Ministry circular.

Lord Silkin said that initially he had been sympathetic to the amendment, and he agreed that most cases of maladministration are concerned with local authority functions. But he now thought that they should start within the confines of the Bill as drafted. When experience had been gained in dealing with cases of maladministration by the Crown, it would be more practicable to devise suitable machinery for looking at complaints against local authorities. He did, however, ask the Minister whether he would be willing 'to have an inquiry into the method by which cases of maladministration on the part of local authorities could be dealt with'.[1]

Lord Harlech and Lady Burton took a similar view to that expressed by Lord Silkin. Lord Shackleton had little difficulty therefore in replying to the amendment since opinion among both Conservative and Labour Peers seemed to be in favour of withdrawal of the amendment. He did not promise that an inquiry would be made into the question of devising a method for investigating complaints against local authorities, but he said that he would draw the attention of his fellow Ministers, and in particular of Richard Crossman, to the suggestion for an inquiry made by Lord Silkin. Lord Wade then withdrew his amendment.

The next amendment was to Clause 5, 'Matters Subject to Investigation'. This amendment was again proposed by Lord Wade and provided that complaints could be forwarded to the Parliamentary Commissioner by Members of either House of Parliament. In speaking to the amendment, he argued that 'the main thing is that we should keep the channels of communication with the Parliamentary Commissioner as open as possible.'[2] He also argued that it would be convenient sometimes, when the senior Minister responsible for a department was a Member of the Lords, for a case involving that department to be sent to the Parliamentary Commissioner

[1] Ibid., Col. 618.   [2] Ibid., Col. 627.

by a peer and for the Parliamentary Commissioner to report back to the peer in question.

Lord Wade was supported in a vigorous speech by a Labour life peer, Lord Willis.[1] He had read the arguments put forward by Lord Shackleton on second reading for excluding peers as a channel for complaints and he thought they were just about the most feeble that he had ever heard.[2] Peers had a traditional right to approach Ministers direct with problems which had been raised with them. They had the right to put questions to Ministers. Why should they not then also be able to approach the Parliamentary Commissioner?

In the lively debate which followed, the line up of speakers was most interesting, The division cut across party lines. Those who spoke in support of the amendment were Lord Somers (Liberal), Lord Citrine (Labour), Lady Burton (Labour), Earl Fortescue, Lord Ogmore, and Lord Moyne.[3] The leading Conservative spokesman on the Bill, Lord Harlech, opposed the amendment as did Lord Conesford and Lady Horsbrugh, both Conservative peers.[4] Two Labour peers who opposed the amendment were Lords Popplewell and Leatherland.

Taking some of the points made by those in favour, Lord Citrine said it would be an advantage to the public at large if peers had the same rights under the Bill as M.P.s.[5] Lady Burton did not accept the argument put forward by Lord Shackleton that peers would not be able to screen the complaints which would be sent to them. Earl Fortescue had the most picturesque argument of all. He reminded

[1] Edward Henry Willis was created Baron Willis in 1963. He is a Director of World Wide Pictures and is a playwright. His film *Woman in a Dressing Gown* (1958) won the Berlin film award. He is best known as the script writer of the television series *Dixon of Dock Green*.

[2] H.L. Deb. Vol. 280, Col. 627.

[3] Walter McLennan Citrine was made 1st Baron Citrine in 1946. He was General Secretary of the T.U.C. from 1926 to 1946. Lt.-Col. David Rees-Williams was made 1st Baron Ogmore in 1950. From 1945 to 1950 he was Labour M.P. for Croydon South. He was Parliamentary Under-Secretary at the Colonial Office from 1947 to 1950 and at the Commonwealth Relations Office from 1950 to 1951.

Bryan Walter Guinness, 2nd Baron Moyne, is a poet, novelist, and playwright. He is also Vice-Chairman of Arthur Guinness & Son Ltd.

[4] Henry George Strauss Q.C. was made 1st Baron Conesford in 1955. He was a Conservative M.P. from 1935 to 1945 and from 1946 to 1955. He was Parliamentary Secretary at the Board of Trade from 1951 to 1955.

Florence Horsbrugh was made a life peeress in 1959. She was a Conservative M.P. from 1931 to 1945 and from 1950 to 1959. She was Minister of Education from 1951 to 1954.

[5] H.L. Deb. Vol. 280, Col. 633.

the House 'that 700 years ago the grievances of the nation were put to King John exclusively by Members of your Lordships' House'.[1]

Looking at some of the arguments on the other side, Lord Harlech maintained that the M.P. had 'a very wide armoury of weapons with which to pursue Ministries'.[2] He could not conceive of a situation in which a peer could not find an M.P. prepared to forward his case to the Parliamentary Commissioner. Lord Popplewell was concerned about the 700 or so peers who do not take an active part in the Lords and would therefore be less able than the active peers to screen the complaints sent to them.[3] Lord Leatherland argued that M.P.s 'feel it their right to take up grievances on behalf of their geographical constituents. I think it would lead to antipathy between the two houses if we the non-elected House tried to usurp those rights.'[4]

Lord Shackleton, in winding up the debate, added no fresh arguments and Lord Wade said that to test the opinion of the House he would ask for a division on the amendment. When it was put to the vote, the amendment was lost by 71 votes to 43. The division list showed as much cross-voting between the parties as had been apparent among those who contributed to the debate. For example, Lord Redmayne and Lady Emmet were two Conservative peers who voted for the amendment while most of the leading Conservatives, including Lord Dilhorne and Lady Brooke, supported Lord Harlech in voting against the amendment.[5]

Labour peers who voted for the amendment included Lord

[1] Ibid., Col. 644. Denzil George Fortescue is the 6th Earl Fortescue. He was a Lt.-Colonel in the 1st Heavy Regt. Royal Artillery from 1942 to 1944.

[2] Ibid., Col. 633.

[3] Ernest Popplewell was made a life peer in 1966. He was Labour M.P. for Newcastle upon Tyne from 1945 to 1966. He was Deputy Chief Whip of the Parliamentary Labour Party from 1955 to 1959. He had been a railway signalman.

[4] H.L. Deb. Vol. 280, Col. 641. Charles Edward Leatherland was made a life peer in 1964. He had been Assistant Editor of the *Daily Herald* until his retirement in 1963.

[5] Evelyn Violet Elizabeth Emmet was made a life peer in 1964. She was Conservative M.P. for East Grinstead from 1955 to 1964. She had been Chairman of the Conservative Women's National Advisory Committee from 1951 to 1954.

Reginald Edward Manningham Buller was made 1st Viscount Dilhorne in 1964. He was a Conservative M.P. from 1943 to 1962. From 1962 to 1964 he was Lord Chancellor, at the time of the Macmillan Government's rejection of the recommendations in the Whyatt Report.

Barbara Brooke was made a life peeress in 1964. She is the wife of Henry Brooke, a former Conservative Minister of Housing and Local Government who is also a life peer. Lady Brooke was a Joint-Vice-Chairman of the Conservative Party Organization from 1954 to 1964.

Chorley as well as Lords Willis and Citrine while the main body of Labour peers voted against.[1] Of the prominent Liberals in the Lords, Lady Asquith joined Lords Wade, Ogmore, and Somers in voting for the amendment.[2]

Lord Wade then moved a further amendment to Clause 5. The effect of this amendment was to provide that an M.P. could send on to the Parliamentary Commissioner a complaint from a member of the public who claimed to have 'sustained injustice which may have arisen in consequence of maladministration', instead of the phrase in the Clause which said merely 'sustained injustice in consequence of maladministration'. He explained to the House that the object of the amendment was to make clear to a person with a grievance that it did not matter if he was not quite sure whether or not there had been maladministration within the meaning of the Act.

He instanced the case of someone who had been to see him the previous week and had told him that a solicitor had advised him that it was no use taking the case to the Parliamentary Commissioner since the decision he was complaining about was a discretionary decision. Lord Wade thought that it should be for the Parliamentary Commissioner and not the complainant to decide whether there was a matter for investigation.

The Lord Chancellor replied that he was not persuaded that the amendment was necessary. He thought that Lord Wade had not given sufficient weight to the word 'claims' in the subsection. The person complaining did not have to produce any evidence, he did not have to prove anything to the Commissioner. However, Lord Gardiner thought that the complainant 'ought to have to screw himself up to say that he is claiming that he suffered injustice in consequence of maladministration'.[3]

Lord Gardiner then went on to say that he did not think the committee, or the public at large, realized just how wide the ambit of the Bill was. In a very interesting passage he listed some of the many matters which would be subject to investigation in a variety of Ministries. For example, in the Ministry of Agriculture the refusal

---

[1] Robert Samuel Theodore Chorley Q.C. was made 1st Baron Chorley in 1945. He was Sir Ernest Cassel, Professor of Commercial and Industrial Law in the University of London from 1930 to 1946.

[2] Helen Violet Bonham Carter was made a life peeress in 1964 as Baroness Asquith. Her father was H. H. Asquith, the Liberal Prime Minister. She was President of the Liberal Party Organization from 1945 to 1947.

[3] H. L. Deb. Vol. 280, Col. 650.

or curtailment of certain agricultural grants or subsidies, on the grounds of eligibility, would be subject to investigation.

As regards the Foreign Office, the withholding of passports, except on the narrow grounds that it was necessary for the prevention of crime or the security of the State, could be investigated. In the Ministry of Health, action taken in the administration of one of the hospitals like Broadmoor, for which the Ministry was directly responsible, was subject to investigation.

Under the Ministry of Housing and Local Government, 'allegations that an appeal against a refusal for planning permission for a house had been dismissed owing to undue influence by a powerful neighbour' could be investigated.[1] The whole vast field of the administration of prisons, which was the responsibility of the Home Office, was also subject to investigation. He did not think really, 'that anybody has sufficiently estimated the "fun" which both the Commissioner and the public are going to have once this Bill reaches the Statute Book'.[2]

Although the Lord Chancellor had said that he was not persuaded that the amendment was necessary, he did say that he was prepared to look at the wording of the subsection again. On the strength of this undertaking Lord Wade withdrew his amendment. But no subsequent change in the wording was made.

The next amendment was proposed by Lord Redmayne. Its effect was really to raise again the issue which had been decided in the division when the amendment to make peers a channel for complaints had been defeated. Lord Redmayne was not ashamed to admit this and told the House that he thought that 'those who argued that your Lordships should have access to the Parliamentary Commissioner won the day in debate, although they failed in the Lobby.'[3]

The amendment was, however, somewhat wider in scope. It would also have allowed a public body such as an association, council, or company to make an approach to the Commissioner through an M.P. The essential point of the amendment was that a complaint did not have to be made by a member of the public, as provided in the Bill. Lord Shackleton urged that the matter had really been decided in the previous division and he hoped that Lord Redmayne would not press his amendment.

Lord Redmayne then withdrew the amendment but went on im-

---

[1] Ibid., Col. 652.   [2] Ibid., Col. 653.   [3] Ibid., Col. 654.

mediately to move a further amendment. This amendment proposed to insert a new paragraph to Clause 5, Subsection (1) providing that complaints sent by members of the public to M.P.s would be referred to a Select Committee of the House of Commons which would have to satisfy itself 'that other means for the redress' of complaints had failed and that there was a *prima facie* case for investigating them, before they were referred to the Parliamentary Commissioner.

Lord Redmayne told the House that the amendment followed from the criticisms of the Bill which he had made in second reading. He argued that making the Select Committee a sieve for complaints to the Commissioner would save M.P.s some of the embarrassments which would otherwise be caused to them under the Bill. It would be the Select Committee which declined to forward a complaint, when it was not an eligible complaint, and not the individual M.P.

The Lord Chancellor argued strongly against this amendment. He did not know how a Select Committee would be able to cope with the vast number of complaints which would come to it. It had been estimated that M.P.s dealt during a year with between 250,000 and 300,000 cases. A high proportion of these would go to the Select Committee.

He advanced two other arguments against the amendment. The quorum in a Select Committee was five. The proposal would give 'enormous power to what may be a very few people to decide exactly what the Parliamentary Commissioner is to be allowed to look at and what he is not'.[1] Again, the Government of the day had a majority on each Select Committee. If the Government did not want a certain matter inquired into they could prevent an inquiry through their majority on the committee.

Lord Redmayne then withdrew his amendment. But he made the telling point that through his lack of knowledge of the Commons, the Lord Chancellor had given a misleading impression of the way in which Select Committees there worked. 'Although there is admittedly a nominal Government majority, Select Committees of this quality perform a most splendid service for the other place with remarkably little bias of any sort.'[2]

The next amendment was moved by Lord Silkin (Labour). It proposed to add a new paragraph giving the Parliamentary Commissioner power to initiate an inquiry if he thought an injustice had

---

[1] Ibid., Col. 666.   [2] Ibid., Col. 667.

been done. Two provisos were proposed. The Commissioner must have a written request from the person who claimed to have sustained injustice and the Commissioner's initiative would only operate in the absence of any written complaint from an M.P.

Lord Silkin argued that there might be special circumstances in which a matter comes to the notice of the Commissioner himself, without the intervention of an M.P. 'The Commissioner may have read something in the Press, or a person may even have made a personal approach to him, and he may think that the case is so bad *prima facie* as to justify an inquiry.'[1] Lord Alport (Conservative) supported the amendment.[2]

The Lord Chancellor replied that 'to accept this proposal would, of course, mean a fundamental departure from the basis of the Bill' since it would allow members of the public to complain directly to the Parliamentary Commissioner.[3] He said that when the Government planned the reform, they had the choice of making it either a public institution or a parliamentary institution.

A public institution, such as the Scandinavian countries have and to which any member of the public could go, would have nothing directly to do with Parliament and would not necessarily be limited to the Central Government, because this public institution might perform services in the field of local government, or of the nationalized industries, or of all sorts of local boards. This would have no particular connection with Members of Parliament.[4]

The other alternative was to 'have a Parliamentary institution to which members of the public would go, through Members of Parliament, and which, being a Parliamentary institution, would be limited to the Central Government. We cannot really mix these two kinds of institutions.'[5] If members of the public could approach the Parliamentary Commissioner directly they would not bother to go through an M.P. Then, 'the present practice which has gone on for centuries, of treating Members of the House of Commons as the repository of the grievances of the people, will cease.'[6] He then

---

[1] Ibid., Col. 688.
[2] Cuthbert James McCall Alport was made a life peer in 1961. He was Conservative M.P. for Colchester from 1950 to 1961. He was Parliamentary Under-Secretary at the Commonwealth Relations Office from 1957 to 1959 and a Minister of State there from 1959 to 1961.
[3] H.L. Deb. Vol. 280, Col. 670.
[4] Ibid.   [5] Ibid., Col. 671.   [6] Ibid., Col. 671.

quoted from the Whyatt Report in support of the Government's position, but he did not quote their recommendation that complaints to the Parliamentary Commissioner should be channelled through M.P.s *and* peers *during a five-year trial period.*

Lord Drumalbyn then suggested that there would be a great deal to be said for the amendment if it were redrafted to provide that a member could only take his complaint 'direct to the Ombudsman' if an M.P. had already refused to forward the complaint.[1] He asked the Lord Chancellor whether he would be willing to look at the possibility of inserting this sort of provision.

The Lord Chancellor said that he would be willing to look at this possibility. Lord Silkin, on his side, said that he would be willing to redraft his amendment. He did not think that it would be 'against the principle of the Bill that, in the last resort, there should be a means of redressing a grievance through the Commissioner himself. It is in the New Zealand Act.'[2] He withdrew his amendment in the hope that he would be able to come back to the subject later.

Lord Wade then moved an amendment to the much-criticized Subsection (4), which had been introduced at report stage in the Commons, and provided that the Commissioner could not review, by way of appeal, any discretionary decision taken by a government department. Lord Wade proposed to add to this subsection words authorizing the Commissioner to review such an exercise of discretion if he was 'satisfied that no reasonable person in possession of all the relevant facts and having regard to any then existing and properly formulated policy of the department or authority would have exercised such discretion in the manner in which it was exercised'.

Lady Elliot warmly supported the amendment. She said that when she spoke on this subject at second reading, Lord Shackleton had implied that her fears about subsection (4) were groundless. She told the House 'I think still they were not groundless and subsequent reading of the papers has confirmed me in that view.'[3] She felt that the Bill as it stands 'and in particular this clause, is a huge disappointment.'[4] She hoped that the Lord Chancellor would take up the point raised in the amendment and look at it again.

[1] Niall Malcolm Stewart Macpherson was made 1st Baron Drumalbyn in 1963. He was National Liberal and Unionist M.P. for Dumfriesshire from 1945 to 1963. He was Minister of Pensions and National Insurance from 1962 to 1963 and Minister of State at the Board of Trade from 1963 to 1964.

[2] H.L. Deb. Vol. 280, Col. 675.   [3] Ibid., Col. 678.   [4] Ibid., Col. 679.

Lord Harlech told the House that his position was different from that taken by Lady Elliot. In the light of the explanations of the clause by Lord Shackleton on second reading, he found the clause less offensive than he did originally. He thought the paragraph should be rephrased to make clear, as Lord Shackleton had said in the debate, that, 'if there has been an improper exercise of discretion, then there is a case on which the Parliamentary Commissioner will be able to pass judgement.'[1]

When the Lord Chancellor rose to reply, he soon made it clear that he intended to make a concession on Subsection (4). He told the House 'Clause 5 (4) has created so much discussion and dissension that I begin to think that it cannot be drafted as we should wish it to be.'[2] He then went over the history of the subsection. 'Although it had been understood throughout ever since the time of the Whyatt Report, there is nothing actually in the Bill which says that the Commissioner is not to be a one-man court of appeal.'[3] When an Opposition Privy Counsellor pointed this out at committee stage in the Commons, the Government decided to rectify the situation on report, only to be told that, 'You have torn the guts out of the Bill.'[4] As there was this extraordinary difference about the way in which the subsection would operate, he thought they ought to do something about it.

He himself had another objection to the subsection.

If we were simply saying, 'If having done all the investigation, there is no maladministration, you must not interfere on questions of discretion', I should have expected to find this provided for somewhere round Clause 10, because that is the part of the Bill dealing with what is to happen when an investigation is over. But this is in Clause 5 and the marginal note to Clause 5 is *Matters subject to investigation.*[5]

He was apprehensive that a Civil Servant looking at Subsection (4) would say, 'If this case has anything to do with discretion you cannot investigate at all, because, obviously, this must be intended to stop your investigating it; otherwise why should they put this in a clause the whole of the rest of which is dealing entirely with what you can investigate and what you cannot ?'[6] He could not accept Lord Wade's amendment but he proposed at report stage to move an amendment

---

[1] Ibid., Col. 680.   [2] Ibid., Col. 681.   [3] Ibid.
[4] Ibid.   [5] Ibid., Col. 682.   [6] Ibid.

deleting Subsection (4) of Clause 5 altogether. He then intended, at a later stage in the Bill, to move an amendment 'to the effect that where there is no maladministration, it is not for the Commissioner to judge on the merits, so to speak, a decision which Parliament has left to the Minister's natural discretion.'[1]

This was a handsome concession to the critics of the subsection and Lord Wade recognized it as such. He said he was extremely pleased to hear of the intention of the Lord Chancellor and he withdrew his amendment. Clause 5 was then agreed to without a division.

On Clause 6 (Provisions Relating to Complaints), the only amendment was moved by Lord Airedale. It merely proposed to replace the word 'sent' by the word 'made' in Subsection (3) of the Clause. It had some importance since, as Lord Airedale pointed out, if the word 'sent' were retained, 'the result might be that a person making a complaint who went to an interview with his Member of Parliament and at the interview handed his written complaint to the Member would technically be in breach of a duty under the subsection because he would not have sent his complaint.'[2]

The Lord Chancellor agreed with Lord Airedale. He said the amendment was an improvement and he had much pleasure in accepting it. Clause 6 was then approved in its amended form and Clauses 7 to 9 were approved without discussion.

On Clause 10 (Reports by Commissioner), an amendment had been put down by Lord Harlech. The object of this amendment was to provide that special reports from the Commissioner would be laid before Parliament instead of merely before the House of Commons as stated in the Bill. He explained that the amendment followed on from a point made by Lord Colville of Culross on second reading.

Lord Colville had raised the case of a Minister who sits in the Lords and whose department is the subject of investigation. Should not a report relating to that Minister's department be debatable in the Lords? Lord Harlech pointed out that not only was the Lord Chancellor of necessity a member of the Lords, but that in recent years the offices of Colonial Secretary, Foreign Secretary, and Defence Minister had been held by peers.

Lord Shackleton replied that Members of the Lords were free to debate anything they wished. They would not be debarred from de-

---

[1] Ibid.   [2] Ibid., Col. 683.

bating the Parliamentary Commissioner's reports. He added that the Government were going to accept a later amendment providing that the Commissioner's annual reports would be laid before both Houses of Parliament, but he did not think the case for accepting the present amendment was a strong one. Nevertheless he was prepared 'to consult my friends on this Amendment'.[1]

Lords Airedale and Harlech criticized the logic of this position. Lord Harlech commented that if Lord Shackleton thought that the Lords were not debarred from discusing the Commissioner's reports, he could not see why the amendment was not being accepted. He would for the time being withdraw his amendment, but he announced his intention of putting it down again at report stage.

Lord Wade then moved the amendment to which Lord Shackleton had referred, providing that the annual reports from the Commissioner would lie before Parliament instead of merely before the Commons. The Lord Chancellor replied that the Government saw no objection in principle to this amendment. He was advised, however, that it was better to say that the report would be laid before 'each House of Parliament' rather than 'before Parliament'. There were also some consequential amendments which would be necessary. He therefore asked Lord Wade to withdraw his amendment and undertook to bring forward the necessary amendments at report stage. Lord Wade then told the House that he was glad his amendment had been accepted in principle and he would accordingly withdraw it.

Lord Wade then moved an amendment to give the Parliamentary Commissioner the protection of a provision of the Defamation Act of 1952 in connection with notices he might issue to the Press or interviews with the Press. The Lord Chancellor replied that the Parliamentary Commissioner designate had been consulted on this question. He had said that he did not require any further degree of privilege than was provided for already in the Bill as drafted. The Lord Chancellor suggested that the amendment was not then really necessary.

Lord Wade, in view of this statement, withdrew his amendment. Clause 10 was then approved and Clauses 11 to 14 and Schedule 1 were agreed to without discussion. A number of amendments had been put down to Schedule 2 (Departments and Authorities Subject to Investigation) but they were of minor importance.

[1] Ibid., Col. 686.

For example, the Lord Chancellor moved to delete the Ministry of Aviation since that Ministry had been abolished. This was agreed. Similarly, he moved to delete the Ministry of Land and Natural Resources and insert the Land Commission. This was also agreed.

Lord Harlech moved to insert 'Chancellor of the Duchy of Lancaster's Office' and mentioned other amendments which provided for the inclusion of the offices of Lord Privy Seal and Minister without Portfolio. The Lord Chancellor replied that all these amendments were unnecessary since all such Ministers, and their offices, were included by the reference in paragraph 6 of Schedule 2: 'the office of any Minister whose expenses are defrayed out of money provided by Parliament for the service of the Treasury'. Schedule 2 was then approved.

On Schedule 3 (Matters Not Subject to Investigation) only one amendment had been put down, but this related to the most controversial of all the exclusions: the hospitals. Lord Wade moved to delete paragraph 8 excluding the hospital boards, hospital management committees, etc., from investigation.

Lady Elliot was the first to support the amendment. She said there were a tremendous number of grievances about the hospital services. She had 'been in touch with the Patients' Association who receive a great many complaints, and they tell me that there is no proper complaints procedure'.[1] The Ministry had issued a leaflet about the handling of complaints but this leaflet was not available to the patients or to the public. She thought that complaints about the hospital service were a vital matter to the public and should come within the orbit of the Ombudsman.

Lord Nugent of Guildford supported Lady Elliot.[2] He recalled that Richard Crossman, in the Commons, had given an undertaking that, before the Bill reached the Lords, the Government would reconsider the question of excluding the hospitals. He only secured the assent of the Commons, on report, to excluding the hospitals once more (after the standing committee had made them open to investigation) by promising to look at the matter again.

The objection had been raised that most complaints about the hospital service would have a clinical element in them. But in

---

[1] Ibid., Col. 694.

[2] George Richard Hodges Nugent was made a life peer in 1966 as Baron Nugent of Guildford. He was Conservative M.P. for Guildford from 1950 to 1966. He was Parliamentary Secretary at the Ministry of Agriculture from 1951 to 1957.

Sweden 'the hospital service complete comes within the sphere of the Ombudsman, and there is no difficulty at all in dealing with clinical points. Indeed, if difficult points were expected to arise, the Ombudsman could always have assessors appointed to assist him in matters of medical and surgical knowledge.'[1]

Another unsatisfactory argument used by the Government was that investigation by the Parliamentary Commissioner was unnecessary since the Minister could set up an independent inquiry as envisaged in the 1966 circular. But if 'the Minister does not set up such an inquiry when a complaint is made, the complainant still has no remedy, and it is here that we feel the Ombudsman should come into the matter.'[2] He thought it was fair to make the point 'that there are great expectations of this Bill. I expect the noble Lord, Lord Shackleton, includes in his reading the *Sunday Mirror* and although they are his constant supporters he will have seen what critical comments they had to make about this.'[3] He felt there was a strong case for putting the hospital service back into the Bill.

Lord Shackleton said that he did not include the *Sunday Mirror* in his reading. He allowed that there was great force in what Lord Nugent had said in favour of including the hospitals. The arguments against were 'simply those of wisdom in relation to the starting of this whole scheme'. There was power in the Bill 'to bring in the hospital service as soon as this or any other Government is ready to do so'.[4]

Two peers with experience of hospital administration then made short contributions to the debate. Lord Auckland said that he was not on a regional hospital board but was a member of two hospital house committees. He believed that to include hospitals within the Bill 'would give protection to the Boards themselves and to the patients they serve'. At present, if things go wrong, the members of the hospital board have very little redress. The hospital boards should be one of the first areas the Ombudsman should cover.[5]

Viscount Addison took a directly contrary view. He disclosed his interest as chairman of a regional hospital board. His board dealt with a very large number of complaints mostly of a minor character. He thought that they would be placing a large additional load on

---

[1] H.L. Deb. Vol. 280, Col. 696.   [2] Ibid.
[3] Ibid., Cols. 696–7. See above p. 206.   [4] Ibid., Col. 697.
[5] Ian George Eden is the 9th Baron Auckland. He is an associate director of a firm of management consultants.

the Ombudsman if they agreed to the amendment. The Government had a strong case for resisting the proposal at this stage.[1]

Both Lord Nugent and Lord Wade then spoke of their disappointment at the Government's attitude. Lord Wade thought that the Government should be able to give some idea of the timing so that they could have an indication of how long they would have to wait until the hospitals were brought in.

Lord Shackleton replied that it was impossible to be definite. 'We do not know what the load on the Parliamentary Commissioner is going to be. I should have thought a great deal would depend on the attitude of the Parliamentary Commissioner himself. We are bound to have regard to his opinion, and although it would be inappropriate for me to say what I believe to be his opinion, certainly the impression I have clearly gained is "not yet".'[2]

Lord Wade then said that he thought the wisest course would be to return to the matter on report stage. Although he did not withdraw any of the observations he had made, he would withdraw his amendment. The rest of Schedule 3 was then agreed to and the committee stage of the Bill concluded just after 7.20 p.m.

[1] H.L. Deb. Vol. 280, Col. 699. Christopher Addison is the 2nd Viscount Addison. He is a director of several companies. He was Chairman of the South Western Metropolitan Regional Hospital Board from 1965 to 1968.

[2] Ibid., Col. 700.

XIII

THE REPORT STAGE AND THIRD READING IN THE LORDS

THE report stage in the Lords was taken a fortnight after the committee stage, on Tuesday, 7 March 1967. The first amendment on report was moved by the Lord Chancellor to Clause 5 (Matters Subject to Investigation). This was the amendment which he had promised at committee stage. It proposed the deletion of the much-criticized subsection (4) preventing the Commissioner from reviewing, by way of appeal, any decision taken by a government department in the exercise of a discretionary power. He told the House that this proposed deletion was coupled with his intention at a later stage of the Bill, of proposing an amendment to make it clear that where, having investigated a case, the Commissioner was satisfied that there had been no maladministration, 'it was not for him to review on the merits a decision taken in the exercise of a statutory discretion.'[1]

Lady Burton warmly welcomed the amendment deleting 5 (4). She said she 'should like to express my great appreciation to the Lord Chancellor for withdrawing it'. The amendment was then agreed to.

The next amendment was to Clause 10 (Reports by the Commissioner) and was moved by Lord Colville of Culross from the Conservative front bench. This amendment proposed that special reports from the Parliamentary Commissioner, indicating that he had found an injustice which was not being remedied, might be laid before each House of Parliament instead of merely before the House of Commons as provided in the Bill. This was substantially the amendment which Lord Harlech had proposed at committee stage and had then withdrawn when he was told that it was unacceptable to the Minister. He had, however, announced his intention of reintroducing it at report stage.

[1] H.L. Deb. Vol. 280, Col. 1329.

Lord Colville repeated the arguments in favour of the amendment which had been used by Lord Harlech in committee. He did, however, introduce one new point. Lord Harlech had argued that there would be occasions when the Ministerial head of a department criticized by the Commissioner was a Member of the Lords. Lord Colville pointed out that it could also happen that a former Minister who was in the Lords could be involved in a case when the department which he had headed was under criticism in a report from the Commissioner. In both types of case it would be desirable for reports to be laid before the Lords so that they could be debated there and a Minister, or former Minister, could answer for the conduct of his department, or former department.

Lords Reay and Airedale supported the amendment. When Lord Shackleton rose to reply, he soon made it clear that the Government had now decided to accept the amendment. He then went on to discuss the question which had been touched on by Lord Colville as to whether a peer could give evidence to a Select Committee of the Commons. He had suggested that there would be grave difficulties in a peer giving evidence to the proposed Select Committee on the Parliamentary Commissioner. Lord Shackleton said that Standing Order No. 22 which was the relevant Order of the House of Lords had been made in 1674. It stated: 'no Lord shall either go down to the House of Commons or send his answer in writing, or appear by counsel, to answer any accusation there.' [1]

In 1805 the House of Lords had summed up the conventions under which this Order operated by saying that it had been the practice of the House to give leave to peers, at their own request, to defend themselves in the Commons 'on any points which that House had not previously passed any accusatory or criminating resolution against them'. [2]

It seemed therefore that there was a long tradition that peers had been given permission to attend the Commons under this kind of condition. He mentioned one instance in which a predecessor of Lord Somers had been allowed to attend the Commons. Nevertheless, he thought it wise that the whole question should be considered by the Lords Committee on Procedure and Lord Colville concurred with this suggestion. Lord Colville's amendment was then approved.

The Lord Chancellor then moved amendments which he had

[1] Ibid., Col. 1336.　　[2] Ibid.

undertaken at committee stage to propose. He explained that they arose from the Liberal amendment at committee stage which had sought to provide that the annual reports from the Parliamentary Commissioner should be made to each House of Parliament. He was now proposing this amendment and certain other consequential amendments which were necessary. Lord Reay said that the Liberals were pleased that the Government had decided to introduce these amendments which were then agreed.

Lord Gardiner then moved an amendment to add a new Subsection (3) to Clause 12 (Interpretation). This was the amendment of which he had earlier spoken when moving the deletion of Subsection (4) of Clause 5. The proposed new subsection read as follows: '(3) It is hereby declared that nothing in this Act authorises or requires the Commissioner to question the merits of a decision taken without maladministration by a government department or other authority in the exercise of a discretion vested in that department or authority.' In introducing the amendment the Lord Chancellor briefly commented: 'I hope it does that which we have all, I think, always intended.' [1] It made clear that the Commissioner is not 'a one-man Court of Appeal from a discretionary decision' but at the same time it in no way restricted what the Commissioner can investigate.

Lord Colville, for the Conservatives, gave a cautious welcome to the amendment. 'It may well be that we have here the clearer statement of the matter which everybody was seeking at Second Reading.' [2] He criticized an amendment to the amendment moved by Lord Airedale for the Liberals. This amendment proposed to add the words 'in good faith' before 'taken without maladministration' in the proposed new subsection.

Lord Colville maintained that this was an attempt to define maladministration and was both unnecessary and unwise. The 'best thing to do is to accept the fact that when we find maladministration we shall recognise it even if we cannot define it in advance'. [3]

The Lord Chancellor agreed. 'We have all agreed that maladministration is the widest possible word. It certainly includes bad faith and delay.' [4] Lord Airedale then withdrew his amendment to the amendment and the House approved the amendment to insert the new Subsection (3) to Clause 12.

[1] Ibid., Col. 1340.   [2] Ibid., Col. 1343.
[3] Ibid., Col. 1342.   [4] Ibid., Col. 1343.

Lord Reay then moved an amendment for the Liberals, to add a further subsection to this clause. This new proposed subsection stated that: 'For the purposes of this Act the term maladministration shall not of itself be understood to exclude those cases where, notwithstanding the fact that administrative procedures may have been properly followed, an arbitrary and unreasonable decision by a government department or other authority resulted in an injustice.'

The discussion on this amendment showed that there were two points of view represented in the House but the Government and Opposition front benches were in agreement. The Lord Chancellor, for the Government, and Lord Colville, for the Conservative Opposition, were in favour of confining the Parliamentary Commissioner to reporting on maladministration and were against any attempt to define the term.

On the other hand, Lord Reay, for the Liberals, was concerned that in cases where no maladministration could be found, there might still be injustice to the individual. Hence his suggestion to allow the Parliamentary Commissioner to report upon 'arbitrary or unreasonable' decisions by government departments. His position was nearer to that found in the New Zealand Act where the Parliamentary Commissioner can report on a decision which, in his opinion, is 'unreasonable, unjust, offensive or unproperly discriminatory'.[1]

Lord Gardiner maintained, in his speech on the amendment, that if you allowed the Parliamentary Commissioner to report that a decision had been arbitrary or unreasonable you would merely be substituting one man's opinion for another's. He went back again to the Whyatt Report with its distinction between maladministration which should be the concern of the Parliamentary Commissioner, and discretionary decisions which should be subject to an extended and improved tribunal system. He told the House that he was hoping under the recently passed Tribunals and Inquiries Act, to lay before Parliament an Order making 'something like a hundred different kinds of ministerial inquiries' subject to supervision by the Council on Tribunals.[2]

Lord Reay was not satisfied by this reply from the Lord Chan-

[1] New Zealand Statutes, 1962, No. 10. The Parliamentary Commissioner (Ombudsman) Act, Section 19, subsection (b).
[2] H.L. Deb. Vol. 280, Col. 1354.

cellor. He asked the House to decide the issue and, on a voice vote, the amendment was defeated.

The Lord Chancellor then moved an amendment to Schedule 2 (Departments and Authorities Subject to Investigation). This amendment proposed to add the Social Survey to the departments or authorities subject to investigation. The Social Survey, which up until then had been a division of the Central Office of Information, was to become a separate department on 1 April 1967. This followed from a recommendation of the Heyworth Committee on Social Studies. The amendment was agreed to.

The final amendment to be moved in the Lords was to Schedule 3 (Matters Not Subject to Investigation). Lord Reay, for the Liberals, moved once again to delete paragraph 8 (Action taken by Regional Hospital Boards, Hospital Management Committees, etc.) and thereby bring back the hospital service within the purview of the Parliamentary Commissioner. A lengthy debate took place on this amendment, but few new arguments were advanced on either side.

In his speech for the amendment Lord Reay brought in many of the arguments which had been used in favour of including the hospital service, in the earlier debates both in the Lords and Commons. One new argument he advanced was an attempt to counter the Government view that the Commissioner would be over-burdened with complaints against the hospitals. He argued that, if the Government were right, the worst that could happen was that there might be delay in the Parliamentary Commissioner's Office in dealing with complaints. He thought that delay was something which the public would mind less and 'would understand more readily than the total exclusion of this source of grievance from any chance of remedy at all'.[1]

Lord Nugent of Guildford supported the amendment on behalf of the Conservatives. He said that he had studied Lord Shackleton's speech on committee stage and thought that his answer really amounted to 'not yet'. He noted 'that part of his answer rested on the opinion of the Ombudsman himself, given informally of course'. He commented drily: 'While I recognise that it is an unusual advantage for Parliament to have the advice of an officer before it appoints him, it still is not enough to persuade me that Lord Shackleton was right.'[2]

[1] Ibid., Col. 1360.   [2] Ibid., Col. 1361.

Viscount Addison had spoken in his capacity of chairman of a regional hospital board, against the amendment, at committee stage, to include the hospitals. He now developed his arguments at greater length. He spoke about the working of the complaints system within the hospitals, and pointed out that very few complaints were found to be justified in relation to the large volume of admissions. For example, in the nine months from April to December 1966, 168 complaints had been found to be justified in his board's area. In the same period there had been 263,000 in-patient and 407,000 out-patient admissions in addition to 401,000 casualties. He also argued that nearly all the complaints have a clinical element and thus the Parliamentary Commissioner's department would need a considerable staff of professionals, such as doctors and nurses, to advise him on clinical questions if the hospitals were brought in.

One new, and very eminent, contributor to the debate was Lord Platt who had been Professor of Medicine at Manchester University from 1945 to 1965 and had also been President of the Royal College of Physicians.[1] Lord Platt spoke against the amendment. He argued that with hospital complaints 'it will be difficult, or almost impossible in many instances, to separate the clinical from the purely administrative.'[2] He also argued that 'to equate the actions of doctors and nurses in caring for their patients with administrative actions carried out on behalf of central Government would be to introduce a new and possible disastrous look at professional duty'.[3]

Lords Mitchison and Grenfell also spoke against the amendment. Lord Grenfell drew on his personal experience as chairman of a hospital management committee. Brief interventions in support of the amendment were made by Lords Somers and Airedale and Earl Fortescue.

The arguments used by Viscount Addison and Lord Shackleton against including the hospitals had for the most part been heard before from Government spokesmen at earlier stages in the Bill. Lord Shackleton did, however, introduce one new argument in his winding-up speech against the amendment. He said that, if the hospitals were brought in, the setting up of the Parliamentary Commissioner would be delayed, possibly for months. This argument

---

[1] Robert Platt was created Baron Platt in 1967. He is a life peer. He was born in 1900. He was President of the Royal College of Physicians from 1957 to 1962. From 1964 to 1967 he was Chairman of the Clinical Research Board of the Medical Research Council.
[2] H.L. Deb. Vol. 280, Col. 1366.   [3] Ibid., Col. 1367.

may have swayed some Labour votes. For when the division took place there was a clear party alignment in the lobbies. Liberal and Conservative peers voted for the amendment, Labour peers voted against, while there was a sprinkling of cross-benchers on either side.

The amendment was lost by a margin of twelve votes, forty-seven peers voting for the amendment and fifty-nine against. The Government was therefore spared the embarrassment of having to apply its majority to have the paragraph restored in the Commons, when the Commons considered the Lords' amendments. This also may have influenced the decision of some Labour peers to vote against the amendment. Another consideration was appreciation of the fact that the Government had made major concessions in the passage of the Bill through the Lords: the curb placed upon the Commissioner by Subsection 4 of Clause 5 had been removed, and the Lords had been given a larger interest in the Commissioner's activities by the amendments providing that his reports would lie before each House of Parliament.

The division on this amendment brought the report stage to an end at 5.39 p.m. It had gone on for 2 hours 25 minutes (allowing for an intervening 17 minutes for a Ministerial statement on another topic).

Third reading in the Lords took place two days later, on Thursday, 9 March. It was completed in ten minutes at the end of the Lords Parliamentary day. The only contributors to this mini-debate were Lord Colville and the Lord Chancellor. The occasion was notable, however, for the valediction which Lord Gardiner gave to the Bill. He thought that the House of Lords had 'substantially improved' the Bill. He thought that 'in the form in which the Bill reached us' it had been open to doubt whether the Commissioner would have adequate powers of investigation. He had no doubt that the Lords had improved this part of the Bill by the amendments they had made. He also thought that they had been right to alter the Bill so that the Commissioner's reports would be made to each House of Parliament.[1]

He ended on a note of personal affirmation for the principle of the Bill.

I have been an Ombudsman enthusiast throughout, and I believe that here we have something which is going to be a considerable arm for

[1] Ibid., Cols. 1636–7.

ordinary Members of another place against the Executive, to a far greater extent than they could ever have controlled the actions of Ministers or Departments before; secondly that this will provide a remedy for grievances of the citizen against the central Government; and, thirdly, while I do not know of any country which has a better Civil Service than we have, everything is always capable of improvement in administration and this step will also, I believe, have that effect.[1]

THE LORDS' AMENDMENTS CONSIDERED IN THE COMMONS

The Commons considered the Lords' amendments six days later on Wednesday, 15 March 1967. The proceedings lasted less than an hour, from 9.34 p.m. to 10.25 p.m. and all the Lords' amendments were agreed to. Some of the opinions expressed on the amendments were, however, of considerable interest.

It was clear that Niall MacDermot, who opened the proceedings, did not share the Lord Chancellor's opinion about Subsection 4 of Clause 5 which the Lords had deleted and which he himself had introduced at report stage in the Commons. He told the House that the Government had accepted that the wording of the subsection might have caused misunderstanding. 'I do not myself take that view, because it is clear from the words, "review by way of appeal" that the subsection was limited in the way that I said when I moved it. However, others have thought otherwise, and the Government are anxious only to achieve the purpose that I stated before, which is to put the matter beyond doubt.'[2]

The reaction on the Conservative benches to this deletion, coupled with the new subsection added in Clause 12, was varied. Sir John Hobson gave a back-handed welcome to the amendments. He argued that the Government had always intended the Bill to be a very emasculated one. These amendments only clarified this situation.

Sir Lionel Heald took a very different view. He thought they should accept the amendments with gratitude. He pointed out that the Lord Chancellor had concurred with the view that Sir Lionel and other Conservatives had voiced at report stage in the Commons. He had agreed that Subsection (4) might have had the effect 'that it would be sufficient to show that there was an exercise of discretion in order to exclude the jurisdiction of the Ombudsman'.[3]

---

[1] Ibid., Col. 1638.   [2] H.C. Deb. Vol. 743, Col. 626.   [3] Ibid., Col. 628.

The situation now was that the Ombudsman would be left in the position of deciding whether there was maladministration or not. He went on: 'I think we would probably agree, certainly as regards the future occupant of the important position of Parliamentary Commissioner, that it would be quite safe to leave it in his hands to decide whether he considers that there has been maladministration or not.'[1] He concluded by saying that they should realize that 'this is one of those occasions when the other place has performed a very important function because the Government adopted a dictatorial attitude which they have so often adopted recently with regard to legislation and in this case it was the Lord Chancellor in another place who was able to put the Government in their proper place.'[2]

This praise for the House of Lords was irksome to Michael English (Labour). He thought that 'the House of Lords has merely served the useful function in being an extra stage in the passing of legislation so that what was always intended to be in the Bill could be inserted in it.'[3] A similar difference of opinion between him and the Conservatives emerged when the House considered the Lords' amendments to provide that the Parliamentary Commissioner's reports should be made to both Houses of Parliament.

Sir John Hobson said that the Conservatives 'greatly welcome these amendments'. They would mean that 'the House of Lords, which has an equal interest in the liberty of the subject and in the rights of citizens and which has always been closely associated, by its judicial nature, with that type of work, will have some part in debating and considering the reports of the Commissioner.'[4] Michael English, on the other hand, said: 'I rather regret that the Government have accepted these Amendments, but I see their point.'[5] The difficulty he foresaw was that the House of Lords would now presumably set up their own Select Committee on the Parliamentary Commissioner. This would mean that the Commissioner would have two Select Committees to listen to, whereas it had been the intention originally that there would be only the Commons Committee with which he would consult. He had no doubt that the two committees would often be in conflict.

Niall MacDermot, replying to this point, said that he understood that 'there is no intention by the other House to seek to set up a Select Committee. I think that it is accepted by them that the

---

[1] Ibid., Col. 629.   [2] Ibid.   [3] Ibid., Col. 629.
[4] Ibid., Col. 638.   [5] Ibid., Col. 639.

Parliamentary Commissioner will be basically an Officer of this House and will report to a Select Committee of this House.'[1]

Dr. Michael Winstanley, speaking for the Liberals, had earlier made it clear that they supported the amendments. It had been argued that there were deficiencies in the Commons which had given rise to the need for a Parliamentary Commissioner. If there were such deficiencies then he believed that it was helpful to associate the Lords with the work of the Parliamentary Commissioner. He believed that there would 'come a time when the Labour Party will honour its election pledge of 1929 to give us a democratic and representative Second Chamber'.[2]

At this stage the Speaker had to use his customary tact and firmness in order to prevent the proceedings from becoming a general discussion of reform of the Upper House and of the relationship between the two chambers. Sir Douglas Glover (Conservative) had been eager to spring to the defence of the Lords and very critical of the view advanced by Michael English that the Parliamentary Commissioner 'should be restricted to the Lower House, the House of Commons'.[3]

When the Lords' amendments had been agreed to by the Commons, all the proceedings on the Bill had been completed. A week later, on 22 March 1967 the Bill received the Royal Assent and was enacted as the Parliamentary Commissioner Act 1967.

CONSIDERATION OF THE PARLIAMENTARY COMMISSIONER BILL BY THE LORDS—AN EVALUATION

We have earlier compared the time given in the Lords to the second reading of the Parliamentary Commissioner Bill to the time given to second reading in the Commons. We saw that there was not much difference: five hours for second reading in the Lords, six hours twenty-seven minutes for second reading in the Commons. When we compare, however, the time taken in the two Houses in considering the details of the Bill there is a vast difference.

The debates in the Lords on the committee and report stages lasted seven hours altogether (four hours and thirty-five minutes for committee stage, two hours twenty-five minutes for report stage). In the Commons, debates on committee stage and report stage went on for twenty eight hours thirty-five minutes altogether (twenty three hours fifty-three minutes for committee stage, four hours

[1] Ibid., Col. 642.   [2] Ibid., Col. 640.   [3] Ibid., Col. 642.

forty-two minutes for report stage). The Commons therefore gave four times as much time as the Lords to discussing the Bill in detail. Discussions in the Commons also took place over a much longer period of time, since the committee stage began in Standing Committee B on 27 October 1966 and the report stage took place on 24 January 1967. In the Lords, the committee stage was completed in one day, 21 February 1967, and the report stage was taken a fortnight later on 7 March 1967.

The much shorter time given to the Bill in the Lords, at committee and report stage, can be justified on the grounds that it was not necessary to go over again everything that had been covered in the Commons. In Standing Committee B, as we have seen, almost every clause and paragraph in the Bill had been probed and debated in an exhaustive fashion. The Lords, instead, concentrated principally on five issues in committee stage and report. These were: (1) the 'maladministration' question, (2) whether local government could be brought in, (3) whether peers could be made a channel to the Parliamentary Commissioner, (4) whether reports from the Commissioner should be made to the Lords as well as to the Commons, and (5) whether the hospital service should be brought back within the purview of the Commissioner.

On the first and fourth of these issues, the peers were able to secure important concessions from the Government. The Lords played an important part in the legislative process, therefore, and made substantial amendments to the Bill in the opinion both of the Lord Chancellor and of Sir Lionel Heald, speaking from the Conservative Front Bench in the Commons.

Is it likely that the Bill would have been similarly improved if there had been no Upper House, but there had been an additional stage of legislation in the Commons? The implication of the remark from Michael English in the Commons, when the Lords amendments were considered, seems to have been that it would.[1]

This question can only be looked at in relation to the maladministration issue since the other group of amendments related to the second chamber itself. The question can therefore be narrowed down to asking whether, if there had been a further legislative stage after report stage, in the Commons, it is likely that Subsection (4) of Clause 5, introduced at report, would have been taken out again?

There can be no conclusive answer to this question but some

[1] See above p. 231.

indications can be noted. On the one hand, there had been, as we have seen, a great deal of Press criticism of Subsection 5 (4) on the grounds that it emasculated the Bill. It is possible therefore that the Government would have yielded to this criticism before a 'fourth stage' of discussion took place in the Commons. On the other hand, in this 'fourth stage', the Minister in charge of the Bill would still have been Niall MacDermot and the influences brought to bear on the Bill from the membership of the Lords would not have been found in the Commons.

There is no doubt that Niall MacDermot and the Lord Chancellor had very different views about Subsection 5 (4). Lord Gardiner told the Lords that it had been a mistake and that there was a serious possibility that it might be interpreted to exclude the Commissioner from considering a great many cases which he would otherwise have been able to investigate. Niall MacDermot, however, when the Bill returned to the Commons, indicated that he was reluctantly accepting the change in the Bill and that he still did not agree with the criticisms that had been made of Subsection 5 (4).

On the question of the influences brought to bear in the Lords, there is no doubt that the different composition of the Lords as compared with the Commons, was important too. In the first place, the Liberals were prominent in discussion of the Bill in the Lords, being ably led by Lord Wade who was himself keenly interested in reform on the Ombudsman model. He and Lord Reay, supported by Lord Airedale, were active in moving amendments which sought to widen the scope of the Parliamentary Commissioner's power to investigate. It was during discussion of an amendment moved, in committee, by Lord Wade to limit the effect of Subsection 5 (4), that the Lord Chancellor announced his intention of moving an amendment, at report stage, to delete the offending subsection.

In the second place, an important part was played in prodding the Government on this question by peers who had special experience not shared by Members of the Commons. In particular, Lady Elliot, with her keen awareness of the needs of the consumer, was as prominent in her support of Lord Wade's amendment as she had been critical at second reading in the Lords of the Government's introduction of Clause 5 (4). Similarly, Lady Burton was highly critical of this part of the Bill, the force of her criticism being strengthened by her position as Chairman of the Council on Tribunals. It can well be argued therefore, that the different party composition of the Lords, and the presence there of eminent people with specialized knowledge and experience, played an important part in subjecting the Bill to a criticism which was, in some respects, more effective than criticism which had been voiced in the Commons.

Part Three

THE PARLIAMENTARY
COMMISSIONER IN OPERATION

XIV

GETTING OFF THE GROUND

ON 1 April 1967, the Parliamentary Commissioner Act came into force and Sir Edmund Compton took up his duties as Parliamentary Commissioner for Administration. He began by giving a Press conference and appearing on television, and was given a reasonably favourable reception in the Press.

For example, an editorial in the *Observer* commented, on 2 April 1967, 'When Sir Edmund Compton starts work tomorrow, in a sedate and modest way he will be making history: a new institution will have come into existence.' This was despite the feeling that, as the editor commented, 'At times during the long debates in Parliament, as the Government hedged in the Parliamentary Commissioner first with one restriction and then another, it has seemed as though it would have been better not to bring such a small, stunted child into the world. But the most important thing about our Ombudsman (as, inevitably, the Commissioner will be called) is that he exists. The barrier against independent investigation of the bureaucracy has been breached.'

On the same day, the *Sunday Times* printed a long and sympathetic profile of 'Sir Edmund Compton, The New Ombudsman'. A sub-heading ran: 'Yesterday the appointment of the Parliamentary Commissioner—or Ombudsman—became official. The powers he has been given are more limited than had at first been expected, and the influence of the job will depend largely on Sir Edmund's personality.'

This mildly favourable reception contrasted strongly with the gloomy comment from the Press before the Bill was discussed in committee in the Lords, only just over six weeks before. The changed atmosphere must be largely explained by the concessions which the Lord Chancellor had made at committee stage and report in the Lords. It is appropriate to give the credit here to the Chancellor, since Lord Gardiner himself had drafted the new subsection on maladministration and discretionary acts, in Clause 12, which had replaced the much-criticized subsection put in at report stage in the Commons.

Sir Edmund Compton's office went into operation on 3 April 1967 and began immediately to deal with complaints which had already been sent to the Commissioner by Members of Parliament. The final proceedings on the Bill had been concluded not much more than a fortnight before, on 15 March. It would obviously have been quite impossible for the Parliamentary Commissioner's Office to have gone into operation so quickly if Sir Edmund Compton had not been appointed well in advance of the passage of the Act.

We have seen that one of the advantages of his early appointment as Parliamentary Commissioner designate was that he was available to advise Ministers about the practicality or impracticality, from his point of view, of various amendments to the Bill put forward from the Opposition benches or by back-benchers on the Government side. Another advantage was that he was able to note closely the hopes and anxieties about his future role voiced by Members during the passage of the Bill. He was, in fact, present in the room in which Standing Committee B met for every one of its ten sittings. On the few occasions when he had to leave before 1.0 p.m., when the standing committee rose, he left a representative to observe and report to him.

The biggest advantage, however, which his advance appointment gave him was the ability to recruit, organize his office, and establish lines of communication with the departments he would be called upon to investigate. By 3 April 1967 all these necessary preparations had been made so that the work of processing and investigating complaints could begin at once.

The staff and its organization will be discussed later.[1] What is interesting to note at this point is the programme which Sir Edmund had set himself, while the Bill was still under discussion, to establish lines of communication with government departments. In his own words, to this author, he undertook 'an assault course around Whitehall'. He interviewed the Permanent Secretaries of all the departments with whom he would be dealing, and arranged the procedures he and they would follow in receiving and investigating complaints. In particular, he agreed with each Permanent Secretary that a

[1] See below, pp. 246–7 and 272–3.

specified person in the department concerned would be the normal channel of communication with the Parliamentary Commissioner's Office.

A further advantage of Sir Edmund Compton's appointment as Parliamentary Commissioner designate was that he was able to use some of the time, before the passage of the Act, for finding out about comparable institutions in other countries. He went, himself, to New Zealand in the autumn of 1966 to discuss with Sir Guy Powles, the New Zealand Ombudsman, the ways in which Sir Guy organized his investigations. He was particularly interested to discuss with Sir Guy the screening process he was using, as well as his relations with departments and his connections with Parliament. He also discussed with Sir Guy the much wider terms of reference given him by the New Zealand Act and his ability to report upon a decision that was, in his opinion, 'unreasonable' or 'wrong'.

Sir Edmund Compton did not himself go to Scandinavia, but he asked the Secretary of his Office, Edwin Sykes, to visit Sweden and Denmark. Edwin L. Sykes had previously been an Assistant Under-Secretary of State in the Commonwealth Office, having served in Pakistan until 1966 as British Deputy High Commissioner.[1] Sykes reported to Sir Edmund that the Ombudsmen in Scandinavia acted as 'administrative judges'. That is to say they did 'review by way of appeal' the actions of public authorities. He also reported that there were no specific statutory definitions of the jurisdictions of Ombudsman in Scandinavia. The small size of each country, in terms of population, also made it possible for the Scandinavian Ombudsmen to operate with small staffs and in an informal manner.

These were the impressions which Sir Edmund received from Edwin Sykes's visit. He and Sykes concluded that there was not a great deal which could be learned from the Scandinavian institution which would be of value to them. Conditions, in their view, were too different. In the first place, the British Parliamentary Commissioner was not meant to be an 'administrative judge'. Secondly, his jurisdiction was closely defined. Finally, the large population with which the British Parliamentary Commissioner would be concerned necessitated a considerable degree of formal organization.

---

[1] Edwin Leonard Sykes was born in 1914. He entered the Dominions Office in 1937. He was Assistant Under-Secretary of State at the Commonwealth Relations Office from 1964 to 1965. From 1965 to 1966 he was Deputy U.K. High Commissioner in Pakistan.

Edwin Sykes also found that the Ombudsmen in Sweden and Denmark had relatively little contact with committees of Parliament. The main concern of the relevant committees of Parliament there was with the question of who would be the next Ombudsman. Here, again, there was a big contrast with Britain since it had all along been intended that the Parliamentary Commissioner would have as close a relationship with a Select Committee of the Commons as Sir Edmund Compton had experienced as Comptroller and Auditor-General in working with the Public Accounts Committee.

The British Parliamentary Commissioner was, in effect, to be in charge of an administrative audit, in central government, working closely with a committee of the House of Commons. Sir Edmund Compton was very well qualified to fill this role. He had had a long and distinguished career in the Civil Service. After taking a First in Greats at Oxford in 1929, he entered the Home Civil Service. He had a year in the Colonial Office from 1930 to 1931, but then transferred to the Treasury, where he stayed until 1940.

In that year, he was seconded to the Ministry of Aircraft Production, where he served as Private Secretary to the Minister, Lord Beaverbrook. From 1941 to 1942 he was in the Ministry of Supply. He then returned to the Treasury as an Assistant Secretary. He was appointed Under-Secretary at the Treasury in 1947 and Third Secretary in 1949. In 1958 he was appointed Comptroller and Auditor-General and held this post for eight years, until 1966, when he was appointed Parliamentary Commissioner designate.

He therefore had a first-rate knowledge of the work of the central government machine as well as of the means by which departments are held financially accountable. He was well used to working with Members of Parliament and, in particular, had established a good relationship with Harold Wilson when the latter was Chairman of the Public Accounts Committee from 1959 to 1963.

It was during this period that Sir Edmund's department pointed to escalating costs in a whole series of guided-missile projects. Shortly after Harold Wilson ceased to be Chairman of the Committee, Sir Edmund Compton and his auditors came up with the discovery that the Ferranti company had made a profit of 63 per cent on cost in developing the Bloodhound Mk. I guided weapon. As a result, the company was induced to return to the Treasury £2,250,000 of the profit it had made. Sir Edmund Compton's vigilance and success in these ways singled him out in Wilson's mind as the ideal man to inaugurate the office of Parliamentary Commissioner.

A very different type of person might have been chosen to be the first Parliamentary Commissioner. The Ombudsmen in Scandinavia always have legal training. Many of them have been judges, while Stephan Hurwitz, the Danish Ombudsman, had been a Professor of Law. Sir Guy Powles, the New Zealand Ombudsman, had been a diplomat and a soldier, but he had also been trained as a lawyer.

British judges are from time to time given 'Ombudsman type' functions. For example, Lord Devlin was made Chairman of the Press Council in 1963. Lord Denning was asked to make a one-man inquiry into the events connected with the resignation of the Secretary of State for War, John Profumo, in 1963, and the trial of Stephen Ward, in the same year. A judge would have certainly been a possible choice as Parliamentary Commissioner.

Another possibility was someone like Lord Shawcross who had been a leading barrister, had had Ministerial experience in the Attlee Government as Attorney General and President of the Board of Trade, and had been prominent in the campaign for a British Ombudsman in his capacity as Chairman of Justice. The choice fell instead on Sir Edmund Compton, because it was felt that the role planned for the Parliamentary Commissioner in Britain would be best filled by someone with experience of the Administrative Class of the Civil Service who also had the confidence of Members of Parliament. It was the fact that he was *persona grata* with higher Civil Servants, and with members of all parties in the House of Commons who had served on the Public Accounts Committee, which seemed to make him a particularly suitable choice for the post.

Sir Edmund Compton had three main tasks when he set up his office. He needed to develop his links with Members of Parliament and improve their understanding of his role under the new Act. He needed to gain the co-operation of government departments and win their acceptance of his investigating activities. Finally, he needed to establish a more favourable image with the Press and the public. We have seen that the welcome he had received from the Press when he took office under the Act was sympathetic, but little more than lukewarm.

On 30 March 1967, two days before he took up his functions officially, Sir Edmund had sent a letter to all 630 Members of Parliament. In this letter he explained his jurisdiction and the procedures he intended to follow in dealing with complaints.

Some aspects of this letter are of particular interest because they follow on closely from issues which were discussed in Parliament during the passage of the Bill.[1] For example, we have seen that Richard Crossman and Niall MacDermot had told the Commons that it was the intention of the Government that M.P.s should act as a screen for complaints to the Commissioner. This concept of their role had given rise to some disquiet among M.P.s, during discussion of the Bill, who felt that it might place them in an invidious position *vis-à-vis* their constituents.

Sir Edmund Compton was clearly concerned to see that Members should not become too opaque a screen for complaints, or, to develop the metaphor, he was in favour of their acting as a sieve but with fairly large holes. He attached to his letter a memorandum setting out the details from the Act so that Members could 'scrutinize a case for eligibility', but he pointed out that the Act provided that any question as to whether a complaint was duly made under the Act was to be decided by the Commissioner. Accordingly, he told Members, 'I shall be ready to receive any case on which a Member feels doubt or wishes me to apply the test of jurisdiction on his behalf.'[2]

In particular, he suggested that reference might be made to him 'in any case which the Member would wish to refer to me if it were eligible, but which can only be investigated if I exercise my discretion'.[3] These were the 'appellate' cases where the complainant has, or had, the right of appeal to an administrative tribunal or has a remedy in a court of law. There were also the cases where the Commissioner had discretion as to whether or not he should investigate a complaint that was 'out of time', that is had been sent in more than a year after the day on which the complainant had notice of the matters alleged in the complaint. In all these matters, where he had discretion, the Commissioner advised that Members should send cases to him.

He explained, too, that since the Act did not anywhere 'give a positive definition of "maladministration"', he did not expect in

---

[1] The text of the letter is given in full in Appendix I of the Parliamentary Commissioner's first report to Parliament: H.C. 6 of 1967–8. First Report of the Parliamentary Commissioner for Administration, pp. 11–12.

[2] Ibid., p. 11.   [3] Ibid.

many cases to form a judgement on the question of whether maladministration had been involved until he had taken the investigation
some way in the department. He therefore advised Members that
it was not necessary for them to decide, on the strength of the
complaint received from the member of the public, whether the
complaint arose from injustice sustained in consequence of maladministration and was not a request for the Commissioner to question
the merits of a discretionary decision taken without maladministration. This, again, was an important statement since it would help to
lessen the possibility that Members would decline to send on complaints to the Commissioner when they thought that there was any
likelihood that maladministration was not involved.

Sir Edmund Compton described the procedures followed by his
office, in carrying out an investigation, in the first report which he
made to Parliament on the basis of the first seven months after the
passage of the Act, and in his first annual report.[1] On receiving a
complaint from a Member, the first task of the Office is to ascertain
whether the Parliamentary Commissioner has jurisdiction in the case.
The officer dealing with the complaint has to ask himself the following questions in order to test whether the conditions required in the
Act have been fulfilled:

Is it a written complaint accompanied by a request by an M.P.
for investigation? Is there evidence that the complainant consents
to the case being referred to the Parliamentary Commissioner? Was
the action complained of taken by a government department subject
to investigation under the act? Was the action *not* excluded by
Schedule 3 of the Act? Was the complaint by an individual or by a
body of persons *not* excluded under Section 6 (e.g. complaints from
local authorities, nationalized industries, or government departments cannot be investigated)? Was the aggrieved person resident
in the U.K., or did the complaint relate to action taken while he was
in the U.K., or did it relate to rights of his arising in the U.K.?

All these questions have to be answered in the affirmative if the
complaint is to be taken up. In addition, the Commissioner may have
to decide whether to exercise his discretion whether to take up the
case if the complaint has not been made within the time limit or if the

[1] H.C. 6 of 1967–8. First Report of the Parliamentary Commissioner for Administration.
  H.C. 134 of 1967–8. Fourth Report of the Parliamentary Commissioner for Administration. Annual Report for 1967.

complainant has the right of appeal to an administrative tribunal or remedy in a court of law.

If all these jurisdictional tests are satisfied, the Commissioner then sends the complaint to the principal officer of the department concerned and asks for his comments on it.[1] When he receives a reply from the principal officer of the department, the Parliamentary Commissioner may decide that there are no grounds for further investigation. If he decides that further investigation is required, he instructs one of his staff to go to the department concerned, availing himself 'of my right of access to the files, and get further evidence from the files and through discussion with the officials who have handled the case'.[2] In the most important cases, the Commissioner takes evidence personally from the officials and the complainants.

When the evidence has been collected, either by the Parliamentary Commissioner himself, or, more often, by a member of his staff, the Commissioner prepares a results report. He sends draft of this report to the principal officer of the department. The department can then check 'the correctness and presentation of the facts concerning them as embodied in the report'. A department can also, at this stage, exercise its power under the Act to instruct the Commissioner not to disclose information which he had proposed to put into the report. This power had not been used at the time of the Commissioner's first annual report (February 1968).

When the Commissioner has received any comments from the department, he draws up the final results report which he sends to the M.P. who has forwarded the complaint, to the principal officer of the department concerned, and to any individual named in the complaint. It is then up to the M.P. concerned to decide how he will communicate the report to the complainant and whether he will inform the Press of the report.

Several features of this procedure are worthy of comment. The members of the Commissioner's investigating staff, of whom there were thirty in 1969 (with twenty-nine supporting staff), are all members of the Civil Service. They are all on secondment from government departments. After a period in the Parliamentary Commissioner's Office, they return to an operational department.

[1] The principal officer of the department is, in the case of a department headed by a Minister, the Permanent Secretary, in the case of a department headed by a Secretary of State, the Permanent Under-Secretary.

[2] H.C. 134 of 1967–8, p. 6 at para. 14.

This arrangement prompts two questions. First, are members of the Executive Class of sufficient calibre for this kind of work? Second, are they sufficiently independent critics of the administration? The answer which can be made to the first point is that the auditors in the Exchequer and Audit Department, who report to the Comptroller and Auditor-General, are of similar calibre and the quality of their work is highly regarded. In answer to the second question, two observations can be made. The Parliamentary Commissioner makes a point of seeing that no member of his staff is asked to investigate his old department. Further, it can be argued that the independent status of the Office is secured by the independent position which the Parliamentary Commissioner himself enjoys and all the reports are his personal responsibility.

A further point of interest concerns the communication of reports to the Press. We have seen that it is the decision of the individual M.P. as to whether the report of a case is communicated to the Press, and in communicating such a report it is expected that he will obtain the consent of the complainant. The effect of this is that publication of material from the Commissioner's reports is quite sporadic. He can himself make a special report to Parliament if a case is of outstanding importance or interest, but he does so rarely. He made two such reports in the session 1967–8, one on aircraft noise and one on the Sachsenhausen case; and one in the 1968–9 session, on the sale of a Duccio painting to the National Gallery.[1] These were the only special reports of investigations which he made to Parliament during the first three years of operation of his office. Material from his other reports was only published when Members thought fit to communicate it to the Press. Otherwise the only information about the Parliamentary Commissioner's investigations is to be found in the brief summaries of the cases he has dealt with given in the appendices of his annual report.

This situation may be thought appropriate to the role which is

---

[1] H.C. 47 and 54 of 1967–8. Second and Third Reports of the Parliamentary Commissioner for Administration. H. C. 316 of 1968–9. Third Report of the Parliamentary Commissioner for Administration.

For a discussion of his report on the Duccio painting case see below Chapter XVI, p. 311.

The report on aircraft noise gave the results of his investigation into complaints against the Board of Trade about the noise caused by aircraft using London Airport at Heathrow. It was published in December 1967. The Parliamentary Commissioner did not find maladministration in the way in which the Board of Trade dealt with complaints about aircraft noise and gave directions to the British Airport Authority.

accorded to the Parliamentary Commissioner under the Act. He is not intended to rival M.P.s in their work in taking up grievances on behalf of citizens, but to supplement and assist them. Sir Edmund Compton has kept closely to this role. Since his initial television appearance, he has eschewed rather than courted publicity. If members of the public write to him, he tells them, quite correctly, that they must take their case to an M.P. Very few members of the public can have found their way to his office which was, in 1970, still unobtrusively housed within a complex of departmental offices in Great Smith Street, behind Westminster Abbey.

He has, then, been careful to see that he does not seem to rival M.P.s or supplant them. This has helped to secure acceptance of his activities by M.P.s, some of whom were, as we have seen, suspicious of the whole idea of a Parliamentary Commissioner. This unobtrusiveness, however could have led him into the opposite danger of seeming ineffective. During the first seven months of his existence he did nothing to catch the imagination or the headlines. But, in December 1967, he completed his report on the Sachsenhausen case. This proved to be of such importance that it is worth looking at in some detail.

THE SACHSENHAUSEN CASE

In June 1964 the British and West German Governments made an agreement for the payment of compensation to British victims of Nazi persecution during the Second World War. The West German Government agreed to pay £1 million to the United Kingdom Government as compensation for British nationals, or their dependants, who had suffered loss of liberty, damage to their health, or death as a result of Nazi persecution.

The British Foreign Office was responsible for deciding who was eligible for payment of compensation under this scheme. The Foreign Office prepared a set of rules for determining the eligibility of claimants, and invited applications from people who considered they were eligible. For compensation to be paid, applicants had to show either that they had been detained in a Nazi concentration camp or, if their place of detention was not a concentration camp, that the conditions they had experienced were comparable to those in a concentration camp.

The Parliamentary Commissioner was asked by Airey Neave, the Conservative M.P. for Abingdon, on 23 May 1967, to examine a complaint from four individuals that they had been unjustly denied compensation under this scheme. These individuals were Group Captain H. M. A. Day, Lieutenant-Colonel J. M. T. F. Churchill, Mr. S. M. Dowse, and Captain S. Payne-Best.

Their case had already been taken to the highest level without any redress. As far back as October 1965, Day, Churchill, and Dowse had approached Airey Neave and shown him the letters from the Foreign Office rejecting their claims. Neave was very well qualified to assess the merits of this case. He had himself been a prisoner of war, imprisoned at Colditz, from which he successfully escaped to Switzerland in 1942. Later in the war, he was concerned with the organization of the London end of escape operations from German occupied territory. After the war, he was an official at the Nuremberg trials of Nazi war criminals and then examined a great deal of the evidence concerned with the operation of concentration camps.[1]

He first took up the case, in October 1965, with George Thomson who was then a Minister of State at the Foreign Office. Thomson informed him, at an interview, that the Foreign Office did not consider that Day, Churchill, and Dowse had been held in the concentration camp at Sachsenhausen since they had been confined at one time in a special camp (*Sonderlager A*) and at another time in the cell block (*Zellenbau*) which were not part of the camp proper. The Foreign Office considered that during their captivity at Sachsenhausen they had not endured conditions of severity comparable to those experienced in concentration camps.

The claimants contested this whole interpretation of the facts. Airey Neave wrote to Thomson in January 1966 asking for an independent inquiry into their case. He also approached Sir Alec Douglas-Home, the Conservative Shadow Foreign Secretary, and Emanuel Shinwell, who was at that time Chairman of the Parliamentary Labour Party.[2] They both agreed to support him in the House.

[1] Airey Neave has been Conservative Member for Abingdon since 1953. He was Under-Secretary for Air in the Macmillan Government from January to October 1959. He is a barrister and is a director of a boilermaker and power station engineering company.

[2] Sir Alec Douglas-Home has been Conservative Member for Kinross and West Perthshire since 1963. He was Prime Minister from October 1963 to October 1964. From July 1960 to October 1963 he had, as Lord Home, been Foreign Secretary in the Macmillan Government. Since June 1970 he has been Foreign Secretary in the Heath Government.

Emanuel Shinwell was a Member of Parliament without a break from 1935 to 1970.

On 28 February 1966, George Thomson said, in reply to questions in the House, that 'The cells in which the men were held, although adjoining the Sachsenhausen Concentration Camp, were quite separate from it and the conditions and treatment in these cases were not comparable with those within the main camp.'[1] Airey Neave later told the Select Committee on the Parliamentary Commissioner that this had seemed to him 'a gross mis-statement of fact' particularly since the Foreign Office had been provided by Group Captain Day with an aerial photograph, taken by an allied plane during the war, which showed the cell block as an integral part of the camp.[2]

Neave's next move was to try and secure an interview for the claimants with Mrs. Eirene White who had now taken George Thomson's place at the Foreign Office as the Minister of State concerned with this sector of the work of the Office. The interview took place on 12 September 1966 and proved to be completely unsatisfactory to Neave and the three claimants. Mrs. White listened to their statements and then told them that nothing could be done as the decision had already been made.

Neave continued his campaign with renewed vigour after this. On 7 November 1966 he asked the Foreign Secretary about the case in an oral parliamentary question. George Brown replied that while the men had been confined in the *Sonderlager* they had received Red Cross parcels and been attended by batmen. Group Captain Day and his friends told Neave that this statement was wholly inaccurate.[3]

On 20 December 1966, George Brown saw a deputation of Members who had joined Neave in his campaign. The deputation consisted, beside Neave himself, of Sir Alec Douglas-Home, Emanuel Shinwell, Jo Grimond (Leader of the Liberal Party), Sir Arthur Harvey (Conservative Member for Macclesfield), David Ginsburg (Labour Member for Dewsbury), William Molloy (Labour Member for Ealing North), and John Mendelson (Labour Member for Penistone). At this meeting, Neave handed to George Brown the

He represented Easington from 1950 to 1970, when he decided not to stand again. He was Secretary of State for War in the Attlee Government from 1947 to 1950 and Minister of Defence from 1950 to 1951.

[1] H.C. Deb. Vol. 725, Col. 890.

[2] H.C. 258 of 1967–8. First Report from the Select Committee on the Parliamentary Commissioner, Sachsenhausen, p. 54 at para. 8.

[3] Ibid., p. 55 at para. 13.

aerial photograph showing the location of the *Sonderlager* and the cell block in which the men had been confined. Brown still maintained that these were not part of 'the Concentration Camp proper', but he agreed to interview the men personally. When this interview took place, on 20 February 1967, he told the men that he was satisfied the decision in their case had been correct and that now 'all the money was gone.'

As a last resort, the eight Members then asked to see the Prime Minister. Harold Wilson, however, wrote back to Neave saying that he could not see any advantage in such a meeting since 'I find myself in complete agreement with the views expressed to you by the Foreign Secretary.'[1] This reply was sent on 6 April 1967.

A motion was then put down on the Order Paper of the Commons asking for an independent inquiry into the case. It attracted the support of more than 350 Members. The Leader of the House, Richard Crossman, was prepared to find time for a debate but, after discussion in private, it was decided that it would be better if Neave were to ask the Parliamentary Commissioner to investigate. This he did on 23 May 1967.

From this summary of Neave's campaign, it will be clear that he had exhausted every weapon in the armoury which an M.P. can bring to bear in criticizing the Executive. He had taken his case right through the hierarchy of Ministers to the Foreign Secretary, and then appealed to the Prime Minister himself, but had drawn a blank at every stage. He had used every parliamentary means available to him and had gained the support of over half the Members of the Commons: all to no result. If, now, the Parliamentary Commissioner could produce a reassessment of the case, it would be a major vindication of his effectiveness.

In view of the importance of the case, Sir Edmund Compton decided to undertake the investigation himself. He examined the Foreign Office files and papers dealing with the case of the three original complainants, together with those relating to Capt. Payne-Best, whose name had been added to the original three. He also examined the files of some of the claimants who had received compensation.

He took oral evidence from all four complainants and from the Foreign Office officials who drew up and administered the compensation scheme. The Foreign Office maintained that the four

[1] Ibid., p. 57 at para. 22.

claimants had not been detained in a concentration camp since the
Sonderlager (special camp) and the *Zellenbau* (cell block), in which
they had been imprisoned, were not part of Sachsenhausen concentration camp. Since the claimants had not, then, in the Foreign
Office view, been held in a concentration camp they had to show
that they had undergone treatment of severity comparable to that
experienced in a concentration camp. The Foreign Office argued
that the treatment they had received in the *Sonderlager* and the
Zellenbau was not of such severity.

The Parliamentary Commissioner was able to contest both these
positions very effectively. He succeeded, by his own investigations,
in providing supporting evidence for Group Captain Day's aerial
photograph which had earlier, as we have seen, been shown to
George Brown, He obtained, from the Ministry of Defence files, a
plan of the camp drawn in August 1944 by an officer who had
escaped from Sachsenhausen. He also obtained a copy of a book,
Damals in Sachsenhausen, which had been published in Berlin in
1961. This gave a valuable insight into conditions in the camp.

From these sources, Sir Edmund Compton was able to satisfy himself that 'the Zellenbau formed part of a compound within the main
camp itself but separated from it by a high wall surmounted by a live
wire. It was adjacent to the punishment squad barracks.'[1] He drew
a map of the concentration camp which he published as Appendix E
to his Report. It shows the *Zellenbau* as within the main compound
and the *Sonderlager* as immediately adjacent to the main compound.[2]

He was also able to produce very strong evidence to refute the
arguments put forward by the Foreign Office about the treatment
which the claimants had been subjected to. The Foreign Office
officials based their position upon evidence found in the following
sources: books by Captain Peter Churchill and Captain Payne-Best
describing conditions in the *Sonderlager* and the cell block, the
written statements made by the claimants after their liberation in
1945, and evidence of conditions in the main camp, in particular,
the evidence of a Sergeant Kemp.

Sir Edmund Compton's investigation showed that Captain Peter
Churchill's book, *The Spirit in the Cage*, gave too rosy a picture of
the conditions in the *Sonderlager*. Peter Churchill had earlier been

---

[1] H.C. 54 of 1967–8. Third Report of the Parliamentary Commissioner for Administration, p. 13 at para. 44.
[2] Ibid., p. 29.

confined in very severe conditions in Fresnes prison and described the *Sonderlager* as a 'paradise' in comparison to what he had previously experienced. Churchill had described early-morning runs and games of netball organized by the prisoners in the *Sonderlager*. But certain of the claimants pointed out to Sir Edmund Compton that these activities were designed to cover the attempt to organize an escape from the *Sonderlager*. They also pointed out that the *Sonderlager* was part of the main camp administration and was guarded by the same S.S. guards who did duty in the main camp.

Captain Peter Churchill had been, at no time, imprisoned in the *Zellenbau*. For conditions in the *Zellenbau* the Foreign Office relied upon the account given by Captain Payne-Best in his book *The Venlo Incident*. This also gave a partial picture. Captain Payne-Best was a British agent who had been kidnapped by the Germans on the Dutch frontier early in the war. He had been imprisoned in the *Zellenbau* since December 1939. Initially, the conditions he experienced were severe, but by the end of the war he had succeeded in establishing such a personal ascendancy over his guards that he had acquired all kinds of personal privileges for himself and lived in comparative comfort.[1]

Sir Edmund Compton was able to establish that conditions elsewhere in the *Zellenbau* were very different. He found evidence of British agents and commandos who were held in solitary confinement in severe conditions and then suddenly executed. The head warder of the *Zellenbau*, at his trial by the Russians, had admitted that towards the end of 1944 he had been ordered to reduce by execution the number of prisoners there. He said that 'of the 100 or more prisoners in the cells in October 1944, only 13 remained in April, 1945, when the camp was evacuated.'[2]

This evidence helped to confirm the accounts given to Sir Edmund Compton by Group Captain Day, Colonel J. M. T. F. Churchill, and Mr. Dowse of their imprisonment in the *Zellenbau*. All three told the Parliamentary Commissioner that during their confinement in the *Zellenbau*, they had been handcuffed and shackled and had expected execution at any time. The Foreign Office had preferred to rely on the 1945 intelligence reports in which the men had made no reference to this treatment.

[1] See S. Payne-Best, *The Venlo Incident* (Hutchinson, 1960).
[2] H.C. 54 of 1967–8. Third Report of the Parliamentary Commissioner for Administration, p. 13 at para. 46.

Sir Edmund Compton, however, was satisfied that their accounts were true. It seems likely that the men had not dwelt on the severity of their treatment when they had made their reports to Intelligence Officers in 1945, because they did not think that this was important to their interrogation. As one of the M.P.s concerned, David Ginsburg, said to the Select Committee on the Parliamentary Commissioner, prisoners held in such conditions were often not willing to give long accounts, after their liberation, of what had happened to them.[1]

Finally, and most telling of all, Sir Edmund Compton found evidence in the Foreign Office files that conditions for some people in the main compound of Sachsenhausen camp had been less severe than those encountered by the claimants when held in the *Zellenbau*. For example, a Captain Starr had received quite favourable treatment from the block chief in his part of the camp because he was employed in drawing murals in the huts. The great variety of treatment experienced by prisoners in the main compound was further attested by a book written by a former Norwegian prisoner, Odd Nansen, and published after the war under the title *Day by Day*. Nansen confirmed that while prisoners of some nationalities, notably Russians, Ukrainians, and Poles, were generally treated very brutally, other nationalities such as the Norwegians and British were often treated relatively well in the main compound.[2]

Sir Edmund Compton summarized the conclusions he reached after his investigation in the following way: '(i) I criticize the process by which the Foreign Office decided against Sonderlager A and Zellenbau being part of Sachsenhausen Concentration Camp, because in my view the original decision was based on partial and largely irrelevant information, and the decision was maintained in disregard of additional information and evidence, particularly as regards Zellenbau.'[3]

He then went on to say:

(ii) I may not question the merits of the general ruling as applied throughout the compensation scheme that claimants judged not to have been held in a concentration camp had to establish detention in conditions

---

[1] H.C. 258 of 1967–8. First Report from the Select Committee on the Parliamentary Commissioner for Administration, p. 66 at para. 418.

[2] H.C. 54 of 1967–8. Third Report of the Parliamentary Commissioner for Administration, pp. 12–13 at paras. 42 and 43.

[3] Ibid., p. 18 at para. 66.

comparable with those in a concentration camp 'as generally understood', meaning severe forms of Nazi persecution treatment. I record that this ruling could mean that a non-camp claimant had to pass a more severe test than a camp claimant, and that this actually happened at Sachsenhausen.[1]

This part of his report was to be closely considered by the Select Committee on the Parliamentary Commissioner. They inclined to the view that the Commissioner had here taken too narrow a view of his investigating role.[2] He had, however, made it clear that although he did not think that it was within his authority to question the merits of a departmental rule, the rule in this case had had unfortunate results.

Finally, he criticized 'the treatment by the Foreign Office of the evidence submitted by the complainants in support of their claims as regards their own conditions under detention in Zellenbau and as regards conditions in the main compound of Sachsenhausen'.[3] There had been maladministration on the part of the Foreign Office and the claimants had suffered injustice in that 'the rejection of their claim and the terms in which the rejection has been defended by the Foreign Office have done harm to their standing and reputation.'[4] This injustice would be remedied by the publication and, he hoped, the acceptance of his finding that the complainants had all been held by the S.S. in premises which were part of the Sachsenhausen complex and 'that as regards Nazi persecution all the complainants suffered loss of identity, risk of liquidation and constant anxiety over their fate, while certain Zellenbau detainees sustained further persecution in the form of different degrees of physical hardship and degradation, with mental suffering from isolation, proximity to the execution of others, and the constant threat that they themselves would be executed without warning'.[5]

He made no recommendation about financial compensation to the claimants. He thought that the next step should be for the Foreign Office to review the evidence and then decide whether a financial award would be appropriate.

The Parliamentary Commissioner's Report on Sachsenhausen was published on 21 December 1967. The following day, *The Times*

---

[1] Ibid.   [2] See below pp. 281–2.

[3] H.C. 54 of 1967–8. Third Report of the Parliamentary Commissioner for Administration, p. 18 at para. 66.

[4] Ibid., p. 19 at para. 68.   [5] Ibid.

gave a summary of the report but commented that there was a difficulty about the payment of compensation since the Foreign Secretary had earlier said that all the money available under the Anglo-German agreement had been paid out. Just over five weeks later, on 30 January 1968, *The Times* reported in a more cheerful vein under the headline 'Nazi victims likely to get £25,000'. It said that the Foreign Secretary was expected soon to announce that compensation would be paid to the survivors of those who had been imprisoned at Sachsenhausen.

The subsidiary headline for this story in *The Times* was: 'Triumph for the Ombudsman'. This was overwhelmingly the verdict of M.P.s who participated in the debate on the Parliamentary Commissioner's Report which took place on 5 February 1968 on a motion from the Foreign Secretary, George Brown. For example, Sir Arthur Vere Harvey (Conservative Member for Macclesfield) told the House: 'I had my doubts when the Government introduced the Bill to establish the Parliamentary Commissioner. I confess I had my doubts, but now, if he has done one thing which justifies his existence, it is this.'[1] Dame Irene Ward was another Conservative Member who spoke in similar vein:

Originally, I was not particularly in favour of having a Parliamentary Commissioner, but after this success I see all sorts of possibilities for extending his powers. However hard my hon. Friend worked, if we had not had the Parliamentary Commissioner we could not have obtained the decision of the Foreign Secretary to compensate these men who were in this portion of the camp. This proves that even in this great Parliamentary democracy of ours we can sometimes improve our constitution to the benefit of the public whom we are supposed to serve.[2]

Two of the Members who had led the parliamentary campaign for the claimants were equally generous in their tributes to Sir Edmund Compton. Airey Neave told the House: 'We could not have got the Government to change their mind without the assistance of Sir Edmund Compton, the Parliamentary Commissioner.'[3]

[1] H.C. Deb. Vol. 758, Col. 130. Sir Arthur Vere Harvey has been Conservative Member for Macclesfield since 1945. He was elected Joint Vice-Chairman of the Conservative Back-Benchers' 1922 Committee in 1964 and Vice-Chairman of the Conservative Parliamentary Defence Committee in the same year. He is a director of electrical, insurance, seed, and other firms.

[2] Ibid., Cols. 161–2. Dame Irene Ward has been Conservative Member for Tynemouth since 1950. She previously represented Wallsend from 1931 to 1945. She is a notable defender of women's rights and of the rights of the back-bench Member.

[3] Ibid., Col. 118.

David Ginsburg commented that 'my colleagues and I would all admit that, without the Parliamentary Commissioner and his very special powers, but also without his great personal skill on this occasion, we might never have broken through.'[1]

George Brown, when he opened the debate, had told the House that he had decided that compensation would be paid to all the claimants. What was surprising about his speech, however, was that he did not accept the Parliamentary Commissioner's finding that there had been maladministration in the Foreign Office proceedings in the case. He said that it was a matter of judgement as to whether the claimants were entitled to compensation. 'The Parliamentary Commissioner's view is that our judgement was wrong. I am willing to accept that. I have therefore reviewed and revised my decision, but this remains a matter of judgement and on a matter of judgement on an issue as narrow as this anyone can be wrong'.[2] He also told the House: 'Having established the office of Parliamentary Commissioner, whether I think his judgement is right or wrong, I am certain that it would be wrong to reject his views.'[3]

In the light of the facts set out in Sir Edmund Compton's report, and in particular of his demonstration that there was evidence in the Foreign Office files that certain prisoners in the main compound had received more favourable treatment than the claimants, it is hard to see how George Brown could argue that there had not been defects in procedure in the handling of the case by the Foreign Office. His attitude can only be explained on the grounds that he felt an overriding need to be loyal to his officials. Indeed, he took his stand on the issue of Ministerial responsibility: 'I think that we have the best Parliamentary democratic system in the world and one of the reasons for this is that our Ministers are responsible to Parliament. If things are wrongly done, then they are wrongly done by Ministers and I think that it is tremendously important to hold to that principle.'[4]

George Brown was not, it seems, convinced by Sir Edmund Compton's report that there had been maladministration in the Foreign Office. For him it was an issue of judgement and a rather narrow issue at that. Members who followed him in the debate, on both sides of the House, did not share this view. Airey Neave put their view succinctly when he said of the claimants' appeal: 'This

---

[1] Ibid., Col. 141.   [2] Ibid., Col. 117.
[3] Ibid., Col. 116.   [4] Ibid., Col. 112.

was a cast-iron case from the start.'[1] But it needed the Parliamentary Commissioner's right of access to the Ministry files in order to prove that it was a cast-iron case.

The Sachsenhausen Report was a triumph for the Parliamentary Commissioner. It got him off the ground and showed beyond doubt that he could be effective despite his limited range of powers. But the report also raised some major constitutional issues: for example about the extent to which officials should be held answerable for their mistakes, and about the desirability of allowing the Parliamentary Commissioner to criticize the merits of a departmental rule. The Select Committee on the Parliamentary Commissioner was ready to take up these, and other questions, which arose from the Commissioner's investigation and his report. It is to the setting up of this Select Committee and its relationship to the work of the Parliamentary Commissioner that we now turn.

[3] Ibid., Col. 117.

XV

THE SELECT COMMITTEE ON THE PARLIAMENTARY COMMISSIONER

THE APPOINTMENT AND COMPOSITION OF THE COMMITTEE

THE Select Committee on the Parliamentary Commissioner for Administration was first appointed by the Commons on 23 November 1967. It had long been envisaged that such a committee would be set up. As we have seen, Harold Wilson, as Leader of the Opposition, had said in his speech at Stowmarket, in July 1964, that 'there should be a high-powered Select Committee of the House who would make it their business to go through the periodic reports of the Commissioner and report to Parliament on them.'[1] During the committee stage of the Parliamentary Commissioner Bill, Niall MacDermot had made a precise commitment that after the passage of the Act, the Government would propose that a Select Committee should be set up and that its Chairman would be a member of the Opposition.[2]

This undertaking had been overlooked by some of the interested Labour Members when the first moves were made to set up the Committee in November 1967. These Members proposed that Douglas Houghton should be the Chairman of the new Committee. The advantages of such a choice seemed considerable. Houghton was no longer a Minister. He had been omitted from the Government when the Cabinet was reshuffled, in January 1967, and in April 1967 he was elected Chairman of the Parliamentary Labour Party. While in the Cabinet, he had chaired the Cabinet Committee which had been responsible for planning the Parliamentary Commissioner Bill.[3] Another advantage of his appointment would be that when he was Chairman of the Public Accounts Committee,

---

[1] See above p. 42.   [2] See above p. 131.   [3] See above pp. 51–60.

from 1963 to 1964, he had worked closely with Sir Edmund Compton who at that time was Comptroller and Auditor-General.

Douglas Houghton was willing to serve as Chairman of the new Select Committee, but the choice was not acceptable to the Conservatives. They recalled Niall MacDermot's statement to the standing committee that the chairman would be a member of the Opposition, and the Government had to honour this pledge. The Conservative choice for chairman was Sir Hugh Munro-Lucas-Tooth. This was apparently a 'safe' choice in that, although Sir Hugh Lucas-Tooth had been a member of the standing committee, he had not then been in favour of a strong Parliamentary Commissioner. His influence had been exerted, on balance, towards defining the powers of the Parliamentary Commissioner rather narrowly although he had been in favour of allowing the Commissioner to look at certain areas, for example the hospitals, from which the Government was concerned to exclude him. Sir Hugh was, therefore, a good choice from the Conservative point of view since many Conservative Members were still distinctly reserved in their attitude to the Parliamentary Commissioner. Sir Hugh had also had Ministerial experience having been Under-Secretary at the Home Office from 1952 to 1955.

When it became clear that Sir Hugh Munro-Lucas-Tooth would be Chairman of the Select Committee, Douglas Houghton decided that he would not accept nomination as a member of the Committee. He felt that his presence there would be an embarrassment to Sir Hugh. The Committee, as finally approved, consisted of eleven members in all. Of these, six were Labour members, four were Conservatives, and one was a Liberal. Of the three Conservatives, in addition to Sir Hugh, two had been, like him, members of the standing committee. These were Antony Buck and Charles Fletcher-Cooke. The fourth Conservative was Dame Irene Ward who had been, as we have seen, initially a critic of the idea of having a Parliamentary Commissioner but became a warm convert as a result of the Sachsenhausen Report.

The one Liberal was Dr. Michael Winstanley who had, in 1966, been critical of the proposal for a Parliamentary Commissioner, on the grounds that it was an unsatisfactory alternative to reforms which would strengthen the role of individual M.P.s, but he had favoured an Ombudsman for local government. Of the six Labour members of the Committee, one, Alexander Lyon, had been a member of the standing committee on the Parliamentary Commissioner Bill. He had been one of the Labour back-benchers who sought to strengthen the position of the Parliamentary Commissioner and he was to be an active member of the Select Committee.

Of the five other Labour members, one, George Lawson, was a Government Whip.[1] One member, Victor Yates, was joint chairman of the Parliamentary Labour Party's Home Affairs Committee.[2] The other three Labour members had all been closely associated with the trade union side of the Labour movement. Kenneth Lomas had been a branch secretary of the National Union of Public Employees.[3] Mrs Margaret McKay had formerly been chief woman officer to the Trades Union Congress.[4] Arthur Probert had been a local government officer and had been secretary and treasurer of the Aberdare Trades Council.[5] He had been a member of the Public Accounts Committee from 1964 to 1966.

The Committee, then, included only one Member, Alexander Lyon, who was known as an advocate of a strong Parliamentary Commissioner. But as a Committee it was reasonably representative of back-bench opinion on both sides of the House. This was probably a more sensible way to construct the Committee than to bring together a group of Members, all or most of whom had been ardent advocates of a Parliamentary Commissioner. It was noticeable that the Committee included three members who had been administrative officers of one kind or another: Arthur Probert had been a local government officer, Kenneth Lomas had been an administrative officer in the Blood Transfusion Service, and Margaret McKay had worked for the T.U.C. and in the national office of a Civil Service union. The Committee included four barristers: Sir Hugh-Munro-Lucas-Tooth, Antony Buck, and Charles Fletcher-Cooke

[1] George Lawson has been Labour Member for Motherwell since 1954. He was appointed a Lord Commissioner of the Treasury in 1964. From 1940 to 1950 he was regional organizer in the West of Scotland for the National Council of Labour Colleges.

[2] Victor Yates was Labour Member for the Ladywood division of Birmingham from 1945 until his death in January 1969. He was formerly a clerk and won scholarships to Ruskin College and Birmingham University.

[3] Kenneth Lomas has been Labour Member for Huddersfield West since 1964. He had been an officer in the National Blood Transfusion Service.

[4] Mrs. Margaret McKay was Labour Member for Clapham (Wandsworth) from 1964 to 1970. She had held administrative posts with the Civil Service Clerical Association and the Transport and General Workers' Union.

[5] Arthur Probert was first elected Labour Member for Aberdare in 1954.

on the Conservative side, Alexander Lyon among the Labour members.

THE SELECT COMMITTEE AND SACHSENHAUSEN

The Select Committee held its first meeting on Wednesday, 29 November 1967. At its second meeting, a fortnight later, on 13 December, it began consideration of the Parliamentary Commissioner's first report in which he gave an account of the work of his Office in its first seven months of operation. The Committee heard evidence from Sir Edmund Compton; the Secretary of his Office, Edwin Sykes, and his Establishment Officer, D. G. Plaister, were also in attendance.

A week later, on 20 December, the Committee resumed consideration of the Parliamentary Commissioner's first report, the same witnesses attending for examination. This was the day on which the Parliamentary Commissioner's report on Sachsenhausen was published. The Committee did not, however, switch at once to consideration of the Sachsenhausen report. There were two reasons for this. For one thing, the Committee had not finished its examination of the issues arising from the Commissioner's first report. For another, as we have seen in the last chapter, it was not at once clear whether the Foreign Office would accept the Parliamentary Commissioner's report on the Sachsenhausen case.

On 24 January and 7 February the Select Committee continued their consideration of the Commissioner's first report. But soon after the debate in the House, on 5 February, on the Sachsenhausen report, the Select Committee decided to give its whole attention to the case. On 14 February, the Committee began a series of meetings on Sachsenhausen.

At the first of these meetings, the Committee heard evidence from Sir Edmund Compton himself, supported by Michael Stewart, a higher executive officer on his staff who had assisted him in the investigation. At the Committee's next two meetings, on 21 and 28 February, it examined the Permanent Under-Secretary at the Foreign Office supported by the Foreign Officer's Senior Legal Adviser.

At its next meeting, on 6 March 1968, the Committee deliberated without calling for further witnesses. A week later on 13 March, it heard evidence from the two M.P.s who had led the campaign on behalf of the Sachsenhausen claimants, Airey Neave and David

Ginsburg. Two further meetings followed, on 27 March and 10 April, at which issues raised in the investigation were discussed but no further witnesses were examined.

On 1 May 1968, the Committee examined Sir Elwyn Jones, the Attorney General, on the issue of Ministerial responsibility as it affected their activities, and on 16 May the Committee approved their draft report on the Sachsenhausen case. On the same day it was ordered by the House to be printed as the first report of the Committee for the session 1967–8.[1]

The Select Committee were critical in this report of the decision to hold a debate in the Commons on the Parliamentary Commissioner's Report on the Sachsenhausen case before it had been considered by the Committee. They recommended that, in future, the House should follow the practice maintained with reports from the Comptroller and Auditor-General which are not debated in the House until they have been examined and reported on by the Public Accounts Committee.

The Foreign Office came in for severe criticism from the Select Committee. In their report, the Committee emphasized that they had been reluctant to retry the case. It would not be appropriate for them, they said, to duplicate the Parliamentary Commissioner's investigating functions. 'On the other hand, owing to the treatment of the Commissioner's report by the Foreign Office, they have felt bound to examine the conflict of judgement between the Commissioner and the Foreign Office.'[2] Having examined the facts set out by the Commissioner in his report, and taken account of evidence given to them by the Permanent Under-Secretary at the Foreign Office, they came to the conclusion that the Commissioner's finding that there had been maladministration in the Foreign Office was justified.

They agreed with the Commissioner's conclusion that 'there were defects in the processes by which the Foreign Office first decided and then maintained their decision not to regard any of the twelve claimants as having been held in Sachsenhausen Concentration Camp.'[3] The Committee supported the Commissioner's other finding of maladministration by the Foreign Office: the damage done to the reputation of the claimants by the Foreign Office's refusal to

---

[1] H.C. 258 of 1967–8. First Report from the Select Committee on the Parliamentary Commissioner for Administration, Sachsenhausen.

[2] Ibid., p. vii at para. 5.   [3] Ibid., p. vii at para. 6.

accept the evidence which the claimants submitted about the conditions they had experienced in the *Zellenbau*. The Committee commented:

Your Committee think it unfortunate that the Foreign Office, by disputing the findings of the Commissioner, might be thought to be reviving the question of the veracity of these complainants. In order to remove any doubts upon this score, Your Committee put it on record that they for their part accept the findings of the Commissioner as set out in paragraphs 68 and 69 of his Report, and regard the standing and reputation of these Zellenbau complainants as completely vindicated.[1]

Sir Paul Gore-Booth, the Permanent Under-Secretary of State at the Foreign Office had kept an impeccably straight bat against all the fast bowling hurled down at him by members of the Committee during the two days on which he was under examination. He had stuck firmly to George Brown's argument that it had been a borderline case, that there had not been maladministration, but that compensation was being paid out of respect for the Parliamentary Commissioner's opinion and for his function as an arbiter. He firmly refused, under pressure from Alexander Lyon, to give the names of the officials who had made the decisions in the claims under question.[2]

The Committee was very much put out by this refusal. Their terms of reference specified that they had power 'to send for persons, papers and records'. But, it was privately pointed out to them that although the Committee had power to send for persons they had no powers to make anyone come and give evidence. Committees of the House of Commons do not have power to subpoena witnesses as Congressional committees do in the United States. It seemed likely that if the Committee attempted to call the individual officials who had been concerned in the case, the Foreign Secretary would not allow them to appear. George Brown had told the Commons on 5 February that he did not think that individual Civil Servants should be held accountable. He had argued that it was the Minister who was responsible for what was done in his department and that it was 'a Minister's job to see that he has all the necessary information'.[3]

The Committee said in their report that Ministers in the Sachsen-

---

[1] Ibid., p. xi at para. 10.   [2] Ibid., pp. 29–30 at question 316.
[3] H.C. Deb. Vol. 758, Col. 111.

hausen case did share the blame for ignoring the evidence which was available to them, for example in the testimony of the claimants and in the aerial photograph submitted by Group Captain Day. The Committee also agreed that the advice given to Ministers on the question was 'the collective responsibility of Foreign Office officials, and there is no evidence or suggestion of personal bias or animosity on the part of any official in the chain.'[1]

They, nevertheless, had thought it important to try and find out what had gone wrong in the Foreign Office over Sachsenhausen. After Sir Paul Gore-Booth refused, on 21 February, to give the names of the officials who had worked on the file, the Committee discussed whether they could get these names from other sources and, in particular, from the M.P.s who had led the campaign to get redress for the claimants. On 13 March 1968, the Committee heard evidence from these M.P.s, Airey Neave and David Ginsburg. Airey Neave was asked by Charles Fletcher-Cooke if he could name the official who had worked on the file. Airey Neave then gave the name of an official who had been present on every occasion when Neave had interviews with Ministers on the case. There is no record of this question and answer in the minutes of evidence published with the Committee's report on Sachsenhausen. At page 70 of this report, questions 439 to 445 have been omitted.[2]

The explanation of this omission is to be found in the minutes of evidence in the second report from the Select Committee for the session 1967-8 when the Attorney General, Sir Elwyn Jones, gave evidence to the Committee.[3] What happened was this. The Clerk of the Committee wrote to the Permanent Under-Secretary at the Foreign Office on 28 March 1968, saying that an official's name had been given to the Committee on 13 March and asking whether the official concerned had 'any comment to make' on the evidence.[4] The Permanent Under-Secretary replied on 10 April that the Foreign Secretary 'earnestly hopes' that the references to the official by name would be removed from the Committee's published report. He also drew attention to an earlier letter to the Committee in which he had informed them that the Foreign Secretary, who was now Michael Stewart, had said that the official concerned 'should

[1] H.C. 258 of 1967-8, p. ix at para. 8.   [2] Ibid., p. 70.
[3] H.C. 350 of 1967-8. Second Report from the Parliamentary Commissioner for Administration, pp. 68-83.
[4] Ibid., p. 70 at question 746.

not comment on the evidence given to the Select Committee'.[1] In view of the attitude of the Foreign Office, the Committee agreed to hold up their report on Sachsenhausen and to consult the Attorney General on the legal and constitutional position.

When the Attorney General, Sir Elwyn Jones, came to give evidence to the Committee, he urged upon them very strongly that the Committee should delete from the published record that part of the minutes of evidence in which the official's name was given, and the Committee agreed to do this.[2]

Elwyn Jones's evidence to the Committee is of very great interest for his enunciation of the convention which he thought the Committee should follow in examining Civil Servants. He argued that the Committee should model itself precisely on the Public Accounts Committee in this matter. That is they should call for evidence from the principal officer of the department and anyone else whom he chose to nominate. The decision, therefore, as to which other officials would appear to give evidence would always be made by the principal officer of the department.

The reasons he advanced for adopting this convention were principally two. First, he argued that it would 'corrode' the sense of Ministerial responsibility if it were possible for the Committee to go down the lower echelons of a department and single out the Civil Servant whom they held to be blameworthy. The Minister would then be able to shrug off his responsibility. He would be able to say 'It was not my fault. It was a fifth grade civil servant who was the offender in this situation.'[3]

Second, it would be very unfair to such Civil Servants if they were to be brought before the Committee to give evidence. The Parliamentary Commissioner is given very exceptional powers under the Act to look at departmental files and to examine officials. Those exceptional powers are not given to the Select Committee. The Commissioner's powers also are exercised in private. He does not, in his reports, give the names of officials except when an official is named in the original complaint. In such a case the Act gives special

---

[1] Ibid.

[2] Sir Elwyn Jones Q.C. was Attorney General from 1964 to 1970. He had been Labour Member for West Ham since 1950, having previously represented Plaistow from 1945 to 1950. He was called to the Bar in 1935 and had been, at different times, Recorder of Merthyr, Swansea, and Cardiff. He had been treasurer of 'Justice' and was a member of its executive committee at the time of the Whyatt Report.

[3] H.C. 350 of 1967–8, p. 77 at question 556.

safeguards to the named official. The Commissioner must send him a copy of the original complaint so that he can comment on it; he must allow the named official legal representation, where this is necessary; and he must send a copy of his report to the official. In addition, the Parliamentary Commissioner operates a 'stop procedure' when it becomes apparent during an investigation that the conduct of an official is likely to be publicly questioned. The same rights are then accorded to him as are accorded to an official named in an original complaint.[1]

The Committee accepted some, but not all, of the Attorney General's argument. In their second report for 1967–8, they said that they recognized that they had a responsibility for maintaining a balance between their function of supporting the activities of the Parliamentary Commissioner and 'the protection of Ministerial responsibility upon which the efficiency of democratic Government depends'.[2]

On the other hand, they did not agree with the suggestion that they should always confine themselves to taking evidence from the principal officer of a department. In particular, when they were considering what a department should do to remedy administrative defects disclosed by the Commissioner's investigation, they thought it might be necessary to call for evidence from 'those officials who are concerned at first hand with the actions in question'. They thought that the occasions when this would be necessary would be infrequent and they said that they were 'satisfied that they would be able to take evidence from subordinate officials for this purpose without exposing them to unfair publicity or criticism, and they feel that they can rely on Departments to indicate the appropriate witnesses'.[3]

The Committee had not been at all satisfied by the answers they had received from Sir Paul Gore-Booth when they asked him what action was being taken to remedy the administrative defects revealed by the Sachsenhausen case. In their first report for 1967–8, they said that

the Principal Officer of the Foreign Office was unable to give Your Committee any specific indication either of the defects of the system

[1] See Sir Edmund Compton's evidence to the Committee, ibid., pp. 68–9 at question 544.
[2] Ibid., p. xii at para. 28.   [3] Ibid., p. xii at para. 30.

that the Sachsenhausen case had brought to light or of the action that
was being taken to mend the system. According to his evidence, a review
had been initiated and no more (Question 378). Your Committee draw
this evidence to the attention of the House, and wish to give notice that
they intend at an early date to call for further evidence from the Foreign
Office in order to ascertain what remedial measures have in fact been
taken as a result of the review.[1]

They took this further evidence from Sir Paul Gore-Booth, in the
following session, on 27 November 1968. On this occasion they
obtained much more satisfaction. Sir Paul told the Committee that,
since the Sachsenhausen case, the claims department of the Foreign
and Commonwealth Office had been increased in size from a staff
complement of ten to thirteen. More important, however, was his
statement to the Committee that the Foreign Office intended that
claims arising from settlements similar to that in the Sachsenhausen
case would, in most cases in future, be dealt with by the Foreign
Compensation Commission.

The members of this Commission are appointed by the Lord
Chancellor and all have wide legal experience. Its chairman at that
time was C. Montgomery White, Q.C.[2]

THE MAIN THEMES IN THE SELECT COMMITTEE'S INQUIRIES

Another important issue to emerge from the Sachsenhausen case,
was whether the Parliamentary Commissioner should, or should not,
question the merits of a departmental rule. This issue was to be
discussed by the Committee with the principal officers of several
departments as well as with the Attorney General and the Chairman
of the House of Commons Select Committee on Statutory Instruments. It forms one of the main themes of the Parliamentary
Commissioner's Committee's inquiries during the first three sessions
of its life: from 1967–8 to 1969–70. These themes can be summed up
under the following headings:

(1) the relationship between the Commissioner and Members of
Parliament;

(2) the ways in which the Parliamentary Commissioner organizes
his work;

---

[1] H.C. 258 of 1967–8, p. xii at para. 13.
[2] H.C. 385 of 1968–9. Report from the Select Committee on the Parliamentary Commissioner for Administration, p. 3 at question 2.

(3) the Parliamentary Commissioner's interpretation of his powers under the Act;

(4) his function in relation to departmental rules and Statutory Orders;

(5) the effects upon departments of his investigations;

(6) the advisability of widening his jurisdiction to include areas exempted under the Act.

(1) *The Relationship between the Parliamentary Commissioner and Members of Parliament*

This theme predominated in the first meeting of the Select Committee at which proceedings were reported. This meeting took place on 13 December 1967, when the Committee heard evidence from the Parliamentary Commissioner on his first report for 1967–8 in which he described the operation of his office during the first seven months of its life. Mrs. McKay indicated to the Committee at this meeting that she was very concerned by the fact that a member of the public could take his complaint to any Member of Parliament. She said that she had an unhappy experience with a constituent whose case she had taken up with a department. After it had been dealt with thoroughly the constituent had insisted that his case should be referred to the Parliamentary Commissioner. Although she was convinced that it was not a case to be sent to the Commissioner she 'eventually in desperation' sent the case to him, only to find that the constituent had now taken his case to a Member in the north of England (incidentally also a member of the Select Committee) who had referred the case to the Commissioner without informing Mrs. McKay.[1]

The other members of the Committee did not support Mrs. McKay's view that the Committee should recommend that the Act should be amended to require complaints to be forwarded only through the M.P. for the constituency in which an individual resided. Arthur Probert, for example, argued that the constituent needed to be 'one hundred per cent protected even against his own Member of Parliament'.[2]

Sir Edmund Compton told the Committee that he had 'no evidence of any Member setting himself up as Ombudsman Member,

[1] H.C. 350 of 1967–8. Second Report from the Select Committee on the Parliamentary Commissioner, p. 5 at question 11.

[2] Ibid., p. 9 at question 24.

as a channel on which the public in general can rely and to whom the public should go. Nothing of this sort is happening.'[1] The fear that this might happen had been quite widely expressed during the passage of the Bill in the Commons.[2] The Commissioner also told the Committee that he doubted whether more than ten per cent of the cases he received came from a Member outside the complainant's constituency.

It is interesting to note that this was the first and last occasion, in the first three sessions of its life, when the Committee discussed this previously vexed issue in the relationship between Members and the Commissioner. That it did not recur is an indication of increasing acceptance of the Commissioner by Members and understanding of his role. Another index of the wider acceptance of the Commissioner by Members is provided by the statistics of numbers of Members who have referred cases to him. The Commissioner commented in his first annual report that 428 Members had referred cases to him in the period between 1 April, 1967, when his office opened, and 31 December 1967.[3] By the end of December 1969 the number of Members who had referred complaints to him had risen to 569.[4] This leaves only sixty Members who had not referred a case to him at the end of 1969.

At its meeting on 13 December 1967, the Select Committee discussed another aspect of the relationship between the Commissioner and Members. The Commissioner had prepared a memorandum for this meeting setting out the procedure he proposed to follow as regards publication of his results reports. In this memorandum, he said that he would not normally publish his results report after an investigation. In those few cases which were 'of special public interest and significance to the performance of my functions under the Act' he would make a full report to Parliament. Such cases would be exceptional.[5] In his annual reports he would include summaries of significant cases but would not mention the names of complainants or of the Members referring the complaints.

He told the Committee that he did not propose to make a general

---

[1] Ibid., p. 8 at question 22.   [2] See above espec. pp. 106–10.

[3] H.C. 134 of 1967–8. Fourth Report of the Parliamentary Commissioner for Administration, Annual Report for 1967, p. 3 at para. 2.

[4] H.C. 138 of 1969–70. Second Report of the Parliamentary Commissioner for Administration, Annual Report for 1969, p. 3 at para. 2.

[5] H.C. 350 of 1967–8. Second Report from the Select Committee on the Parliamentary Commissioner, p. 1 at para. 4.

practice of sending his results reports to the Press because he thought this would be unfair to Members since the reports were made personally to them.[1] There was also the point that his results reports were, under the Act, absolutely privileged when communicated to Parliament, to the Member, to the department, and to any person complained against, but they would be subject to the law of defamation if published to the Press. Nevertheless, he did intend to issue the text of a results report to the Press when 'a partial or misleading reference' to the investigation had been published.[2] This memorandum from the Commissioner was approved by the Committee with little discussion.

Since this first meeting of the Select Committee, at which evidence was taken, little consideration has been given to the relationship between the Commissioner and Members. One of the few later discussions on this theme was really concerned with an oddity but is of some interest. The Commissioner reported to the Committee, on 22 May 1968, that he had received a complaint from a Member on his own behalf. The Commissioner had replied that he could not receive this complaint since, under the Act, a complaint must be made to a Member of the House of Commons by a member of the public. The Member concerned was complaining that he had not been invited to the opening of a hospital in his own constituency. He had complained to the Minister and asked him to instruct all hospital authorities that they should invite their local M.P. to every local hospital function. The Minister had refused to do this and the Member then complained to the Commissioner. Sir Edmund Compton refused to investigate this complaint because it was made by the Member on his own behalf. If, however, the Member had forwarded his complaint through another Member, the complaint would have been made in proper form and would have been capable of investigation.[3]

(2) *The Ways in which the Parliamentary Commissioner Organizes his Work*

While the question of the relationship between the Commissioner and M.P.s has declined in importance as an issue in the Select Committee, the Committee has understandably taken a continuing interest in the ways in which the Commissioner organizes his work.

---

[1] Ibid., p. 14 at question 42.   [2] Ibid., p. 1 at para. 5.
[3] Ibid., pp. 92–4 at questions 615–21.

For example, the Committee has from time to time asked the Commissioner about his caseload and the adequacy of his staff for dealing with this load. The Commissioner told the Committee, on 13 December 1967, that the caseload had not proved to be as high as he had expected but that the amount of work per case had been higher than he had anticipated. The number of staff at 59 had 'almost by luck' remained right. If, however, the Act were to be modified to bring the hospital service within his scrutiny, he would expect to have to double his staff overnight.[1] On 22 May 1968, when the Committee were asking him about his first annual report, he told them that the flow of work remained about the same. 'I get something like 28 cases a week.'[2] When the Committee examined him on his second annual report, on 12 March 1969, he reported that the intake of cases to his office had dropped. In 1967, he had received an average of 120 cases a month, in 1968 an average of 94 a month. But the load in terms of work had been fully maintained.[3]

He has from time to time given insights into the way in which his staff undertake investigations. All his investigators, are, as we have seen, members of the executive grade of the Civil Service on secondment from other departments.[4] They are 'divided into investigation units, units of staff who are concerned with different areas of Government departments'.[5] Where the complaint is against an official in an outstation of a central department, for example a local office of the Department of Health and Social Security, the investigating unit normally goes to that office rather than asking the official complained against to come to London. When an investigating team goes to Scotland, it gets the assistance of the Parliamentary Commissioner's officer in Scotland, Mr. Diack, particularly when the complaint is against one of the departments in the Scottish Office rather than a Whitehall department.[6]

The Parliamentary Commissioner only exceptionally takes part personally in an investigation—as we have seen he did in the Sachsenhausen case. But he sees every case at an early stage, when he sends a copy of the complaint to the principal officer of the department concerned. The Commissioner also, in every case, examines the evidence collected by his staff and arrives at a personal

[1] Ibid. p. 10 at question 25.　　[2] Ibid., p. 85 at question 592.
[3] H.C. 385 of 1968-9. Report from the Select Committee on the Parliamentary Commissioner for Administration, p. 70 at question 271.
[4] See above pp. 246-7.　　[5] H.C. 350 of 1967-8, p. 11 at question 32.
[6] Ibid., p. 10 at question 28.

conclusion as a result of the investigation. He then draws up his results report.[1]

The Parliamentary Commissioner does not have his own legal adviser. Charles Fletcher-Cooke asked him to comment on this to the Committee at its meeting on 22 May 1968. Sir Edmund Compton replied that he mainly received legal advice from the Treasury Solicitor. His other sources could be the legal advisers of the department concerned in the complaint and the Law Officers of the Crown.

He preferred this situation to a hypothetical one in which he had his own team of legal advisers. There would then be 'a kind of adversative attitude towards the legal opinion of the Department being looked at'.[2] This he thought would delay cases. There was also the problem of getting specialist legal advice. The departments had such advice and 'if I were to equip myself with an independent legal adviser, he would have to be a most remarkable legal adviser if he were going to stand up to the specialist knowledge of the law which exists in all the Departments investigated.'[3] Sir Edmund also pointed to the relevance of his experience as Comptroller and Auditor-General. He had not had legal advisers in the Audit Office, whereas in most foreign countries the equivalent of that office would be heavily staffed with lawyers. He found, however, that in the British context this kind of staff was not necessary.

Another aspect of the Commissioner's organization of his investigations interested the Committee. They questioned a number of the principal officers about the arrangements made in their departments for dealing with Parliamentary Commissioner cases. Most principal officers replied that the task of coordinating work on such cases was given to the Establishment Officer of the department under the supervision of the principal officer himself who is required by the Act to see the original letter of reference from the Parliamentary Commissioner and the text of the Commissioner's results report after the investigation.[4]

The Foreign Office was one department which had set up a different form of organization. Sir Paul Gore-Booth, the Permanent

---

[1] H.C. 134 of 1967–8. Fourth Report of the Parliamentary Commissioner for Administration, Annual Report for 1967, p. 6 at para. 14.

[2] H.C. 350 of 1967–8, p. 87 at question 598.

[3] Ibid.

[4] See for example evidence from G. H. Daniel, Permanent Under-Secretary at the Welsh Office, on 4 December 1968 (H. C. 385 of 1968–9, p. 15 at question 38).

Under-Secretary, told the Committee that the Foreign Office had set up a separate Parliamentary Commissioner Unit under a First Secretary. This officer also dealt with business concerning other Parliamentary Select Committees.[1]

(3) *The Parliamentary Commissioner's Interpretation of his Powers under the Act*

The Parliamentary Commissioner's interpretation of his powers is a matter of continuing interest to the Committee and it naturally bulked very large in the first two years of the Committee's life. Their interests can be summarized under three main headings: the Commissioner's interpretation of his jurisdiction, his interpretation of his discretionary powers to look at cases which are out of time, or are subject to appeal to the courts or to administrative tribunals, and his interpretation of maladministration.

On the question of his jurisdiction, perhaps the most interesting and important issue was his power to investigate complaints against the Home Secretary in relation to police matters. The Committee heard evidence on this question from Sir Edmund Compton himself, on 20 December 1967, and then decided to invite the Permanent Under-Secretary of State at the Home Office, Sir Philip Allen, to give evidence to them on 24 April 1968.

The Parliamentary Commissioner told the Committee, at the first of these two meetings, that he was assured that there was a firm legal distinction between a police authority and a police force.[2] Thus a local authority cannot intervene with the functioning of a police force in carrying out its duty of preserving the peace by investigating crime, controlling traffic, etc. Similarly, although the Home Secretary is himself the police authority for the Metropolitan Police, he cannot intervene in the functioning of the Metropolitan Police.

When asked to define the powers of the Home Secretary in relation to police forces, Sir Philip Allen told the Committee that, as far as the Metropolitan Police was concerned, the Home Secretary is required by the Police Act, 1964 (Section 50), to keep himself informed about the manner in which complaints against the police are investigated. The Parliamentary Commissioner could, therefore, investigate a complaint that the Home Secretary had not satisfied

[1] H.C. 358 of 1968–9, pp. 6–8 at questions 3–7.
[2] H.C. 350 of 1967–8, p. 30 at question 99.

himself that the Commissioner of Police had adequate machinery for dealing with complaints.[1]

As far as all other police forces are concerned, the Home Secretary's powers may be summarized under the following three headings. First, he is empowered to call for reports from chief constables on matters connected with the policing of their areas (Section 30 of the 1964 Act). Second, he has power to cause a local inquiry to be held, by a person appointed by him, into any matter connected with the policing of an area (Section 32). Third, he can direct that an officer from another area shall investigate a complaint against the police (Section 49).[2]

The Parliamentary Commissioner could investigate a complaint about action taken by the Home Secretary under these powers, but Sir Philip Allen thought it was unlikely that he would be brought in in this way. As for the Home Secretary's other powers in police matters, such as his responsibility for senior appointments and his final responsibility in disciplinary cases, these are excluded from consideration by the Parliamentary Commissioner by paragraph 10 of Schedule 3 of the Parliamentary Commissioner Act (Action taken in respect of discipline, personnel matters, etc. in any office or employment under the Crown).

Similarly, the Home Secretary's power to recommend remission of sentence or a free pardon, in case of a wrongful conviction, is excluded from consideration by the Commissioner under paragraph 7 of Schedule 3. Again, his power, in certain cases, to refer a case to the Criminal Division of the Court of Appeal for retrial is excluded from consideration by the Commissioner under the same paragraph. One is left with the impression, after reading Sir Philip Allen's evidence to the Committee, that the Civil Servants who drafted the Parliamentary Commissioner Bill had done their homework very well in excluding almost all possibility of reference to the Parliamentary Commissioner in relation to the police and criminal proceedings.

After hearing this evidence, the Select Committee apparently saw no reason for disagreeing with the views on the Parliamentary Commissioner's jurisdiction in police matters expressed by the Commissioner himself and by Sir Philip Allen. In their second report for the session 1967–8, the Committee said they accepted the Parliamentary Commissioner's view that he could not investigate

[1] Ibid., pp. 57–8 at question 485.   [2] Ibid., p. 59 at question 493.

action taken by the Metropolitan Police or by any other police force. Neither did they recommend that the Commissioner's powers should be extended in this area.[1] It is worth noting, however, that when Arthur Probert asked Sir Philip Allen about the adequacy of the system for investigating complaints against the police, he replied that Parliament could change the complaints system. 'There are plenty of people who would like to see that done', he commented.[2]

The Parliamentary Commissioner's interpretation of his discretionary powers has not been a matter of major interest to the Committee. On his discretion whether or not to investigate a case which is out of time (that is a complaint which was more than a year old when reported to an M.P.) the Commissioner told the Committee, on 22 May 1968, what was his standard procedure in such cases. He said that, to a large extent, he did not decide whether to exercise his discretion to investigate a case which was out of time until he had gone into it and seen whether there was evidence and whether there was material which he could usefully investigate.[3] The Committee did not in any way question this procedure.

The other aspect of his discretionary power is more complicated. He has power, at his discretion, to look at cases which could go to an administrative tribunal or a court of law. It would not appear that he has used this discretion at all frequently. For example in his annual report for 1968, he recorded that out of the 727 cases which he had rejected during the year, as outside his jurisdiction, 13 per cent were cases in which he saw no justification for using his 'discretion in relation to appellate procedure'.[4]

On the other hand, in a case in which the complaint is against a government department, the fact that there is a tribunal aspect to the case does not deter him from investigating it. As Niall Mac-Dermot forecast during debates on the Bill, he considers that it is appropriate for him to investigate whether the department has followed fair-minded procedures in preparing a case for a tribunal. For example in his annual report for 1969, he summarized, in Appendix B, a case in which he found that the information given by the Ministry of Social Security to the Pensions Appeal Tribunal was not entirely correct. He was satisfied, however, that there had

[1] H.C. 350 of 1967–8, p. xiii at paras. 33–5.
[2] Ibid., p. 62 at question 510.   [3] Ibid., p. 86 at question 592.
[4] H.C. 129 of 1968–9. Second Report of the Parliamentary Commissioner for Administration, pp. 3–4 at para. 5.

been 'no attempt, at any time, to prejudice the hearing of the appeal by the deliberate withholding of information'.[1] He did not find maladministration in this case, but clearly any such deliberate withholding of information would have constituted maladministration.

When the Commissioner finds that a complaint is against a tribunal, rather than the government department, he advises the M.P. concerned to take the complaint to the Council of Tribunals. His *ex officio* position as a member of the Council on Tribunals then enables him to observe the subsequent history of the complaint. He told the Committee, on 12 March 1969, that he had, in 1968, advised M.P.s in twenty cases to take them to the Council on Tribunals and in thirteen instances this had been done.[2] An effective liaison is, therefore, being maintained between the Commissioner and the Council on Tribunals.

By far the greatest interest has been shown by the Committee in the Parliamentary Commissioner's interpretation of 'maladministration'. In his first ever report, his first report for the session 1967-8, the Commissioner gave his interpretation of the key section of the Act (Section 12 (3)) which states that the Commissioner may not 'question the merits of a decision taken without maladministration by a government department or other authority in the exercise of a discretion vested in that department or authority'.

The Commissioner reported that he interpreted this Section of the Act to mean that he should confine himself to investigating

the administrative processes attendant on the discretionary decision: collection of the evidence on which the decision was taken, the presentation of the case to the Minister and so on. If I find there has been a defect in these processes, detrimental to the complainant, then I do enquire into the prospects of a remedy by way of review of the decision. But if I find no such defect, then I do not regard myself as competent to question the quality of the decision, even if, in an extreme case, it has resulted in manifest hardship to the complainant.[3]

The Commissioner told the Committee, on 24 January 1968, that in such cases where there had been injustice but no maladministration, although he was not able to recommend a review of the

[1] H.C. 138 of 1969-70, p. 32 at paras. 12 and 13.
[2] H.C. 385 of 1968-9, p. 72 at question 272.
[3] H.C. 6 of 1967-8. First Report of the Parliamentary Commissioner for Administration, p. 9 at para. 35.

decision, the mere fact of his investigation had brought out a situation in which hardship was being caused.[1] Some members of the Committee clearly felt that this was not enough. For example, Charles Fletcher-Cooke asked the Commissioner whether he could not criticize a decision, even though the processes by which it was taken were correct, if that decision was 'so wrong that no reasonable man could arrive at it'. He noticed that the Commissioner had, in his report, used the words 'my practice so far'. Did this mean that he had an open mind about whether he might extend his range of criticism of discretionary decisions in this kind of way?[2]

Sir Edmund Compton replied that he had used the words 'so far' advisedly because 'I did want to expose my practice so far to this Committee and to obtain guidance from this Committee.' But he then went on to say that Ministers had said, during the passage of the Parliamentary Commissioner Act, that he was not to review discretionary decisions 'because in the words, if I may quote them, of Mr. MacDermot, then Financial Secretary, this would mean not government by Government but government by Commissioner'.[3]

The Committee continued to probe the Commissioner on what could constitute maladministration, producing some interesting comments from him. He discussed, for example, the 'Crossman catalogue' of forms of maladministration and expressed the view that most instances of maladministration were not like this 'rather horrific catalogue of crimes' that Crossman had given, such things as bias, perversity, or the taking of bribes. The 'more common form of maladministration is just making a mistake, losing the file, defects in administration really'.[4]

Sir William Armstrong, the Permanent Secretary of the Treasury, gave support to this view when he was examined by the Committee on 29 May 1968.[5] He said that the Treasury had anlaysed the 19

---

[1] H.C. 350 of 1967–8, p. 39 at question 134.   [2] Ibid., p. 39 at question 135.
[3] Ibid.   [4] Ibid., p. 44 at question 152.

[5] Sir William Armstrong was Third Secretary and Treasury Officer of Accounts from 1958 to 1962, and from 1962 to 1968 was Joint Permanent Secretary of the Treasury. In 1968 he was appointed Permanent Secretary of the newly created Civil Service Department.

Sir William Armstrong was supported at this meeting by K. E. Couzens, an Assistant Secretary at the Treasury, whom Sir William introduced to the Committee as 'the person on the Management side of the Treasury who has been concerned with the development of the procedures relating to the Parliamentary Commissioner' (Ibid., p. 96 at question 631). He had also been, although Sir William Armstrong did not mention this, one of Niall MacDermot's principal Treasury advisers during the passage of the Parliamentary Commissioner Bill.

cases of maladministration which the Parliamentary Commissioner had found in his first year and had summarized in Appendix B of his annual report for 1967. They found that the cases of maladministration could be grouped in the following ten categories:

(i) Failure by a department to correct an error when discovered (2 cases).

(ii) An incomplete or ambiguous instruction from the department to an operating officer (1 case).

(iii) Departmental instructions or circulars to local authorities were unclear or ambiguous (2 cases).

(iv) Misleading statements were made to citizens of the legal position (3 cases).

(v) Departments got the facts in the case wrong (2 cases).

(vi) Departments did not take certain relevant facts into account (3 cases).

(vii) There was delay which amounted to maladministration (3 cases).

(viii) A letter written to the citizen showed bias (1 case).

(ix) Papers in the case were lost by the department (1 case).

(x) The department failed to reply to a letter (1 case).

Sir William Armstrong particularly commented on the fact that in only one instance did the Commissioner find that the official in the case had been biased.[1]

The Committee examined a number of Principal Officers on the Commissioner's interpretation of maladministration in the cases with which their departments had been concerned. They discussed several instances in which the Commissioner had recommended a review of the decision because faulty procedures had been involved, although he would not have considered himself empowered to recommend a review if the procedures followed had been correct. For example, they asked Sir Matthew Stevenson, Permanent Secretary at the Ministry of Housing and Local Government, about the Solihull case in which the Minister allowed a planning appeal without hearing representations from the Tenants' Association in a nearby local authority.[2] Sir Matthew Stevenson admitted to the Committee that there had been 'a human slip in the Department'

---

[1] Ibid., pp. 100–1 at question 643.

[2] Sir Matthew Stevenson was Deputy Secretary in the Ministry of Power from 1961 to 1965 and Permanent Secretary from 1965 to 1966. He was Permanent Secretary at the Ministry of Housing and Local Government from 1966 to 1970.

in that the officials concerned had not taken note of the fact that this Tenant's Association in a neighbouring authority had objected to the proposed development which was the subject of appeal. This was a proposal to erect an eight-storey office block. There had also been an administrative defect, in that the Ministry's circular to local authorities had not made it sufficiently clear that representations should be invited at the appeal stage from all parties who had objected to or supported the proposed development at an earlier stage. A new circular had now been sent out making this point.[1]

It was because the Parliamentary Commissioner found these errors of administrative procedure that he was able to recommend, in his results report, that a new inquiry should be held into the proposed development at Solihull. Sir Matthew Stevenson told the Committee that a fresh inquiry was being held 'with a different Inspector from the first time and with an assurance that the parties previously neglected will be heard.'[2]

The Committee asked Sir Matthew Stevenson, as they did when they examined other principal officers, whether he thought that the concept of maladministration should be widened to enable him to look at the quality of decisions. Sir Matthew Stevenson said that he saw grave objections to this: 'the idea that somebody who is not responsible for the administration and is not responsible for the carrying out of policy will enter in to give a different kind of balance on the same facts, and on established facts, seems to me to be very difficult.'[3] Many of the cases with which his Ministry was concerned were in fact 'rather finely balanced'. This was the situation when, for example, it came to measuring individual hardship as against a policy about Green Belts. It would, in his view, result in a 'pretty considerable slowing down of the whole process of planning' and 'would result in persons who carry no responsibility for the policy giving evidence on it by expressing views on where the balances lie'.

Having heard evidence of this kind, the Committee went on to say in their report that they were not encouraging the Commissioner to substitute his decision for that of the Government. They did suggest, however, 'that if he finds a decision which, judged by its effect upon the aggrieved person, appears to him to be thoroughly bad in quality, he might infer from the quality of the decision itself that there had been an element of maladministration in the taking of it and ask for

---

[1] H.C. 350 of 1967–8, pp. 45–6 at question 156.   [2] Ibid., p. 46 at question 158.
[3] Ibid., p. 53 at question 196.

its review'.[1] The Commissioner, in his first report for the session 1968-9, told Parliament that he was acting on the Committee's recommendations in this question.[2]

However, when he came to make his annual report for 1968, he commented that the effect of considering the quality of the decision itself had so far been slight.[3] It would seem that it has had as yet little effect in widening his interpretation of what constitutes maladministration.

(4) *The Examination of Departmental Rules and Statutory Orders*

The Committee produced a more immediate effect through the recommendation in their second report for 1967-8 that the Commissioner should be able to criticize a government department for not reviewing a departmental rule which was found to be causing injustice. We have seen that the Committee had been concerned about this aspect of the Sachsenhausen case: that the Parliamentary Commissioner had not felt himself empowered to criticize a departmental rule even though he clearly considered that its effect was inequitable.

The Committee looked at other instances in which the Commissioner had not felt himself able to criticize a departmental rule. For example, on 7 February 1968, they discussed with Sir Matthew Stevenson, the Permanent Secretary at the Ministry of Housing and Local Government, the Ministry condition whereby, once planning permission had been given for building a house in a rural area for agricultural purposes, it could only be resold to an agricultural buyer. In the 'Battle' case the owner of a cottage had complained to the Parliamentary Commissioner that he was suffering injustice through maladministration in that the Ministry was refusing to waive this rule although the owner had retired from farming and wished to sell his cottage.[4]

When the Committee discussed this question with the Parliamentary Commissioner, on 22 May 1968, the Commissioner said that it was an area where he was 'hoping for assistance and for guidance

[1] H.C. 350 of 1967-8, viii at para. 14.
[2] H.C. 9 of 1968-9. First Report of the Parliamentary Commissioner for Administration.
[3] H.C. 129 of 1968-9. Second Report of the Parliamentary Commissioner for Administration, Annual Report for 1968, p. 6 at para. 16.
[4] H.C. 350 of 1967-8, pp. 50-2 at questions 175-93.

from this Committee'. He asked: 'where a rule has caused hardship, should I test the Department administratively for not having taken action to review this rule?' Similarly, as regards subordinate legislation he had 'seen it stated by a distinguished academic lawyer that the making of statutory orders is one way in which Departments administer Acts of Parliament and is, in that sense, part of the administrative process.'[1] Sir Edmund Compton said he would want to look very closely at how far this would take him if he were encouraged to act on this advice.

Sir Edmund was here referring to a letter, published in *The Times* of 11 April 1968, from Geoffrey Marshall. In this letter, Marshall had asked whether the Parliamentary Commissioner was not restraining himself unnecessarily in holding that he could not investigate the exercise of a ministerial power to make an order under the Rent Act, on the ground that he could only examine administrative and not legislative functions.

In their Second Report for 1967–8, the Committee recommended that where the Commissioner found that a departmental rule was harsh in its effect, he should consider whether the department had taken action to revise the rule.[2] The Commissioner reported on 7 November 1968 that he was acting on this recommendation.[3]

In his annual report for 1968, he described the way he had modified his practice. He said that he now felt entitled to inquire whether a department had reviewed a rule in the light of the hardship sustained by the complainant. But he pointed out that the decision whether or not the rule should be changed would rest with the department and not with him. He also pointed out that 'there might be grounds of public need which in the judgment of the department over-rode the hardship to the individual whose complaint had been referred to him.'[4] He instanced a case (summarized in Appendix B of his report) where he thought it reasonable for the Ministry of Transport to maintain their rule of not buying up property in advance of their motorway programme, even though owners of houses along the projected motorway were suffering hardship due to 'blight' caused by the motorway proposals.[5]

In the session 1968–9, the Committee went on to consider whether

[1] H.C. 350 of 1967–8, pp. 90–1 at question 611.
[2] H.C. 350 of 1967–8, pp. viii–ix at para. 17.   [3] H.C. 9 of 1968–9.
[4] H.C. 129 of 1968–9. Second Report of the Parliamentary Commissioner for Administration, Annual Report for 1968, pp. 6–7 at para. 17.
[5] Ibid., pp. 139–40.

to recommend that the Commissioner should also inquire into the operation of statutory orders, on similar lines to the practice he had developed in relation to departmental rules. They heard evidence on this question from the Parliamentary Commissioner himself, from the Chairman of the Select Committee on Statutory Instruments, from the Counsel to the Speaker, who advises this Committee and from the Attorney General.

The Committee found that there was a distinction between Statutory Orders which are Statutory Instruments and are, therefore, subject to the scrutiny of the Select Committee on Statutory Instruments and those which are not. Statutory Instruments are mostly the exercise of legislative functions but other Statutory Orders are not. The Parliamentary Commissioner told the Committee, on 5 February 1969, that, in his view, it would be a reasonable step for him to look at complaints against Statutory Orders which were not subject to scrutiny by the Statutory Instruments Committee. It would be administratively possible for his staff to check, when screening a complaint against a Statutory Order, whether it had been to the Statutory Instruments Committee.[1]

When the Committee heard evidence from Graham Page, the Chairman of the Statutory Instruments Committee, and from Sir Robert Speed, the Counsel to the Speaker, Sir Hugh Munro-Lucas-Tooth was at pains to point out for his Committee that they wanted to avoid any clash between the two Committees.[2] But the Chairman of the Statutory Instruments Committee did not think there need be a clash. He thought that it would be a useful supplement to the work of the Statutory Instruments Committee if the Parliamentary Commissioner were to examine the administrative processes which led to the formulation of a Statutory Instrument or Order.[3]

The Attorney General, Sir Elwyn Jones, told the Committee that in his view the making of a Statutory Instrument was itself part of the legislative process and was not an administrative act and that, accordingly, the Commissioner has no power to examine the form, content, or merits of Statutory Instruments.[4] He did think,

---

[1] H.C. 385 of 1968–9. Report from the Select Committee on the Parliamentary Commissioner for Administration, pp. 44–5 at question 169.

[2] Graham Page has been Conservative M.P. for Crosby since 1953. He was Chairman of the Select Committee on Statutory Instruments from 1964 to 1970. He is a solicitor.

Sir Robert Speed, Q.C., has been Counsel to the Speaker since 1960. From 1948 to 1960 he was Solicitor to the Board of Trade.

[3] H.C. 385 of 1968–9, p. 39 at question 157.   [4] Ibid., p. 65 at question 254.

however, that it would be proper for the Parliamentary Commissioner, after a Statutory Instrument had become law, to see whether complaints about the way it was operating had been looked at. He also thought that failure by a department to review an Instrument which was causing hardship could be considered maladministration.[1]

The Committee, after collecting these opinions, came up with the following recommendation in their report for 1968–9. They suggested that 'it would be proper for the Commissioner to investigate any complaint of maladministration in the administrative process leading to the making and subsequent reviewing of Orders which are not Statutory Instruments.' As regards Statutory Instruments, they suggested that the Commissioner should look at the effect of any Instrument, in a case under investigation, and inquire into action taken by the department to review the operation of the Instrument. By implication, however, he would not look at the making of Statutory Instruments.[2] In his first report for the session 1969–70, the Parliamentary Commissioner said that he was acting on these recommendations of the Committee.

(5) *The Effect upon Departments of the Parliamentary Commissioner's Investigations*

Sir Matthew Stevenson, the Permanent Secretary at the Ministry of Housing and Local Government, was the first Permanent Secretary to be questioned by the Select Committee about the effects the Parliamentary Commissioner's inquiries were having on his department. On 7 February 1968, he told the Committee that, at a rough estimate, he thought that the Commissioner's investigations cost, in terms of departmental time, about $1\frac{1}{2}$ man days per case.[3] Sir William Armstrong's estimate of the effect of the Commissioner on the public service in general was very similar. He told the Committee on May 29 1968, that the Treasury estimated that Parliamentary Commissioner's cases might cause $1\frac{1}{2}$ to $1\frac{3}{4}$ man days extra work per case. He thought that the Inland Revenue would probably think this was an underestimate and that more time was spent on their cases.[4]

Sir Matthew Stevenson also told the Committee that because the Parliamentary Commissioner worked within quite a short time limit, his cases tended to disrupt other work in the department. He thought

---

[1] Ibid., pp. 69–70 at questions 266 and 267. [2] Ibid., p. vii at para. 11.
[3] H.C. 350 of 1967–8, p. 54 at question 197. [4] Ibid., p. 98 at question 634.

that there had been a noticeable tendency, in the very early stages, for the work of the department to proceed more slowly and more carefully. Finally, he found, personally, that the Parliamentary Commissioner's cases took up a good deal of his time since he felt that it was necessary for him to go through many of the cases 'wherever I have reason to believe that there are genuine difficulties; wherever I think there is a problem about protecting the legitimate rights of the officers involved on the one hand, and the need for candour with the Parliamentary Commissioner on the other'. This was, he said, a time consuming business but there was, perhaps, a compensation since he had probably learned things 'about the operation of that part of the office that I might not otherwise have learned'.[1]

Sir William Armstrong, on the other hand, said he thought that the Parliamentary Commissioner's inquiries had not made Civil Servants more meticulous. He said that he doubted if the arrival of the Parliamentary Commissioner on the scene had made much difference in this respect. The Public Accounts Committee, the other parliamentary committees, and Members' letters to Ministers already had the effect of making Civil Servants meticulous.[2]

Immediately after Sir William Armstrong gave this evidence to the Committee, Sir Edmund Compton volunteered his own assessment of the effect of his investigations on departments. He thought that he could discern three credit and two debit items. The first credit item was that where he found maladministration, the failure was detected and put right. Second, the result of his work was that complaints which otherwise might have gone on plaguing departments were finally disposed of. Third, he was having, he hoped, 'a tonic effect' on the departments in the sense that Permanent Secretaries would organize their administrative procedures with a sense of awareness that the Parliamentary Commissioner might at any time subject them to investigation. This tonic effect on administrative procedures he compared to the similar effect over accounting procedures which was exerted by the investigating powers of the Comptroller and Auditor-General.

On the debit side, his investigations must result in additional work for the department and 'inevitably that means either more staff or longer time taken'. The second debit item was the possibility that his investigations might make departments 'less forthcoming and

[1] Ibid., p. 58 at question 197.   [2] Ibid., p. 109 at question 664.

helpful in the work they do for the public'. Departments often give advice to the public which is outside the limit of their statutory obligations. He was concerned that they might not now be willing to do this in case there were complaints that they had given wrong advice. He hoped that departments would not become over-cautious in this way and said he would very much like to encourage them not to be over-cautious 'even at the risk of some additional complaints coming my way on account of it'.[1]

The somewhat gloomy view of the effects of the Parliamentary Commissioner's investigations on his department, expressed by Sir Matthew Stevenson, was not echoed by the Permanent Secretaries who gave evidence to the Select Committee in the following, 1968–9, session of Parliament. Sir Philip Allen, the Permanent Under-Secretary at the Home Office, told the Committee on 19 March 1969, that the burden on his department was less than he had anticipated when, as a member of the Treasury, he was concerned with planning the Bill.[2] Sir Anthony Part, Permanent Secretary at the Board of Trade, said that the Parliamentary Commissioner's cases had not placed an enormous extra load on his department but his cases were to some extent concentrated on relatively few sectors of the Department and tended 'to put under greater pressure people who are already under some pressure as a result of the business of their sector in the Board'.[3]

Sir Clifford Jarrett, the Permanent Under-Secretary of State for the Department of Health and Social Security, told the Committee that the Commissioner's investigations had not resulted in the slowing down of decisions taken in his department in relation to such matters as social security benefits.[4] G. H. Daniel, Under-Secretary at the Welsh Office, told the Committee, on 4 December 1968, that he thought Civil Servants in his department might 'perhaps spend fractionally longer' over a decision because they thought it

[1] Ibid., pp. 112–13 at question 673.

[2] H.C. 385 of 1968–9, p. 82 at question 305. Sir Philip Allen chaired the committee of officials concerned with planning the Bill which paralleled Douglas Houghton's committee of Ministers. See above pp. 51–2.

[3] Ibid., p. 53 at question 213. Sir Anthony Part has been Permanent Secretary at the Board of Trade since 1968. He was Deputy Secretary at the Ministry of Public Building and Works from 1963 to 1965 and Permanent Secretary from 1965 to 1968.

[4] Ibid., p. 108 at question 448. Sir Clifford Jarrett was Permanent Secretary at the Admiralty from 1961 to 1964. Since 1964, he has been Permanent Secretary at the Ministry of Pensions and National Insurance, then at the Ministry of Social Security, and finally Permanent Under-Secretary at the Department of Health and Social Security.

might be investigated, but he did not think this was a serious problem.[1]

Several of the Civil Servants examined indicated that they thought the Parliamentary Commissioner was, in general, having a beneficial effect on administration. G. H. Daniel told the Committee that 'he would think that it is in fact salutary for our Department to know that at any moment a complaint can be taken up and looked at by the Parliamentary Commissioner in some detail. This keeps the whole Department on its toes.'[2] It was clear from his subsequent evidence that he thought that the Commissioner's investigating powers could have a greater effect than, for example, an adjournment debate in the Commons. For an adjournment debate, he told the Committee, the Minister would call for a report from the department, a draft speech, and notes for dealing with questions that might crop up. The Minister might ask to see some of the papers, to clarify a point which he did not quite understand, but he would not examine all the papers as the Parliamentary Commissioner, or his investigator, could.[3]

Several Permanent Secretaries gave evidence to the effect that they regularly tried to follow up the Parliamentary Commissioner's findings and review their administrative procedures where this seemed necessary. The Chairman of the Select Committee asked Sir Philip Allen on 19 March 1968, whether, in the Home Office, they regularly had a review of the case, after an investigation by the Commissioner, to see if their administrative procedures needed any amendment. Sir Philip Allen replied that they did. 'We always look with great care at the final Decision Letter, and in the cases where this has pointed to something, we certainly consider what changes are necessary in order to avoid a recurrence or to diminish the chances of a recurrence' of an administrative failing.[4]

Sir Anthony Part, for the Board of Trade, gave certain instances of areas in which the Parliamentary Commissioner's inquiries had led the Board to review and improve their procedures. On the liquidation side of their work, they had given particular attention

---

[1] Ibid., p. 15 at question 36. Sir Goronwy Hopkin Daniel was Permanent Under-Secretary of State at the Welsh Office from 1961 to 1964. He had been a Lecturer in Economics at Bristol University from 1940 to 1941 and from 1941 to 1943 was a Clerk in the House of Commons. Since 1969 he has been Principal of Aberystwyth University College.

[2] Ibid., p. 15 at question 35.   [3] Ibid., pp. 23–4 at questions 73–82.

[4] Ibid., p. 86 at question 336.

to trying to get cases handled more speedily. In the area of investment grants, they had given prolonged care to the question of re-
conditioned machinery. This was a difficult area to which the
Parliamentary Commissioner's inquiries had drawn attention.[1]

The Committee heard about one case in which the department
concerned decided to pay a really substantial sum of compensation
to an individual who had been found by the Commissioner to have
sustained injustice as a result of maladministration. Sir Edmund
Compton told the Committee, on 26 March 1968, that as a result of
his report, the Ministry of Transport had decided to pay around
£7,900 to a doctor who claimed that he had to pay this amount in
betterment levy on a property which he was selling to a local authority for road improvement. Due to unreasonable delay in the Ministry of Transport, loan sanction for the purpose was slow in being
approved and, as a result of this delay, the doctor became liable
to betterment levy which he would not otherwise have had to
pay.[2]

A spectacular contrast was provided to this case by the Parliamentary Commissioner's experience in relation to the demolition
of a station near Nottingham. Trevor Park, the Labour Member for
South-East Derbyshire, complained to the Commissioner on 6
January 1968, against the action of the Minister of Transport in
approving the closure of Trent railway station. He also told Sir
Edmund Compton that although the Minister's approval had only
been given five days previously, on 1 January, preliminary demolition of the station had already begun. The Parliamentary Commissioner took up the case, but by the time he had concluded his
investigation, in September 1968, demolition of the station was
already complete.[3]

Alexander Lyon asked Sir David Serpell, the Permanent Secretary to the Ministry of Transport, whether there should not be a
code of conduct that irreversible action of this sort should not
proceed when a matter was under investigation by the Parliamentary

---

[1] Ibid., p. 60 at question 240.

[2] Ibid., p. 95 at question 371. See also, for a summary of this case, H.C. 129 of 1968–9.
Second Report of the Parliamentary Commissioner for Administration, Annual Report
for 1968, pp. 125–6.

[3] Trevor Park was Labour M.P. for South-East Derbyshire from 1964 to 1970. He
was a university lecturer before entering Parliament. He was not mentioned by name by
Sir Edmund Compton in giving evidence to the Select Committee, but his action in
taking the case to the Parliamentary Commissioner was reported in the Press.

Commissioner.[1] Sir Edmund Compton had already made clear in his annual report for 1968 that the Parliamentary Commissioner Act did not give him power to 'freeze' any situation which he was investigating. Section 7 (4) of the Act says that any investigation by the Commissioner should not affect the power of the department 'to take further action with respect to any matters subject to the investigation'.[2]

The question was whether, despite this provision in the Act, there should not be a code of conduct between the departments and the Commissioner in cases where the action being taken by the department was irreversible. Sir Edmund Compton did not propose that there should be an understanding that action should not proceed. He told the Committee that he was glad, in such a situation, to consult with the department 'to enable them to judge whether it is their duty to go ahead with an action or whether there is scope for them to suspend action'. But the decision remained with the department. The department might reasonably ask him to expedite his investigation in which case he would do his best to comply. There was also the question of the pressure and priority of other cases and the case in question might be a complex one to investigate. He had to admit that, in the Trent station case, the investigation had taken him nine months to complete (well above his average). He had had to go into the question of what economic advice had been taken by the Ministry before reaching their decision to approve the closure. This had proved a complex matter. He hoped that he would not take so long in looking into any other railway closure case.[3]

It was fortunate, perhaps, that the Parliamentary Commissioner did not find any maladministration in this case. He found, for example, that the confidential reports of the Transport Users Consultative Committee showed that the Ministry had fully considered each aspect of hardship to passengers which it was claimed would follow from the closure.[4] When the Select Committee came to draw up their report on this issue, they concluded that where continued action by a department during the Parliamentary Commissioner's investigation would prejudge the issue, 'it is for the department to hold the balance between the efficient process of Government on

[1] H.C. 385 of 1968–9, p. 100 at question 401A.
[2] H.C. 129 of 1968–9. Second Report of the Parliamentary Commissioner for Administration, Annual Report for 1968, p. 8 at para. 24.
[3] H.C. 385 of 1968–9, pp. 99–100 at questions 397 and 398.
[4] H.C. 129 of 1968–9. Annual Report for 1968, p. 130.

the one hand and the rights of the citizen on the other.'[1] One may sum up the position by saying that a department may continue with an action which the Parliamentary Commissioner is investigating but it does so at its peril. Sir David Serpell admitted to the Select Committee that the Ministry of Transport might even have had to tell the Railways Board to rebuild Trent station if the Commissioner's findings had been adverse. Alexander Lyon questioned, however, whether the Treasury would have allowed this to be done.[2]

The impact of the Parliamentary Commissioner on administration in the departments is of such importance that it seems appropriate here to supplement what can be gleaned from the evidence given to the Select Committee by Permanent Secretaries with some of the author's own findings from interviews with Civil Servants and Ministers. First, G. H. Daniel's evidence that greater impact is made by the Parliamentary Commissioner than is made by the traditional methods of parliamentary pressure can be amply confirmed. For example, it is clear that in the Department of Health and Social Security much greater attention is given to a complaint coming from the Parliamentary Commissioner than is given to finding an answer to a Parliamentary question. A departmental circular, issued in 1968, informed all members of staff that Parliamentary Commissioner cases should be given absolute priority, as a reply had normally to be sent to the Commissioner within fourteen days of the date on which it was referred to the department. The circular also stated that the internal investigation of complaints, from the Commissioner, should be thorough and at least supervised (if not conducted) by a senior officer. The discovery of an error or of additional relevant information by the Commissioner or his officers after the formal departmental reply had been sent to him would obviously, the circular emphasized, reflect serious discredit on the department.

All replies from a department to the Parliamentary Commissioner are vetted by the Permanent Secretary of the department and are signed by him. It is, therefore, inevitable, as was brought out in evidence to the Select Committee, that the Permanent Secretary's work load is made heavier in a department which receives a good

[1] H.C. 385 of 1968–9, p. ix at para. 18.
[2] Ibid., p. 100 at questions 401 and 401A. Sir David Serpell became Permanent Secretary to the Ministry of Transport in December 1968. From 1963 to 1968 he was Second Secretary and then Second Permanent Secretary at the Board of Trade.

many Parliamentary Commissioner cases. Permanent Secretaries also keep continuous supervision of progress in the department on Parliamentary Commissioner cases. Ministers too tend to keep 'a weather eye' on the progress of these cases.

The author's second main finding supports the evidence given to the Committee about the need for maintaining a balance of advantage between the individual and the public interest, when there is an issue of whether or not administrative action should be delayed. Successive Ministers of Transport, in the period from 1968 to 1970, have had to make some awkward decisions here. For example, when Fred Mulley was Minister of Transport, the Parliamentary Commissioner was investigating a complaint against a projected route for road development. As a result of the delay which his investigation occasioned, the road contractor who had made the lowest tender told the Ministry that he would have to withdraw his tender if the project was not confirmed. The Minister then decided to order that work should begin without waiting for the Parliamentary Commissioner's report. If the Parliamentary Commissioner had then reported against the Minister's route, the Ministry would have had to explain to the Select Committee how a greater expenditure of public money would have been incurred if they had waited for the report. Mulley conveyed to the author some sense of exasperation about this case but he was, none the less, quite clear that the general effect on the administrative system of having a Parliamentary Commissioner was a good one. But he thought that if the Parliamentary Commissioner did not come to sensible conclusions, then a Government should have the courage to say so.[1]

(6) *The Advisability of Widening the Commissioner's Jurisdiction to Include Areas Exempted under the Act*

(i) *The Hospital Service*

We have seen that much of the discussion in standing committee on the Parliamentary Commissioner Bill had centred on Schedule 3, the schedule which listed the areas of central government to be exempted from the Commissioner's jurisdiction. A major concession wrung from the Government had been the provision, added at

[1] Frederick Mulley has been Labour M.P. for Sheffield Park since 1950. He was Minister of Transport from 1969 to 1970. He had previously been a Deputy Secretary of State and Minister of Defence for the Army from 1964 to 1965, Minister of Aviation from 1965 to 1967, and Minister of State at the Foreign Office from 1967 to 1969. He is a barrister and economist.

report, under which exempted areas could be brought within his jurisdiction merely by passage of an Order in Council. It was to be expected, therefore, that the Select Committee should give early consideration to some of these areas and not in the least surprising that they should look first at the hospitals, since the standing committee had voted to bring the hospital service within the Commissioner's jurisdiction—a decision which the Government had used its majority to reverse at report stage.

The Select Committee devoted a whole sitting to this question on 12 June 1968. They heard evidence from Sir Arnold France who was, at that time, Permanent Secretary at the Ministry of Health.[1] He was assisted by J. C. Hales, the Principal Assistant Solicitor at the Ministry of Health. Sir Arnold France's evidence related to the hospital service in England and Wales. R. E. C. Johnson, the Secretary of the Scottish Home and Health Department, was present to speak for the hospital service in Scotland.

Sir Arnold France explained to the Select Committee the application of the memorandum on complaints machinery which the Minister had sent in 1966 to hospitals in England and Wales. This memorandum had been mentioned by Niall MacDermott during discussion of Schedule 3 in standing committee.[2] Sir Arnold France now explained its operation more fully and gave some figures of the numbers of complaints which were made in writing to hospital management committees, or boards of governors, in England and Wales during the course of the year. There were 8,000 complaints in all. Of these more than 7,300 were dealt with by hospital officers without the management committees or boards of governors being brought in. Another 500 were dealt with by the management committee or the board of governors itself, 70 went to the regional board, and about a dozen were the subject of an independent inquiry (such inquiries examine complaints of the gravest character).[3] He estimated that of the total of over 7,000 complaints, between 1,000 and 1,500 were raised with the Ministry of Health through M.P.s.

He then went on to give three reasons why he did not consider it would be appropriate for the Parliamentary Commissioner to look at complaints against the hospital service. First, the tripartite

[1] Sir Arnold France was appointed Chairman of the Board of Inland Revenue in 1968. He was Permanent Secretary to the Ministry of Health from 1964 to 1968.

[2] See above pp. 154–5.

[3] H.C. 350 of 1967–8, p. 117 at question 680.

structure of the service would mean that the Commissioner would be 'coming up against a brick wall every now and again' when a complaint overlapped into the general practitioner service or the local authority service, neither of which is a direct responsibility of the Minister of Health. Second, he thought that in quite a substantial number of cases there would be a possibility of an action in the law courts. Third, there was the problem of cases in which clinical judgement had to be assessed. It would be possible to exclude such cases but there was still then the problem of borderline cases when the complaint was partly against an administrative failure and partly against a clinical judgement.[1]

Alexander Lyon then questioned him very effectively on the first of these two arguments. On the tripartite nature of the service, Lyon asked 'was it not the case that there were a large number of complaints where it was clearly a hospital service responsibility and the executive council service and local authorites were not concerned?' Sir Arnold France agreed that there were cases which were wholly a hospital responsibility. On the second point, Lyon asked whether it was not true that over large areas of administration, the citizen might have redress to a court of law but this was not, therefore, held to be a reason for excluding the Parliamentary Commissioner. The Permanent Secretary agreed that this was so.[2]

On the question of clinical judgement, the following points emerged. Sir Arnold France agreed with Alexander Lyon that there is a whole area of administration in the hospital service in which clinical judgements are not involved, for example, the ways in which waiting rooms or appointment times are arranged. Another member of the Committee, Kenneth Lomas, drawing upon his experience as a former administrator in the Blood Transfusion Service, argued that it would be desirable for the Parliamentary Commissioner to investigate all the complaints which came to him from within the hospital service where a clinical judgement was not involved.[3]

Finally, the Chairman of the Committee, Sir Hugh Monro-Lucas-Tooth, asked Sir Arnold France what had been the experience with the four hospitals which are placed within the Parliamentary Commissioner's jurisdiction under the Act. These hospitals are Broadmoor, Rampton, Moss Side, and Carstairs. Ministers have

---

[1] Ibid., p. 119 at question 690.   [2] Ibid., p. 120 at question 694.
[3] Ibid., pp. 129–30 at question 737.

a direct responsibility for each of these hospitals, their employees are Civil Servants, and they are all special security mental hospitals.

Sir Arnold France and R. E. C. Johnson told the Committee that the Parliamentary Commissioner had received three complaints from these hospitals. One of them, France said, 'presented a clinical difficulty and the Commissioner did in fact arm himself with medical advice on it'.[1]

Taken as a whole, this session on the hospital service showed up the arguments in favour of excluding the Parliamentary Commissioner from the hospitals as lacking in substance. Something of the same ground had been covered in standing committee on the Bill. The Select Committee now, however, had two advantages. First, it could cross-examine the senior Civil Servants concerned on the arguments used for excluding the Parliamentary Commissioner. Second, enough time had elapsed for there to be some experience of complaints reaching the Commissioner from the four special hospitals where he has jurisdiction. Although he had only received three complaints from these hospitals, one of them had involved a clinical judgement and had not, on that account, been discontinued by the Commissioner.

In view of the trend of examination in the Committee, it was not surprising that, in their report, the Select Committee came out strongly in favour of inclusion of the hospitals. 'Your Committee do not consider that the reasons given by the Principal Officers justify the exclusion of the hospital service from the jurisdiction of the Parliamentary Commissioner.'[2] They took note, however, of the fact that discussions were proceeding at that time about the unification of the three arms of the Health Service: the hospitals, the general practitioner services, and the local authority service. They thought that it would be appropriate if the position of the Parliamentary Commissioner were to be reconsidered when discussions about the unification of the Health Service had reached a more advanced stage.

In the same month which this report from the Select Committee appeared, July 1968, the then Minister of Health, Kenneth Robinson, published his Green Paper making proposals for merging the three branches of the Health Service. It proposed that area boards should be set up for administering a unified service and suggested some alternative methods which might be adopted for examining

---

[1] Ibid., p. 130 at question 742.   [2] Ibid., p. xiv at para. 37.

complaints by the public against area boards. The first possibility was that the activities of the boards might be brought within the ambit of the Parliamentary Commissioner. Another possibility was that a Health Commissioner, or Commissioners, might be established whose functions would be similar to those of the Parliamentary Commissioner but who would only consider complaints against Health Service authorities.[1]

The Robinson Green Paper came in for heavy criticism for proposing that the unified Health Service should be administered by appointed boards, much on the lines of the existing hospital boards. Robinson's responsibility for health passed later in 1968 to Richard Crossman who, as Secretary of State for Social Services, took over responsibility for both health and social security. His Green Paper, published in February 1970, took account of the criticisms. It proposed 90 area boards for England, as against the 40 to 50 proposed by the first Green Paper for England and Wales. Each of the boards would consist one third of members appointed by the Secretary of State, one third appointed by local authorities, and one third of people chosen by the health professions in the areas. It was proposed that the boards should appoint district committees, bringing the administration of the Health Service one stage again nearer to the patient.

As far as the complaints machinery was concerned, the second Green Paper made no new proposals. It announced that consultations were taking place with professional and other interests about the proposal for a Health Commissioner.[2] The return of a Conservative Government, at the general election in June 1970, cast a doubt on the future of this proposal. Sir Keith Joseph, the Conservative Secretary of State for Social Services, had not, by the end of April 1971, announced proposals for a unified Health Service or for a Health Commissioner, although it was known that both projects were being considered by his department.

(ii) Personnel Matters in the Civil Service and Armed Forces

The exclusion of personnel matters in the Civil Service and in the Armed Forces had also been strongly criticized during the passage of the Parliamentary Commissioner Bill. The Select Committee

---

[1] Ministry of Health, National Health Service, The Administrative Structure of the Medical and Related Services in England and Wales (July 1968), pp. 24–5.

[2] Department of Health and Social Security, National Health Service, The Future Structure of the National Health Service (Feb. 1970), p. 26.

heard evidence on this question from Sir William Armstrong, as Head of the Home Civil Service, and Permanent Secretary to the Civil Service Department, on 14 May and 15 October 1969. They also heard evidence from Sir Arthur Drew, Second Permanent Under-Secretary of State (Administration) to the Ministry of Defence, on 18 June 1969, on the exclusion of personnel matters in the Armed Forces.[1]

Sir William Armstrong was assisted on the second occasion by K. E. Couzens who was at that time responsible, in the Machinery of Government Division of the Civil Service Department, for Parliamentary Commissioner matters. For the first of the meetings with the Select Committee, the Civil Service Department and the Ministry of Defence each submitted a memorandum to the Committee.

The Civil Service Department memorandum referred back to the arguments given by Ministers, during the passage of the Bill through Parliament, for excluding personnel matters in the Civil Service. These arguments, it said, could be summarized under four headings:

(a) The Parliamentary Commissioner is concerned with relations between government and the governed, not with relations between the State, as employer, and its employees.

(b) Civil Servants ought not to be made a privileged class among employees by being given the right to have recourse to the Parliamentary Commissioner against their employer, when employees outside the Civil Service have no such right.

(c) There are well tried arrangements, through the Whitley Council machinery, by which Civil Servants can ask for redress of grievances within their departments with the assistance of their staff associations. 'These arrangements would be damaged by superimposing on them another channel for the pursuit of grievances through Members of Parliament and the Parliamentary Commissioner.' Further, the Staff Side of the Whitley Council did not think it appropriate for the Parliamentary Commissioner to be brought into Civil Service personnel questions.

(d) There would be 'a clear risk of damage to the non-political

---

[1] Sir Arthur Drew has been Permanent Under-Secretary of State (Administration) to the Ministry of Defence since 1964. From 1961 to 1963 he was Deputy Under-Secretary of State at the Home Office. From 1963 to 1964 he was Permanent Under-Secretary to the War Office.

character of the Civil Service if recourse to the Parliamentary Commissioner via Members of Parliament became a regular and recognized procedure' as it would do if Civil Service personnel matters were brought within his scope.[1]

Examination of this memorandum by the Committee followed a similar course to their examination of the arguments for excluding the hospitals. The arguments advanced by the Civil Service Department were critically scrutinized and found wanting. Sir Hugh Munro-Lucas-Tooth first asked Sir William about argument (b), that Civil Servants ought not to be made a privileged class having rights against their employers which were not enjoyed by employees outside the Civil Service. Sir Hugh wanted to know how this argument could be reconciled with the practice under which Civil Servants could have recourse to Members of Parliament when they had complaints about their treatment in the Service.

Sir William agreed that this practice had grown up informally over the years. Ministers and departments would look into complaints from Civil Servants forwarded to them by Members of Parliament. There were areas where the Clerks at the Table of the Commons would probably not allow questions, for example a question about why a constituent was not selected by the Civil Service Commissioners would not seem admissible. But, on matters such as superannuation, Ministers could, and did, answer questions.[2]

Antony Buck then asked Sir William about argument (d), that reference of complaints to the Parliamentary Commissioner might damage the non-political character of the Civil Service. Buck pointed out that in his constituency, Colchester, he received complaints from employees of the Ministry of Works working on defence installations. He regularly took up these complaints with the Minister and did not think this did much harm to the non-political character of the Civil Service.

Sir William then frankly acknowledged that the argument was overstated, 'I think that perhaps we are seeing bogies under the bed at that point.' He asked leave from the Committee to withdraw paragraph (d) of the memorandum. Leave to withdraw the paragraph was immediately granted.[3]

Antony Buck also asked Sir William about the argument (argument

---

[1] H.C. 385 of 1968–9, pp. 121–2.   [2] Ibid., p. 126 at paras. 513–5.
[3] Ibid., p. 128 at paras. 525 and 526.

(c) in the memorandum) that the superimposition of recourse to the Parliamentary Commissioner on the Whitley machinery would damage the latter. Had the Whitley machinery, he asked, been affected by recourse by Civil Servants to Members of Parliament? Sir William replied that he thought it had not been affected; 'they both have grown up together.'[1] He maintained, nevertheless, that complaints were best dealt with through the Whitley machinery and staff representation.

Finally, the Chairman asked Sir William whether he knew that most Ombudsmen abroad investigate complaints from Civil Servants in personnel matters. Sir William replied that he did know this. He understood that it had 'produced a somewhat legalistic approach to the terms of their employment by Civil Servants.' Their complaints had swamped the Parliamentary Commissioner, 'or the corresponding apparatus,' and finally, in such countries there was nothing comparable to the Whitley machinery in the British Civil Service.[2]

The effect of these questions to Sir William Armstrong, largely put by Antony Buck and the Chairman, was to demolish three of the four arguments put forward in the Civil Service Department memorandum. Argument (d), damage to the non-political character of the Civil Service, had in fact been withdrawn by Sir William. Arguments (b) and (c), that Civil Servants should not be put in a special position as employees, and that recourse to the Parliamentary Commissioner might damage the Whitley Council machinery, were shown to be very lame. Civil Servants, it had been conceded, were already in a special position as employees since they could take their complaints to Members of Parliament. The fact that they did have this recourse could not be said to damage the Whitley Council machinery. The Civil Service Department were left with only the first argument in their memorandum, that the Parliamentary Commissioner system is concerned with relations between government and the governed and not with relations between the State and its employees.

The Select Committee, having thus effectively directed its fire against the Civil Service Department's memorandum, came up against an obscurity when it turned from the question of Civil Service personnel matters to the third exclusion in paragraph 10 of Schedule 3 of the Act. This paragraph excluded 'service in any

[1] Ibid., p. 127 at question 517.   [2] Ibid., p. 129, questions 533 and 534,

office or employment, or under any contract for services, in respect of which power to take action, or to determine or approve the action to be taken, in such matters is vested in Her Majesty, any Minister of the Crown or any such authority as aforesaid.' The Chairman asked Sir William whether he could give any kind of analysis of the range of appointments that this might cover. Sir William Armstrong replied that he regretted he could not. He had come prepared to talk about personnel matters in the Civil Service; he was not really well equipped to talk about the final section of paragraph 10.

The Chairman commented that this was clearly a matter of some importance since the Parliamentary Commissioner had found that a large number of complaints under paragraph 10 had come from the 'appointments under the Crown' area. Of the 160 complaints which he had had to reject in the preceding year under paragraph 10, seventy-five had come from people who were appointed under the Crown but who were neither Civil Servants nor members of the Armed Forces. Sir William Armstrong then suggested that he should gather the material for such an analysis and present it to the Committee on another occasion. It was agreed that this should be done.[1]

The Select Committee met to consider a further memorandum from the Civil Service Department on 15 October 1969. The memorandum did little more than set out the effect of sub-paragraph (c) of paragraph 10 of Schedule 3 of the Act. This was the nub of the memorandum:

'Very broadly, the effect of sub-paragraph 10 (c) is to exclude from the scope of the Parliamentary Commissioner all Government action on personnel matters in the public sector which is not already excluded by sub-paragraph 10 (a) or 10 (b)' (personnel matters in the Armed Forces and in the Civil Service). The memorandum then went on to say that it would not be practicable to give an exhaustive list of personnel matters involved but it gave the following examples:

(a) administrative action in relation to the pay or pensions of teachers, National Health Service employees, and members of the Metropolitan Police.

(b) appointments, pay, or pensions of members of the boards of

---

[1] Ibid., pp. 131–3 at questions 541–9.

nationalized industries and appointments to such bodies as the Arts Council and the new town development corporations.[1]

Before the Committee began to question Sir William Armstrong about this memorandum, they heard evidence from Sir Edmund Compton who gave an analysis of the 75 cases which he had rejected under sub-paragraph 10 (c) in 1968. Of these, 25 complaints were from overseas government employees, 17 from Health Services employees, 17 from teachers, 7 from local government employees, and 9 were miscellaneous. Most of the complaints, 42 in fact, related to superannuation or pension matters, 13 were about appointments or removals, and ten were about pay. Only one was a complaint about an appointment by a Minister to a public body. This was a complaint about the appointment of the chairman of the Rural Development Board of Wales.[2]

When Sir William Armstrong came to give evidence, he pointed to a number of difficulties which might ensue from ending the exclusion of 'appointments under the Crown'. He foresaw possible difficulties of demarcation particularly in relation to local authorities and the Health Service. The Government had stated that it intended to bring in an Ombudsman system for local government and a Health Commissioner for the Health Service. Who then would be given the task of looking at complaints in personnel matters in these areas? It was a problem that would need some thought, but he did not imply that it was an insoluble problem.[3]

On the question of 'patronage' appointments, that is appointments by Ministers to public boards, Sir Edmund Compton also pointed to a difficulty. He could see that a complaint could be made, by someone who had been passed over for an appointment, that the appointing process had been infected by maladministration and an injustice had been done to him. He would, therefore, be an 'aggrieved person', and complaints were only receivable by the Commissioner from aggrieved persons. But he thought that it was 'doubtful whether a complaint would be investigable if it was in effect a complaint from, say, a user of water that he had suffered injustice because the irregular process of appointment had resulted in the appointment of an incompetent chairman of the water board'.[4]

---

[1] H.C. 127 of 1969–70. Second Report from the Select Committee on the Parliamentary Commissioner for Administration, p. 1.

[2] Ibid., pp. 3–4 at questions 2–5.   [3] Ibid., p. 4 at question 7.

[4] Ibid., p. 8 at question 21.

Having heard this evidence on 'appointments under the Crown', the Select Committee published its conclusions on the whole subject of exclusions under paragraph 10 of Schedule 3. In its second report for the session 1969–70, published in February 1970, it came out in favour of ending the exclusion of personnel matters in all three categories: the Armed Forces, the Civil Service, and 'appointments under the Crown'. 'Your Committee, having given the matter careful consideration, conclude that the exclusion of personnel matters in relation to the Crown set out in paragraph 10 of Schedule 3 to the Parliamentary Commissioner Act is not justified.'[1]

They pointed out that 'civil servants and members of the Armed Forces are already in a special class of employee since Members of Parliament can question Ministers about them.'[2] They also noted that the practice of Members questioning Ministers had not impaired the non-political character of the Civil Service nor done damage to the Whitley Council machinery. They saw no reason why reinforcing the role of Members by giving the Parliamentary Commissioner investigating powers should damage the Whitley machinery.

On Crown appointments, the Committee said that they did not consider that demarcation difficulties, for example in relation to local authority and Health Service employees, were sufficient to justify exclusion of this category. 'Demarcation problems already exist for the Commissioner, particularly in the planning area, and these have not proved insurmountable.' On difficulties which might arise in the area of 'patronage appointments', the Committee said that they thought the Parliamentary Commissioner's strict view of the definition of an 'aggrieved person' (instanced by him in evidence to the Committee) (see above p. 300), would 'prevent any danger of the extension of his powers into this area being abused'.[3]

Nothing has been said so far of the evidence given to the Committee by Sir Arthur Drew, on 18 June 1969, about the exclusion of personnel matters in the Armed Forces. Sir Arthur Drew, giving evidence as Second Permanent Under-Secretary of State (Administration) at the Ministry of Defence, was asked by the Chairman to indicate which personnel matters would, in his opinion, be embarrassing for the Parliamentary Commissioner to investigate. He replied that he thought appointments and discipline would be

[1] Ibid., p. v at para. 11.   [2] Ibid.   [3] Ibid., p. vi at para. 14.

difficult, but he did not see any great difficulty in regard to super-annuation.[1]

The Committee, in their conclusions on this question, recognized that there were difficulties in relation to the Armed Forces. They concluded, however, that the Parliamentary Commissioner's investigations would not affect the operation of the internal Service machinery for dealing with personnel grievances. 'His investigations would be directed towards seeing that the machinery had been properly used.' On purely disciplinary matters, they accepted that recourse to the Parliamentary Commissioner might be considered embarrassing. But they were satisfied that there was an adequate safeguard in that the Parliamentary Commissioner Act provided, in section 12 (3), that the Commissioner could not substitute his decision for that of the Government. By implication, therefore, his interest would be in the process by which a decision in disciplinary matters had been arrived at, and in considering whether there had been maladministration in the disciplinary process.[2]

THE WORK OF THE SELECT COMMITTEE SURVEYED

When we survey the work of the Select Committee on the Parliamentary Commissioner in its first three years of operation, it is at once apparent that the Committee has had a considerable impact. It is also clear that its influence has been exerted in one general direction. The Committee has become a powerful influence in favour of enhancing the role of the Parliamentary Commissioner and widening his sphere of operation.

Its report in January 1970 recommended, as we have just seen, extension of his powers of investigation to personnel matters in the Armed Forces, the Civil Service, and in other areas of administration under the Crown.[3] Its report in July 1968 recommended bringing in the hospital service.

As regards the powers enjoyed by the Parliamentary Commissioner, the Committee has been successful in getting his powers widened in certain directions. On the Committee's suggestion, he can now consider whether a departmental rule, or a Statutory Instrument, is giving rise to injustice and can say whether or not the department concerned is taking steps to review that rule.[4] On their suggestion also, the interpretation of maladministration

---

[1] H.C. 385 of 1968–9, pp. 151–5 at questions 640–60.
[2] Ibid., pp. v–vi at para. 12.   [3] H.C. 127 of 1969–70.   [4] See above pp. 282–4.

has been a little widened. The Commissioner can now report upon a decision which has been arrived at by the correct procedures but is so bad in quality that it can be deemed maladministration.[1] So far this change of interpretation has had little effect, but potentially it may be important.

The Committee's investigations have been skilfully conducted. In general, its relations with the Civil Service have been good. There was a period during which a distinct coolness developed. This was at the time of its inquiry into the Sachsenhausen case. The Committee's attempt to take evidence from the middle-rank Civil Servants who had taken the initial decision to turn down the claimants' applications, was, as we have seen, successfully resisted by the Government on the advice of senior Civil Servants.

The Committee's position at this time was probably unwise. In the first place, it was by no means clear that the Civil Servant who was named by Airey Neave to the Committee (although his name was expunged from the record at the instance of the Attorney General) had actually played any part in turning down the original applications. He was the one Civil Servant who was present at all the interviews which Neave had with Ministers. Neave got to know his name and made the assumption that he was the Civil Servant who had taken the initial decision.

In the second place, experience has shown that there are advantages in following the practice, enjoined upon the Committee by the Attorney General, of taking evidence either from the Permanent Secretary of the Department or from the official whom he deputes to give evidence. It means that the evidence given is authoritative. If a Permanent Secretary makes a concession to the Committee, as for example, Sir William Armstrong did when withdrawing part of his department's argument against allowing personnel matters in the Civil Service to be looked at by the Parliamentary Commissioner, it is a meaningful concession.

In general, we may say that since the dust over Sachsenhausen subsided, relations between the Committee and senior Civil Servants have been good. The attitude of officials giving evidence to the Committee has been generally co-operative and they have not adopted an inflexible attitude towards arguments in favour of extending the Parliamentary Commissioner's powers. Here, no doubt, the Commissioner's own background and Civil Service experience

[1] See above pp. 280–1.

have been a help. His experience in working with the Public Accounts Committee has also been of value. It was logical from his point of view, as a former Comptroller and Auditor-General, that the practice of taking evidence from Permanent Secretaries should be carried over into this new committee. Obviously, too, it was more acceptable to the Permanent Secretaries to carry over a practice which had become familiar to them.

The Parliamentary Commissioner's own relations with the Select Committee have also been very good. At times, the more ardent members of the Committee may have seemed to have been prodding him. For example on 20 December 1967, Alexander Lyon said to Sir Edmund Compton during the course of his evidence: 'I think on occasion you have interpreted rather strictly your jurisdiction and I am rather sorry about it.'[1] Collectively, the Committee have indeed been prodding him: to widen the interpretation of maladministration, to question departmental rules, etc. But the Parliamentary Commissioner has not been unwilling to go in these directions when prodded.[2]

As on the Public Accounts Committee, and on the Select Committee on Statutory Instruments, party allegiances have counted for nothing on this Committee. On the Labour side, Alexander Lyon, has been the most vigorous advocate of a strong Parliamentary Commissioner. But, as we have seen, a Conservative Member, Antony Buck, was the main interlocutor of Sir William Armstrong and advocate for the Parliamentary Commissioner being brought into Civil Service personnel matters. Another Conservative, Charles Fletcher-Cooke, was the member of the Committee who urged the Commissioner to look at the quality of a decision.

It is significant that all three of these members were on the standing committee on the Parliamentary Commissioner Bill. In a real sense, the Select Committee has carried on the debate which was begun on the standing committee on such issues as the areas from which the Commissioner was excluded and the interpretation of maladministration. The advocates of a strong Parliamentary Commissioner on the standing committee have their representatives on the Select Committee. They have been joined, in practice, by Sir Hugh Munro-Lucas-Tooth who was, as we have seen, a somewhat lukewarm supporter of the idea of a Parliamentary Commis-

[1] H.C. 350 of 1967–8, p. 27 at question 88.
[2] See also below p. 313.

sioner, but emerged, as Chairman of the Select Committee from 1967 to 1970, as an advocate of a more powerful Commissioner.

Dame Irene Ward was, as we have seen, converted to the Parliamentary Commissioner idea by the Sachsenhausen Report. As a member of the Select Committee she has been a consistent supporter of a strong Commissioner. George Lawson, Kenneth Lomas, Arthur Probert, and Dr. Michael Winstanley have also indicated, in Committee proceedings, their support for moves which would enhance the role of the Commissioner.

Something close to a consensus of outlook has, then, emerged in the Select Committee and this consensus has not been modified by the changes in membership which have occurred. There were no changes of membership during the first session of its life, 1967–8. During the session 1968–9, Stanley Henig came on to the Committee in place of George Lawson.[1] For that session only, 1968–9, Roy Roebuck came on to the Committee in place of Kenneth Lomas.[2] In the session 1969–70, Dan Jones was appointed to the Committee in place of Victor Yates who had died in January 1969.[3] In the same session Frederick Lee took the place of Roy Roebuck.[4] These changes in Committee membership did not alter the balance of the Committee in any significant way. It continued to provide steady support for the Parliamentary Commissioner and to advocate a wider role for him.[5]

[1] Stanley Henig was Labour Member for Lancaster from 1966 to 1970. He was a University Lecturer in Politics, having studied at Oxford at Corpus Christi and Nuffield Colleges. He was born in 1939. He was a member of the Labour Committee for Europe and is assistant editor of the *Journal of Common Market Studies*.

[2] Roy Roebuck was Labour Member for Harrow East from 1966 to 1970. He was born in 1929 and was educated at Manchester College of Commerce. He is a journalist and a member of the Central London Committee of the National Union of Journalists.

[3] Daniel Jones was first elected Labour Member for Burnley in 1955. He was born in 1908 and was a trade union official in the A.E.F. At one time he was a lecturer in the National Council of Labour Colleges. He was Parliamentary Private Secretary to the President of the Board of Trade in 1964.

[4] Frederick Lee was born in 1906. He represented the Hulme division of Manchester for Labour from 1945 to 1950. Since 1950 he has represented Newton. He was Minister of Power from 1964 to 1966 and Secretary of State for the Colonies from 1966 to 1967. He had been an engineer's turner before entering Parliament and was a member of the National Committee of the Amalgamated Engineering Union.

[5] The Select Committee was reappointed after the 1970 General Election on 26 November 1970. The new Committee included five members of the previous Committee. These were Antony Buck, Charles Fletcher-Cooke, Dan Jones, Frederick Lee, and Dame Irene Ward. The five other members of the new Committee, who had no previous experience of the Committee, were Captain Walter Elliot, Mark Hughes, Angus Maude, Michael Stewart, and Sir Richard Thompson. The new Committee chose

In this chapter, we have looked at the institution of Parliamentary Commissioner largely through the eyes of the Select Committee. This is an excellent vantage point to take, since the Committee has probed energetically and its reports are a mine of information. There are features, however, of the operation of his office which the Committee has overlooked or has little touched upon. It has also, understandably, made very few international comparisons with Ombudsmen abroad. It is largely to these aspects which we shall now turn, in the next and final chapter, in attempting to sum up the operation of the Office of Parliamentary Commissioner in its first four years.

Michael Stewart as its Chairman. Michael Stewart had been Secretary of State for Foreign Affairs and Secretary of State for Economic Affairs in the Wilson Government. He had been a strong advocate of a Parliamentary Commissioner before the 1964 General Election. See above p. 83.

XVI

THE PARLIAMENTARY COMMISSIONER: AN EVALUATION

THE BRITISH AND NEW ZEALAND PARLIAMENTARY COMMISSIONERS COMPARED

When this final chapter was written the British Parliamentary Commissioner had been in operation for over four years. His counterpart, the New Zealand Parliamentary Commissioner, or Ombudsman, had been at work for more than eight years.[1] It was possible, therefore, to make some worthwhile comparisons between the two offices, the more usefully since they operate within basically similar parliamentary systems.

On balance, the comparison was not favourable to the British Parliamentary Commissioner. The accompanying table shows the cases dealt with by the British Parliamentary Commissioner in 1970 and by the New Zealand Ombudsman in the year ended 31 March 1970. It shows also the cases which they found to be outside their jurisdictions, the cases they investigated, and the number of instances where they found the complaint to be justified.

In Britain, which has a population of more than 53 million, the Parliamentary Commissioner dealt with 651 complaints, investigated 259, and found 59 cases of maladministration. In New Zealand which has a population of $2\frac{1}{2}$ million, the Ombudsman dealt with 663 cases, investigated 366 of them, and found 78 complaints to be justified. It is apparent that in the British system the Parliamentary Commissioner is, in effect, shielded from receiving complaints to a much greater extent than is his New Zealand counterpart.

This shield operates in three ways, compared with the New Zealand system. First, the fact that there is no provision for direct access to the Parliamentary Commissioner by members of the public

[1] The New Zealand Parliamentary Commissioner (Ombudsman) began work on 1 October 1962.

has clearly cut back the flow of complaints severely. Second, the provision in the British Act which limits the Parliamentary Commissioner to looking at maladministration means that he cannot investigate cases which the New Zealand Ombudsman can consider under his power to report on 'unreasonable' actions by government departments. Third, the British Parliamentary Commissioner is excluded under Schedule 3 of the Act from areas of central government from which the New Zealand Ombudsman is not excluded.

The last of these three is the least important difference. The main area from which the Parliamentary Commissioner is, at present excluded, and the New Zealand Ombudsman is not, is personnel matters in the Civil Service. Otherwise, the areas within which

TABLE I

The British Parliamentary Commissioner and the New Zealand Ombudsman compared

	The British Parliamentary Commissioner*	The New Zealand Ombudsman†
Period	1970	Year ended 31 March 1970
Cases dealt with	651	663
Found outside jurisdiction or discontinued after partial investigation	392	297
Cases investigated	259	366
Complaints found justified	59	78

* Source: H.C. 261 of 1970–71. First Report of the Parliamentary Commissioner, Annual Report for 1970, pp. 3–5.

† Source: Report of The Ombudsman (New Zealand) for the year ended 31 March 1970, pp. 6 and 7.

they have jurisdiction are similar. Both are excluded from local government and from personnel matters in the Armed Forces.

Clearly, it is the denial of direct access by the public to the Commissioner, and limiting him to maladministration, which have curtailed his role so markedly in Britain. It is worth considering how these two factors operate.

The absence of direct access makes the Parliamentary Commissioner much less intelligible to the ordinary member of the public. The Parliamentary Commissioner operates behind the scenes. Although newspapers give good publicity to material which they receive on the Commissioner, this material is, as we have seen, sporadic because publication is dependent, in most cases, on the decision of the M.P. who has taken the case to the Commissioner. Therefore, both the method by which the Parliamentary Commissioner is put into action and the result of his investigations remain obscure to the ordinary person.

Limiting the Parliamentary Commissioner to maladministration has a similar effect. It makes it very difficult for even a well-informed Member of Parliament to predict whether the Commissioner is likely to find for the complainant. It also makes the system haphazard in operation since, if the Commissioner can find a defect of procedure, he can say there has been maladministration even if the hardship suffered by the complainant is relatively trivial. On the other hand, if he cannot find a defect in procedure, he cannot say there has been maladministration even if a complainant is suffering hardship as a result of a decision by a government department.

The complexity of the system is illustrated by the Parliamentary Commissioner's own leaflet explaining his functions which his office supplies to inquiring members of the public. This leaflet covers five columns of small print. It explains that the Commissioner is concerned with government departments only, but that some central government services, such as the hospitals and personnel questions in the Armed Forces and the Civil Service, are excluded. It explains that the Commissioner cannot look at matters which have gone to the courts or to administrative tribunals, and normally cannot investigate cases which *could go* to the courts or tribunals.[1] It explains the twelve-month time limit within which complaints must be made, and that complaints must be made in writing to a Member of the House of Commons. It then describes other features of the system such as the stages of investigation and the provisions in the Act which empower the Commissioner to provide expenses where necessary and, abnormally, legal costs for a complainant.

This information covers the first three columns of the leaflet. In the last two columns, the texts of Schedules 2 and 3 of the Act are given listing the departments and authorities which are subject to investigation and the matters within those departments which are not subject to investigation.

This whole system is obviously less easily understood than the

[1] My italics.

New Zealand system. There, the Ombudsman, Sir Guy Powles, is very much in the public eye. He can be approached directly by members of the public. He, like the British Commissioner, works within the limits of his Statute, but the limits are much less confining since he can report on any unreasonable action of a government department. The personal contact which he has with the complainant enables him to explain directly why he cannot take up a case, when it is outside his jurisdiction. Even when a case is outside his jurisdiction, he sometimes uses his good offices informally to try and get help for the complainant. Walter Gellhorn has pointed out, for example, how the New Zealand Ombudsman, in 1965, helped a foreign teacher who was having difficulty with the currency regulations. Although the question was outside his jurisdiction, Sir Guy Powles took it up 'personally and unofficially' with the Governor of the Reserve Bank.[1]

It should not be thought, however, that a comparison between the British and New Zealand systems is in every respect favourable to the latter. There are features of the British system which appear in a more favourable light. For example, the New Zealand Act requires the payment of a £1 fee whenever a complaint is lodged with the Ombudsman. No fee is payable when a complaint is taken to the British Parliamentary Commissioner. The fee, in New Zealand, must deter poor people and occupants of institutions. It is probably significant that the New Zealand Commissioner receives few complaints from the inmates of mental hospitals and virtually none from people in prisons or other places of detention. By contrast, such people provide an important element in the case load of Ombudsmen in Sweden and Denmark where no filing fee is required.[2]

Another aspect in which the British system comes out well is in the ability of the British Commissioner to look at the actions of Ministers. The New Zealand Ombudsman can investigate recommendations made to Ministers, but he cannot investigate the decisions of Ministers. The British Parliamentary Commissioner is not inhibited in this way. Thus in his special report on the Sachsenhausen case he was able to say that the claimants had suffered maladministration in that the rejection of their claim 'and the terms in which the rejection has been defended by the Foreign Office' had done harm to their standing and reputation. This finding re-

---

[1] Walter Gellhorn, *Ombudsmen and Others* (Harvard University Press 1967), p. 133.
[2] Ibid., p. 122.

ferred primarily to the statements made by Foreign Office Ministers including the Foreign Secretary himself.[1]

Again, in the Duccio painting case, part of the complaint was about statements made by the President of the Board of Trade, Anthony Crosland. This case concerned a painting which was sold in October 1968 to the National Gallery for £150,000. The painting had been bought by a dealer seven months earlier, at an auction at a private house, for only £2,700. The President of the Board of Trade told the Commons that his department's inquiries into the matter would have been greatly helped 'if we had not met a wall of silence . . . on the part of many people'.

Two of the complainants claimed that these statements were not true as far as they were concerned, and that they were discreditable to them and to other members of the Society of London Art Dealers. The Parliamentary Commissioner took evidence on the case from the Minister himself, as well as from Civil Servants and the Director of the National Gallery. In his report, Sir Edmund Compton concluded that the Minister's reference to 'a wall of silence' did not apply to the complainants themselves but to 'some other possible sources of information to which the investigators were directed by the complainants and other informants'.[2] He did not find maladministration in this case, either in the Minister's statement or in the actions taken by the Board of Trade to investigate information about an alleged 'ring' of dealers at the original auction of the painting.

These two cases illustrate the way in which the Parliamentary Commissioner's inquiries are assisted by his ability to look at the actions of Ministers as well as of Civil Servants. He would have had to proceed in a much more roundabout way if he had only been able to look at the recommendations made to Ministers and not at the actions of Ministers themselves.

THE PARLIAMENTARY COMMISSIONER HAS THE ROLE ENVISAGED IN THE WHYATT REPORT

While, however, the British system has advantages in some details, the overall impact of the British Commissioner is undoubtedly inferior to the impact which the New Zealand Ombudsman is

[1] See above pp. 249–51.
[2] H.C. 316 of 1968–9. Third Report of the Parliamentary Commissioner for Administration, p. 17.

11+B.O.

having as a 'grievance chaser'. This lesser impact is largely due to the way in which the British Parliamentary Commissioner is insulated from contact with the public and is confined to a narrow sector of 'maladministration'.

When one says this, however, one must be aware that the British Parliamentary Commissioner has very much the role which was envisaged for him by those who first advocated the reform in Britain. Professor Lawson, as we have seen, argued that the 'Inspector General', whom he proposed in 1957, should be concerned with maladministration.[1] The Whyatt Report proposed that the Parliamentary Commissioner should be confined to maladministration, although it said that, as a concomitant to this, administrative tribunals should be greatly extended to deal with appeals against discretionary decisions in the whole field of central government.

The Whyatt Report recommended also that, during an initial five-year period, access to the Parliamentary Commissioner should be only through M.P.s and peers. A large section of M.P.s themselves seems all along to have favoured making access only through M.P.s, and has supported the argument put forward by the Government during the passage of the Bill that the role of the Commissioner should be to supplement the activities of M.P.s, not to rival them.

This argument was strongly reinforced by the prediction that, if direct access to the Commissioner were allowed, in a country the size of Britain, he would be swamped by the volume of complaints. In fact, however, the opposite has happened. Whereas Sir Edmund Compton, when he began work, anticipated receiving 6,000 to 7,000 complaints in a year, in 1969 he only received 761 complaints through M.P.s. A further 814 written complaints were submitted to him directly by members of the public.[2] Under the terms of the Act, these complaints were not validly made and could not be investigated. It would seem that the limitations placed upon him by the Act have proved too severe.

It could be argued that it was wiser to err on the side of caution, in the early stages, since there was a real danger that if the Commissioner had many more cases than he could deal with, an enormous back-log of cases would quickly develop. This danger has

[1] See above p. 7.
[2] H.C. 138. Second Report of the Parliamentary Commissioner for Administration, Annual Report for 1969, p. 3.

certainly been avoided, since the Commissioner is on average able to make his results report within about three months from the date on which he first receives a complaint from an M.P.[1]

Another danger was that the Commissioner's activities would not prove acceptable to M.P.s or Civil Servants. It was, perhaps, then, prudent to begin in a modest way and demonstrate that his investigations would not, as the Macmillan Government had feared, be detrimental to efficient administration in the departments. Sir Edmund Compton indicated privately to the author in an interview in July 1968 that he thought that, in time, the role of the Parliamentary Commissioner should broaden and develop. It was harder for him to say this in public.

When interviewed, for example, on 10 March 1970 in a programme on B.B.C. television, he took the cautious position that his office was doing what Parliament intended and that most of the expectations of those who had planned the reform had come right.[2] He, clearly, did not feel able to say that once the Office of Parliamentary Commissioner was established it would be possible to extend his scope. Consequently, to the viewer, his performance was disappointing and his attitude seemed complacent.

THE IMPACT OF THE PARLIAMENTARY COMMISSIONER IS NOT READILY APPARENT

Up until the end of April 1971 there had been no recurrence of a case like Sachsenhausen which could demonstrate the Parliamentary Commissioner's effectiveness in a dramatic way to the general public. The record of his achievements was largely buried in the appendices of his annual reports where anonymity of the individuals who complained was carefully preserved, and only the bare bones of each case was given. The cases were grouped by departments and, in a self-effacing way, the cases in which the Commissioner had found maladministration were not singled out and given prominence. A member of the Select Committee, Alexander Lyon, asked the Parliamentary Commissioner, on 12 March 1969, whether he would consider highlighting the cases in which maladministration was found, by an asterisk, or by placing the letter

[1] Sir Edmund Compton in an address to the Society of Individual Freedom, on 9 February 1970, gave three months as the average time he took to dispose of a case. See *Freedom First*, May 1970, p. 13.

[2] See the *Listener*, 19 March 1970, p. 368.

'M' against the heading of the case. Sir Edmund Compton was opposed even to giving this degree of prominence since, he argued, maladministration covered a wide range of defects in administration. By implication, his reasoning was that 'to brand all cases of this kind with a big "M" would be unfair to the departments concerned.[1]

If the reader ferrets hard among the Commissioner's annual reports, he can find instances where, for example, the Ministry of Social Security had acknowledged that there had been maladministration in giving wrong advice to a pensioner and had agreed that arrears of pension, previously refused, would now be paid.[2] Even a close perusal of these reports, however, would not give a full impression of the effect which the Commissioner can have on the public service.

In some cases which the author has been able to follow up with M.P.s, an investigation by the Commissioner in which he found no maladministration has, nevertheless, resulted in a government department giving redress to a complainant. For example, in South Wales in 1967, the Commissioner investigated a complaint from a group of householders that the new motorway which passed their houses, on an embankment, constituted a danger to them since there was no crash barrier to prevent vehicles, or objects dropped from vehicles, from falling into their gardens. The Parliamentary Commissioner found that refusal by the Welsh Office to erect a crash barrier did not constitute maladministration since the standard Ministry practice was to erect a barrier if an embankment was at least 20 feet high. The embankment in this case was only 15 feet high at the highest point. The Commissioner therefore found that there had been no maladministration. The investigation of the case, nevertheless, resulted in a reappraisal by the Welsh Office who, not long after, erected the desired crash barrier.

This instance of a case in which redress was provided by a department, even though the Commissioner did not find maladministration, leads to a tentative conclusion that the impact made by the Parliamentary Commissioner is not fully measured by the proportion of cases in which he finds maladministration. This proportion

---

[1] H.C. 385 of 1968–9. Report from the Select Committee on the Parliamentary Commissioner for Administration, p. 75 at para. 282.

[2] For an example of such a case see the Parliamentary Commissioner's Annual Report for 1967 (H.C. 134 of 1967–8), p. 63.

was 10 per cent in 1968, 16 per cent in 1969 and 23 per cent in 1970. In 1968 he found maladministration in 38 out of 374 cases which he investigated, in 1969 there was maladministration in 48 out of 302 cases and in 1970 in 59 out of 259 cases investigated.[1]

The proportion of complaints found justified by Ombudsmen in Sweden and New Zealand is broadly similar. In Sweden, the Ombudsman finds roughly 10 per cent of the complaints which he investigates are justified.[2] In New Zealand, the proportion is higher than in Sweden. For example, in the year ended March 1969, the New Zealand Ombudsman found that out of 285 complaints which he investigated 66 were justified. The proportion in that year then was around 23 per cent. In the following year, ended March 1970, he investigated 366 complaints and found 78 were justified. This gives a proportion found justified of about 22 per cent.[3] This would seem to place the British Parliamentary Commissioner nearer to the New Zealand than to the Swedish Ombudsman, judging by the proportion of cases he has investigated in which he has found maladministration.

When estimating the effect of the British Parliamentary Commissioner on administration in the central departments we must bear in mind, in addition to the cases where maladministration is found, also what Sir Edmund Compton has called the 'general tonic effect' upon the departments in improving the standard of administration, and those instances, impossible to show statistically but probably not negligible, when a department has subsequently provided redress after the Commissioner had found that there had not been maladministration. Nevertheless, although the impact of the Commissioner can be reckoned important and salutary, the small number of cases which he receives, in a country with so large a population, is a clear indication that he is not being given sufficient scope.

Should members of the public have direct access to him?

The Select Committee has, as we have seen, recognized that the Parliamentary Commissioner's sphere of operation could be

---

[1] See H.C. 129 of 1968–9, Annual Report for 1968, p. 5, H.C. 138 of 1969–70, Annual Report for 1969, p. 4 and H.C. 261 of 1970–71, Annual Report for 1970, p. 5.
[2] Gellhorn, op. cit., p. 213.
[3] Report of the Ombudsman for the year ended 31 March 1970 (A. R. Shearer, Government Printer, Wellington, New Zealand), p. 7.

extended without overstraining his office and has recommended, in particular, that he should be given, by Order in Council, power to consider complaints in personnel matters from Civil Servants, members of the Armed Forces, and from people who hold office under the Crown.[1] It is appropriate to consider at this point some of the arguments for extending the scope of the Parliamentary Commissioner still further and to do this by posing a series of questions on the main possibilities for expansion.

First, should direct access be allowed to the Commissioner by members of the public? We have argued that one great benefit of this reform would be to make the Commissioner much more intelligible to the average citizen. It would be likely to make him the natural recourse of many people who are dissatisfied with their treatment by a government department instead of being someone who is invoked only in the last resort. This does not mean, however, that he would be likely to supplant M.P.s in taking up grievances. The British M.P. is so well established in this field that he would be unlikely to see a big falling off in his post-bag from constituents. Indeed, the M.P. has certain advantages in that he is an all-purpose grievance man. It is customary for M.P.s to give some help to constituents even when they have complaints against local authorities. Here the M.P. has, in theory, no status, but he will often write to the Town Clerk, or other senior officer, drawing his attention to a constituent's complaint. The Parliamentary Commissioner, even if direct access were allowed by the public, is bound to be tied more closely to his jurisdiction under the Act. This, as we shall see, is unlikely to include local government and may not include the Health Service if a separate Health Commissioner, or Commissioners, should be set up for this sphere.

On the other hand, the Parliamentary Commissioner can delve much deeper in investigating a complaint than an M.P. can. It seems reasonable to argue that access to the Parliamentary Commissioner should be *either* through an M.P. *or* directly from a member of the public. When this is said, however, it should be recognized that this would greatly increase the number of cases reaching the Commissioner. This problem could be met, in part, by having different Commissioners for different spheres, as has been suggested for local government and the Health Service. The Parlia-

[1] See above pp. 301–2.

mentary Commissioner would then continue to deal only with a defined sphere of central government. If the case load still proved very heavy for him, he could be assisted by a series of deputy Commissioners. Sweden is an example of a country which already has a system of multiple Ombudsmen. In 1968 Sweden appointed a third full Ombudsman.[1] There are also two deputy Ombudsmen and the Chancellor of Justice, who is, in formal terms, the Royal investigator of grievances as distinct from the Ombudsmen who are Parliament's investigators, but who in fact looks into complaints from citizens in much the same manner as the Ombudsmen do.

Sir Edmund Compton, as Parliamentary Commissioner, came out strongly against providing for direct access to him from members of the public. In February 1970, he told the Society for Individual Freedom that he had three reasons for taking this view. First, he did not want to find himself 'competing with Members of Parliament in those areas of central government where Members can themselves question Ministers'. Second, his connection with Members of Parliament solved 'the collection problem'. If he had direct access he would need to have a widespread local organization for the collection and local processing of complaints. His third reason was that he depended 'on the Parliamentary follow-through for introducing remedies'.[2]

There does not seem to be a great deal of force in these arguments. It seems highly likely, perhaps certain, that the Parliamentary follow-through would remain even if direct access to the Commissioner were allowed. When the Commissioner found that a grievance was not being remedied, in a case which had come directly to him, he would report the fact to the House of Commons just as he does in cases which have come to him from M.P.s. It is inconceivable that M.P.s would not then press for the grievance to be remedied as strongly as if the case had come through an M.P.

The point about collection has little substance. On the Commissioner's own testimony in his Annual Report for 1969, he received in that year more complaints directly from members of the public than he received through M.P.s. These complaints are not vetted as, in theory, they are by M.P.s. But many of the complaints sent on by M.P.s are not, in practice, vetted by them.

The argument that he might be seen to be competing with M.P.s

[1] See Neil C. Elder, *Government in Sweden* (Pergamon, 1970), p. 185.
[2] *Freedom First*, May 1970, pp. 12–13.

has the greatest weight. The opposing view is that redress of a grievance for the citizen is desirable whether it is achieved by the action of an M.P. or by direct approach to the Commissioner. Presumably, however, direct access to the Commissioner will not be introduced until the majority of M.P.s come to accept this view.

HOW HIS REPORTS COULD BE GIVEN MORE PUBLICITY

Short of allowing direct access, are there other changes which would make the work of the Commissioner more intelligible to the public? A good deal could be done to give more publicity to his reports. At present, as we have seen, his results reports are only published if he decides that the case is of such importance that it warrants a special report to Parliament, as in the Sachsenhausen and Duccio cases, or if a misleading report has appeared in the Press and the Commissioner thinks that this should be corrected. In more than four years the Commissioner has only published three special reports on his investigations: those on aircraft noise, Sachsenhausen and the Duccio painting. The vast majority of his results reports, therefore, are not published and are regarded, in effect, as the property of the M.P.s to whom they are made. A report is only published if the M.P. decides that it should be communicated to the Press.

There is much to be said for taking the opposite course. That is, the Parliamentary Commissioner could, as a normal practice, say to the M.P. when sending him the results report: 'I propose to send a copy of this report to the Press unless you, or the complainant, object to my so doing.' In some cases, an objection would be made which the Commissioner would respect. It is likely, however, that in numerous cases there would not be an objection. Many more reports would be published and the public would become more aware of the Commissioner's activities.

This would not be a radical change, but it would be a change of some importance in the Commissioner's practice. A less far reaching, but still valuable, change would be for him to group together in his annual reports all those cases in which he has found maladministration. His present practice of leaving them scattered amongst the general body of reports without any special emphasis or highlighting, is to lean over backwards in protecting the image of government departments.

SHOULD HE BE EMPOWERED TO REPORT ON
UNREASONABLE ACTIONS BY DEPARTMENTS?

More publicity, therefore, could be given to the Commissioner's reports without making a radical change in his role and relationship to M.P.s. It would be a radical change to amend the Act to allow him to report on 'unreasonable actions' by government departments instead of confining him to 'injustice in consequence of maladministration'. Should this be done?

Earlier in this chapter, we noted some of the advantages which might flow from such a change. What are the arguments against it? They were, in effect, well stated by Sir Matthew Stevenson in his evidence to the Select Committee on the Parliamentary Commissioner on 7 February 1968. He argued then that the Parliamentary Commissioner should not, for example, be empowered to weigh up the balance of hardship caused to an individual by not allowing development of property in a Green Belt against the Government's policy of maintaining protected areas of countryside around cities.[1] To do this would be to allow someone who carried no responsibility for the making of policy to make a judgement on the desirability of that policy.

On the other hand, it can be suggested that if the Parliamentary Commissioner were allowed to compare the advantages of different courses of action, in considering whether the Government's decision was unreasonable, he would not be taking decisions for the Government. He would be acting as an independent critic of Government decisions. Against this, the argument can be advanced that since he is neither an expert in town planning nor an elected representative, he has neither the expertise nor the accountability which would justify him in making such criticisms. The advocate of the Parliamentary Commissioner being given power to consider unreasonable decisions could then reply that the role of the Commissioner would be to assess the merits of rival arguments and the views of experts. If, when he presented his report, the conclusions he reached could be shown to be unsound or unacceptable, then his report could be shelved.

To say this, however, is to concede that, if the Commissioner were given power to report on unreasonable action by government departments, there might sometimes be room for considerable

[1] H.C. 350 of 1967–8, p. 53 at para. 195.

difference of opinion about what constituted reasonable action and whether the Commissioner's view was a sound one. At present, since the Commissioner is concerned largely with whether fair-minded procedures have been followed, his results reports are often incontrovertible and are normally, as we shall see below, implemented.[1] There have been occasions, however, when his findings have been contested, as for example by George Brown over Sachsenhausen. We have seen too that Fred Mulley, as Minister of Transport, took the view that if a Government thought that the Parliamentary Commissioner came to a wrong conclusion, then it should have the courage to say so.[2] Nobody has, after all, promulgated a doctrine of Parliamentary Commissioner Infallibility, at least publicly.

It is likely, anyway, that it would not at this stage be practical politics to try to amend the Parliamentary Commissioner Act so as to allow the Commissioner to report on 'unreasonable' action by government departments. The Select Committee on the Parliamentary Commissioner has shown realism in the stand it has taken on this question. As we have seen, they have accepted the concept of maladministration but have attempted to broaden its scope by suggesting that, if the quality of a decision taken by an adminstrator is bad, that, in itself, can constitute maladministration. In other words, a decision which is clearly very unreasonable is maladministration.

We have seen that acceptance of the principle that the Parliamentary Commissioner can look at the quality of a decision has, as yet, had little effect upon his role.[3] This must mean that he is 'looking at the quality of a decision' in a narrow way. This is certainly the view of Geoffrey Marshall who, in a recent essay, has commented that, 'the Commissioner seems on the face of it still to be fighting shy of the quality and merits of the decision.' He points out that, in his results report on his investigation of a railway station closure, the Commissioner said that the merits of the decision were not for him to question. Obviously, the merits of the decision must be open to question if the quality of the decision is really to be assessed.[4]

---

[1] See below, pp. 324–6.   [2] See above p. 291.   [3] See above p. 281.

[4] Geoffrey Marshall, 'Parliament and the Ombudsman', Chapter 6 in A. H. Hanson and B. Crick (eds.), *The Commons in Transition* (Fontana, 1970), p. 127. The Parliamentary Commissioner's report on the station closure was made in October 1968. It is summarized in his Annual Report for 1968, pp. 129–31. For this case see also above pp. 288–90.

It does seem logical now to expect the Parliamentary Commissioner to look at the merits of a decision and to categorize as maladministration any decision which seems to him to be very unreasonable. If he were to adopt this interpretation of looking at the quality of a decision he would be able to recommend redress for many complainants for whom he has not been able to find in the past. Perhaps, with time and encouragement, he will come to adopt this interpretation.

EXTENSION OF THE ADMINISTRATIVE TRIBUNAL SYSTEM

The Whyatt Committee recommended that the Parliamentary Commissioner should only be concerned with maladministration, but it did say that 'a decision so harsh and unreasonable as to offend a sense of justice' might be termed maladministration.[1] In this way it foreshadowed the Select Committee's advice to the Parliamentary Commissioner that he should look at the quality of a decision. An important feature of the Whyatt Report was their recommendation that a concomitant to confining the Parliamentary Commissioner to maladministration should be a major expansion of the system of administrative tribunals to consider all kinds of complaints against discretionary action by government departments, where maladministration was not involved. The Report recommended that the Council on Tribunals should be given power to recommend the creation of new tribunals, where it found a gap in the system of tribunals, and that a general tribunal should be set up to consider miscellaneous complaints against discretionary decisions where it was not appropriate to create a specialized tribunal.

This recommendation of the Whyatt Report was not acted upon by the Wilson Government. In his speech on the second reading of the Parliamentary Commissioner Bill in 1966, Richard Crossman claimed that the Tribunals and Inquiries Bill, then in process of becoming law, implemented this part of the Whyatt Report.[2] Later, during the passage through the Lords of the Parliamentary Commissioner Bill, Lord Shackleton corrected this statement.[3] The Tribunals and Inquiries Act, 1966, as it became, was, in fact, a modest, although useful, reform. It enabled the Lord Chancellor and the Secretary of State for Scotland to bring within the scrutiny

---

[1] 'Justice', *The Citizen and the Administration*, p. 35 at para. 72.
[2] See above p. 78.　　[3] See above p. 202.

of the Council on Tribunals certain types of inquiry which were not included under the 1958 Tribunals and Inquiries Act. Under the 1958 Act, inquiries which a Minister was statutorily *required* to hold came within the jurisdiction of the Council of Tribunals. Inquiries which Ministers had, by statute, a *discretion* whether or not to hold did not come within the jurisdiction of the Council. The 1966 Act brings such discretionary inquiries within their jurisdiction where the Lord Chancellor, or the Secretary of State for Scotland, makes a designating Order.

The effect of this Act, therefore, has been to bring within the ambit of the Council on Tribunals certain discretionary inquiries which would otherwise not be subject to scrutiny by the Council. For example, in March 1967 an Order brought 65 classes of discretionary inquiry within the Council's jurisdiction.[1] There remain, however, many areas of departmental decision making where a dissatisfied citizen does not have the right to appeal to an administrative tribunal. The tribunal system, in other words, is far from being a comprehensive one as the Whyatt Committee recommended it should be.

Lord Gardiner was fully aware of this. In response to the feeling, particularly among lawyers, that there should be a comprehensive system of administrative justice, he encouraged the Law Commission to carry out a preliminary investigation of this question. The Law Commission is itself a product of the zeal to undertake reform of the law and legal institutions, which Lord Gardiner and his associates had expressed when Labour was in opposition.[2] Soon after Labour came to power, the Law Commission was set up, under the Law Commissions Act, 1965, in order to promote reform of the law. The Lord Chancellor appoints its chairman and four other members all of whom are lawyers of high standing. Its chairman, in 1969, was Mr. Justice Scarman and one of its members was Norman Marsh who had earlier, as we have seen, played a key role in the introduction of the Parliamentary Commissioner to Britain. As Secretary General of the International Commission of Jurists, he had, in 1958, published an article by the Danish Ombudsman on his work, and later had been the chairman of the committee of 'Justice' which helped to prepare the Whyatt Report.[3]

---

[1] Statutory Instruments 1967, No. 451.
[2] See Gerald Gardiner and Andrew Martin (eds.), *Law Reform NOW* (Gollancz, 1963).   [3] See above pp. 16 and 19.

The Law Commission sought the opinion of judges, public officials, and practising and academic lawyers on the question of whether there was a need for a major reform in administrative justice. In its report to the Lord Chancellor, published in May 1969, it recommended that a Royal Commission should be set up to consider the citizen's rights and remedies against the State.[1] The appointment of a Parliamentary Commissioner had given the citizen additional protection, but, in their view, more was needed. The Royal Commission, they said, should undertake a wide-ranging inquiry and should consider, for example, how far 'changes should be made in the organization and personnel of the courts in which proceedings may be brought against the administration'.[2] It was clear, from the Explanatory Working Paper which the Law Commission published as an appendix to their Report, that the Commissioners had in mind the need to examine the possibility of instituting in Britain something on the lines of the French *Conseil d'État*.[3]

We have seen that some of the advocates of a *Conseil d'État* type system for Britain had, before 1967, opposed the introduction of a Parliamentary Commissioner on the ground that it was a less satisfactory alternative to setting up some form of *Conseil d'État*.[4] With the passage of the Parliamentary Commissioner Act, some lawyers who, like Professor J. D. B. Mitchell, had taken this view came to feel that there would be a role both for the Parliamentary Commissioner and for an administrative court comparable to the *Conseil d'État*. For example, Mitchell argued, in 1967, that the Parliamentary Commissioner, like the Council on Tribunals, was 'a partial solution'. There remained a need for an administrative court which would have jurisdiction over administrative tribunals, would review the legality of administrative acts, and would have jurisdiction in public contracts and in reparation for administrative fault.[5]

THE PARLIAMENTARY COMMISSIONER AND THE *Conseil d'État* COMPARED

Experience has also shown that some of the criticisms of the hite Paper on the Parliamentary Commissioner made in 1966, by

---

[1] Cmnd. 4059. The Law Commission, *Administrative Law*.
[2] Ibid., p. 2 at para. 3.   [3] Ibid., p. 7 at para. 9.   [4] See above pp. 62–4.
[5] J. D. B. Mitchell, 'Administrative Law and Parliamentary Control', *Political Quarterly*, 1967, pp. 360–74.

advocates of a *Conseil d'État* type reform, were unsound. For example, the Inns of Court Conservative and Unionist Society had argued that since the Commissioner could only recommend, and not require redress, he would be a 'toothless Ombudsman'. In fact, experience has shown that the moral force of the Parliamentary Commissioner's recommendations is normally sufficient to secure compliance by the government department concerned. If we survey all the cases in which the Parliamentary Commissioner found maladministration, during the first four years of operation of the Act, we find that the government department has always acted upon the Commissioner's recommendation except in one relatively narrow, although important, area. This exception is found in certain types of complaint against the Inland Revenue.

Many of the instances of maladministration which the Parliamentary Commissioner has found relate to the Inland Revenue. For example, during the first three and three-quarter years of operation of his office (from 1 April 1967 to 31 December 1970) he found no less than 77 cases of maladministration among the complaints against the Inland Revenue which he investigated. (See Table II on p. 325).

In most of these cases the remedy which the Commissioner suggested was provided by the Inland Revenue. In some cases, however, there was, in the Commissioner's view, inexcusable delay by the department in repaying tax which had been overpaid. Sir Edmund Compton pressed the department to pay interest to the complainants on their overdue refunds of tax. The Inland Revenue replied that they had no statutory power to do this 'and that payment of interest in such cases would involve a fundamental change in established practice which they were not prepared to consider without legislative cover'.[1]

The Select Committee on the Parliamentary Commissioner, on 21 May 1969, asked Sir Arnold France, the Chairman of the Inland Revenue, about the department's position on this question. Sir Arnold France told Alexander Lyon that Parliament had many times discussed amendments to Finance Bills which proposed to give the Inland Revenue power to pay interest on tax repayments. 'Ministers of neither party', he told the Committee, 'have thought fit to take powers to do it.'[2]

---

[1] Memorandum by the Parliamentary Commissioner submitted to the Select Committee on the Parliamentary Commissioner for its meeting on 21 May 1969. H.C. 385 of 1968–9, p. 135.   [2] H.C. 385 of 1968–9, p. 146 at question 614.

As the accompanying table shows, the Parliamentary Commissioner found 164 instances of maladministration in the first four years of operation of his office. That, during this period, there was only one area in which the injustice he found to be consequent upon maladministration was not adequately remedied is a good indication of his effectiveness. Even in this area, a partial remedy was in many cases supplied in that the department agreed to repay the tax overpaid, but it was, in the Commissioner's view, an incomplete remedy since the department refused to pay interest on the overpayments. Further, the Inland Revenue had some reason for its refusal in that it claimed that Parliament had refused, on several occasions, to legislate for payment of interest in such cases.

These cases, therefore, provide only a partial exception to the

TABLE II

*Cases investigated by the Parliamentary Commissioner
in which he found maladministration, 1967 to 1970**

	1967	1968	1969	1970	Total over 4 years
Inland Revenue	6	13	26	32	77
Dept. of Health and Social Security (Until 1968 Ministry of Social Security)	5	7	6	6	24
Dept. of the Environment (Until 1970 Ministries of Housing and Local Government, Public Building and Works, and Transport)	3	5	6	5	19
Dept. of Employment and Productivity (Until 1968 Ministry of Labour)	3	1	1	3	8
Customs and Excise	1	—	3	3	7
Home Office	—	4	2	—	6
Foreign and Commonwealth Office (Until 1968 Foreign Office only)	1	3	—	1	5
Dept. of Trade and Industry (Until 1970 Board of Trade and Ministry of Technology	—	1	2	2	5
Ministry of Agriculture	—	1	—	3	4
Ministry of Defence	—	1	1	—	2
Land Commission	—	1	—	1	2
Scottish Office	—	1	—	1	2
Dept. of Education and Science	—	—	1	1	2
Public Trustee	—	—	—	1	1
Totals	19	38	48	59	164

(Source: Parliamentary Commissioner's Annual Reports for 1967, 1968, 1969 and 1970.)
* Listed by department.

general conclusion that, in the four years since he started work, the Parliamentary Commissioner's recommendations for remedying injustice, when he has found maladministration, have always been followed by the department concerned. This finding is certainly not consistent with the view that the Parliamentary Commissioner is 'a toothless Ombudsman'. Indeed, if the Parliamentary Commissioner is compared for effectiveness with the *Conseil d'État* he comes out well. It should not be thought that the *Conseil d'État* has power to enforce its decisions. L. Neville Brown and J. F. Garner comment that, at least in theory, the *Conseil d'État* itself has 'no effective means of enforcing compliance against an administration which is determined not to give way'.[1] In practice, the administration in France very seldom fails to comply with decisions of the *Conseil d'État*. But, then, British government departments very seldom fail to comply with recommendations from the Parliamentary Commissioner.

When we compare the Parliamentary Commissioner with the *Conseil d'État* for speed in handling a case, the Parliamentary Commissioner comes out very favourably. In 1966 the average time taken over a case by the *Conseil d'État* was eighteen months, according to Brown and Garner.[2] The average time taken by the Parliamentary Commissioner to dispose of a case is about three months.[3]

The arguments set out here comparing the Parliamentary Commissioner with the French *Conseil d'État* should not be construed as arguments against instituting in Britain an improved system of administrative justice. There is need, in the author's view, both for an extended system of Ombudsmen and for a more effective, comprehensive, system of administrative tribunals. It is significant that some countries which have a well-developed Ombudsman system also have an extensive system of administrative courts: Sweden and Finland are examples of such countries.

The question what type of case, or what area, is more suitable for an Ombudsman, and what for an administrative court, is more difficult to answer. The Whyatt Report's criterion of giving maladministration to the Ombudsman and discretionary decisions, without maladministration, to tribunals is not a satisfactory one. Perhaps a better criterion is to say that where examination of a dis-

[1] L. Neville Brown and J. F. Garner, *French Administrative Law* (Butterworth, 1967), p. 137.

[2] Ibid., p. 136.

[3] This is Sir Edmund Compton's own estimate given in an address to the Society for Individual Freedom printed in *Freedom First*, May 1970, p. 13.

pute requires much specialist knowledge, a tribunal on which the appropriate specialists, such as medical men or scientists, can sit is more appropriate. Again, where a dispute involves two or more parties, in addition to a public authority, a tribunal seems appropriate. Examples here are complaints against general practitioners and disputes about the granting of planning permission. This does not mean to say, however, that an Ombudsman might not also have a role in relation to such tribunals. We have seen that the Parliamentary Commissioner does investigate complaints about the way in which government officials have behaved before a matter has gone to a tribunal and he has reported upon a failure, for example, to invite all interested parties to give evidence at a planning inquiry.[1] It might be appropriate in some circumstances for a Commissioner to investigate complaints about the functioning of tribunals. The Department of Health and Social Security's 1970 Green Paper on Reorganization of the Health Service, for example, suggested that a Health Service Commissioner should examine the way in which the complaints machinery in the Health Service was working. This had the implication that he would investigate, in some instances, allegations that tribunal proceedings had not been fairly conducted. His role here in relation to the Council on Tribunals would need to be examined. But there is plenty of evidence that the existence of the Council is not of itself a guarantee that tribunals are being properly supervised. The Council's work would be usefully supplemented by a Health Commissioner who would have an apparatus, and an expertise, for investigating complaints about the functioning of Health Service tribunals which the members of the Council on Tribunals do not possess.

Returning to a comparison between the Parliamentary Commissioner and the *Conseil d'État*, there is one respect in which the *Conseil d'État* clearly scores. This is in the area of government which it covers. Not only does the *Conseil d'État* take in a large sector of central government (foreign relations is one of the few excluded spheres) but it is also concerned with most of local government. This lies entirely outside the Parliamentary Commissioner's sphere except when a central government department has become involved through, for example, a planning appeal to the Minister of Housing and Local Government against a local authority's refusal of planning permission.

[1] See above pp. 279–80.

PROPOSALS FOR OMBUDSMEN FOR LOCAL GOVERNMENT

Harold Wilson in his Stowmarket speech on 3 July 1964 had warned that it would be necessary, in order to prevent the Parliamentary Commissioner and his Select Committee from being swamped by too many cases, to limit their sphere of activities to central government. Later, their powers could be extended 'into the field of other public bodies and local authorities, though there is, of course, a very strong case for providing at least the larger local authorities with their own Ombudsman'.[1]

The Leader of the Labour Party, had, therefore, committed himself to the principle of having Ombudsmen for local government, but he had left the options open between having a central government Commissioner who would investigate complaints against local authorities, or establishing Ombudsmen responsible to local authorities, or having a combination of the two systems. The situation was complicated, after Labour took office in 1964, by the decision to undertake a major review of the structure of local government. The Labour Government decided that the piecemeal revision of local government areas which had been going on in England since 1958 was inadequate. They advised the Queen to set up a Royal Commission on Local Government Reform under the chairmanship of Sir John Maud (later made a life peer under the title Redcliffe-Maud). The Royal Commission was appointed in May 1966 and reported in June 1969.[2]

The terms of reference of the Royal Commission empowered it to consider the structure of local government in England and to make recommendations about authorities and boundaries and the division of functions. It was not empowered to consider the desirability of introducing an Ombudsman system for local government. The Wilson Government, nevertheless, took the view that it would not be appropriate to draw up proposals for such a system until the Redcliffe-Maud Commission had reported and the outlines of the new structure of local government had been decided.

In the month of publication of the Redcliffe-Maud Report, the Prime Minister, Harold Wilson, announced in the Commons, on 22 July 1969, that the Government had decided that an Ombuds-

---

[1] See above, Chapter IV, p. 43.
[2] Cmnd. 4040, Report of the Royal Commission on Local Government in England 1966–9.

man system for local government should be established by law. The system would be separate from the Parliamentary Commissioner system, but it would be analogous since its function would be to investigate complaints of maladministration by local authorities. Reports of investigations would be considered by the appropriate local authorities.[1]

The Prime Minister told the Commons that the Government was going to enter into discussions with the local authority associations and other bodies concerned. It would then present proposals for legislation to set up an ombudsmen system in the context of reorganized local government.

Meanwhile, 'Justice' had been at work on this question. Towards the end of 1968, the Council of 'Justice' had asked Professor J. F. Garner 'to direct an enquiry into the need for and potential scope of the ombudsman principle in local government'.[2] Professor Garner was well qualified to do this. He is a member of the Council on Tribunals and an authority on administrative law.[3] He had also at one time been Town Clerk of Andover and therefore knew local government from the inside. He was helped by a committee of ten which included Professor Stanley de Smith, Geoffrey Marshall, and Miss M. N. Rendel.[4] The committee included one Queen's Counsel, David Widdicombe, and had Graham Arran as its research assistant.

The committee's report appeared in November 1969 under the title *The Citizen and his Council. Ombudsmen for Local Government?* It recommended the appointment of one chief commissioner, and five or six commissioners, for local administration. These they suggested should be 'based at a central office with a small secretariat in a convenient central location'.[5] They thought it better that the commissioners should not be based in the regions since centralization of the office would 'make easier an effective liaison between the

[1] H.C. Deb. Vol. 187, Cols. 1501–3.

[2] 'Justice', 12th Annual Report, June 1969, p. 14.

[3] J. F. Garner is Professor of Public Law at Nottingham University. His published works include *Administrative Law* (Butterworth, 2nd edn. 1967).

[4] Stanley de Smith has been Downing Professor of the Laws of England at Cambridge University since 1969. His published works include *Judicial Review of Administrative Acts* (2nd edn. 1968) and *The New Commonwealth and its Constitutions* (1964).

Miss M. N. Rendel is Lecturer in Government at London University Institute of Education.

[5] 'Justice', *The Citizen and his Council. Ombudsmen for Local Government?* (Stevens, 1969), p. 10 at para. 19.

Commissioners for Local Administration and the Parliamentary Commissioner'.[1] They envisaged that in some branches of government such as education, planning and housing an investigation into alleged maladministration might involve both local and central government and liaison of this kind would be essential. They also suggested that the Chief Commissioner, like the Parliamentary Commissioner, could be an *ex officio* member of the Council on Tribunals.

The Commissioners would investigate complaints by members of the public (or by local authorities themselves) that they had suffered injustice in consequence of maladministration by a local authority. A local authority was defined as 'any agency financed directly or indirectly under statutory authority from local rates. This would include such bodies as river authorities, drainage boards, joint planning or sewerage boards and water boards and, in education, the Boards of governors as well as the committees themselves.'[2]

The Commissioners would receive complaints direct from members of the public and from local authorities. A Commissioner in investigating a complaint would have a right of access to all relevant local authority documents. Having investigated a complaint, he would send a copy of his report to the complainant and to the clerk of the local authority concerned. The clerk would be required to show the report to his council within a specified time, and the item would have to appear on the agenda for the next council meeting.[3]

The Chief Commissioner would be required to prepare an annual report for the Lord Chancellor, which should then be laid before each House of Parliament. 'In this Report the Commissioner should be expected to include summaries of more important cases investigated by himself and his colleagues, and he should also draw attention to any general matters where injustice may have been caused as a consequence of statutory provisions or the terms of regulations or the exercise of discretions vested in local authorities.'[4] The report argued, however, that it would not be appropriate to make the Commissioners for Local Administration subject to the House of Commons Select Committee on the Parliamentary Commissioner.

This 'Justice' report had many admirable features. It could be particularly commended for placing the Ombudsmen outside the

---

[1] Ibid.   [2] Ibid., p. 13 at para. 23.
[3] Ibid., p. 15 at para. 30.   [4] Ibid., p. 12 at para. 21.

local authorities themselves. The notion that local Ombudsmen should be responsible to and be employed by the local authorities themselves is fundamentally unsound. The analogy here with the Parliamentary Commissioner for Administration is not exact. The Parliamentary Commissioner is responsible to the House of Commons the majority of whose members have no part in the administration of government departments. A local Ombudsman who was responsible to a local authority would be reporting to a body of councillors the majority of whom were themselves concerned in administrative decision making. An Ombudsman who was responsible to, and employed by, a local authority could not be an effective and independent critic of that authority.

Another good feature of the 'Justice' report was their proposal that there should be direct access to the Commissioners for Local Administration by members of the public. They were a good deal more cautious in their close adherence to the concept of maladministration as employed in the Parliamentary Commissioner Act. They quoted the 'Crossman catalogue' of examples of maladministration and followed closely the Parliamentary Commissioner precedent by suggesting that the bad rule should be included in maladministration.[1]

Early in 1970, the Wilson Government published a White Paper on *Reform of Local Government in England*.[2] The primary purpose of this White Paper was to set out the Government's proposals for reform of the structure of local government broadly on the lines of the Redcliffe-Maud Report but with certain modifications of detail. However, the White Paper also stated that the Government proposed to set up ten, or more, 'Local Commissioners for Administration'. Whereas the Commissioners proposed in the 'Justice' report were to work from one central office, the White Paper preferred the suggestion that they should be based in different parts of the country. There is much to be said for this suggestion which would enable each Commissioner to become known in the region for which he had concern.

Certain other features of the White Paper proposals were inferior to the scheme set out in the 'Justice' report. In particular, the White Paper proposed that the public should not have direct access to the Commissioners. Instead, complaints would be made to

---

[1] Ibid., p. 13 at para. 24.   [2] Cmnd. 4276.

councillors who would act as a filter to the Commissioner, as M.P.s do to the Parliamentary Commissioner. Similarly, the White Paper proposed that the Commissioners should only report to the local authorities with whom they were concerned. They would not, as the 'Justice' report recommended, also report to Parliament. Both these provisions would tend to weaken the role of the Commissioners as independent critics of local government.[1]

With the defeat of the Wilson Government at the General Election in June 1970, their White Paper on Local Government Reform became a dead letter. The Heath Government announced in July 1970 that new proposals for the reform of local government would now be made after full consultation with local authorities, and their associations. The Conservative Government was not committed to implement the proposals put forward, in December 1968, by a committee of the Society of Conservative Lawyers, for regional Ombudsmen to examine complaints against local authorities.[2] It was likely, however, that the idea would receive sympathetic consideration particularly since their 1968 pamphlet had had a foreword from Edward Heath commending the proposals for study and debate.

Individual initiatives in favour of setting up regional Ombudsmen for local government had been attempted by parliamentarians of all three political parties in the period 1966 to 1970. In 1966 Lord Wade, one of the leading Liberal peers, introduced a Private Members' Bill in the House of Lords which would have established regional Commissioners for local government. Evelyn King, the Conservative Member for Dorset South, introduced a similar Bill in the House of Commons in 1967.[3] Robert Maclennan, the Labour Member for Caithness and Sutherland, introduced a Bill in December 1968 to set up a regional Ombudsman for Scotland to investigate complaints against local authorities.[4] All these initiatives,

---

[1] See Charles D. Drake, 'Ombudsmen for Local Government' in *Public Administration*, Summer 1970, pp. 178–9 for a comparison of the 1969 'Justice' report and the Wilson Government's 1970 proposals.

[2] Conservative Political Centre, *Rough Justice* (1968), pp. 11–12.

[3] Evelyn King has been Conservative Member for Dorset South since 1964. He was Labour Member for Penryn and Falmouth from 1945 to 1950 and was Parliamentary Secretary at the Ministry of Town and Country Planning from 1947 to 1950. He joined the Conservative Party in 1951. He is a farmer.

[4] Robert Maclennan has been Labour Member for Caithness and Sutherland since 1966. He was called to the Bar in 1962 and is a member of the Society of Labour Lawyers.

of course, failed and were designed to prompt the Government to action.

OMBUDSMEN IN NORTHERN IRELAND

The first official move to set up a regional Ombudsman came from the Government of Northern Ireland in response to the turbulent events there from 1968 onwards. In 1969, the Parliament at Stormont passed the Parliamentary Commissioner (Northern Ireland) Act, 1969, setting up a Parliamentary Commissioner for Northern Ireland. With the passage of this Act, the United Kingdom Parliamentary Commissioner, Sir Edmund Compton, was invited also to become Parliamentary Commissioner for Northern Ireland. On accepting this duty he set up an office in Belfast, with a staff of eight, which he visited once a week.

Before the passage of this Act, Sir Edmund, in his capacity as Parliamentary Commissioner for the U.K., had investigated complaints from citizens in Northern Ireland in those spheres of central government where Westminster has responsibility, for example Defence and Customs and Excise. In his capacity as Parliamentary Commissioner for Northern Ireland, he can receive complaints against administration by departments of the Northern Ireland Government. An approach to him in these matters has to be through an M.P. of the Stormont Parliament.

Relatively few complaints reached him by this route in his first three months of office. He told a press conference in Belfast on 1 October 1969 that during this period he had received only eight complaints.[1]

The volume of complaints against local authorities in Northern Ireland was likely to be much greater. The Northern Ireland Government, in December 1969, appointed a Commissioner for Complaints with the function of investigating complaints against the actions of local authorities and other public bodies, including hospitals and other health authorities, but excluding departments of the Northern Ireland Government for which Sir Edmund Compton as Parliamentary Commissioner for Northern Ireland is responsible.

The Commissioner for Complaints, then, combines the functions

[1] *Guardian* report, 2 October 1969. When the Heath Government announced, on 14 December, 1970 that Sir Edmund Compton would be retiring from the office of United Kingdom Parliamentary Commissioner at the end of March 1971, the announcement also made clear that Sir Edmund would continue, after that date, in his office as Parliamentary Commissioner for Northern Ireland.

of a regional Ombudsman for local government and of a Health Service Commissioner. His method of operation is different from that of the Parliamentary Commissioner. He receives complaints direct from members of the public. If after investigation of a case, no remedy is provided, his report provides the material upon which the complainant can go to the court and ask the court to make an enforceable award against the local authority, health authority, or other public body.

The first Commissioner for Complaints was appointed in December 1969. He is J. M. Benn who had formerly been Permanent Secretary of the Northern Ireland Ministry of Education. Between his appointment and November 1970 he investigated well over 100 complaints. He found no instances of maladministration, but in a number of the cases he investigated a settlement was achieved between the complainant and the public body against which the complaint had been directed.[1]

COMPLAINTS AGAINST THE POLICE

One area in which, on *a priori* grounds, we would most expect to find provision for an Ombudsman is in the police services. The function of an Ombudsman is to investigate complaints from citizens that they have been treated by the public authorities in an unfair or arbitrary manner. The police, in the nature of their work, are likely to occasion many complaints of this type. Ombudsmen in Sweden, Finland, Denmark, New Zealand, and Norway investigate complaints against the police. The British Parliamentary Commissioner does not, except when a complaint lies against the Home Secretary on the grounds that he has failed to adhere to the statutory machinery for setting up an inquiry into examining a complaint against the police, or when the Home Secretary has failed to exercise some of his other general powers of surveillance of police forces.[2]

Under the Police Act, 1964, serious complaints against police officers are investigated by a senior officer from a different police force, not, as before the passage of the Act, by the Chief Constable of the police force concerned. Widespread dissatisfaction has been expressed about this system in which only police officers undertake such investigations, even if they are officers from a different force.

---

[1] See K. P. Poole, 'Ulster's Local Government Ombudsman' in *Municipal Review*, November 1970, p. 455.

[2] See above pp. 274–5.

In July 1969, for example, 160 M.P.s signed a motion asking for amendment of the Police Act so that an independent element, representing the public, would be introduced into the machinery for investigating complaints against the police.

In October 1969, the National Council for Civil Liberties published a pamphlet advocating independent regional tribunals, with legally qualified chairmen, to hear complaints by the public against the police.[1] 'Justice', in the same year, set up a special committee under the chairmanship of Lewis Hawser Q.C. to make recommendations on the investigation of complaints against the police. These recommendations were published and submitted to the Police Advisory Boards' Joint Working Party on the Investigation of Complaints in January 1970.

The 'Justice' memorandum suggested that complaints should continue to be investigated by the police themselves, but where a complainant was not satisfied with the handling of his complaint he should be able to ask an independent investigator to look into it. The independent investigator would do so and would then report to the Chief Constable concerned. The police officer complained against would, at this stage, have the right to appeal to a central review tribunal consisting of a legally qualified chairman and two senior police officers from another force.[2]

An Ombudsman is an independent investigator and the 'Justice' proposals seem to be close to what was reportedly the Home Office view, at this time, on the question. On 23 July 1969, the *Guardian* reported that Elystan Morgan, a Parliamentary Secretary at the Home Office, had told the Parliamentary Labour Party Home Office group, on the preceding day, that the Home Secretary was considering setting up a system for investigating complaints against the police on the lines of the proposed Health Commissioner. The Home Office seemed, at this stage, therefore, to be favouring the idea of a form of Ombudsman for the police rather than the suggestion for independent regional tribunals.

AN OMBUDSMAN FOR THE COURTS?

Whereas there has been considerable discussion in this country of proposals for some kind of Ombudsman system to investigate

[1] Mervyn Jones, *The Police and the Citizen* (National Council for Civil Liberties, 1969).

[2] 'Justice', Recommendations Submitted to the Police Advisory Boards' Joint Working Party on the Investigation of Complaints, January 1970, pp. 4. 5, and 7.

complaints against the police, there has been very little consideration of the possibility that an Ombudsman might investigate complaints against the courts. Two countries, Sweden and Finland, have Ombudsmen who can investigate complaints against judges.

British judges are, in practice, remarkably immune from criticism. High Court judges sometimes show remarkable discourtesy towards those who appear before them. For example, Justice Melford Stevenson when sentencing, on 3 July 1970, six Cambridge students for their part in an anti-Greek demonstration at a Cambridge hotel, was reported as having said: 'I must say these sentences would have been heavier if I had not been made aware you have been exposed to the evil influence of some of the senior members of the university—one or two of whom I have seen as witnesses for the defence.'[1]

Six college Fellows who had appeared as witnesses for the defence then wrote to *The Times* expressing 'profound astonishment' at the judge's remarks. They concluded their letter by saying: 'We know there is no legal redress against statements made by a presiding judge in court, but each of us emphatically denies the charge.'[2]

An Ombudsman with power to investigate complaints about the behaviour of judges would clearly have been of value here. Similarly, at the other end of the scale from the senior professional judges, the unpaid amateurs on the local bench sometimes leave much to be desired in courtesy and fairness towards witnesses or the accused. Provision for appeal to a higher level, of course, enables the worst abuses to be checked. But the existence of an Ombudsman, who could investigate complaints against all kinds of judges, from Justices of the Peace at one end of the scale to High Court judges at the other, would help to improve the standards of courtesy and humanity in British courts.

ACCEPTANCE OF THE PARLIAMENTARY COMMISSIONER

An Ombudsman to investigate complaints against judges would clearly have to have legal training. So would an Ombudsman to investigate complaints against the police. Lawyers were not slow to criticize the fact that Sir Edmund Compton did not have a legal background and no member of his staff had legal training. There are strong arguments, however, for the view that it was more important that the first Parliamentary Commissioner in Britain should

---

[1] The *Guardian*, 4 July 1970.   [2] *The Times*, 6 July 1970.

be an experienced Civil Servant who would have the necessary expertise to assess the administrative situation in the cases he was investigating. His Civil Service background also made it more likely that he would receive the ready co-operation of the Civil Servants he, and his staff, would have to investigate.

That co-operation he has certainly achieved. Our main conclusion, in surveying the first four years of operation of the Parliamentary Commissioner Act, can indeed be that the reform has been accepted. The Parliamentary Commissioner and the role he performs have been accepted by those who work the central government machine. They have also been accepted by the Conservative leadership, whereas the leadership of the Party under Macmillan was, in 1962, hostile to the whole idea.

We have already noted the pamphlet published by the Conservative Political Centre in December 1968 under the title *Rough Justice*. This pamphlet was the work of the Society for Conservative Lawyers but had a foreword from Edward Heath commending the proposals for study and debate. In their comments on the Parliamentary Commissioner, the Conservative lawyers retained some echoes of the Macmillan Government's view in 1962. They said, for example, that the activities of the Parliamentary Commissioner 'may impair the traditional doctrine of Ministerial responsibility which protects the civil servant who cannot defend himself publicly from denigration'. But they went on to say:

We recognize the need for using and developing each and every institution capable of helping the redress of grievances and, accordingly, we take the view that if we are to have the Parliamentary Commissioner we should at least make him as effective as possible. We think that the powers of the Parliamentary Commissioner to investigate complaints of maladministration by central government ought to be made the subject of as few restrictions as possible.[1]

After the Conservative success at the General Election of 1970, Edward Heath offered Quintin Hogg the office of Lord Chancellor. Hogg accepted and became Lord Hailsham again, although this time he was made a life peer, having renounced his hereditary peerage in 1963. Hogg, as we have seen, had described the Parliamentary Commissioner as 'a swiz' during the passage of the Bill. But by 1970 he had changed his opinion. In an interview in the *Sunday Times*,

[1] Conservative Political Centre, *Rough Justice*, pp. 10–11.

on 19 July 1970, less than a month after taking up his office as Lord Chancellor, he was asked if he was completely happy with the way the Ombudsman's office works. He replied: 'I think it works extremely well, within limits.'

There were, he said, two important areas which were beyond the Ombudsman's competence. The first was local government and M.P.s found that a very high proportion of the complaints they received were against local authorities. The second area which was closed to the Ombudsman was the area of complaints against statutory instruments. He frequently found that the action complained against was made under an order or instrument within the terms of an Act. For this reason, Lord Hailsham advocated a Bill of Rights. This would give to the courts the power to decide whether orders or regulations were in conflict with entrenched legislated rights.

The first lacuna which Lord Hailsham observed could be filled by the appointment of regional Ombudsmen to investigate complaints against local authorities. This was, as we have seen, the remedy advocated by the Committee of Conservative Lawyers. This leads on to another finding we may derive from the experience of the first three years of operation of the Parliamentary Commissioner. This is that the success he has achieved, although limited and in a limited sphere, has led to a wide support for the Ombudsman idea. Thus we find proposals for extending the scope of the Parliamentary Commissioner to personnel matters in the Civil Service and the Armed Forces being advanced by the Select Committee. We find the Wilson Government committing itself, in principle, to the institution, by law, of Ombudsmen for local government, and a committee of the Society for Conservative Lawyers taking a similar view. We find the Department of Health and Social Security proposing, in its 1970 Green Paper, a Health Commissioner for a unified Health Service. Again, the idea of an Ombudsman to investigate complaints against the police was, in 1969, being considered by the Home Office.

The United Kingdom may, then, be on the way to establishing a system of protection of the public through multiple Ombudsmen. If this happens, the Parliamentary Commissioner is likely to be strengthened and given more scope but will probably continue to deal only with certain specified central government functions. Alongside him there could be, in time, Ombudsmen for local government and a Health Commissioner, or Commissioners, for the Health

Service. These developments should be complemented by major reforms in the system of administrative tribunals.

A great deal has changed in this field from the day in 1957 when *The Times* returned to Professor Lawson his letter, proposing an Inspector General for Administration, on the ground that it was 'not topical'. This book has attempted to trace the way in which these changes have come about. It is not possible to say that, in carrying through the reform, any group or individual played the major part. Certainly, 'Justice' has been the most important of the pressure groups but on its own it could have achieved little. A major role was also played by individual party leaders and Ministers: by Harold Wilson, Lord Gardiner, Douglas Houghton, and Niall MacDermot in particular. Backbenchers in the House of Commons also played a very important part, among them especially Dr. Donald Johnson, in the early stages, and Alexander Lyon in the standing committee and on the Select Committee on the Parliamentary Commissioner. The first chairman of this Committee, Sir Hugh Munro-Lucas-Tooth, and other members of the original Committee, also did a great deal to strengthen the position of the Parliamentary Commissioner. Sir Edmund Compton, himself, as the first Parliamentary Commissioner, ensured the permanence of the reform by seeing it safely through the proving stages. He has been assailed for showing excessive caution and discretion. But caution and discretion were needed, at the outset, and were coupled in him with pertinacity and determination to see the office established. The British Ombudsman is unlike any other Ombudsman in the world. He is not even officially called an Ombudsman, even as a subsidiary title. But by popular consent this is how he is known. It is a title he deserves.

The Act provides that the Parliamentary Commissioner must retire in the year in which he attains the age of sixty-five. Sir Edmund Compton would be sixty-five in July 1971, but he decided to retire from office at the end of March 1971. When the Prime Minister, Edward Heath, told the Commons on 14 December 1970 of Sir Edmund Compton's impending resignation, he announced that the Queen had approved the appointment as his successor of Sir Alan Marre, at that time Second Permanent Secretary in the Department of Health and Social Security. The Heath Government therefore followed the precedent set by the Wilson Government in choosing someone with Civil Service experience as

Ombudsman. When the Liberal Member, John Pardoe, asked why the possibility had been turned down of appointing someone from outside the Civil Service, the Prime Minister replied that, in his view, the advantages of appointing a Civil Servant, who knew public administration inside out, were overriding and this did not, in any sense, weaken the independence of the office of Parliamentary Commissioner.

THE PARLIAMENTARY COMMISSIONER ACT AND THE LEGISLATIVE PROCESS

This has been a study of an important reform in the British system of government and it has also been a case study of the legislative process. What light does it throw on issues which have been raised in this field?

One of the few analytical studies of the process of legislation is S. A. Walkland's *The Legislative Process in Great Britain*, published in 1968.[1] This study of the Parliamentary Commissioner Bill does not, on the whole, support Walkland's thesis. Walkland argues that the main deliberative stage of legislation is carried on between government departments and pressure groups. When a Bill reaches Parliament it is, more or less, cut and dried. Legislation 'is not now effectively a Parliamentary function'.[2]

This picture does not fit the Parliamentary Commissioner Bill. As we have seen, only one pressure group, 'Justice', was important in the campaign for a Parliamentary Commissioner. The other pressure group, the Society for Individual Freedom, was more marginal, its influence being, in practice, only exerted on certain individuals on the Conservative front and back benches. The 'Justice' report of 1961, *The Citizen and the Administration*, was very influential, being in effect, the Wilson Government's starting point for legislation. The memorandum which 'Justice' sent to Lord Gardiner in 1964 was also influential, but less so.

Although, then, 'Justice' played a major part in influencing informed opinion in the period before the Wilson Government began to rough out its Bill, once the Government had started on this there was no interchange between the Government and 'Justice', or any other pressure group. That is to say the deliberative process in drafting the Bill went on, not, as Walkland suggests it does, between

---

[1] S. A. Walkland, *The Legislative Process in Great Britain* (Allen and Unwin, 1968).
[2] Ibid., p. 8.

the Government and pressure groups but within the Government itself.

Then again, whereas Walkland argues that Parliament itself nowadays plays a very minor part in the legislative process, we have seen that discussion of the Parliamentary Commissioner Bill led to important changes in the Bill, both in the Commons and the Lords. The Bill was also very fully discussed, especially in the standing committee sessions in the Commons.

Walkland is, of course, right when he says that the main purpose of the Parliamentary stages of legislation is 'to dissect and expose the Government's intentions and to clarify the consequences of them for the electorate'.[1] In the case of the Parliamentary Commissioner Bill, this kind of probing and exploration had a further dimension in that M.P.s were seeking to shape the development of a reform, not only through the Bill itself, but also in the subsequent operation of the Parliamentary Commissioner and his office. We have seen that many of the discussions in the Select Committee on the Parliamentary Commissioner have been in effect continuations of discussions begun in standing committee, for example on the inclusion of the hospitals or of personnel matters in the Civil Service, or on the role of the Commissioner in relation to discretionary decisions.

It could be argued here that the Parliamentary Commissioner Bill was in a special category in that it introduced a reform which was of special concern to M.P.s, since it would influence their relationship with constituents and their own roles in taking up constituents' grievances. It could also be argued that the Bill was in a special category since it was not a partisan measure. Although the Labour Party was committed to the reform and the Conservative Party was not, the Bill had support from elements in both parties and also had critics, indeed, opponents in both parties.

The argument could then run that on a Bill which was not concerned with a reform in the system of government, and on which the two parties were clearly divided, Walkland's thesis might be more accurate. For example, on a Bill to which a Labour Government was heavily committed and which was concerned with the reorganization of industry, it might be shown that the main deliberative stage took place between the government department and pressure groups, be-

---

[1] Ibid.

fore the Bill reached the Commons, and that Parliament itself played only a minor part in the legislative process.

An example of such a Bill would be the Bill which was enacted as the Transport Act, 1968. This was a major Government Bill which was strongly supported on the Labour side. It had been extensively discussed with pressure groups, before it reached the Commons; but in its passage through Parliament it was very fully discussed and extensively amended. Around 700 amendments were made to the Bill during its passage through both Houses. Many of these amendments came from the Opposition or from Government backbenchers, or were drafted by the Government in response to criticisms made in debate.

In this instance, therefore, Parliament can be seen, apparently, taking as important a part in the legislative process as it did on the Parliamentary Commissioner Bill. Walkland's generalization would not seem therefore to stand up very well. On the other hand, his generalization undoubtedly does apply to some Government Bills. Two possible conclusions can be suggested therefore. First, there is a great deal of variation in the handling of Government Bills by Parliament. Some Bills are perfunctorily discussed and little amended, some Bills are extensively discussed and little amended, some Bills are extensively discussed and extensively amended. Second, to produce a generalization about which types of Bill come in which category may not ever be possible, and is certainly not possible in the present state of the art, since there have as yet been so few detailed case studies of the passage of legislation in Britain.[1]

One conclusion can be made from this study, however, with some confidence. This is that Parliament's handling of the Parliamentary Commissioner Bill gives no support to the theory that Parliament is in decline as a legislature. In discussion of this Bill, M.P.s and peers showed an independence of outlook, a high degree of relevant knowledge, and an ability to influence the outcome which does not fit in with the view that Parliament no longer has a legislative role of any significance.

[1] A recent study of great interest is Malcolm Joel Barnett's *The Politics of Legislation. The Rent Act 1957* (Weidenfeld and Nicolson, 1969). Barnett sees his case study as an example of a failure of a government department to size up the problem adequately for which it was trying to legislate, and a failure of both Houses of Parliament to supply themselves with adequate information to make an effective critique of the Bill.

INDEX